Vet in the Vestry

with

Poultry in the Pulpit

By the same author
Dog Collar Diary

Vet in the Vestry

with

Poultry in the Pulpit

ALEXANDER CAMERON

Vet in the Vestry first published 1987 by Lochar Publishing
Poultry in the Pulpit first published 1988 by Lochar Publishing

First combined edition published 1995 by House of Lochar

British Library Cataloguing in Publication Data
A catalogue record for this book is available from the British Library.
ISBN 1-899863-04-4

Printed in Great Britain
by BPC Wheatons Ltd, Exeter
for House of Lochar, Isle of Colonsay, Argyll PA61 7YR

Vet in the Vestry

ALEXANDER CAMERON

To my parents
who sacrificed so much for their family
and to my wife
who has shared to the full in my "Two lives".

CONTENTS

The Devil They Know

ONE

Andrew warmly shook my hand, helped me off with my gowns, neatly folded them and put them back in their case.

"You'll be the seventh minister I've dressed these past Sundays," he announced. I was startled. I had already realised the general public's idea of a minister was a pretty wet, helpless creature, but I was unaware somebody had to dress him. He explained,

"Weel, ye ken, help him on and off with his robes."

"Hold on" I said, "I'm not your minister yet; they've got to vote on it," something that at that moment was being conducted in the Church.

"Ach!" exclaimed Andrew, with enough force and vigour to counter any argument, "Ach! Efter that the day there's nae fear." Then he added, "You're jist like the gude ministers we've had before." I perked up, preened myself, and said that was a compliment indeed, recalling some of the fine men who had occupied that pulpit. I enquired in what way I resembled my predecessors. He told me

"You're gey sweaty under the ocksters!"

So he had noticed. My shirt was in fact sticking to me, and might even have been steaming, a common experience of men who have undergone 'the weekly ordeal of public exposure', even more of an ordeal when one is preaching for a Charge and aware of the keenest scrutiny.

"Mind you" Andrew went on, "maist gude ministers sweat an awfu' lot. The yins that have the gift o' the gab an' just blether on when they've nothing to say don't sweat."

Well, he should know, I thought, after a lifetime as a Church officer, and in a way I was quite pleased that I had joined the select band of the sweaty shirt brigade.

"How long do you think they'll be?" I asked.

"No long" he replied, "just you sit doon and rest yoursel' for a bit."

I gladly obeyed. I had come to realise that preaching, contrary to public opinion, took it out of you, even if you didn't pound the bookboard and perform everything but handstands in the pulpit. Andrew peeped through the curtained window which gave a view of the Church, a procedure he was to repeat every Sunday thereafter, informing himself and anyone else in the vestry, who, what, and how many were in their pews. Everything Andrew the Beadle did was with dignity, and somehow he managed to have his weekly peek and endue it with the solemnity of a sacrament.

"Aye," he mused aloud, "it's a while since I've seen the Kirk sae fu'. Oh, that's them done noo; here comes the committee."

The Committee squeezed into the small vestry, which also served as a choir room and session room, while Andrew discreetly withdrew. Revd George, acting as Interim Moderator in place of Revd Andrew, the appointed Interim Moderator who was on holiday said,

"Well, Mr Cameron, after an open vote of the congregation, you'll be glad to know that the vote was unanimously in your favour. May I congratulate you, and wish you every blessing." Then he gave a smile and said,

"I think this must be nearly unique — a vet in the vestry!" I thanked him in stammering words, then the committee led by Duncan came forward to shake me by the hand, or thump me on the back according to their inclination, and one and all wished me well, in subdued or boisterous fashion.

"Of course," said one of the committee, "we never had any doot aboot it, but efter a gude sermon like that, the voting was a formality." The congratulations over, some of the elders turned to the important task of counting the offering.

"A gran' collection the day. Notes in the plate" said one. I thought it time to depart before they passed the plate to me again . . . so took my farewells and headed for my car, case in hand.

"Have you no' a hat?" queried one.

"Never wear one," I replied.

"Ah, times change" sighed my questioner. "I mind when Mr MacDonald came to preach for Moorton before the war, he arrived in a baby Austin wi' top hat an' tails on." My mind grappled in vain with the picture of a car so attired.

"Mr MacDonald managed to get oot o' the car withoot knocking his hat off, and he was as big a man as you." I just grunted "Good for him," realising I would probably hear a good deal about Mr MacDonald in the years to come, a natural thing for he and the speaker would have been young men together. I demonstrated that I too could negotiate a car with some elegance, albeit not wearing a hat. I was about to drive off, when Duncan came up the Church pathway in a 'pelting heat', as John Bunyan would have described it.

"I was busy with the collection" he explained. "There hasna been one like that since Mr Cruickshank left. When you've no a minister o' your ain, the folk don't come the same."

"When the cat's away, the mice play," I suggested. He agreed, reached in the car, warmly shook my hand and said,

"Man, you were jist gran the day! Bring Mrs Cameron ower the morn an' we'll go through the Manse an' see what's to be done, an' you can pick some wallpaper. Though," he added cautiously, "we've no' got too much to spend. I'm the Treasurer an' it's me has to balance the books" . . . a phrase I was to hear often in the years ahead. But Duncan was a kindly soul, and with final handshakes from him, from yet another Andrew, the saintly old Session Clerk whose cherubic face just beamed, and faithful Andrew the Beadle, I was off.

It felt good! I had just been voted their Minister, in the democratic Presbyterian manner, by the congregation of Moorton. This was a humble country church, but a church very much the centre of the scattered community it served, which dwelt in the villages of Moorton and Waterfoot, and on the one hundred farms in the sixty square miles of parish. It was also an historic church, founded in the 'killing times', and had suffered greatly in those terrible yet valiant years when men fought and died for freedom of the faith. In a few weeks, I would be ordained, with due solemnity, by the local Presbytery, but that was yet ahead. I wondered, as I drove homeward, if I should stop and phone Janet? I decided against it, and in fact pulled into a layby for a few minutes to let it all sink in. I, Alexander Cameron, M.R.C.V.S., was now elected, and soon would be formally appointed minister of my first Charge. Yes, truly it felt good! But it was still unreal, and I knew not what lay ahead. I didn't care where, if anywhere else, we might be called in future, but what was behind me I remembered well.

Three years ago I had been a country vet . . . hence the letters after my name. Now I was to be a country minister . . . as brother George had said, I would be a vet in the vestry. I remembered the short interview I'd had with the selection board before they had decided that, subject to passing the Bible and Greek entrance exams, they would accept me.

"Were you really a vet, Mr Cameron? I mean did you practise?" asked the Chairman. "Still do," I replied. There had been smiles around the group, and a murmur of 'Really!' For the life of me I couldn't see anything odd about it. After all, other vets had gone into other churches. A fellow student had become a priest, and indeed the founder of my Devon practice was now a Canon in the Church of England. But everywhere there had been this same mixture of surprise and amusement, presumably because I was apparently the first of my kind, so far as people knew, in the Church of Scotland. I recalled being rudely interrupted while doodling during a Psychology of Religion lecture.

"Perhaps Mr Cameron, you could tell us of your experiences in this field with animals," suggested the lecturer. Mr Cameron could not. I had replied to the effect that I had never encountered a neurotic nanny goat or a schizophrenic sow, whereupon my pal Charlie had passed along an instant portrait of a cow weeping copious tears, and saying 'Cameron doesn't understand that what I need is a good psychiatrist!' But for the most part the banter had been good natured, and I had usually answered that I would be doing the same job; only the species, homo sapiens, was different. I was all in favour of men having had to work out in the big wide world, face difficulties, and understand the problems and trials of ordinary people before they tried to minister to them. It seemed to me that we had the best possible warrant for this, in that the founder of the Christian faith had worked as a carpenter to the age of thirty before becoming a wandering preacher. One thing I knew for certain as I sat musing in the layby, was that I was still exactly the same person I had been as a vet, and that if a halo was to be conferred to somehow produce instant holiness on becoming a minister of the Gospel, then mine had somehow been lost in transit! I was the same fellow who had worn a calving coat, even though I would now have a different uniform. I was no better a Christian for having become a minister — only a better informed and trained one.

Three months ago my training had ended, and I had been cast adrift with my fellow students like so many ships seeking a harbour. I had been surprised to find that the way to reach a haven was to answer advertisements in the *Glasgow Herald* or *The Scotsman*, and these adverts had really astonished and somewhat disappointed me. They might have come straight from *The Veterinary Record* as churches vied with each other in offering the inducements of modern manses, up-to-date kitchens, central heating, beautiful outlooks, stipends so much above the minimum, and altogether desirable situations. I had applied for a couple in the country, for I would have been lost in a city, and meantime to keep my family, had taught English in a comprehensive school. English included Geography, and each night I swotted up to keep one step ahead of the class. I thought I was doing rather well too, till one day, showing a film strip and waxing eloquent about the Canadian prairies I became aware of a disturbance behind me, and discovered a good going card school in the back seat. So much for my teaching knowhow! I hadn't long to wait, mercifully, for I had a wife and four children to maintain. In a month the first Charge for which I'd applied had invited me to be their minister. After ten days of consideration, and feeling rotten about declining the honour these folk had paid me, I'd had to refuse for the remoteness of the place would have presented schooling and family problems. I'd applied for another Charge in my native Ayrshire, and meantime with the coming of summer holidays, been asked to take pulpit supply in various churches.

I first suspected that I had a visiting committee at an evening service in Kilmarnock. They were there again the next Sunday — and the next. On that third occasion, a glorious summer evening, few of the devout had come to Church, no doubt preferring God's good sunshine to the *Revised Church Hymnary, 2nd edition,* and my eloquence! But I had a congregation nonetheless, consisting of my visitation committee of four, and a group of about sixteen seated closely together near the front. Obviously another committee — in force. Who were they? I don't know how I preached — nor indeed how I maintained any kind of concentration, for I was highly amused by the glances darting from one committee to the other, and the intense scrutiny bestowed on me. I could almost read their thoughts . . . 'Does he read his prayers?' . . . 'Does his voice carry?' . . . 'Is he reasonably presentable?' (I'd heard of one student turned down because he had fiery red hair!) . . . 'I wonder if he believes in visiting?' . . . 'Has he a wife?', the million dollar question. (One of my friends waited a year for a Charge largely because he lacked this all important attribute . . . but eventually he got a fiancée, and a church!). So the service proceeded, and shaking hands at the door, as was my custom, my four regular visitors whispered that they were holding a meeting a week on Tuesday, and I was one of a short leet of two. They were from the Ayrshire Church, it seemed.

I discovered a deputation from the other committee awaiting me in the vestry, who explained they were from Moorton, and had only that morning appointed their committee. They already had fifty applicants . . . had I not seen their advertisement? . . . If I was interested, would I apply, to keep the matter in order. I recognised one or two of them now, for Moorton was a neighbouring parish to Kilmarton, where I had acted as a student pastor during most of my three years at Trinity College, for the minister there had died, and there were prolonged negotiations about the union of the two churches. We had even lived in the enormous, but very gracious manse, camping out in a few of its twenty rooms. This identification explained the far from charitable looks that had passed between the two committees, for clearly the farmers of Moorton recognised the farmers of the other parish, not twenty miles away. Here was a dilemma! I had applied for one Charge, was one of a leet of two, it seemed, and was now being urged to apply for Moorton. What did one do? It all seemed so . . . what was the description? Worldly? Materialistic? All on the human level? I suppose I felt a dove should wing its way downwards with a message in its beak. And yet, how could God work except through men and women, be they bishops or committees? As I thought about it all that summer evening, I recalled the words of Revd Andrew Eastham, my parents' Minister, who had been, and was to continue to be a friend, adviser, and father in God to me.

"Our system of electing ministers has its faults," he had said, "but I honestly believe the Holy Spirit does guide in all this. . . and that's a miracle." So I sent in the application for consideration, and left it there. I had no means of knowing whether I would be the selected one in the other short leet.

The following Sunday evening, preaching at Mochrum, where I had begun as a young vet years ago, there was the Moorton Committee again, the entire seventeen this time. I've no idea how they knew where I was preaching, but the Scot is noted for his 'speirin', and someone had found out. The Service over, I made a leisurely journey homewards, calling at my widowed mother's on the way to spend an hour or two with her. She greeted me with a message that I was to go straight home, since 'a minister and some men . . . (it seemed doubtful what ministers were in the human spectrum!) were awaiting me and would like a word.' The minister proved to be Revd George, the acting Interim Moderator, and every inch a man . . . the other men were two of the Moorton Vacancy Committee. They explained they were from Moorton, had held a meeting that night, and invited me to be their 'sole nominee'. I listened carefully, but with an assumed air of nonchalance, as if even St Giles wouldn't tempt me (I was learning fast), and subdued a smile when they, without giving a reason, asked

"Could you let us have your decision before Tuesday?"

Clearly farmers discussed other things at the market besides the price of beasts and the poor pig subsidies! Janet had been valiantly supplying them with tea, and making polite conversation till I arrived, and had withdrawn to let the men and the minister talk business. I asked that she should join us in the discussion, for from the beginning, our Call had been a joint thing. I protested, I hope sincerely, that they had been less than fair to their other fifty applicants, some of whom were probably friends from Trinity.

"Och, don't worry about that" said one of the delegation, "we decided we wanted somebody in his thirties, and we've been scattered like the Israelites across the face of Scotland this morning, hearing the ones we'd considered."

"But you've heard me twice ... and even more, for I preached at Moorton about a year ago, when we were staying at Kilmarton. That's hardly fair to all the others?" I reiterated. "Besides, I've applied for another Church too, and it's possible they might be interested." They looked down, hesitated, then one said

"Aye, we heard aboot the ither Kirk, but we're unan... unani...a' agreed we'd like you."

I assured them I'd think about it, let them have an answer within the deadline, and gravely showed them out. Then Janet and I hugged one another, and did a few waltz steps round the room ... most unseemly behaviour for a Sabbath evening!! Somebody wanted us; maybe even two congregations. Still, we'd had no official approach from the other, and as we thought it over, prayed it through, and slept on it ... a trinity of excellent actions ... it seemed we should say yes.

All that had been three weeks ago. Now, as I sat in the layby and reached for the ignition key, it had come to pass. The congregation had endorsed their Committee's recommendation. Maybe God did indeed work in mysterious ways ... anyway it was time to pass on the good news to my waiting wife, and tell the boys the far more important thing to them. They could soon have the addition to the family for which they had been clamouring for three years, and to which I had always answered ... "You'll get it when Mummy and Daddy have a home of their own ... you'll get your puppy then."

There was jubilation on my return, my attempt to convey gloom and despondency signifying rejection being a flop. It felt grand, to be wanted, to be settled, to be faced with a challenge, to be trusted by a congregation . . . even, my ego whispered, to be preferred to fifty others. Revd Andrew when he returned from holiday, and came to congratulate me, put the ego in its place, when he remarked

"I felt sure Moorton would go for you. You see, a congregation nearly always goes for the devil they know, rather than one they don't."

That about summed it up!

The Deep End

TWO

I was doing a surprising thing — in fact a daft-like thing! I was sitting at a telephone and longing for it to ring with news of trouble! Here was I, Alexander Cameron, complete with the letters, M.R.C.V.S. after my name, positively God's gift to mankind — or at least to animal-kind — and the world out there didn't seem to know what it was missing. Nobody needed me! True, in two weeks I would be able to display my talents to the full, for I was then to start work as assistant vet in the little town of Mochrum, where I had completed my schooling, and near which my parents still lived — but that was two weeks away. Today, and for the next fortnight, I was locum for Len Simpson at Glenafton, where I'd been born, had lived till I was 14, and where I'd seen most of my practice as a student. A student . . . my mind went back four days to that scene at the old Vet College in Buccleugh Street, and to the longest hour of my life. We had all just completed our oral finals, and had to wait for the results to be posted. With exaggerated nonchalance we wandered about to put in the time. We tried table tennis, but somehow the spins and smashes wouldn't work. Every few minutes we drifted back to the courtyard to glance at the notice board or the clock. It must be bad, all this time they were taking! There were two theories about the orals. One was that if you had not been asked many questions, you were clearly home and dry on the written and practical exams. The other theory was that few questions meant it wasn't worth the examiners' time quizzing you for you were beyond hope and no amount of questions would alter the result, and you were therefore doomed to re-sits, or maybe repeating the final year. We all tried to recall how many questions we'd been asked, and wondered what comprised a safe number. The air was thick with tobacco smoke, as men feverishly, with shaking hand, lit one cigarette from another. Nobody knew about the cigarette-lung cancer connection then, and it is questionable as to whether it would have altered the position anyway in this frantic waiting period. At least the nicotine masked the odour of formaldehyde from the adjacent anatomy lab! We gravitated into the small groups of pals we had made over the years, and tried to console one another, but each of us, as time passed, was becoming convinced we'd failed the lot!

"They asked me how to treat conjunctivitis in an elephant" said John. An elephant! We pondered that one deeply, and decided John was heading for honours — or wait a minute — maybe the wretched external examiners were taking the mickey out of such an appalling student!

"Twice when I answered, the Principal put his head down" announced Joe. That sounded bad, but we tried to persuade Joe the Principal was just tired after a long stint. As time dragged past, we became more cynical and 'who cares anyway!' The die was cast!

"There they go!" came a shout and we looked up to see the two external examiners hurry away, to mingled cheers and whistles from about thirty suffering students. We knew now we had about twenty minutes to wait, for it was decreed that no results be posted until the examiners were safely away, ever since an irate student who'd failed in some past era had assaulted and caused grievous bodily harm to one of the blighters. Never were more cigarettes consumed, nor such inane chatter uttered, in any twenty minutes since — well — since last year anyway! Some of the suffering throng had been there then too. You could tell them by the extreme pallor of the cheeks in thirty faces virtually devoid of colour — except Bill — who'd had a few too many, and was glowing pink. We all knew he'd passed, for Bill was brilliant, had gained honours all along the way, and this was despite the fact that a friend had left him propped against his front door, out cold, the night before the written finals. He'd turned up seeing two exam papers — and probably passed both with distinction!

But the longest day passes, which was what some of us had not, and eventually there was a sudden silence as the Secretary emerged from the office, sheet of paper in hand, and headed, in a deathly hush, for the notice board. Then there was an almighty rush, and a series of shouts of relief or groans of agony, as we studied that notice. No names appeared, for we all, like the prisoners we were, had numbers, and there, in an unrepeatable moment of ineffable joy, was number eight — me! I was quick, but I wasn't quick enough, for the others had beaten me to the phones, in college and surrounding streets. I hared across several Glasgow streets before finding an empty phone box, and there, all pretence gone now, had sent the glad tidings forty-five miles across the air to my mother. There was a hush at the other end, while she swallowed a few lumps in her throat, before she managed to say

"Well done, son! Your dad will be pleased?'

Then a mad rush back for the closing ceremony, a quick look at the notice — yes, eight was still there, and into the Board room where I had missed all the speeches and was just in time to get in the tail of the queue to pay the registration fee which made one a Member of the Royal College of Veterinary Surgeons. Since the College had not then been taken over by the University, which a few years later for the same course, in the same antiquated buildings was issuing the degree of B.V.M.S., with a full scale graduation ceremony, we had to be content with a simple M.R.C.V.S., and pay for it. Now I was itching to treat my first patient, but, as if fearful of what might befall their beasts, the farmers of Glenafton parish were lying low. I glared at the phone again, and a thought came to me! That could be the only explanation, so I picked the instrument up to find out,

"Number please" came a cheerful voice, too cheerful, I thought in the circumstances.

"Er... operator ... I think this phone must be out of order"

"Why do you think that, sir" she asked. That was better ... 'sir!'

"Well, you see ... eh ... er ... it hasn't rung for two hours now, and it's a busy number ... rings a lot ... " I ended lamely.

"What is your number?" I told her.

"Oh, that's the vet's number, and I expect everyone knows Mr Simpson is away on holiday so they are not ringing," she answered brightly.

"But I'm here!" It sounded a bit pathetic.

"Yes, but you are just a student or something, aren't you, so ... " Was there anything these country operators didn't know, I wondered? A 'student' or a 'something' indeed.

"I'm not a student ... I'm a qualified vet ... I'm Mr Simpson's locum" In my indignation I must have raised my voice, for back came the 'polite to the public' tone.

"*I'm* hearing you loud and clear ... very clearly indeed," I could picture her holding her earphones back further, and probably the whole Exchange listening in. "However, if you just replace your receiver, I'll ring you back."

"Right." I grunted, and put the thing down.

In a minute it rang. "Aftonvale 153" I said hopefully, though forlornly.

"Just testing" came that wretched female voice. "The phone seems to be quite alright, Mr Cameron. I expect someone will ring you up eventually." She hung up, and I stood gaping. She even knew my name, and that 'eventually' seemed to imply anybody would have to be pretty desperate to risk me. "The wee besom" I thought, "probably she had been to school with me — even worse, had been in a lower class." I gnashed my teeth at her condescension, took a few turns round the room, and flung myself down in a chair with *The Veterinary Record*. I came to the 'wanted' column and read 'First year student desires to see general practice, south Scotland preferred!' That sent the wheels of memory whirling. A few years ago I had been a first year student about to see my first cases. I recalled coming to this very house all eager anticipation, shiny new wellington boots under one arm, lab coat under the other, and the only two instruments I possessed, a thermometer and a stethoscope, stuffed in a pocket. A long, lean, bronzed individual had answered the door, and hauled me into the room with the warmest of welcomes. This figure, with his wiry frame, open-air face, and aura of authority about him exactly fitted my image of a country vet, all the more so since he was dressed in riding breeches and a tweed jacket. The impression I gained that morning of Sandy Gray was confirmed by the passing years — a first class vet who had 'put up his plate' and carved out a new practice with his skill, enthusiasm and warm personality. Farmers felt they could trust this man both on a professional and personal basis, and they were right. There had been two other students there that first time, a third year student from Rhodesia, and Alec Milroy, a final year student, who in contrast to most final year men, treated first year students like myself as fellow human beings with some common sense, and not as creatures from some lower order of the animal kingdom. Three students at one time was unusual, and I've no doubt I was simply a nuisance, with, as yet, no theoretical knowledge, let alone practical experience. I'd become an expert at cutting up worms and cockroaches, but since the number of these that a vet is called to treat is somewhat limited, I couldn't for the life of me see how they would help me calve a cow or treat a lame horse.

"You may not see much practice here, but you will see life" said Sandy, an expression I was to hear him use with many students over the years. I did see life — but also a deal of practice too, and my list of case histories which had to be presented to the final year examiners was wide and varied.

At all hours of day or night, we would be on the job, and we recorded in the casebook every kind of presentation in calving: breech, head back, transverse, locked twins, and bizarre cases which baffled even Sandy. I remember the examiner picking on one of these, and asking in some surprise,

"What's this . . . plough handle in the stomach?"

It had been just that! A stirk maybe eight months old had been let out on grass for the first time after a long winter indoors. With its fellow Ayrshire stirks at Grassyards Farm, it had run pell mell about the field, in sheer joy at this new world of freedom. The owner had found it collapsed in the field, brought it in, and phoned Sandy. From the beginning it was a puzzle, and also a very sick animal. Early on, Sandy had diagnosed a ruptured diaphragm, the sheet of muscle that separates abdomen from chest. It was weird to listen with my brand new stethoscope at the stomach, and hear respiratory sounds, and at the chest and hear gastric gurgles. Sandy had suggested he try surgery, but to his relief the farmer had declined, and decided 'jist tae leave her alane an' see hoo she'll dae". We visited her every day for nine days, when inevitably, she died. A post mortem discovered a wooden plough handle in the abomasum or fourth stomach. The little stirk had, unknown to the farmer, run full pelt into a single furrow horse plough sitting in the field, and the force of the impact had snapped off the handle, which had been forced between two ribs — we had noticed this small wound in the chest but it had seemed of little consequence — then gone on right through the diaphragm into the stomach. The farmer had missed his plough handle, but hardly expected to find it in a beast's stomach! That case had been the first one of many to illustrate the astonishing durability of bovines, as against almost any other animal. The stomach contents were actually sploshing about in the chest, one lung was completely useless, the other almost so, yet it had lived for nine days! I could remember the quizzical look the examiner gave me when I explained the details. I couldn't blame him. For improbability, it beat any fishing story by a mile! Two things I recalled about that first 'seeing practice'. One was doing my first pregnancy diagnosis — or rather non diagnosis. Sandy had, by rectal examination, felt the size of the uterus through the rectal wall and pronounced four months in calf. Alec Milroy had done plenty of P.Ds and didn't bother, but the third year student and I were invited to have a go. "Yes, about four months," agreed the other, and I had vaguely nodded when my turn came. I hadn't felt a thing except rectal wall, and cow dung going up my sleeve. I later asked the Rhodesian lad how he could tell it was four months in calf, and confessed I hadn't felt a thing I was supposed to. He grinned at me and said, "that makes two of us". I must say he was a superb actor, because he had emphatically concurred with Sandy's estimate.

The other big memory of that first time was Sandy's wedding. He had gone off on honeymoon to sunny Devon, leaving Alec Milroy in charge. One night the phone rang and on answering, I was asked by a distant voice "Will you accept a long distance call from Devon and pay for the call?" I was still humming and hawing when Sandy's voice came over the line. The operator in Devon had taken my grunts as signifying agreement — he probably thought I was talking Gaelic! Sandy was brief and to the point.

"Alec" he said, "go into the top drawer of the dressing table upstairs, and get the three table tennis balls there, and post them on. They've a table in the hotel here, but no balls." In those closing years of the war T.T. balls were almost unobtainable.

"Oh . . . eh . . . righto, Sandy. Everythings OK here! We had a couple of calvings yesterday, a horse with colic and . . ."

"Cheerio, Alec, try and get these balls off tonight."

I looked at the phone in astonishment. What a queer vet; he didn't want to know about the work we'd done! Eighteen years old and still starry eyed with the novelty and excitement of treating animals, I found this inconceivable. Sure, it was his honeymoon, but I mean to say, we might be ruining his practice, or stuck and needing his advice! I had yet to learn how completely demanding single man practice was, and didn't appreciate that this was the first holiday Sandy had enjoyed for years, since the day he'd 'put up his plate'.

Brm, brm . . . brm . . . brm . . . brm, brm. I sat up with a jerk. The phone was ringing.

"Aftonvale 153" I almost shouted, in eagerness.

"This is Polquhirter Mains. We've a cow to clean tomorrow."

"Tomorrow? Oh, I can come out today and clean it"

"No, tomorrow is the third day. We always leave it till the third day"

"Sure you're wise?" I queried. "She's not off her food or anything?"

"Not her! See you tomorrow."

My hopes were dashed — tomorrow! Polquhirter Mains, (pronounced, as any sensible person knows, Pawhirter) that was Mr Aird. I knew the farm, just half a mile from where we'd lived in Glenafton; in fact we'd bought our eggs there. A cow to clean — a nice easy case — I stretched out my arm and rehearsed the job, meticulously removing the afterbirth from the rows of cotyledons, known as 'berries', which stuck out from the wall of the womb in a cow. To remove the placenta was a bit like peeling about fifty little oranges blindfold. I shuddered when I recalled the student who'd just pulled the 'berries' off, and the cow had almost bled to death. Oh, well, I couldn't get a much easier case for a first, I thought, but decided to check the car to make sure I'd put pessaries in. I'd already checked the contents three times. Why couldn't the case have been today?

I went back to my easy chair, looked round the familiar room, and recalled an incident which even after three years made me fidget uncomfortably. Like table tennis balls, cars were also at a premium, waiting period for new cars being about five years. But Sandy had discovered that one particular make of sports car could be obtained with just a few months wait. The time had passed, and daily he expected news of the car. Being a good vet and willing teacher, Sandy had a student almost every holiday period. That Easter there were three of us again, and on our way to the house, on the morning of 1st April, we thought it would be a fine idea to phone Sandy, say this was So and So's garage, that his new car had come, and would he collect if that afternoon. Being the only Scot in the three, I was appointed to disguise my voice and be the salesman. All went well; the fish took the bait, and when we arrived at his home, Sandy was one big smile.

"Great news, lads! The car's arrived, and I'm going for it this afternoon!" We shared in his joy, and kept our faces with just the right amount of smile on them. All morning, Sandy was in a ferment of excitement, wondered about the car's colour, what its top speed would be, how much she'd do to the gallon and so on.

"It's just as well your holidays are nearly over" he said thoughtfully, "for being a sports job, there's just two seats. I'll need to take just one student after this."

He was like a kid with a new toy, and we let him ramble on, and laughed behind our hands. What an April fool! He rushed through his cases, to be free for the great expedition of the afternoon, when he spotted the two of us sniggering surreptitiously in the back seat. He liked a joke, and he asked us to tell him this one. We did, thinking it was a pretty smart piece of work that we'd been able to keep it going so long. The car stopped with a screech of brakes, and Sandy went crimson, then a deathly white. He was furious, and really tore into us, which we deserved. He demanded to know who had made the call, and his wrath fell on me as I tried to curl up and look insignificant. Suddenly, we saw the thing for what it was, a rotten trick which had gone sour, and caused this man whom we all respected, and who had gone out of his way to help us, a lot of embarrassment, for he had apparently rung his bank immediately after the 'garage' call, and arranged an overdraft. His anger soon passed, but clearly he had been deeply hurt. Even now, sitting in that room where he had so often sat I felt bad about it, and remembered all I owed him. He had even taught me to drive! Sandy was now a vet with the Ministry of Agriculture — a reluctant Ministry man, for he had loved general practice. It had almost cost him his life. Giving a horse a pill or bolus, as it was called — balling a horse to the farmers — his hand had been badly gashed as the horse clamped down on him with its back teeth. He'd given the wound a dab of iodine, and then gone on for a few days, calving and cleaning cows, lancing abscesses, paring horses' feet — all the day-to-day tasks of the profession. His wound had become infected, a raging septicaemia developed, and in hospital, even with the new wonder antibiotics, his life had hung by a thread for days, and his convalescence was slow and frustrating. His illness had illustrated the vulnerability of a vet in a single man practice. All was well when you were fit, but there was just no time for illness or even regular holidays. So he'd advertised and sold the practice to Len Simpson, and taken a five-days-a-week job.

I'd seen practice with Len once or twice, and while a different build of man, and different style from Sandy, he too had taught me, and as my course at college drew near its end, increasingly gave me my head in cases. Now he was entrusting his practice to me, for a fortnight, and I appreciated that, especially as there would be a wage at the end — my first pay!

The day slowly dragged on, with lunch providing a break from the monotony of *The Veterinary Record*. I yawned my head off, and reconciled myself to the fact that in my first day on the job I'd done nothing before I was roused from my reverie by the phone. I couldn't believe it was a case — but it was — a cow with a torn teat at Mid Brockloch. I glanced at my watch, five o'clock, but better late than never.

It might have been a torn teat; I couldn't say, for we never found the teat. Where it had been was a great gaping hole in the udder, big enough to put your fist in, and pouring out a mixture of milk and blood which made the channel run red. Not only had the teat gone, but a great strip of udder skin was flapping about as the cow moved its legs. I kept my head down looking at that wound for a long time, to allow me to get over the shock and think. Never before, or indeed since, had I had to cope with such an udder wound — and to think that all day I had been longing for trouble of some kind!

Well, I'd got it now, big trouble. I was thrown in at the deep end with a vengeance, and I was trying madly to think how to swim!

"How did this happen?" I asked, trying to gain a few more moments to think. "She tried to jump a barbed wire fence" said Mr Barclay, the farmer. He was a quiet man, an excellent farmer, one of the most respected men in the district, a church elder, and a man who would seldom criticise anybody. He had known of me since I was a wee laddie, and must have realised I was just very recently qualified, but he'd received me with his customary quiet courtesy, as if I was some famous consultant come to treat his cow, and had even apologised for troubling me. The dairyman joined us at the cow, and gave the whole story.

"It was a young collie I'm training that chased her, the stippit dug. The beast's only a week calved, and just about our best milker. I hope you can dae something, veet."

I hoped so too, and looked at Mr Barclay again with added respect. Most men would have been cursing their dairyman and his dog, but no word of reproach had he uttered. He looked at me now, and said.

"I know it's a bad wound. I can only ask you to do what you can. What will you need?"

I shook myself from my mental paralysis and realised that this man of vast experience was awaiting the orders of a mere novice. At another time I'd have enjoyed this new position of power, but truth to tell, that ghastly wound had so shaken me, I wanted just to crawl away.

"I'll need lots of hot water, soap and towel, a rope and two strong men."

"Right," said Mr Barclay, "I'll get Bill the ploughman to give us a hand. Peter, leave the milking for now. The cows can wait." The dairyman nodded and departed.

"Bring a halter too!" I called after him. "Now, Mr Barclay, let's see where we can cast her — somewhere reasonably clean." He led me to the hayshed.

"Will this do?"

"First class," I nodded, "let's just make a good soft bed of straw for her." The dairyman's wife arrived with water, soap and a snowy white towel, Bill the ploughman came with a long rope, then he and Peter brought the patient, leading her with a struggle on the halter, to our improvised operating theatre. Meantime I'd laid out suture materials, needles, disinfectant, a great roll of cotton wool and so on, in gleaming white trays on top of some bales of straw. The trays wouldn't be white for long, I thought.

I'd never actually cast a cow myself before, but I had assisted often, and fixing the ropes in Reuff's method around the cow, told the men to pull. She went down exactly as the book said she should. That was encouraging. Soon we had her hind legs pulled forward, and trussed up like a parcel. I splashed disinfectant liberally into the bucket and started to clean the wound. I had only just cleaned away the outer crust of dirt and semi-congealed blood, when a great spurt of blood hit me in the eye. Two large vessels were sticking out of that hole, and pouring blood. You could grip them with your fingers easily and temporarily stop the flow. I did not know what damage I might be doing to the udder's blood supply, but these big vessels simply had to be tied off.

"I don't remember seeing such a bad tear before" said Mr Barclay.

"And I hope you won't again"

"I admire you men, the way you can stand up to this kind of thing" he said. He evidently couldn't hear the thunder of butterflies wings in my stomach, and the cow's blood must have been giving me a nice ruddy complexion I didn't possess. I was slow, painfully slow, but then it was my first suturing. It had all been done on dead greyhounds at college, and they don't bleed! The flapping skin was first stitched back where it belonged. The hole was a different problem.

"I'm afraid I can't do much about where the teat was, Mr Barclay. I can only try to make the hole smaller, but the pressure of milk will be bound to keep a hole open."

I put twenty-two stitches in her, puffed some antiseptic powder over a now dry, and reasonably neat wound, gave her a shot of penicillin, and said cheerfully, "Right, you can take the rope off and let her up now."

Sixty seconds later my cheerfulness had disappeared, for as the cow lurched to her feet, Peter's dog galloped out from some corner where he'd been lurking. The cow kicked up her heels, broke into a trot, and bang went half my sutures. There was an almighty hullabaloo, shouts from Mr Barclay and his men, and a weary moan from me. It didn't help now that the byreman had caught his dog, and was kicking it round the yard. We'd to catch the cow, cast her again, re-clean, and re-stitch the wound. At last it was done — I'd been one and a half hours on my first case.

"Keep her in the byre for a few days, and I'll see her tomorrow . . . and keep that dog out of the way."

So it was done. The first case was over, and as I drove home I reflected that one thing about going in at the deep end was that you had to swim, mighty quickly, and were unlikely to be so shocked again. The next day I cleaned the Polquhirter cow, and as he held the cow's tail, the byreman remarked "I heard about that job you did at Brockloch yesterday, sixty stitches, I was tellt!" I modestly protested that was a bit of an exaggeration, and marvelled at the speed of the bush telegraph in the country. It appeared others heard too, for I was kept respectably busy for the next fortnight, and the Brockloch cow was a frequent opener of farmers' conversation. It seemed that 'the student or something' had been accepted. The cow did fine, the wound healed without infection, and on my last visit, Peter the dairyman grinned and said "She's the quickest cow to milk in the place. As soon as I put the teat cups on her, the milk just pours out that quarter in two minutes. You've got to be gey smart wi' a bucket to catch it. We use that milk for feedin' calves."

One thing the case did teach me, a lesson I've never forgotten. Never look at a phone or it might ring and do a Brockloch on you!

Growing Pains

THREE

"You'll have to stitch it." said the boss, holding out a hand encased in a dish towel which was getting bloodier by the minute.

"We've phoned every blessed doctor in the place and they're all either on holiday or out and can't be reached" He took the towel off his hand to reveal a badly gashed thumb, blood welling up in it and dripping to the floor, at which sight his wife fled, saying "I can't bear to look!" I felt like fleeing after her!

"I couldn't do that" I quailed. "I could drive you to the hospital. It's only ten miles."

"And sit in Casualty bleeding like a stuck pig for two hours? No fear!"

"But I've done hardly any suturing" I wailed, "besides eh, er . . ." I paused helplessly.

"And I'm your boss so you feel on a hiding to nothing. Come on, Alec, I'm asking a lot, but you can do it" and he plonked himself down in a chair and said "Get busy!"

Then followed one of the most harrowing half hours of my life, yet one of the most momentous of my vet career. I cleaned the wound, soaked it with Ethyl Chloride local anaesthetic, and forceps in one hand, needle in the other, began. He jumped as the needle went in, so I said "Sorry," and applied more Ethyl Chloride. Slowly, painfully slowly, I sutured his thumb which was cut along almost its entire length. He must have felt it plenty, but said not a word except at the end "Well done," as I finished tying on a bandage. I noticed there were beads of perspiration on his forehead, but they were nothing to the rivers of sweat running down my back. Never, I'm sure, did two men welcome more the cup of tea that arrived at that moment.

The next morning he greeted me with the news that he'd been to his doctor the previous evening, and the Doc had said "A first class job" and jabbed him with an anti-tetanus shot. I don't know whether the doctor really said any such thing, and daily I waited for the boss to appear with his arm in a sling and say he had the beginnings of gangrene, or his wife to inform me some morning that he'd been carted off in the night with blood poisoning. But no, it healed perfectly. From that moment, I was trusted with almost any kind of case. It was a sticky start, and not one I'd recommend to any budding vet, but there's no doubt it was a turning point in my career.

I'd been Mr Buchan's assistant for some weeks before 'the case of the boss's thumb', but all I'd had to do were very routine jobs such as injections in calves, cleaning cows and all the cat work. He reckoned I couldn't do much damage with the first two and the cats didn't matter! Mind you, I could understand his attitude. He had come into an almost dead practice some years before, and by his hard work, youthful vigour and modern methods had built up the practice to the point where it was too much for one man and barely enough for two. It was still growing, and he reckoned that shortly it would keep two men fully occupied. Ian Buchan's clients came to him because he was a good vet with a strong personality. It was not going to be easy for him to trust another with his clients, nor the clients to accept anyone but himself. The position had been made worse by the one assistant he'd had for a few months, my immediate predecessor, who, by all accounts, had been a disaster. 'Pansy', 'Cissy', 'Dreep', were some of the words I'd heard used to describe him. I'd only met him once, but he was a city bred lad whose long hair, foppish ways and superior manner, had not exactly impressed the hard headed farmers of Ayrshire. Typical of the stories told me, no doubt by way of warning, concerned Mrs McQueen and her pigs. That worthy woman had conducted the young vet round to her piggery, where he had gazed vaguely and dreamily into the pen in question, and then taken out his comb to sleek back his long hair. Mrs McQueen had suggested he might like a mirror, to which he had replied "thank you all the same but I'll manage". The pig owner had then asked him if he knew anything about pigs, and he'd replied "Not much", whereupon, being a woman of bold speech, sterling character and bulging muscles, she'd run him off the farm. All this explained why I'd had my cases hand picked for me, that while the boss did eight, I was given two, and consequently spent much of my time making up stomach mixtures, scour powders, bloat drenches and the like, and when I had the shelves groaning with about a year's supply of the various remedies, I'd then been given a supply of Westerns and a comfortable armchair to while away the hours. Many boring days I'd put in, just sitting in the surgery, which was, in fact, an annexe of their bungalow home, the hours brightened somewhat by the appearance at regular intervals of Mrs Buchan with tea or coffee.

I told myself this was only to be expected, that these were merely the growing pains of becoming a vet, and that eventually things would change, but they were not changing quickly enough . . . till the thumb! "Some of my colleagues' initiation into practice was that they had been rushed off their feet while my gripe was that I was getting next to nothing to do. However, for a week, the boss was limited in what he could tackle and I'd to fill in for him. It seemed that agonising half hour we'd shared had altered my position completely and gained his confidence". In that week amongst other things, I treated two milk fevers, calved three cows, including an embryotomy (where a calf has to be dismembered inside the cow by means of a fine wire like a cheese wire) in a bloated dead calf, an operation I'd been dreading. Also in that week I cleaned my first mare at Mr Anderson's farm at Garpin. He patiently held the mare, and though he said nothing, I suspected he knew this was my first, and it was with considerable satisfaction that I ran my fingers between the placenta and the wall of the uterus, and peeled off the placenta in one piece. I'd laid it out on the ground afterwards, and with relief saw the 'pair of breeches shape' that had been described at College, with the warning that if we didn't have that, we'd left a bit behind, which in a mare, in complete contrast to a cow, could produce metritis and death in a short time.

But if I'd come good with my boss, though I still regarded him with some awe akin to fear, it was a different story with the farmers. I found there weren't many Mr Andersons about in courtesy and confidence. As far as the farmers were concerned, there was nobody like Mr Buchan and when I appeared their faces perceptibly fell, and they'd enquire if Mr Buchan was ill or away, and had I seen anything like this case before. My position was made more difficult by the fact that I'd gone to the local Academy with sons and daughters of some of them. My parents still lived in the area, and in a little town like Mochrum, well, 'a prophet hath no honour in his own country', so what hope was there for a vet? But bit by bit, with a few cases under the belt on each farm, one came, at least to be accepted. Mind you, there were many growing pains to be endured, difficulties to be overcome.

For example, while attending a cow at Merkland one day, I'd diagnosed an impacted rumen, the first of a cow's four stomachs. I knew various stomach drenches would do the job of starting it churning over again, but that Carbachol would be quicker. So I got out my syringe and injected a few cc's into the cows neck, and closed my case. The farmer continued to glance at me expectantly. Finally he asked "Are you no' goin' tae drench her?"

"No need now. That injection will do instead."

He treated me to a look of withering scorn, and demanded, "Hoo can a jag in the neck get tae a coo's stomach?"

"Give it twenty-four hours and you'll see," I said, fingers crossed.

I looked in next day and he greeted me with a huge smile, and took my arm to conduct me up the byre.

"Man," he said, "that jag fair did the trick. There's a barrow load o' dung ahin' 'er. See," he pointed, and we both stood admiring as if it were gold!

One or two farmers were openly hostile. Many had pedigree herds of Ayrshires or Aberdeen Anguses; most were first class farmers, and the majority had some knowledge of the various diseases and their treatments. They tended to phone up and ask the vet to come and inject some particular drug, and he had to be mighty sure of himself, if he deviated from their stated orders. Old man McNulty was like that. He had a cynical outlook and seemed to think he was doing the vet a considerable favour by calling him, and he should note that fact! My first brush with him was sticky. It happened to be the afternoon milking time when I walked up the byre, and I was looking round about me for signs of human life when a loud gruff voice demanded to know "Who the hell are you, and where do you think you might be going?"

I told him I was Mr Buchan's assistant, and I'd been sent to see a sick cow. He didn't look at me, but through me, and jabbing a finger in the air, announced:

"When I send for the veet, I expect the veet, an' no boy (I was twenty-four!) just learnin' the trade at my expense!"

I explained that Mr Buchan was away at a calving case, and he couldn't cover all the work himself.

"Well, he kens damn fine to come himsel' to me!"

This seemed either to imply that he was some close buddy of the boss or had very precious beasts indeed. I had been sent to do a job, and I was going to try to do it, so asked, "Could I see the sick beast now I'm here anyway, Mr McNulty?"

"Och, it's no seeck — it's stawed — it just wants a bottle o' your glucose. That's her second fae the end."

A 'stawed' cow in Ayrshire was a case of acetonaemia, very prevalent towards the end of winter, when the beasts had been housed for six months, and stall fed on concentrates. I took her temperature. The old man spat derisively (it was soon apparent he was a spitting addict) and asked what I was playing at. I ignored him and took her pulse. Both were slightly above normal. I caught her by the horns and smelled her breath; there was acetone there alright, but I had a vague uneasiness about her, and wasn't satisfied that the acetonaemia was the prime cause of her going off her food. She had a pained look about her, back slightly arched, elbows pointing outwards. I gave her a poke just behind the diaphragm and got a decided grunt. The old man, meantime, was alternating between cynical laughter and derisive spitting at my antics. He really was a shocker!

"I'm not sure but there's something more than acetonaemia" I said.

"And I'm telling you she's stawed! Get the glucose into her!"

"Oh, I'll do that alright, but I'd like to put the Cintel on her." (The Cintel was our metal detector . . . earphones . . . a sensitive diaphragm that picked up the presence of any ferrous metal which might be lodged in a cow's stomach. At Glenafton we had, in fact made do with an old wartime mine detector.) "I think she's got a wire or nail in her."

"Damn the fear o' it!"

"I maybe wrong, but I'd like to see what Mr Buchan thinks"

"Well, see he comes himsel', an' disnae charge me for twae visits."

The boss was just back from his calving when I walked in the Surgery. I told him of old man McNulty and his cow.

"I'll nip up with the Cintel after tea" he said. "Away you go home and get yours and don't worry about either McNulty, father or son."

So I departed for home three miles out in the country where my father was Station Master of two small railway stations. My times off duty were strictly limited to Friday evenings, and one weekend a month. Otherwise I was on duty at the surgery, or on call, which meant I had to be by a phone. The summons came about eight o'clock. "Rumenotomy at McNulty's; come and give me a hand" said the boss.

In those days when straw and hay was held in bales by wire instead of string, and in an area where there were principally wire fences as opposed to hedges or dykes, a foreign body was quite common. Indeed a rumenotomy was the in operation of the time. What happened was that the cow, a non selective feeder, would scoop up a piece of wire or nail in hay or grass, and this metal would make its way to the reticulum or second of the four stomachs, where it would sometimes, but by no means always, cause trouble. A long list of unusual objects including an umbrella frame had been discovered in cows' stomachs, many of these foreign bodies only being discovered at slaughter, and apparently having caused no discomfort to the beast. The only unusual object apart from nails and wires that we had so far found was a sixpence, which was causing no trouble, but had some bits of wire for company which were. Anyway, the sixpence was better in the vet's pocket than the cow's stomach. Symptoms of the presence of a foreign body only occurred when it was actually lodged in the wall of the reticulum, and causing pain and sepsis. But the real danger was that a fall, or some violent muscular effort like calving, would force the metal right through the reticulum, diaphragm, and into the pericardeum, the sheath surrounding the heart. Many a sudden death in an apparently healthy cow was due to the object reaching the heart itself, the distance between reticulum and heart being a matter of a few inches. A rumenotomy was only successful when the foreign body was still in the stomach and could be removed. If it had passed into the chest cavity or pericardeum, it could not be reached and the cow was doomed.

I drove with the boss up to the farm where the whole squad was mustered — the old man, who never looked at me or spoke to me the whole night, the son who briefly nodded, plus two farm labourers who were still human enough in that sour farm, to raise a smile of welcome. The rumenotomy proceeded normally, an opening being cut in the cow's left side (under local anaesthetic) and the contents of the massive rumen removed and carted away in a barrow. Then reaching through the incision in the rumen wall, the vet searched about in the reticulum for whatever he could find. The boss nearly always did this part of the proceedings himself, and in this case, after a few moments, he gave a grunt of satisfaction and brought forth a three-inch nail.

"It was through almost right to the head. A few more days and we'd have been too late, Mr McNulty" he announced, and went on "in fact we might still be too late for that nail could possibly already have set up a pericarditis, that's an inflammation round the heart!"

Old man McNulty was examining the nail feverishly, running it round in his hands, holding it up to the light. In fact he did everything but test it with his teeth. I think he'd have liked to have accused me of planting it, but that being impossible, he rounded on his two workers.

"Damn carelessness, you lazy devils! One of you must have left that lying when you were fencing. If that happens again, I'll have your hides and then it will be doon the road for the pair o' you." His choice of words gave me a picture of two skinless men walking down the road. Mr McNulty was the kind of man who must always have someone to blame.

"Well done, Alec" said the boss as we headed away. 'I'll charge the old rascal double for doing the operation after hours. He insisted it be done tonight. You should have seen him when the old Cintel started buzzing. He nearly had a fit, swore for five minutes, then demanded that I do something right away. You made a good job of the suturing, by the way"

I'd appreciated that. Having got the nail out, he had very pointedly told me to stitch her up to show that he had confidence in me.

"Och well, I did my practice sutures in a nice tender skin!" He grinned.

A few days later we had another rumenotomy, but the atmosphere and circumstances were totally different. For a start, it was at Willie McCulloch's farm, and that meant that we were welcomed warmly, for Mr and Mrs Buchan and the McCullochs were very friendly and socialised together. Willie was a gentle, canny soul who would seldom speak ill of anybody. He had a droll manner, and having been endowed with a rather long face by nature, when he had the cares of the world on his shoulders, his expression was not unlike a friendly bloodhound. Mr Buchan had told me that when the McCulloch's child, now a growing boy, had arrived, he had cried more or less solidly every night for two years! Father and mother took night about walking the floor with him, and on one occasion Mrs McCulloch, at her wits' end, appealed to her somnolent spouse "what will I do with him?" to which she got the weary reply "throw him out the window!" However, Willie had survived the rigours of parenthood though it was maybe significant that they had but the one child.

It appeared that often a deal of leg pulling went on between Willie and Mr Buchan, and on the occasion of the operation, the boss decided to play a trick on Willie. At the appropriate moment when he withdrew his arm to clean and re-soap it preparatory to the search in the reticulum, I was to slip him a great long, thick spike, something like a tent peg in appearance, which I duly managed without Willie spotting me. The boss played up well, muttering to himself as if perplexed, and finally, explosively shouting

"Good life! What have we here?"

"What is it, Ian," demanded Willie excitedly, "have you found something?"

The spike was slowly and solemnly brought forth and handed to Willie, whose large eyes opened another couple of inches while his face fell another foot, making him look more than ever like a sorrowing blood hound who has just seen his quarry escape up a tree. It was sometime before Willie found speech, "Would you credit it! Nae wonder the beast was no' weel" he finally pronounced. The boss had meantime turned his face cow-wards and was guddling about in the reticulum, while I discovered I had to bend over the bucket for some time and slowly wash my arms, each thus successfully for a few minutes managing to hide our humour, for Willie's expression would have made the dourest mortal laugh. A piece of wire was found, genuinely, and removed, and the boss could hide his joke no longer, for in truth the situation had become solemn. "I'm sorry, Willie, we had you on. There was just the wire" he said.

It was some time before this dawned on Willie who was still gazing awe-struck at the spike. "So it wisna' this at a'?' he finally managed.

"No, Willie it was the wire" said the boss "and though I'm not certain, I think, Willie, that's just a bit of it, and there's another bit already broken off in her chest. Keep your fingers crossed."

Stories should have happy endings, but in real life it is not always so. In this instance old McNulty's cow survived, while likeable, friendly Willie's beast died a few days later, which maybe supports the old Scots maxim that "the de'il's kind to his ain!"

Go And Learn To Be Vets

FOUR

"Go out now from this College and learn to be vets" our Principal had said to us as we left with the letters M.R.C.V.S. after our names. We had smiled at his paternalism: "Dear old boy. Learn to be vets indeed. What does he think we've been doing for five years. We are vets. We know it all now."

So youth, in its innocence, or arrogance, has always answered. But after some months as an assistant vet in a general, mainly farm practice, the words had come back to me and hit me smack between the eyes, for every week I was realising there was a very great deal still to be learned. Much I was learning from watching my boss at work. Some of it I was finding out by trial and error and getting away with it. A great deal I was learning the hard way. The growing pains were still mighty sore at times.

The boss came in chuckling one morning.

"You know wee MacFarlane down the road at Blackbyre?" he asked. I nodded. "I was out there at a Milk Fever this morning and as we were coming out the door he stopped and pointed up at a beam in the roof.

"Do you see that?" says he "do you think I could reach it."

"Never" says I. "Oh well I reached it last nicht" he told me. "Seemingly he and his dairyman had just come out to start the evening milking, when the bull came at them. He'd broken his chain, and you know he's a treacherous brute. Well, they both turned and ran for the door, the dairyman got there first but slammed the door behind him. So with the bull breathing down his neck, MacFarlane jumped, caught the beam, and sat there looking down at his bull. glaring up at him, and pawing the floor. Eventually MacFarlane walked along the rest of the beams which go on into the next byre and got out the door there. It was some jump, Alec. It's amazing what you can do with a bull at your back." He paused, and lit his pipe, then went on. "I mind when I was blood testing the herd at Dalwhinnie — I don't think you've been there yet — but the couple there have a wee boy who's a mongol child. They've also got a notorious bull. The wee fellow didn't like me 'jaggin' his coos', so he walked away saying 'I'll get somebody that'll sort you.' He did too, for he came back leading this big brute with a piece of binder cord through its ring. He led him right up the byre to me and said "There he's, Jock. Get him,' and when I looked round, the boy's father was up on the milk pipe."

"What did you do?" I asked.

"Stayed put where I was between two cows where the bull couldn't get at me. The farmer spoke quietly to his boy, still hanging on to the milk pipe, and at last he went away, and that bull followed him like a pup on a lead."

"How do you account for something like that?"

"I don't know, Alec, but I think it's just that these kids don't know any fear, and the animal senses it. Take Spike (his Springer Spaniel.) You know how he'll let nobody get in the car unless I'm there?"

"I know fine; he nearly took the hand off me the other day when I opened the door" I recalled.

"The only person who ever got in there without me was wee James McKendrick;"

"And he's a mongol too."

"He is, and the first time I was on the farm, I said to his father he'd better keep James away from the car or Spike would go for him; but the old man shook his head and said 'I don't think the dog would touch him'. 'Well, you don't know Spike,' says I, and off we went to the byre. When we came back, James was sitting in the car and Spike was licking his hand. I was flabbergasted, and asked his father how he had known the dog wouldn't harm him? He told me that one day when he came into the farm close, he couldn't find him. He looked about, and saw the stable door open, so in he went, and there was James actually standing between a horse's front and back legs, and that horse would not let nobody except one certain ploughman near him, not even McKendrick himself. 'Animals don't hurt James' was all he said." He paused and puffed at his pipe, "Maybe there's something in the saying that there's a special Providence that looks after drunk men and helpless bairns!"

I thought about the stories as I set off on my morning round. I knew plenty about Ayrshire bulls. As a boy I'd spent a lot of time going about farms, and I'd known of several instances where a bull had attacked its owner. In two instances, the farmer had actually been killed. I made a mental note to tread warily when around bulls. But pigs now, they were safe. So I thought as I drove into Applegrove, a bonny wee farm run by two sisters. I was told that the patient was a pig about six weeks old, one of a litter of eight. I rang the farmhouse bell, got no reply, so walked round the buildings shouting "Hello! Anybody about?" I couldn't find a soul so went looking for the patient, and came to a pen with a sow and seven piglets. "Aha," I reasoned, having O level maths, "I bet the patient's the one that's missing. It will be lying in the house." It was a typical pig pen with a concrete exercising yard and feeding trough, with the pig house built on with a low door for the pigs to get out and in. There was another door round the back, but it seemed to be all blocked up, so I jumped into the pen, and crawled through the wee low door, my black case in my hand. Sure enough, there lying on the straw was a piglet. He wasn't all that sick for as soon as I'd inserted the thermometer into his rectum, he hollered loudly, there was a great snort from outside, and in came mother, at the trot, mouth open, heading straight for me. She had a fine set of teeth, and she evidently meant to use them. I leapt to my feet as she took a snap at my leg. She missed, but only just, and got a mouthful of corduroy trousers. She stood looking at me as much as to say 'the corduroy is just for starters, now for the main course', while I fended her off with my case. I licked my lips and glanced around nervously. The proper door really was all blocked up with bales of straw, and I wasn't going to turn my back on that wild beast, to remove them, I sort of sidled along the wall towards the low door I'd come in. The sow sidled along too. It was stalemate, and for some time we just stood and watched each other, neither of us liking what we saw. When I thought her eyes wavered just a fraction from me towards her offspring, I made a sudden dive for that door and crawled through it. No rabbit ever disappeared down its burrow quicker than me exiting from that pig-house. I didn't stop to look behind me, but with coat tails flapping and black case bursting open, I leapt the wall. I just made it too, as she came after me for another tasty bite. I was vaguely aware of a figure standing before me as I jumped who turned out to be female, and bent double with laughter. I assumed — rightly, that this was one of the Misses Wilson, and she was having the best laugh she'd had for a long time.

"Miss Wilson?" I enquired, with a sort of 'we are not amused' note in my voice. She nodded, and then laughed some more, her large well padded frame quivering like a jelly. "If you'd seen yourself . . . Ha.Ha.Ha. A vet six feet tall jumping a wall, chased by a wee pig; oh . . . Ho.Ho.Ho!

"She nearly had me too," I said in an aggrieved tone, "look at my trousers!" She did, sobered up, then said

"That'll teach you, young man, never to molest a piglet when its mother is about." It did too; ever afterwards when handling babies that were likely to squeal, I made sure there was a good stout door between the sow and myself.

Yes, some things were learned the hard way, like being too casual, even with seemingly quiet animals. Just finishing a herd Tuberculin test, at the end of a hard day, I came to this obviously ancient beast, with great spreading horns. Thinking her quiet, I got a bit too near her head and she came round in a flash and caught me on the jaw with the base of one horn, sending me staggering into the middle of the byre. Cassius Clay would have been proud of that left hook. I honestly thought my jaw was broken, but apparently it was only bruised. Being too confident was just as risky as being too casual, I discovered. I'd gone to McNulty's to inject a cow for Foul in the Foot, known in Ayreshire as Clit-ill. For some reason, McNulty seemed to get a lot of it. It was summer, there wasn't a man about the place, but Mrs McNulty told me I'd find the cow in the byre, the only beast there. I'd injected many beasts before in the mammary vein, but if the animal was hale and hearty and in full possession of its faculties, as this one was, I usually got somebody to push the beast's tail straight up, or hold its nose, both traditional means of restraint. Today I just boldly went forward, flutter valve on the sulphamezathine bottle at the ready, and stuck the needle into the vein. The next moment I was flat on my back in the middle of the byre. I'd never even seen the foot come up, but I sure felt it. Getting kicked by cows, or toes trodden on, was an almost daily occurrence, but that was the father and mother of all kicks. She looked round to see the effect of her nifty back heeler, then went on chewing the cud, satisfied she'd done a good job, and given a typical McNulty welcome in the old man's absence. I searched around the byre for some time before I found the needle, shuddering to think what the old boy would say if a further rumenotomy disclosed a hypodermic needle and, taking a clean one from the box, injected the drug subcutaneously behind her shoulder, a safe position half way between horns and hind legs. I didn't know whether the drug was effective this way, since it had always been given straight into the bloodstream before, to hit the bug hard and produce a knock out blow, emulating the cow's style! Apparently it did work, so I'd learned that fact, and more important, never again to attack the mammary vein of a fit, unrestrained cow.

What with the risk of contracting brucellosis, anthrax, rabies, psittacosis, mange, tape worms, and a host of other cheerful things, I was discovering that my profession was somewhat hazardous. But it was fascinating too, and as I bumped along the side roads of my native county, I was learning all the time, and content with my lot. I was even learning how to handle the car I'd be given, an ancient Standard whose back springs were gone, so cornering produced a decided tilt, a horrible rubbing sound and the smell of tortured rubber. In fact, it was not unlike the motion of a ship, and to add to the nautical illusion, there was a regular splash of water. Just above my head was a hole in the roof. I kept it stuffed with a rag, and when it rained (which it does quite a lot in Ayrshire) I rolled down the window, pulled out the dripping rag, squeezed its excess moisture out the window and stuffed it back in the roof, all with one hand while at the same time, keeling my torso sufficiently far over to prevent the rain pouring straight down my neck through the unguarded hole. It certainly gave one a new slant on the passing scene! The boss was impatiently waiting the delivery of a Land Rover, when I would fall heir to his Ford Prefect but meantime the Standard staggered on. Compared to the old Austin at Glenafton, however, my car was positively hale and hearty. We had a visit from my friend Mike, who had gone as Mr Simpson's assistant to Glenafton, and he arrived with a roar one evening to see us, driving the same old car in which I'd learned to drive, and which I'd used when acting as *locum*. It was now in such a state that it was in line for being declared a disaster area. I wondered why Mike came out the passenger door,until I saw the intricate arrangement of string and wire keeping the driver's door still attached to the body. There was a hole in the floor which no doubt helped ventilation but provided a water hazard from beneath. To start the car, Mike laid a brick on the accelerator pedal, cranked the startling handle like mad, then leapt into the car, removed the brick and replaced it with his foot. If he didn't manage this without the engine stopping, he had to begin the brick work all over again. Apparently the brakes, long suspect, had now all but given up the ghost. Mike enlivened the evening by telling us some of his experiences in his brakeless car such as an occasion when a bus drew into a stopping place to pick up the waiting passengers. Coming in the opposite direction was a car, and just behind the bus came Mike, hauling like mad on the Austin's hand brake, which slowed him sufficiently to allow him to swerve on to the footpath and nip out in front of the bus, to the astonishment of passengers and driver. In those days before M.O.T. tests on a car's roadworthiness, there were as many dangers to the budding vet just driving to the farm, as awaited him on it.

The days were full of interest and incident, with new cases and the occasional new client. Came the day when I gained one. Mrs Buchan came through from the telephone looking extremely worried, and not for the first time, I realised what a strain was imposed on the wife in a practice which could not afford a receptionist/secretary. It seemed that Mr Wallace had a cow choked on a potato, and badly swollen with the build up of gas. He had phoned for his own vet who was miles away, and unable to be contacted, as was Mr Buchan. Now Mr Wallace was an important man in the area, in his business being an employer of many men, but he also farmed. So I could understand Mrs Buchan's anxiety when she asked me if I could go, and if I knew what to do. I knew alright, but didn't tell her I'd never seen, far less treated a Choke before. However, after throwing a probang and trocar and canula into the car, I hurried at the Standard's full rate of knots to the farm, where I was received somewhat suspiciously by Mr Wallace himself. He was used to experienced vets, and I could read the doubt in his glance. The case was fairly desperate, and the cow on the point of collapse. I got the long probang over the beast's throat, and gave the potato a few taps, but it was stuck fast, and the animal was ballooning by the minute to bursting point.

"I'll have to stick her" I said.

"I think you will," he agreed.

So, recalling from our college lectures how to work out the spot for stabbing the rumen, I tried, and only then realised how tough a cow's hide could be. I couldn't get the trocar through the skin, so had to use a scalpel. The cow never felt it; she was in too much agony in other ways, liable either to float up into the air or explode in our faces, it seemed to me. The skin cut, I plunged the instrument in, withdrew the trocar, and like a dam bursting, the gas came hissing out of the canula. When she had reached reasonable proportions again, I had another go at shifting the potato, and with the inside pressure now considerably reduced, it went first shot into the stomach. Mr Wallace looked at me and said, "I bet you were sweating the first time you had to do that." I smiled and agreed, omitting to tell him this was it. When I got back the boss cross-examined me on that case. Clearly he had been hoping to get a foothold in the Wallace establishment for some time; he was pleased, and said so. This increased his confidence in me, for soon after that he began asking me which cases I'd like to do. He phoned one evening shortly afterwards, and cheerfully announced I could take my pick between lambing a ewe in a blizzard of snow up the hills at Greenwell, or driving twelve miles to treat a mare with colic. I knew which one I preferred, but thought it prudent to say "whatever you like".

"I'll do the lambing then" he decided. I was relieved, for it really was a perishing night. The colic proved to be quite a violent one, with the mare sweating, and kicking every few minutes at her abdomen. I listened and could hear plenty of gurgles and squeaks; in fact I reckoned there was about as much wind inside her as even now would be blowing round the boss up at Greenwell. However, to be certain there was no twist, I did a rectal. All seemed straightforward, an ordinary flatulent, spasmodic colic, treated with a jab of Pethidine, followed by some Carbachol. Fairly quickly the Pethidine brought relief, and I felt that she could be safely left, and that during the night, there would be sundry explosions coming from her rear, and by morning, a good load of dung.

So the weeks and months sped past, full of interest now. Except for the precious Friday evening off, it was strictly duty. If there was nothing pressing, I could stay at home and have any calls relayed, but one day the boss decided it would be a considerable asset to have a few kennels in a small brick building at the top of his garden. I'd never been a bricklayer or plasterer before, but the kennels shot up in no time — it's amazing how quickly you can work just in order to keep warm! With two of us working, and with a small number of kennels, the boss was able to encourage the small animal side of practice, something he'd wanted to do for a few years. An evening consulting hour was started, the first boarders arrived, and dogs could be left for a couple of days after whatever surgery they'd undergone.

Small animal operations were always done in the evenings, sometimes it being ten o'clock before we were able to start. The boss, initially, did all the surgery; I was anaethetist and general factotum! I thought him a good surgeon, and certainly he was in farm animals. Comparing him with Kenneth later, Ian was not in the same class with small animals — but in relation to both of them, I was a complete dud, my fingers being all thumbs, and my general surgical technique leaving a lot to be desired. I recall the evening when the boss told me to spay a cat, while he would assist. A simpler operation can hardly be imagined, and I'd seen him do a fair number. With my patient safely anaesthetised, I made my incision, and poked about looking for ovaries and uterus. I kept finding loops of small intestine, but no uterus. I looked at the cat again to make sure it was a female, then enlarged my incision and groped and guddled some more. Finally, with sweat blinding me, I said to the boss, with what dignity I could muster "I think there must be something abnormal about this cat. Maybe you better do it" He took over and found ovaries and uterus immediately. So much for my abnormal cat!

This business of learning to be a vet could be humiliating, as well as dangerous. I had my failures too on the farms. Twice I'd had to admit defeat at calvings; both were great big, ugly bulldog calves, an abnormality certain strains of Ayrshire threw up occasionally. In both cases, I'd had to ask the farmer to phone the boss, and felt very small indeed when he managed to complete an embryotomy, where I'd failed. In each case, he'd tried to console me my saying 'it was a right stinker!', but needless to say, this didn't help my reputation with these particular farmers.

Having learned that danger was part of my profession, seeing this man work made me realise that dedication and sheer determination were also necessary, and I pledged myself after that second defeat that henceforward determination would be part of my makeup. Many, many times there at Mochrum and in the years to follow in Devon, I was on the point of giving up at calving, having lain on my side and had each hand and arm in turn numbed by the pressure of the calf on them, pinning them to the pelvic bones. More than once I felt like saying 'phone for Mr Buchan', if only to get relief after two or three hours hard labour, and only sheer cussedness kept me going. I learned to grit my teeth, and fight on, and gradually, over the two years there, I came to be accepted by all but a few farmers and there would be a welcome 'Hello, Alec!' or 'Good morning, Mr Cameron!' It felt good. The apprentice was gradually becoming a tradesman, with every now and again something that would knock the pins out of me and cut me right down to size.

Now that we had the kennels, if a client turned up with a dog through the day, Mrs Buchan would put it in a kennel till one of us came in. One morning I was told there was a Labrador in kennels, to be destroyed. The boss liked to use a humane killer in large dogs and the gun was one of the captive bolt type. I hated it, but an assistant has to do as he's told. I went into the kennels with the humane killer, brought out a handsome looking Labrador, held him firmly by the collar, put the gun to his head, and pulled the trigger. At the very last moment, he jerked his head, let out a howl as the gun went off, and he was off. I was left with his collar in one hand, and a smoking gun in the other. I'd forgotten to make sure the outer door was properly closed, and he was out, down the drive and away. It was horrific, for I knew the bolt had broken the skin and drawn blood. As white as a ghost, I'm certain, I ran after him, weapon still in one hand, collar in the other. He was headed for the town, and had anyone been about, very likely they would at once have phoned the police or the nearest lunatic asylum, with a wild looking man charging about the place with a gun. Fortunately there was not a soul on the street; equally fortunately I had been told the dog's name was Rex, so hollering "Rex . . . Rex . . . here boy" . . . I kept going and miracle of miracles, he eventually stopped at the sound of his name. I slipped the collar back on him, tried not to look at this poor beast with a small hole in his skull spurting blood, then took him back to kennels, shut the door, and finished the job. I had to grit my teeth to do it, and felt the biggest rotter in creation. That trusting dog had stopped at the sound of his name, let me lead him back to a place of terror — and there I'd betrayed his trust. Ugh! I must have looked pretty ghastly when I went in the Surgery door, for Mrs Buchan asked me what was wrong, and I told her the tale. She also said "Ugh!", then poured a strong cup of tea. Later in the day, the boss cornered me, "I've been hearing about your experience this morning, Alec," he said.

"I made a right mess of it . . ." I began, but he interrupted.

"Now, I've been meaning to talk to you about this. You're far too careless in these kennels. You must always shut the outer door, as I do."

I nodded dumbly.

"We can't have escaped dogs running all over the town. It will give the kennels a bad name." 'Especially when they have a hole in their head,' I thought. "Don't you agree, Alec?"

"Yes . . . oh, yes, I'm sorry. It was sheer carelessness."

"Well then, we'll say no more about it."

A few mornings later, as I was heading towards the surgery to begin another day's work, I met the boss driving furiously down the hill that led to Mochrum's shopping centre. 'A pretty urgent case', I thought. I got into the Surgery, hung about for a time, and finally Mrs Buchan came through and said I should just tick where I was going, and go on.

"Ian isn't here," she said. "He was taking the dogs out of the kennels this morning to exercise them, when three got away from him. He might be some time."

He might indeed, I thought, searching the town for three runaways.

"How did it happen?" I asked innocently.

"He didn't stop to tell me." she answered, truly innocently.

No word was spoken about the runaways, but I knew, and the boss knew I knew he'd forgotten to close the outer door!

Learning to be a vet could be a long process, I thought.

New Beginnings

FIVE

"Mr Cameron", a lass said to me the other day, "Brian and I are getting engaged a year come June the first on my birthday."

I had a quiet smile to myself at her earnestness, but when she had gone, I sat at my desk and thought back over the years. That girl seemed part of the modern way; you fix your engagement in advance. It seems so matter-of-fact, so staid, so planned, so seemingly lacking in romance.

My mind went back over the years to a bright summer day in June. Janet and I had gone to the Heads of Ayr for a swim, a picnic, an afternoon away from the grind of veterinary practice and teaching maths. On the way back up over the hill to the car, as I watched her swinging on ahead of me, I realised I could not live without this girl any longer and there and then asked her to marry me. Her eyes sparkled, she drew a great, deep breath, a smile seemed to engulf her whole being, and she said

"Oh yes!"

Mind you, it was to be expected, even if the culmination was unplanned and unrehearsed. We had known each other for seven years; we had 'gone together' since our later years at school, ever since I spotted this lass with the dark mass of hair, the sparkling green eyes and the warm figure in my father's Junior Choir at the local village Church where he was organist. I walked her home from choir practice, and after that first night, we walked many miles, for without cars, with no money, most of our courting consisted of walks to the Grove, beside the river Doon, or cycle runs up into the hills. In due course the village took notice that Janet Morrison and the Station Master's son were 'gey weel acquaint'.

In time Glasgow University claimed Janet to study for an M.A., while I went to the old Glasgow Vet College. She stayed with her aunt in Paisley, while I travelled the forty-five miles each day, but there were stolen moments when we would meet in the Mitchell Library, watching out for 'the Gestapo', the attendants who prowled around and sternly commanded you to stop talking. Eventually she graduated, and in these halcyon days when there were jobs aplenty, she immediately got a post in the Academy at Byneton, while I started as assistant at Mochrum.

Now we had a car between us, and occasionally I could plan my afternoon round to meet her at four at Byneton. I had only one evening off in the week, a Friday, and usually we went to the Ice Hockey at Ayr . . . a precious few hours together in our busy lives. We had no money, for neither of us was well paid, and we both felt we ought to pay back some of what our parents had given to us. My mother, starting with six hens, had built up a veritable poultry farm of hens, ducks, turkeys, geese, guinea fowl . . . just to see her three sons educated.

We still had no money on that shining day at Heads of Ayr, but we wandered up the Ayr High Street, wrapped in our own dream world, walking on a pink cloud, looking in furniture shops and deciding what we would have in our own home. (Some of the articles we haven't got yet). The sun often shines on the Ayrshire coast, but never did it shine more brightly from a magically blue sky as on that glorious day. One week later we bought the ring and all was official. My father thought we were rushing things . . . after seven years! But he was fond of Janet, as was my mother, and they gave their blessing. In a state of extreme trepidation, I approached Mr Morrison and asked for leave to marry his daughter, and to my profound relief he raised no objections. I left with my legs trembling, but my heart singing.

Now something had to be done about the future. I was not overpaid at Mochrum at £10 a week, and although Ian Buchan dropped occasional hints about a future partnership, there was nothing concrete, and more important, much as I respected him, I felt I could not happily work in partnership with him the rest of my life. I would always be very much the junior, and having had a church upbringing, I felt if I was going to enter into a partnership, it should be, if possible, with a more kindred spirit.

So I advertised in *The Veterinary Record* — and wonder of wonders — in a few days came an offer to come to Bristacombe and discuss a possible partnership there. It was March, one of the busiest months in the vet's year, but Ian gave me a weekend off and, none more Scottish than a

Cameron, I set off by train for the foreign land of England. I was met at Bristacombe Station, North Devon, by an enormous individual and a very small one: Major Kenneth Davidson and a student, Tom Atkins.

We had a short drive to Chade Lodge, I was shown to my bedroom, and then to my utter surprise and somewhat embarrassment, this strange new man dropped to his knees and prayed that we would be guided as to our future. My Scottish reticence was a bit shocked, but this was my first experience of a man who was to mean a very great deal to me . . . a man to whom prayer was as natural as breathing, a very unusual vet in a not notoriously godly profession . . . A man to whom his Lord was a constant companion and friend.

It was a hectic weekend. Before that night was out (I had arrived about seven), I had seen several cases and watched two Caesareans in sheep, one operation performed on a farmhouse kitchen table, the other on a 'table' of straw bales with a hanging Tilly lamp for light. I was astonished at the dexterity of this large man, and somewhat fearful, for we had never done a Caesar at Mochrum. Late at night Kenneth produced sheets of paper showing the takings and outgoings of the Practice for the last three years, and I performed a creditable piece of acting, pretending to understand them, for I had never seen a balance sheet in my life. Before the weekend was over, in a dazed state, I had agreed to become a partner, an act of sheer audacity for I possessed barely £100 in all the world. So we talked of bank loans, life policies, insurance brokers and other mysterious and quite unknown creatures to me, and in a whirlwind I departed from Kenneth and Susan and headed back north, due to start in May — a partner in the Practice of Davidson and Cameron.

Janet was delighted on receipt of the news, my parents were pleased for me but sorry I was going so far away, and Ian Buchan thought I had fairly landed on my feet. He seemed genuinely sorry to lose me and perhaps for the first time came out clearly and said I would have had a partnership there in due course.

I lodged with Kenneth and Susan and their three young sons for three months, and I needed that time to adjust to a totally new experience, almost a new culture and a different kind of farmer who talked a strange language. Phone calls for weeks needed an interpreter as I could not understand the Devonian dialect and the Devon farmers found my Scots tongue equally bewildering. The farmer's names for diseases were different from Ayrshire — every bovine was a 'he', whether male, female or neuter, and I remember holding the telephone away from my ear in total astonishment when asked to go and see 'a bullock bad to calve'

I learned much in these early months, just watching Kenneth at work, for he was a fine vet, a good diagnostician and a magnificent surgeon, beside whom I was a bungling amateur. I also learned that his faith was the mainspring of his life, and while some of his clients pulled his leg and others shared his beliefs, all respected him. Every day before afternoon surgery we would meet, compare notes on cases, read a few verses of the Bible and have a short prayer, and in time my embarrassment and awkwardness gave place to a very real admiration, and some of the naturalness of Kenneth's faith became mine. He tried to run his Practice as a genuinely Christian concern, in every way, right down to his moderate charges, and refusing to take advantage of drugs like the new wonder penicillin, over which vets had a monopoly, and some were charging extortionate prices. We were very different in personality and background — he was a colonial, a native of Kenya, a product of a public school, a former Major in the Indian Army, a man of substance, a big man in every way — while I had grown up in a council house, gone to the local school, and was as ordinary as it is possible to be. Yet we were one, bound together by a common bond, not just as vets, but as brother Christians.

My brother Fergus came down to Bristacombe to share the long drive north for the wedding, in those days before any motorways. A few days later, on 15 August, with two bridesmaids, and my twin brothers Graham and Fergus as Best Man, Janet and I were married in the little village Church of Maryshall, where we had first met and worshipped week by week. I remember little of the wedding, for I was in a state of nerves and ignorance as to procedure, not having had a rehearsal or seen a minister. I just knew I had to say 'I do' at some point, and duly managed to croak the words.

After the reception we took the high road north, spending the first night of our life together at Luss (Glendarroch of the famous Scottish Soap Opera), then on to Morar with its white sands, and finally to beautiful little Plockton, with which we had both fallen in love the previous year, when we rented rooms from the Misses Montgomery. These were two elderly sisters whose prayers in Gaelic filtered up to our bedrooms each night. That year before we had required two rooms, but now we were truly one and it must have been plain we were a honeymoon couple; but with the manners of Highlanders, the sisters made no comment. All too soon we were again heading south to Ayrshire, where the car was loaded to the roof with wedding presents.

We set up house in a four room flat, which we loved for its beauty and peace. We had more furniture than we had expected, thanks to the generosity of parents and the kindness of friends. Our sitting-room was a bit sparse with one armchair and a tea chest for the other, but our first home was a place of calm and deep, deep happiness. Janet continued her teaching and gradually I learned the way to all the various farms and holdings, of which latter there were many, for farming had not yet changed from small family farms to bigger units. We were still using many of the time honoured drugs, with the one great addition of the still new antibiotics.

I learned a lot from Kenneth in these early days, and gradually my dexterity as a surgeon improved. From the beginning Ken treated me as an equal, and trusted me to get on with the job as if I was as experienced as he was. The practice was still at the growing stage, far too much for one but just barely enough for two so, building for the future, I at first just took £6 a week from the takings, and we lived on Janet's salary. Kenneth and I had great dreams of branch practices and expansion, and were sure we would grow. This indeed happened, we soon opened two branch surgeries. We worked very hard indeed to sow the seed for future growth.

Right from the beginning, Kenneth tried to involve me in the life of his church, the Church of England. So I taught in the Convenanters, a youth movement which was a Bible class for older teenagers on a Sunday, and a Youth Club through the week. My initiation into the first Club night produced some pain and not a little mirth. It was a cricket night, and I was fielding at mid-on to the smallest boy in the Club. He gently hit a ball in my direction, I got down on my knees casually to gather it, and at the last minute it bounced and hit me whack on the nose to the delight of the youngsters and the embarrassment of the new leader. Some fielder! I had a swollen nose for a time afterwards, which did not look too good on a newly married man! So far as teaching was concerned, I was a novice. I had once, when I was a serious sixteen-year-old, taken the tiny tots in the Sunday School at Maryshall, when my father couldn't be there. I took the task very seriously, prepared a talk on 'the love of God', and by way of illustration explained to the children "You know your Mummy loves your Daddy, they love you, and you love your brothers and sisters, I hope; well, God loves you like that."

"That's right, Mr Cameron" (Mr! I'd never been addressed like that before) "my Mummy does love my Daddy. She sits on his knee!"

Embarrassment of one earnest teenager!

We worshipped at Kenneth's Church, but although we did try for a time, we found the C of E with its liturgy so very different from the plainness of our Presbyterian Kirk of Scotland, that we eventually joined Brookfield Free Church, whose worship was more like home, and where we were welcomed by several young couples like ourselves. Although no longer young, they remain friends to this day. Ken was also a lay preacher in great demand, and one day I walked in the surgery door to hear him say on the phone he was sorry he couldn't come that particular Sunday, but he was sure his partner would! His partner was horrified, and terrified, having no ambitions whatever to climb into a pulpit. But under the coaxing of my persuasive and powerful partner, I did eventually go out and take the service, marvelling that a congregation could listen to one of such abysmal ignorance. I had no thoughts then of one day becoming a preacher, but the passing years were to change that and lead eventually from dog to dog collar. Four of us in time formed a group, and went out conducting services in North Devon's many picturesque villages, singing as a quartet (how those poor folks must have suffered!) and preaching, and three of that group were eventually to become full time ministers.

So Kenneth Davidson not only taught me much as a vet, and showed me the gladness of walking close to God, (something I had first seen in another former Major, Ian Thomas – the evangelist, of Capernwray Hall who greatly influenced both Janet and I in our teens and early twenties). It was Ken who first sent my footsteps toward the ministry, though he himself remained a vet. After our three years together, he got the opportunity to return to his native Kenya as a vet, and we parted. His place was taken by Bernard Paterson, who had been a student with us, and who then became my assistant, and finally my partner for the rest of my time in practice. He still works away in glorious North Devon. However all this comes later in the story.

I owe much to Kenneth, more than I can ever express, and likewise to Bernard. Who, though a totally different character, quiet, unassuming but with the same sure faith, took Kenneth's place in every way. I don't believe I ever expressed my thanks and my indebtedness to them; perhaps if they ever read this, they will accept a belated 'thank you' for our marvellous years together.

By the spring of the year after our marriage, it was clear a baby was on the way. We prepared for its coming with all the joy and anticipation of every young couple. Janet was sometimes far from well . . . indeed had a rough time in pregnancy, but she was uncomplaining, and buoyed up with the thought of the new life that was at the end of it all. Two days after our wedding anniversary, on 17 August, I drove her to the local Maternity Hospital and left her. It was quite out of the question in those days for a father to be present at the birth, even though he was a vet who had delivered many young things, and was not likely to faint at a childbirth. I returned from some visits, which I had flown round in my excitement, to be met by a very agitated Kenneth, who told me the doctor wanted to see me. With sinking heart I visited the doctor, not knowing what his news would be, but certain it must be bad. The doctor was uneasy and I've felt to this day he had a right to be uneasy. The baby had been stillborn, which, of course, still happens from time to time, despite our many advances. But the doctor had allowed Janet to go three weeks over her time, the baby was very large for a first, its heart had been beating fifteen minutes before the birth, but it had been lost in the delivery.

We mourned for our little babe, and comforted one another as best we could, with Janet as always, doing most of the comforting. The baby was a girl, perfect in every way, and so much the image of her mother that she has been forever baby Janet. It hurt deeply, and brought me face to face with the question that has been asked of me more than any other in my ministry . . . the 'why?' of suffering and sorrow. Even today, after more than thirty years, I can never see a little white coffin without a lump in my throat, and a pricking behind my eyes. How much harder for my Janet . . . but time does ease the pain. Time also was to bring us four other children, all boys . . . Neil, Ian, David all born in England, which fact, as fervent Scots they have forever been trying to forget! I did see David's birth and recorded his first cries, threatening to play them over to them when he first brought a girl home! Of course I never did. The baby of the family, Alan, was born in Scotland while I was a Divinity student. So we were deprived of our daughter, but have been blessed in four healthy, handsome and strapping sons, now, of course, men.

Bristacombe was the scene of several new beginnings, and remains in our hearts always for its beauty, its olde world charm, the warmth of its people . . . and as the place where an apprentice vet became a journeyman, and a journeyman vet became an apprentice preacher.

Kennel Capers

SIX

"Ow. . . ooo. . . !Ooooo! Ow. . . ooooo. . . ooo. . . oo. Ow. . . ooo. . . Wow-wow-wow-oooooooah!"

Thud! . . . My feet hit the bedroom floor.

Bang! . . . An upstairs window was flung open.

"Shut up, you noisy dog or you'll be sorry!" My dulcet tones floated over Chade Valley. This was the ritual almost nightly now in our lives. Gone were the days of tranquillity in that delightful little flat at Langleigh Farm where Janet and I had begun our married life. The farm, nestling at the foot of the mighty Torrs, and sheltered in its ring of trees, had been a perfect haven of peace, a delight to come home to when the day's work was done. The only sounds were the bleating of sheep grazing the Torrs, or the contended cluck of hens as they strolled about the yard. Periodically farmer Conibear's voice would be raised as he called directions to his dog rounding up the sheep, and in the mornings before breakfast we would hear Mrs Conibear calling the hens to their feed of grain or mash. But those halcyon days had lasted an all too brief eighteen months, and we had moved to Chade Lodge. The reason for the turn up in our domestic bliss was that the surgery premises we rented on the High Street and the house above had come on the market, and Kenneth felt he ought to buy the property. This he did, and he, Susan and their family moved to the more commodious house above. Reasoning that if he was prepared to stay above a surgery, we should be willing to live beside the kennels, Kenneth had suggested we move into Chade Lodge, which he had just vacated. We could hardly refuse.

I had always associated the description 'Lodge' with a large property on a Highland moor, much favoured by Cabinet Ministers, American oil tycoons and the like from 12 August onwards for the annual slaughter of grouse, partridge, deer and the almost tame pheasants that abounded in these parts. Alternatively, I had pictured an attractive gatehouse at the entrance to some large estate, with roses round the door. The only resemblance Chade Lodge bore to other lodges was that it did have some roses in the minute plot of front garden with iron railings around it. The property was in fact a rather tatty, far from convenient, jerry built house of brick and roughcast, erected by the local council for their abattoir superintendent. The rooms were tiny, the lighting was gas, and behind us stretched a mass of buildings, open yards and narrow passageways which had once been the local slaughter house but was now rented by us for use as kennels. Above us was a railway line, a spur or off-shoot of the main line, along which the giant West Country class locomotives came daily to let off steam, take on water and generally hang about till their time came to head back to the railway station and be linked to their coaches. Below us at the foot of the steeply sided valley was the little township of Chade, composed of new council houses and much older terraced dwellings, but now part of Bristacombe itself. So our days were made hideous by sudden explosions of escaping steam from the monsters above us, though over the years we also got grins and waves from the engine driver and his fireman, who could look right in our bedroom windows. Night brought a cessation of steam explosions, and it was then that some horrible canine, thinking that things had gone a bit quiet, would decide to bay the moon or recite poetry to his fellow inmates, and rouse us and the dwellers in the valley below, seemingly on the principle that if you couldn't sleep, it was much cheerier to have someone awake with you. So nightly, as Kenneth had done before me, I bellowed at the brutes! Generally the blood curdling threats I uttered had the desired effect as the beast got the message. But there were often the crafty ones who would wait till you were nicely tucked up in bed again, about to drop off and then recommence their nightly song, invariably with others joining in the chorus. So frequently, feet had to be shoved into slippers, a dressing gown or coat thrown on, and with set face and fixed purpose I would have to enter the dark kennels, locate the culprit if possible — not always easy for very quickly they could look like a class of innocent children when the teacher whirled to find the offender. If located he/she heard my threats uttered at close range; if unlocated they were all bawled out. If verbal reasoning failed, then one had to try manual persuasion, that terrible thing corporal punishment, now seemingly regarded as a grisly relic of man's barbaric past. If all else failed, the dog had to be sedated by injection, and a Mickey Finn slipped into his supper the following night.

There are two types of kennels. There are those purpose built as kennels, preferably situated miles from anywhere, and run, for profit by sufficient staff, as a board residence. Then there are the kennels like ours, which were an extra, an adjunct to a veterinary practice, useful for hospitalising patients, boarding some dogs, but scarcely a paying proposition.

When I first joined the Practice, we had a kennel maid, a girl who was crazy about dogs, and happily spent the whole day there, cleaning kennels, playing games with the residents, clipping or stripping such dogs as required these forms of hairdressing, and generally keeping a kennel of contented canines. In a separate building, in their cages, were the cats, and these comfort loving creatures had all the caressing and care a cat could crave. She did all this for a mere pittance. But alas, she left us for another, transferring all the affection so freely lavished on our delightful dogs and charming cats, to some blighted male of the human breed! We couldn't replace her. We tried various part time kennelmaids, at one time combined the post of surgery assistant with kennelman, but these experiments proved unsuccessful. We simply could not afford to pay anyone full-time, the kennels barely covering themselves as it was, with feeding, disinfectants, rent and lozenges for my larynx! So with Janet's help, Kenneth and I would take week about at feeding, cleaning and exercising the animals.

When the mantle of night fell on the scene, the responsibility to keep the peace was mine. Such was the vehemence with which I at times verbally assaulted these dogs, daily threatening to 'come and knock their blocks off', 'murder them', or generally cause life to be unpleasant for them, that I was sure I heard the words 'Shut up!' uttered by our infant son in almost his first coherent utterance. This indeed was a sobering thought. Suppose he used the phrase to either of his grandparents, or treated the minister to his party piece? From a very early age, he would sit in his high chair, and when dogs were giving tongue in their premises, he would sit in his, point an accusing finger in their direction and sternly order "Quiet, wow, wows!"

As for the cats they were transferred to back premises of the surgery — more escape proof than their former abode for more than one seemingly innocent feline had done a Colditz on us and 'gone away', making it a trifle awkward when the owner returned.

In a steeply sloping one-acre field which ran parallel with the drive up to Chade Lodge we also kept two sows, Susan and Veronica, respectively a Large White sow and a black-and-white Wessex Saddleback sow. With them I was already well acquainted before we moved into the Lodge. While Kenneth drove his very new Triumph saloon car, yours truly had the antiquated van, so when either Susan or Veronica expressed a wish to visit their mutual husband who dwelt on a farm just outside the town, there was only one vehicle that could be used to transport them. So from time to time S or V, or occasionally S and V together would be coaxed, cajoled and generally heaved into COD 330's interior, something that long suffering vehicle had known many times before, having in fact previously been a butcher's van. I will always remember those hair raising trips with pigs as my companions. No partition separated the driver from the rear of the van, and since there were no windows in the sides, naturally enough, my passengers, eager to view the passing scene, would speedily gravitate to the front. Veronica was a good natured creature, Susan a bit temperamental, so whenever a pig snout appeared over my shoulder, to peer out my side window, I greatly trembled for the safety, even future existence of my ears, for Susan was liable to sample any tasty looking morsel she came across. We would not be any great distance on our trip, before half a pig would be leaning over the driver's seat, so that it must have appeared to any onlooker that a pig was driving the van, an impression enhanced by the erratic, swaying course of the little vehicle if both pigs were present and lurching about with the movement of their carriage. I tried to make these trips in the early mornings or latish evenings, and I recall one half-awake worker stop dead in his tracks, rub his eyes, shake his head unbelievingly, as he stared after a blue van driven by a black pig. Even more startling was the effect on a couple of revellers as they lurched their way homewards late one summer even, (and held one another upright) at the sight of a van driven by an enormous white sow with a black one as passenger. If that didn't make them hive off with all possible speed to sign the pledge, nothing would!

When not with their husband, the doughty pair dwelt peaceably enough in their little shed, grazed the field and produced their young, which we sold as weaners. There was little profit in pigs at the time, but they helped pay the rent. They might have been allowed to graze a few years longer, had not their nusisance value outweighted the profit after a morning adventure. It began with a knock at the door as I was having breakfast. There, on the doormat, stood one excited little boy, ably supported by a bevy of kindred spirits, of both sexes, in an arc behind.

"Hey, mister," announced our visitor, "there's some little pigs running about on the main road!"

"How many?" I asked. A daft like question, as if it mattered, but I'm not at my brightest, unbreakfasted. The spokesman said three, but his attendants quickly corrected him, in numbers varying, so far as I could make out, from one to thirteen. Something had to be done, so accompanied by my self-appointed assistants, I hurried down to the scene of the action. It was a graphic scene, though to tender eyes was worthy, I'm certain of an X certificate. What had happened was that sometime during the night Veronica had felt her time to produce another litter had come. I suspect that she was turfed out of their house by Susan, always the boss, and probably in one of her moods. Now the field was very steep indeed and apparently the only reasonably level, sheltered and seemingly private bed Veroncia could find was right under the hedge, which grew, Devon style, on top of a wall, whose top was some ten feet above the main Chade-Bristacombe highway beneath. There she had given birth, and continued to do so, producing at regular intervals another little black and white minstrel. Since sows frequently take some time to deliver the complete litter, the early arrivals felt they couldn't hang about for ever to see how many brothers or sisters they would have, and had set about the immediate task of finding food, readily available from any one of the teats neatly arranged on Veronica's undercarriage for that very purpose. The trouble was, that with her feet sticking through the hedge, this was a hazardous journey for the newly born. The easy way was to walk over mother, but on that already steep gradient her side acted as a shute, propelling her off-spring out into the unexplored depths below, where they hung about waiting for something to happen. The craftier members of the litter some-how tip-toed their way along the top of the wall, until, finding a teat, they hung on, some of them with their back legs dangling into space. This was the scene which greeted the douce inhabitants of Chade as they proceeded to work and school. Below the wall stood a group of the little minstrels singing a harrowing song in soprano, or perhaps rather more falsetto voices, while above, our brainless sow continued to lie there, producing pigs periodically, while barnacle-like, a few hardy specimens clung tenaciously to her abdominal and thoracic appendages. To some of the onlookers it must have seemed that those piglets clinging to their mother's teats by dint of suction and determination, were trying to pull her over the precipice to join the chorus below. The din of squealing pigs pursued by squealing children was accompanied by the honk of cars seeking to avoid both parties, and the chatter of the ever increasing crowd, some of whose comments I could make out.

"Look at em go — oh, there's another gone over!"

"Poor lil ol things!"

"Should have been in a house, poor beast!"

"Taint right, ah tell ee. Enough fur the cruelty man, vur zertain."

Through it all Veronica lay blissfully on, grunting contentedly, though it time it must surely have penetrated even her thick skull that she was on an endless task. As fast as she produced pigs, these same pigs disappeared. That's what I proceeded to do — disappear fast — before the Cruelty Man, the Police, the Fire Brigade or any other body was summoned to the scene. The van was hastily driven down the road, and assisted by dozens of children having the time of their lives, I tried to round up the now scattered minstrel chorus, and pop them in the van. The two remaining 'barnacles' were removed, pushed in front of V's snout, and my poor wife, using these two as bait, proceeded to shoo the lady of the moment to her shed, where she was reunited with her offspring, or most of them. For all I know, some family on the Chade housing estate had roast sucking pig for supper that night, but we had a fair number, and Veronica seemed well content with her brood, and a job well done. That was the last straw. Vets and their wives couldn't regularly be collecting piglets from the public highway, so a few weeks later, with relief, tinged with regret, we sent our two sows to market. Our pig farming days were over.

At the kennels we also had a motley collection of feathered and furred fauna. The former were hens, two hundred of them of different breeds, which I kept in the 'deep litter' system in one large shed unused for anything else. Since a lad, I'd always known hens about the place, and they were a decided source of revenue with a nice tidy profit, if you forgot the hours in daily washing eggs. As well as giving me endless pleasure in sitting, of an evening, watching them, they gave us some extra cash. After having electricity installed in the house, the poultry profit provided a brand new electric cooker to displace the enormous gas monstrosity we had purchased at a sale room for £5. I recall the pleasure the purchase of that new cooker gave us, virtually the first new article we'd bought for our home since we'd set up house with £150 between us, and a flat half furnished by wedding gifts. Night by night, we'd examine the cooker, lest any hint of a scratch should mar its shining surface, stroking it almost like a family pet. Ah, me, the simple pleasures of yesterday! Next we managed a fridge, then, with the family growing, a washing machine, then a real luxury, a tape recorder, all furnished by courtesty of our feathered flock, and all still in use today. Quite frequently, after a long day in the Practice, it would be very dim or even dark when I went round the nest boxes to collect the eggs. I collected more than eggs one night. Reaching into a dark laying box — I very quickly withdrew my hand with a howl. I'd been well and truly bitten, by a rat. It slithered out, eyed me malevolently as if I'd bitten it, and slowly disappeared. The wound, in fact, required hospital dressing and the usual tetanus injection. This act of aggression was the opening shot in a war that raged ceaselessly thereafter. Rats produce the same reaction in me as snakes and stoats — a kind of quiver that starts in the soles of the feet, and progresses upwards till the hair finally stands up 'like the quills on the fretful porcupine', as P.G. Wodehouse would put it. So war it was, and if our feathered friends gave us endless pleasure and profit, our furred kennel dwellers produced a smouldering anger and periodic frenzied activity.

There were rats on the railway embankments, and, of course, the presence of any dog food brought them into the kennels at night. Going in with a torch, one could spot them speeding up pipes or disappearing down drains. The poultry, with their easily available food, and warm deep bed of moss litter, attracted still more. Of course we tried the Pest Control Officer, but with so many dogs around, he could not use poison readily, and there were too many exits to use traps effectively. So clearly if there was to be any action, it had to come from us, and regularly of an evening, father, mother and the two under-fives would sally forth to a rat hunt. It seemed our first two offspring had some terrier blood in them somewhere. We would all don wellington boots, tuck trouser legs into stockings, and wear gloves, self-armed with a large garden fork or spade for digging purposes, while the rest of the army sported long sticks or shovels. There was a surprise diversion one evening, as Mum, who kept her boots in a shed at the back door, having eased her feet into them, suddenly leapt skywards, and to the infinite amusement of our senior boy, Neil, aged four, gave a very passable demonstration of a Zulu war dance, complete with yells. It was only when she succeeded in kicking off her boots and one somewhat dazed rat staggered out that we learned the reason for the antics. Mercifully she had not been bitten, but ugh! Then we would proceed in formation to the deep-litter house and while father dug out the obvious tunnels, mother and children would guard the escape routes, and those brown rats which escaped my weapon were enthusiastically chased by the family, with loud yells, shouts, and the thump of descending sticks, all to a deafening background of cackles, cries and fluttering from the poultry. Our record kill was thirty-nine in one night. We never completely mastered them, only kept them within bounds, and in the process probably completely ruined our sons for life, what with yells of 'Shut up!' and 'There he is, hit him!'

But of course, kennels are the dwelling place of dogs, and our inmates came into one of three groups. Those in for hospitalisation, generally following surgery, boarders from the local populace or visitors; and dogs under sentence of death, and kept by us for the RSPCA. Strictly speaking these dogs should have been kept only for a week, and if unclaimed, destroyed but this was something I was most reluctant to do, for while occasionally we had a genuine stray, the majority were poor creatures which had simply been turned loose by uncaring owners, quite often when their Dog Licence fee of seven and sixpence was due. So, because of the good offices of the local RSPCA secretary, a very large, florid, but gentle woman, we came to an arrangement that we would keep these dogs almost indefinitely for virtually the cost of food, while Mrs Gorman would insert an advert in the local paper: 'Good homes wanted for Labrador, Sheepdog cross, Corgi type and so on'. I suspect much of the total cost was met by this generous woman from her own funds, just as after some years she insisted on donating a portable X-Ray to us.

The hospital patients, seldom stayed long enough to become characters or personalities — all except one, a lovely Boxer bitch called Paula. She had been a boarder on a previous occasion, and I was very surprised to find her in kennels one evening, and be given the message that 'she was in for a spay and would be collected in ten days'. I thought it a crying shame to sterilise such a pedigreed beauty, but dutifully did the deed. In ten days her owner rolled up in his large car to fetch her. We went into the kennels and he asked,

"Why has she a bandage on?"

"Oh, it could come off now really. We just left it on to keep dirt out of the wound."

'Bandage? Wound?" he looked at me completely flummoxed.

"Yes, it is usual for a few days after surgery."

"Has she been ill then?"

"We . . . ell, not ill. Just a bit quiet for a few days. That's usual after an op."

"Operation for what?" he persisted.

Our lines had been crossed somewhat, and I feared what would be revealed when the tangle was unravelled.

"The operation you asked for, the spay, the sterilisation," I said guardedly. He looked at me a long time, at least thirty seconds, I'm sure, before he snapped "I said no such thing!" I couldn't really blame him for snapping; I'd have bitten under the circumstances.

"Well, Mr Mooney, I'm very sorry indeed, but the message I received was that Paula was in for a spay and would be collected in ten days. If something is amiss, I can only apologise."

"I said she was in for a stay — and would be collected in ten days."

He was a well to do hotelier, and could afford a dozen pedigree Boxers, but that was beside the point. Paula was his pride and joy, he'd planned to let her have pups, and we'd ruined his plans. I must say he took it astonishingly well, for she was a really lovely animal. I suppose he might have sued us, but he didn't. It was a genuine telephone message mistake, and he did have a rather quiet voice. Needless to say, there was no charge for either spay or stay! He even forgave us, and boarded Paula with us again. I suppose he reasoned we couldn't do any more damage.

Many of our boarders, were regulars year after year, and sometimes several times a year. Some owners even reserved certain kennels, and the majority of their pets settled in reasonably well to communal life, with their favourite toys or rubber bones, baskets and favourite rugs from home. With many came hints that Fifi, or Charles, or Boko was particularly partial to sweet tea, or a leg of lamb, or a stout at bedtime, and that darling Mimi could never sleep till she'd had her good night cuddle. Cat owners would be even more fussy, as a rule. I remember one owner insisting that her pussy would only eat pancakes, and only then if freshly cooked. We duly noted all requests, and fed the dogs on biscuits and meat, the cats on meat, fish and milk. We had only one privileged, regular boarder, a Pekingese called Chota. Our kennels were really designed for larger dogs, and since most Yorky, Pom, or Peke owners 'couldn't bear to be separated from the little darling', we had few lap dogs to cosset. Chota was an exception. In a weak moment I'd said we would keep him in the house, so in the house it always was. I had never been a Peke lover before, largely being put off by Peke owners. But with Chota I gained a real admiration for the intelligence, resourcefulness and particularly the courage of the lion dog of Peking. He was a grand wee chap. One day his owner phoned to say that Chota's right eye had come out of its socket, and what should she do? She was told to bring it right in, and we prepared the surgical kit just in case, though, frankly, I was sceptical. We had been told at College that, if shaken sufficiently hard by the scruff of the neck, a Peke's eyes could, in fact, pop out. But neither in my student or assistantship days had I seen this, nor had I ever met any other student who had. It would be a blood clot, or maybe a bad gash in the cheek at which the poor lady could not bear to look properly. But one glance at Chota as she came in the surgery door confirmed that Mrs Kerr's diagnosis had been spot on. The eye was resting grotesquely on Chota's cheek. Mrs Kerr looked almost on the point of collapse, but assured me a neighbour was driving her home, so we sent her off, took the little fellow in, and within minutes had him out of his world of pain, if only for a time. Mrs Kerr had told us before departing that she had been away all morning, had come home to be told by a neighbour that an Alsatian had attacked Chota that morning, then the little fellow had disappeared, so it was evident that the eye had been displaced at least five hours before. The amount of swelling confirmed this. I vaguely recalled that the surgery book had indicated that, if treated in time, it was sometimes possible to replace the eye-ball in its socket. We could but try. Mrs Drury who was assisting was, as always, unflappable, as if eyes lying about were an everyday occurrence. She watched the anaesthetic, and from the other side of the table was ready, as always, to give me whatever instrument I might require. That I didn't yet know. I had, of course, removed a few diseased or badly damaged eyes before, but I confess I quailed before that eye staring fixedly at me from its resting place on the dog's cheek, as if daring me to touch it while its owner was out for the count. But touch it we did, gently bathing and cleaning, then with plenty of antiseptic cream for lubrication, lashings of patience, and firm, but gentle pressure tried to coax the eyeball back.

"He's coming round," said Mrs Dru's voice.

"We can't have that; more pentothal, Mrs D." She moved to get it. My normal form of anaesthesia for reasonably short operations was pentothal, (the so called truth drug), followed by a mask with Ether-Oxygen mixture to keep the patient at the desired depth of unconsciousness. But to fix a face mask to a snub nose dog was difficult, and to one with an eyeball lying on its face impossible. So more pentothal was put in a vein. I cannot recall now how long we worked on that eye. To hurry would be to damage it irreparably, yet every instinct was to put the horrible object back in its right place. Bit by bit it yielded, till with a slight plop, it was back in its socket. It hardly could be described as a beautiful eye as yet, but at least it was an eye again, not a thing. We packed the eyeball around with antibiotic and anaesthetic cream, then sutured upper and lower eyelids together, to keep out all light and dirt.

In ten days, in fear and trepidation, I removed the sutures and gently prised the eyelids apart to reveal the squint to beat all others! But the eye was surprisingly clean and clear and was reacting to light. Clearly one or more of the ocular muscles had been damaged, but I was sure Chota was seeing with that eye, even if all he could see was his own tiny snout. Over time, the squint improved markedly, and if his two eyes never quite matched again, at least he had two functional eyes.

Another regular boarder was Sandy, a handsome Staffordshire Bull Terrier. Now the Staffordshire can be a tricky customer to handle because it is very much a one-person dog. Sandy lived for his master, and when master chose to leave him in these kennels, Sandy would look at the world with a jaundiced eye, put his chin on his paws, heave an enormous sigh, and indicate that until his master returned, he was prepared to put up with this existence, but certainly not going to enjoy it. Towards the other dogs he maintained a degree of aloofness, but no aggression. He co-existed, and made it clear that was the way he wanted it. His frequent sojourns with us all passed peacefully, he was absolutely no trouble whatever, and he was a real character. All would have been well had not a party of holidaymakers arrived one Saturday evening with their black Cocker Spaniel. They had come on holiday to find their Boarding House did not permit dogs, and so hastened to us to plead for boarding space. It was the height of summer, we were very full, but we made room. They were humble folks, informed us they came from Wolverhampton, and the dog was called Whisky. He proved to be a Grade A, Category 1 nuisance, a barker with a capital B. Fortunately for everyone's peace of mind, most days his owners took him off our hands, to return him in the evenings, when he proceeded to bark incessantly at all and sundry, albeit wagging his tail as if to say 'No offence, chums'. But it was apparent that Sandy had taken offence. I imagine he had told the new arrival to 'pipe down', and been, from the safety of his strong Sandy-proof kennel, told where to get off by Whisky. Nobody spoke to Sandy like that in any language; it was doubly insulting to his West Country nature to be addressed in the language of Wolverhampton!! Sandy morosely brooded, and thought dark thoughts. During morning exercise one day, Sandy had a go at Whisky, who not imbued with the spirit from which he took his name, fled for dear life. Fortunately the chase was spotted, and Sandy restrained in time. But he waited, glaring and muttering threats at this upstart, who, brave as always in his secure kennel, barked back his abuse. There came a day when Whisky's owners left him behind while they went on a coach trip. All was peaceful in the warmth of a Devon summer afternoon, thought Janet as she pottered in the little garden, between rests in a deck chair, for in a few days our babe was due. Suddenly the summer calm was shattered by a growl, then a scream. followed by the barking of every dog in the kennels. Hurrying as fast as circumstances would allow, Janet went into the kennels. Somehow, Sandy had escaped from his pen, managed to get into Whisky's and had him pinned to the ground. The poor girl fled for the phone, to be told at the surgery that both vets were miles away in the country. She had it all to do herself. Hardly realising what she was doing, she struck and poked Sandy again and again with the little garden fork still in her hands. She might as well have used a feather duster. The Staffordshire's hour of vengeance had come, he had the spaniel by the throat, and he was not letting go. Almost sobbing with fear and helplessness, the poor girl shouted 'Sandy' — and miracle of miracles, where the pain of the fork had failed to move him, the voice of command did. He left the spaniel lying, and with a look that suggested 'that was just for starters, look out next time', he walked majestically back to his own abode and lay down as if nothing had happened. Returning later to the surgery, I was advised by Mrs Drury to proceed with all due haste to the kennels. The battle was over. The spaniel had several wounds, but nothing that ordinary dressings wouldn't heal, while Sandy was sporting several deep puncture wounds. My poor wife had recovered from a state of near collapse, and could now look back and laugh; without her presence, there would certainly have been one dead spaniel. As it was, I wondered what I would tell the folks from Wolverhampton when they arrived in a body to take their Whisky out for evening walkies. I told them exactly what had happened, and to my astonishment, they were tickled pink. Whisky had never fought any dog before, they said and when they saw the deep wounds he had seemingly inflicted on that terrible animal, their pleasure increased even more. I did not disabuse them as to Sandy's wounds. Their dog was a hero, head bloodied but unbowed. He was also a non barker for the remainder of his stay. Sandy bore no grudge to my wife; on the contrary in retrospect, he appeared grateful, and I was sure the grunts deep in his throat indicated 'Sorry about that shemozzle in there; got carried away, what! But I couldn't stand the fellow. Just as well you stopped me when you did.'

Another canine was the young St Bernard who appeared with visitors to be boarded for a fortnight, his front legs resplendent in full length leather boots, which his own vet had recommended for a tendency to rickets. As everyone knows, a St Bernard with rickets would not be much cop carrying his barrel up Mont Blanc to succour some stranded mountaineer. We had another St Bernard, Carlo, boarded with us for a year, a great, lolloping hunk of good nature. His owners had moved to London and it was a full twelve months before they could find premises suitable to have him with them again. Then there was Boris the Borzoi. Carlo was everybody's friend, Boris nobody's. Carlo was one of the gang; Boris would not so demean himself. He was evidently a prerevolution Borzoi, a real Czar, who went about on his own every day from first to last, with his nose in the air. None of your proletariats for Boris! He didn't even sleep beside them, seemingly preferring the side of the kennels which was seldom used and where he could keep his own company. I did not like the dog, but I was sorry for him. He reminded me of some European monarch, displaced from his throne, and with nowhere to go.

Of all our characters, Cindy was the favourite. She was a gentle brown, black and white mongrel, with hints of spaniel, sheepdog, foxhound blood in her, and maybe a dash of some kind of terrier far back. She came to us as a tiny puppy, one of eight that had been found, with their mother, under a hedge, and rescued by the RSPCA Inspector. The mother made a good job of rearing her large brood, and quite quickly, she herself and seven of the puppies had found good homes. One little one was left, Cindy. She grew, appeared regularly in the papers with the others in the 'Good homes wanted' advert, but nobody wanted Cindy. She was nobody's child. She saw other waifs come and go, she would amble up to visitors and look up, but always they chose another. I could not understand it, for she was gentle, obedient, loving, with excellent manners, and was, in her own way, quite a character. Then she was taken — at last. She came back to us maybe nine months later. It had not been a good home, she had been turned loose, and in the time away had been thoroughly neglected. She had a beaten, hang dog expression, and she was about to become a mother any day. She produced her pups, and like her mother before her, proved a first class parent, but in the process lost her figure! 'No home for Cindy now', I felt sure. She was given the run of the kennels for there was no fear of her wandering off. She came and went in and out the gate as she pleased, with her puppies behind her. One day I received an urgent call, dashed out to the car, reversed, and felt a sickening bump. One of her pups had been lying under the car, unknown to me. Cindy came over, licked her dead puppy, then her soulful brown eyes looked up into mine, she put out a paw as if to reassure me, gathered her other offspring around her, and trotted into the kennels to mourn in secret. All her puppies eventually found a niche in some home and only Cindy was left and we continued to let her roam. Cindy never wandered. I would not put her down — I could not. Then one day he came, Prince Charming himself. He didn't have a white charger; he was dressed fairly roughly, but he was looking for a dog, and clearly from his talk, a genuine dog lover. He'd lost his last one, and wanted a replacement. His eyes wandered over a Collie, a Labrador, an Alsatian, then stopped at Cindy. His face lit up. "That's the one," he said, and as if she knew it, Cindy stood on her hind legs to greet him. The stranger had at last come in from the cold and Cindy never needed to come back.

The Consulting Hour

SEVEN

Every February and March in the town there was much blowing away of cobwebs, washing of bed linen and splashing about of paint as Bristacombe prepared for its annual invasion of visitors. Being a seaside town with no industry, everything revolved round 'The Season'. Signs offering B and B from seven and sixpence to a guinea sprouted everywhere. Hotels that had been shuttered and desolate suddenly came to life, amusement arcades re-opened and in numerous Curio-Present-from-Devon-shops, proprietors arranged their window displays with great care. Along the sea front and in the main streets where in winter every face was known, there now appeared thousands of strangers conversing with one another in the greatest conglomeration of languages and dialects since the day of Pentecost! The Season was Bristacombe's harvest time. If you didn't make money then, you didn't make money; if tradesmen's bills, including ours, were not settled then, they were not settled till next Season.

The town and its adjacent caravan sites were filling up, and as I passed our waiting room for afternoon consulting hour one spring day, I knew without question that 'The Season' was upon us once more. The room was full, and half the customers seemed to be poodles. The poodle was the 'in' breed of the decade. We had quite a few as permanent residents in the town, but the poodle population multiplied enormously with the coming of summer. I wasn't too fond of the breed — a nice enough and quite intelligent wee dog, but some a bit neurotic like half the owners! The only dog I'd seen go completely round the bend, after producing a litter of pups had been a poodle. The strain of motherhood seemed to unhinge completely what brain it possessed, and where in a human mother post-natal depression was fairly common, I'd never heard of post-natal hysteria, until seeing it in that poodle. The wretched little creature howled incessantly, an unearthly kind of screech that caused the occupants of houses within one hundred yards of the *locus* to talk of mass evacuation, or poodlicide! We'd had to keep the dog under morphia no less, for a week, as other tranquillisers or sedatives proved powerless against that appalling cry.

Sure enough the first case that day was a white poodle carried by a glamorous blonde. Though it was a warm day, she was sheathed in a fur coat, her companion dressed in a pink ribbon. I recognised the glamour girl as Tanya or Melinda or some such name, the leading lady of the Summer Show in the Pavilion. She had been here last year too. In a voice so refined that I could only comprehend about every fourth word, she gave me to understand that Chi-Chi's blood seemed overheated and she was scratching herself more or less non stop. I looked at the dog's skin, then looked more closely, an unholy joy taking possession of me.

"Where does she sleep?" I asked.

"Well, really she has her own little bed, but you know how it is. She usually cuddles in beside me."

"I'm afraid she's got fleas"

The flush started down the lady's visible skin — and that was far down. For all I know, it maybe began at her feet, and gradually engulfed her.

"Fleas! Really! You are most insulting! How dare you suggest such a thing! Where could she possibly get fleas?"

"Oh, from other dogs, or a chair — or her bed." I looked heavenwards till the full significance of my words sank in, and when I looked down again, instead of a faint flush was a deep crimson. The lady, it seemed, was not amused, but fleas it was.

"But don't worry," I purred, "just give her a shampoo with this. That should do the trick, but you can take this dusting powder too, and use it on her and any place you think they might be hiding."

The lady was scratching now. Imagination is an amazing thing, and my imagination was working overtime as I pictured her shaking flea powder all round her hotel bedroom, and then dusting herself from head to foot before taking to the blankets that night.

"That will be two pounds, ten shillings, please!"

"Two pounds ten. That is scandalous for a shampoo and powder!"

"Oh no they only come to ten shillings, with consulting fee. The two pounds is for last year's bill which has not been paid. Perhaps it was not re-directed to you?" I smiled serenely.

She paid up, unwillingly, then said in a husky voice, and with a languishing look of tender appeal, usually reserved for Chi-Chi,

"You won't let this out, will you?"

I assured her our little secret was safe, and so it has been, until now.

I understood the reason for the tender appeal bit, for the next customer was also from the Summer Show, and also a poodle owner. She was, I imagined, one of the chorus girls, and came clad in just the bare minimum allowable for walking the streets. I didn't know what her stage name was, but as soon as she opened her mouth, I recognised her place of origin. I grinned and asked, "What part of Glasgow are you from?"

"Hill Street," she replied. I told her I had been to the College in Buccleugh Street, which was next to Hill Street. We said 'fancy that' and 'it's a wee world', 'just imagine', and 'would you credit that', then the lady informed me,

"We used tae see the greyhounds goin' in there, so we did so, but we never saw ony come oot!" She was right too. The penalty for being an unsuccessful greyhound was to end up an anatomy specimen in Buccleugh Street.

"I've just had another of your cast in," I informed her.

"Och, aye-Tanya! She's fae Glesca tae!"

"No!"

"Aye!"

"She doesn't sound like it."

"Maybe no in here; she can fair pit on the la-di-da, but you should hear her when she's no pleased — pure Gallagate then! Her richt name's Annie McGonigle! Me, a'm Mary Bell, but a'm jist in the chorus so a' don't need a fancy name. Whit wis wrang wi' her dug? She said it wis its high breedin', that the bluid wis ower rich — wis that richt?"

Mindful of my promise, and professional etiquette, I hastily changed the subject.

"And what's wrong wi' your wee dog?"

"Och, it's jist his lugs — they're needin' a guid cleanin' oot." I peered in the ears with my auriscope; they were indeed needing 'cleanin' oot'.

"A lot of poodles get ear trouble," I explained, "usually just because the hair inside their ears holds the dirt or causes an irritation." I cleaned them out, and gave her some drops to use on them. She returned to her former question.

"Wiz it really heated bluid wi' Annie?"

Remembering that lady's blush, I could truthfully answer,

"Something like that. Seven and sixpence please."

"Och, is that a'? You're cheap! The last man a went tae took fifteen bob, so he did. Fancy you kennin' Hill Street. Aye, it's a wee world, i'nt it?"

As a change from poodles, next we had a shoe box, borne carefully in by a little lady of maybe seven, who solemnly handed it to me.

"What's this?" I asked, lifting the lid. Inside was a great mass of cotton wool. Wondering what would pop up, I moved it rather gingerly. Kids had all sorts of strange pets. Maybe it was a lizard or grass snake. However it proved to be a squirming mass of naked mice, hundreds of them — or so it seemed, though I suppose the number would be nearer fifteen. The mouse owner was blinking up at me very earnestly. She smiled and revealed a large gap in her front teeth, through which she lisped,

"Pleath thir, my mummy mouth had baby mouthes, and could you pleath tell me the oneth that will be daddy mouthes and what oneth are mummy mouthes?" This presented considerable difficulties. First there was the difficulty of picking them up, second the problem of marking males and females, and third I didn't know anyway! I replaced the cotton wool.

"You come back in about six weeks and I'll tell you then." Sexing mice, let alone newly born ones, was a new request. The wee hand was clutching a minute purse.

"How many pennieth ith that?" she enquired. I grinned at her, and handed back the box.

"You keep your pennieth . . . eh . . . your money; that's alright, my dear."

The next customer was a boy with a tortoise.

"It's got a sore eye," he announced.

I peered at the beast. I was willing to believe him, but at the moment its head was inside the shell, and no eye visible. I poked at it, and nothing happened. I knocked on the shell; it did not answer my knock. I hadn't at that time treated many tortoises, in fact the last one had been brought, not for treatment, but to be put to sleep. Its owner had rung up, in horror, to say that her tortoise had just come out of hibernation, minus three legs, which had been eaten by a rat, and what was she to do. My wife had advised her to hit it on the head! I'd had to administer a gentle rebuke that you didn't speak to clients that way. The poor creature had been brought in, and we'd chloroformed it and put it out of its misery. I remember initially trying to get its head out – though I hadn't tried hitting it on the skull. "Look, son," I said in my most professional manner, "I think it will be best if you go back to the waiting room, and my assistant will help me to do this." So, summoning Mrs Drury from her desk, I turned to her in the surgery and asked,

"Any ideas how to make a tortoise stick its head out? What does Major Davidson do?" For once that mine of information was stumped. It seemed that Kenneth and Mrs Drury's lives had been pretty well tortoise-free too, and so far as veterinary husbandry, surgical and medical textbooks were concerned, the tortoise had apparently not been invented when they were compiled. So, left to our own devices, we turned it on its back, tapped its shell with various instruments, and even tried to gently pull its head out with forceps. I was baffled, and picked it up off the table to consider the problem – when lo and behold, its legs came out, and its head. It seemed legs and head worked together. So we ended up with Mrs Drury contriving to hold the creature and pull on its legs at the same time, to keep the head from slipping back out of sight, while I had a look at the eye. It was a nasty conjunctivitis. With difficulty I managed to get some eye ointment directed on to the general area of the eye, summoned the boy back, gave him the ointment and told him to insert some twice a day, as if it was the easiest thing in the world.

"You know, of course, how to get the head out?" It seemed he did not.

"You a tortoise keeper and don't know that! Well, you have to pull its legs out and you'll find its head comes too, O.K.? Get your wee sister or somebody to hold it up for you."

"Right!" he replied, and departed, clutching his baffling beast.

Poodle number three was led in on a lead by a little man wearing a bonnet, preceded by a woman of vast proportions, wearing blue hair, matching the colour the dog had been dyed. When the small man took his bonnet off, his head wasn't the same shade of blue, but bald.

"Our little dog has developed a large black lump on its head. Come, Charles, show the gentleman."

Charles obligingly lifted the dog on to the table, and stood to attention holding it. Charles' principal function in life was clearly that of dog handler, daily trotting behind his wife, as if he too was on a leash. Every year we had examples of this syndrome where dog apparently had displaced man in a wife's affections, and making the cry for women's liberation appear ridiculous.

"Would you care to show me the lump?" I asked the lady, for nothing was very obvious through the hair.

"Charles, show the veterinary doctor the lump."

At the command, Charles leapt into action, scrabbled about among the hair, and pointed. I wondered if Charles was naturally dumb, or only when his wife was present to speak for both of them.

"When did you notice this?" I asked.

"Only this morning. It was horrible then, and has grown since."

"And it will go on growing too!" I said.

"Oh dearie me," she wailed in a high soprano — surprising really, for with her build I'd have thought she was more a contralto, if not a baritone. She wrung her hands, and I gazed fascinated, for this was a spectacle often referred to in melodramas, but seldom actually witnessed. The action produced quite a clink and jingle as her many bangles, rings and trinkets met head on. "Can nothing be done?" she bayed.

"Oh, yes, quite easily. I expect you were walking on the Torrs yesterday?"

"Oh, you wonderful man! How did you guess?"

She gazed at me in wonderment, and for one awful moment I thought she was about to embrace me, so I backed away hurriedly and picked up a pair of forceps. I dare say it was alright for her to embrace Charles, if she ever did, for he only came up to her shoulder, but since I was as tall as Charles' owner, I feared for my ribs in such a bear hug.

"Now don't worry, if your dog gives a little yelp. I'm about to pull the lump out" — and before she could protest at this cruel act, I did it, and held it up for her to see.

"It's a tick . . . very common around here, especially on the Torrs. They fasten on to sheep, dogs, or any animal, and suck its blood, and so grow quite dramatically, something like a vampire," I smiled. I held it in front of her and said, "If you look carefully, you can probably see its legs moving." She gave a yowl, and pushing Charles effortlessly aside proceeded to kiss and cuddle "Mama's poor darling little baa lamb," who it appeared, had been a "brave little dinkums". As I mentioned, a dog had to be something special to preserve a vet's admiration, with owners like this around. Charles was commanded to pay up, which he did, replaced his bonnet, and wearily trailing the dog's lead, followed his lady who was clutching her "clever little poppet", to her vast bosom and sallied forth like a battle cruiser. It was a frightening spectacle, enough to turn any discerning male permanently against matrimony.

There followed in rapid succession three Bristacombites. The first had a female cat to neuter, and was advised to bring it back on operation day, Wednesday, actually the next day. The second carried a Basset Hound with a haematoma (blood blister) in its ear, a condition common in long eared dogs, prize fighters and front row forwards in a rugby scrum. The Basset's owner was also advised to return on the morrow. The third was yet another poodle with Entropion, a condition where the eyelids tend to turn inwards, so that their eyelashes constantly irritate the eyes, and produce infection. Whatever else we said about the breed, we had to admit they were good vet's dogs, boosting the income considerably. If only they could pick their owners, I thought there might be some hope for the species!! The Entropion was also scheduled for the next day. Since we already had a bitch and two other cats booked in for spays, clearly either Kenneth or I would spend most of the next day 'in theatre'.

That seemed to be the lot, and I was just taking off my white coat, preparatory to starting the afternoon visits, when the door burst open and the blue poodle owner and little Charles bearing the dog, arrived again in a state of near hysteria. Dinkums, it appeared, had suddenly gone round the bend. They'd returned to their nearby Boarding House, and the lady had proceeded forthwith to reward her brave little dog with a slap up feed, when poppet, or baa lamb, had quite suddenly rushed round the room, yelping, pawing his mouth, rolling over, jumping up, and generally giving every sign of having flipped his lid. The battle cruiser seemed about to do likewise, or explode any minute, so I called to Mrs Drury to take her into the waiting room and calm her.

"Sit on her, if you need to, but keep her out of the surgery,"I whispered. Mrs Drury, who was about a third of the size of Charles' helpmeet, gave me a pained look. "You can cope," I assured her with a smile, as she led the sobbing lady by the arm, like a tug with a liner in tow.

"Now, Mr . . . er . . . Charles; let's have a look at your dog!"

I prized open the poppet's mouth, then reached for the forceps again, stronger ones this time. I'd guessed what I would find, the description being fairly typical of the trouble.

"Hold him tightly," I said.

The little man did this with great gusto, gripping the dog by the scruff of the neck in a manner I'm sure his lady would have not liked at all, and which caused the dog to yelp loudly. Charles seemed to be enjoying it. I only hoped Mrs Drury was sitting firmly on the lady next door, or I fancy if she'd appeared and seen her man doing what he'd clearly wanted to do for some time to his rival, there might have been another instant haematoma! A quick yank, and I drew out the forceps with a chop bone in their jaws. It had been lodged firmly across the dog's hard palate, and produced the same sort of effect as raspberry seeds or nuts getting under a person's false teeth, only more so.

"Strewth!" exclaimed Charles, the only word he uttered during our entire acquaintanceship.

The Volks From Away

EIGHT

"Hello! Is thack the veterererinary . . . click surgeon?"

"Yes — Cameron here." I was trying to place the voice with its odd clipped pronunciation, and background of clicks.

"This is Mr Badger." Ah, I had it now. Mr Badger had considerable trouble with his dentures, which at times stuck out like a boxer's gum shield, and when he made a speech of any length, they slid up and down, clicking like castanets. He must have had these teeth forty years!

"What can I do for you, Mr Badger?"

"I do nock know if you can do anythink."

"As bad as that, eh? Well, what does the trouble seem to be?"

"I very much fear I have foot . . . click and mouth disease."

"You have foot and mouth, do you say?" I knew about the mouth . . . the foot was a new development.

"Well, so far I seem to have escaped, but one of my cackle, my shorthorn, ackchually, has contracted it."

"What makes you think it's foot and mouth?"

"I do nock think — I know, Mr Cameron. The signs are exackly . . . click . . . click as the book describes." He paused, as if gathering his verbal resources to have a run at the next bit. "She is lame, and blowing bubbles."

"Blowing bubbles, eh?"

"Yes, bick ones too, and has clearly acuke discomfort . . . click . . . click . . . in the mouth and foot."

"Any other animals affected?" I enquired.

"No . . . o . . . o . . . . jusk the cow. Do I phone the Police or the Minister of Agriculture?"

I could just picture the Minister of Agriculture in some lofty Whitehall office trying to make sense of a cow blowing bubbles in Devon, reported by a man with 'shoogly' teeth.

"Don't phone anybody! I'll be out to see her within the hour. It may not be as bad as you fear."

"Thank you, Mr Cameron, I know you mean well, but I fear it is a for . . . for . . . forlorn hope."

I could picture Mr Badger sitting at his phone, one hand gripping the instrument firmly, the other at the ready as a tooth catcher or manipulator. Mr Badger was a solemn little man who wore at all times a hat so firmly planted on his head, one felt it was part of his anatomy, while across his round little abdomen hung an enormous watch chain. He blinked at the world through horn rimmed spectacles, and generally gave the impression of having just returned from a funeral. His Anthony Eden hat, if now somewhat green with age, was undoubtedly his distinguishing feature. What a cigar was to Winston Churchill, an umbrella to Neville Chamberlain, or a pipe to Harold Wilson, so a hat was to Edwin Badger. He was one of the large contingent in the area, who were described by the Devonians as the 'volks from away'. Away was a delightfully vague term denoting Somerset, Scotland or Swaziland! If you weren't from North Devon, you were 'from away'. This band of immigrants was a mixed bag. Some were ex-servicemen, officers from any of the three Services, who had sunk their demob payment in a farm, and for the most part were doing well, being keen, intelligent, genned up on their new life and willing to learn. We had farmers who had come from other parts of the country, and almost without exception had proved outstanding, since although Devon was exceedingly beautiful and its land fertile, some of the farming methods were fairly primitive, and with the modern methods of the incomers allied to Devon's rich soil, they very soon forged ahead. There were also others, of humbler lineage from away. By and large these were 'volks' who had longed for a little place in the country, and there, in the glories of sunny Devon, with its gentle people, and slower pace of life, were enjoying a more leisurely, if at times precarious existence. Mr Badger was of this latter breed. He was a retired greengrocer from London, who had apparently cherished a secret desire to settle down in the country, own his own little piece of 'England's green and pleasant land' and with great daring had taken the plunge, retired early, and bought about fifteen acres. His smallholding was at

Martincombe, a district of patchwork fields stretching up the steep surrounding hills, famed for its warm climate and early strawberries; it has a honeycomb of lanes leading to the various cottages and little farms perched so precariously on ledges and outcrops, that one felt that any sleepwalker stepping out of his front door, would disappear into the abyss hundreds of feet below.

I had only been at the Badger residence once before, and it had struck me on that occasion that although Mr B. was very likely a first class greengrocer, with every brussels sprout accounted for each night, he was not exactly a ray of sunshine, and his knowledge of cattle was probably nil.

He was consulting his famous watch when I arrived, perhaps a parting gift from 'The Allied Society of Costermongers and Greengrocers', or some such worthy body. Beside him stood Mrs Badger, whom I had not met before. She might have been his twin, being exactly the same size and shape, with a matching pair of spectacles and abdominal bulge. Only the watch chain, and of course the hat, distinguished the male Badger from his mate, with perhaps a suggestion in Mrs B's expression that she had come from an even more tragic funeral than her man. They were a cheerful pair but then if you have spent a lifetime receiving complaints from an unfeeling public that one orange was bad, an apple had a worm in it, and a lovely juicy lettuce had harboured an even juicier slug, you were entitled to feel that life was a bit on the grim side.

"Well, then, let's see the Shorthorn," I said in my cheeriest manner, endeavouring to spread a little sunshine around the sorrowing Badgers. They led me silently to their tiny shippen, which only held four cows. There was the cow drooling saliva, and every now and then smacking its lips and blowing a bubble. She seemed to be standing firmly enough on all four feet, so I suggested he turn her loose and let me see her walk. Sure enough, she had a slight limp. Examination of the offending foot produced a stone lodged between her clits.

"That's all that was wrong with her foot, Mr Badger. Now for the mouth. Grabbing her by the nose, I swung her head round, looked in the mouth, felt the tongue, and palpated the submaxillary glands of the throat, then announced in my spreading-joy-around tone,

"Nothing to worry about. No ulceration in foot or mouth. She has Wooden Tongue, due to a germ called *Actinobacillus lignieresi,* affecting the tongue and soft tissues around. I'll give her an injection, and leave you a bottle to give her a dose every day, and in ten days or so, she'll be as sound as a bell."

"But her symptoms are so like foo . . . click and mouth disease," he said despondently. I think he was genuinely disappointed, and looking forward to writing to some greengrocer friend, saying

'Dear Jack, or Bill, or Bert, I'm afraid I've got bad news to report . . . '

"Well, Mr Badger, a lot of diseases have similar symptoms. If you look at a medical dictionary, you can imagine you have any number of things wrong with you, and rush off to make your will." Over the ritual hand washing in the kitchen, I enquired, "How was the lambing this year?"

"Quite good," he replied lugubriously (it would have been an education to find him on a bad day) "We had ten twins, but the trouble is the ewes will keep lambing at night. However," he added, some excitement coming into his voice and transforming his expression from deep solemnity to a kind of sombre deadpan look (this was the expression which in former times he reserved for his wholesaler when he was a pomegranate short). "I'm having no more lambings at night. Next year they will all lamb through the day."

"Good for you!" I congratulated, "what's the secret?" He looked at me rather pityingly, as if I should have known by now.

"Why, I'll only put the ram out with the ewes through the day this autumn, then all the lambs are bound to arrive by day. It's so simple, really!" I tittered, then hastily changed it to a fit of coughing, for he was absolutely serious. Hastily I bade them goodbye, then laughed non stop for about three miles. A childless couple, they fondly imagined they had discovered a secret that had remained hidden from sheep breeders since first sheep walked the earth. If Mr Badger announced to his neighbours his master plan, as I'd no doubt he would, I could imagine the comments in 'The Fox and Grapes', and 'The Jolly Huntsman' for the next months as the locals discussed 'the plan o' that yur zhopkeeper from away'.

I was dreading the next call, for a very odd reason. The Old Mill was one of my favourite farms, a delightful spot I'd marked out in my pipe dreams as the little farm I'd buy one day when the finances would allow it. The Horne Family who lived there were very friendly, always welcoming me like some long lost brother, and no matter the hour of my arrival, by day or night, miraculously the coffee seemed ready waiting. The farm only extended for forty acres, but Mr and Mrs Horne, having come to that haven of peace to escape the city rat race, were somehow making it pay, with their herd of Guernseys and intensive pig farming. There was nothing terrifying about the case I'd to see, being merely a cow with bursitis of the hock joint. It was my other patient who worried me. The last time I'd been there, which was some two weeks previously, when I'd been cleaning a cow, I'd noticed Uncle, who lived with the family, had been anything but his usual bouncy self, resembling, in fact, a half shut knife as he draped himself over a cow.

"What's the trouble with you, Uncle?" I'd enquired. He groaned and spread himself even more listlessly on the cow.

"It's my water. This gravel in it is murder, and the blasted doctors can't seem to do anything. They don't look at you, just write a prescription and say 'Here! Try this!'" He looked at me piteously. He was a little terrier of a man, and moaning was foreign to his nature. He went on, "Could you not give me something?"

"Oh, sure" I replied in a moment of bravado — one up on the medics — but I soon realised I was playing with fire. "We've got the very pill for you." We had, in fact, an excellent diuretic which flushed out the kidneys like a hose! We had used it successfully on numerous dogs, and had even had success with stones in the kidneys, the drug appearing sometimes to dissolve or break up the calculi.

"Give me some to try," he pleaded, and foolishly, I did. I warned him that if anything went wrong, to contact his doctor, stop the pills right away, and left him. I'd been a worried man since, and had even scanned the obituary notices. But he was still there, looking as grey as before, walking straddle legged, and doubled up over the cow I'd come to see. I was sorry to find him like that, but relieved to find him there at all. Casually I asked,

"How did you get on with the pills?"

"Tremendous," he said, "they worked marvellously. The only trouble was that they brought such lumps of stone down, it took me about an hour to pass each one. I tell you, you could have put them in a rockery. Look!" — he rummaged in a waistcoat pocket — "Did you ever see anything like these?" I goggled, and gulped. "Never!" then added hastily, "I think you better stop these pills, and get to your doctor and ask for an X Ray."

"Ach, doctors!" he snorted, condemning the whole medical profession in two words. I talked to him for a time, managed to persuade him to do as I suggested, relieved him of the remainder of my pills, and went on my way, considerably shaken by these jagged calculi the old man had passed.

As it happened, my next call was actually to a doctor's farm. Dr. White was an easy-going, friendly soul, with a limitless fund of stories. He had retired relatively young from a busy Midlands practice, and with his Irish wife, kept about the muckiest farm in the area. It was quite a feat to walk across their yard without having a wellington sucked off in the slime! I was constantly surprised at the cases to which I was called, many being akin to conditions in man, but it seemed that the doctor, having hung up his stethoscope, so to speak, was determined never to take it down again. He used to peer over my shoulder at whatever beast I was treating, and give me some racy anecdotes about comparable cases he'd had. Today I was setting a broken tibia in a calf, and he enlivened the proceedings with a tale of a former patient whose leg had been put in plaster by some orthopaedic surgeon in Birmingham. Later, examining the leg set with several layers of gypsona, the doctor ran his finger between the leg and the top of the plaster, and explained that the said surgeon in Birmingham had put the plaster on too tightly.

"Leg went gangrenous," said the Doc, puffing at his pipe as if gangrene was no worse than chicken pox, "and of course he lost the leg."

A visit to Blackhill was apt to be a long drawn-out affair, since Mrs White generally had a piece of paper with a list of cases to be seen 'when you're here anyway'. I don't know how she did as a doctor's wife, but clearly she was right at home in the role of farmer, and constantly wore an old pair of corduroys which were so stiff with dirt, that I'm sure at night they stood upright in her bedroom like a suit of armour. Today she had lined up about a dozen cows for pregnancy diagnosis. Again the doctor accompanied me, and told me a long involved tale of a Polish soldier who had married an English girl during the war. They had come to him when the wife was pregnant, and Dr White had worked out the date the baby was due. At five minutes past midnight (some months later) the doctor had been roused from slumber to hear the Pole state in accusing tone 'Dr White! You told me my wife would a baby have on July twenty first. It is now five minutes past that, and no baby there is. What are you going to do about it?'

The thought crossed my mind, as I continued my P.Ds, that what with Badger's cure for night lambings, and the Pole's insistence that if a doctor said a day, he should keep to it, one way and another sex education had been badly neglected in our land. I was spared from any further 'Revelations of a Midlands Doctor', by Mrs White coming with a message that I was to go with all speed to Major Biggleswade's farm, where four heifers had been found dead, and others were very bad. Hastily washing my arms, I leapt into my jacket and my car, and put the foot down. Four dead! What could it be? Staggers possibly . . . Bloat, unlikely . . . What? The yearlings had apparently died without a struggle, as if poleaxed. A further half dozen were staggering about, or down, twitching and groaning. There was a fair old hiatus, and those awful few moments when the vet is surrounded by a sea of anxious faces, waiting for some word of hope. Major Biggleswade, another of our 'from away' people, was a first class farmer, who had but recently moved from a small farm to a large one, indeed one of the best in the district. He tended to get a bit red in the face when agitated, and he had every reason to be bright red now. Four fine, fat, Devon yearlings was a considerable loss. Another six would be catastrophic. At such a time the grey matter is strained to the limit, as one attempts to recall, and mentally tick off, all the differential diagnostic features. Botulism . . . anthrax . . . magnesium deficiency . . . lightning stroke or electrocution . . . there was just nothing be seen externally. It could only be a poison of some sort, I thought, and my heart, already pretty low, went right into my boots, for the world of poisons, apart from reasonably obvious ones like bracken or lead, was a maze. The toxicology book was a most discouraging thing to read, for most of the poisons had similar symptoms, most resulted in death, and in the vast majority of instances, the book mournfully recorded that treatment was unavailing, and a positive diagnosis could only be made on post mortem. I didn't think the Major's blood pressure would stand up to me telling him: "I'll be able to tell you what it was when they're all dead!"

Something had to be done. I looked in the mouths of all the dead beasts, and in the fourth I found something — a twig with some chewed up leaves on it. Animal dead without a struggle — sometimes twigs still in mouth . . . Far back in the limbo of forgotten things, something stirred.

"Show me where they were grazing," I asked, for all the sick beasts had been brought into the barn. Major Biggleswade took me round to a little paddock, and there in a corner was what I sought — a pile of hedge clippings. I poked about in it, brought out some twigs, and held them up.

"There's the trouble!"

"Hedge clippings?" he asked in bewilderment. "Surely these don't kill."

"This kind do; they're yew clippings, absolutely lethal. Beasts can die in five minutes, some still with leaves in their mouth."

The poor fellow sat down on a large stone, and put his head in his hands. But not for nothing was he a Major. He had been at El Alamein, fought his way up Italy, and later in Germany. Within moments he was in command again.

"Can anything be done?" he asked.

My mind was frantically trying to recollect the few paragraphs in our course that had dealt with yew poisoning. My memories were not comforting.

"Look, Major, it's no good building up your hopes. Yew is nearly always fatal, and a quick killer. Our only hope is to get that yew out of them as quickly as possible. So far as I can recollect, the books advise a rumenotomy, but by the time we'd opened up one of your beasts, and taken the yew out of the stomach, I reckon the others would be dead. What I do know is that yew kills by direct action on the heart, so let's have a go with heart stimulants."

We injected the six survivors with adrenaline, then poured all the purgatives I had in my car down the poor beasts' throats — linseed oil, epsom salts, a bloat mixture with turpentine in it, everything remotely resembling a purge, proven and unproven, to try to shift that yew quickly, but I feared it was a hopeless business. I stayed a while, then went home, ostensibly for tea, but in reality to look up the poisons book. It was cheerful! It seemed yew was invariably fatal, but a case had been recorded in 1859 when somebody had saved a beast. As an added item of interest, the author further informed us that yew poisoning also occurred in man, but only in lunatics! I've often ridiculed the phrase in newspapers 'that doctors were fighting to save' somebody or other. Whenever somebody is ill, it appears doctors don't treat, they battle for the patient's life. We did actually fight for these beasts' lives, almost hourly keeping them going with stimulants, in the hope that our various charges of dynamite would work in time. Two more died but four survived . . . just. They had diarrhoea for about a fortnight, but they lived.

So, in the ever-changing kaleidoscope of patterns that made up our lives, I had spent an afternoon with 'the volks from away', had begun with a serious disease that wasn't, had learned of the great secret of daytime lambings, learned how not to treat humans for renal calculi, how not to predict a delivery date, and how to face crisis and loss with dignity, as had Major Biggleswade.

The men of Devon were, and are, a delightful, friendly race. Their rich, rolling tongue is music in the ear. But in the main, critical as this may sound, the farming standards of Devon thirty years ago were poor and primitive, and their improvement is certainly, in part, due to the 'volks from away'. Of that I'm 'sartin sure, m'dears!'

Never!

NINE

"Crowbars" wrote Jimmy in his letter. I could see by the blot he had really stabbed the word out with his pen. Then to make sure I'd grasped the horror of it all, he wrote it again: "Crowbars! He actually used crowbars at a calving. I ask you?" I sat back and tried to picture the scene, and before me came a dreadful picture of a vet, probably with a horrible sadistic leer on his face, actually levering a calf from a cow. "That couldn't be right" I thought. If the man had done that, either he had a dash of Frankenstein in his heritage, or he had gone round the bend; I'd heard of such things, especially when clients didn't pay their bills and drug firms were getting decidedly shirty about 'your outstanding account with us, to which we referred one month ago'. I shook my head to rid myself of the nightmarish pictures. Jimmy had been a pal at the old Vet College, and while I had remained doucely in my native Ayrshire as an assistant, Jimmy had departed for the warmer clime of Somerset there to learn the trade, and I've no doubt, cause a flutter in a few feminine hearts, for there's no doubt he was a real charmer. We didn't correspond very often, but out of the blue had come this racy letter from him, most of which, in the manner of assistants in every profession from time immemorial, had been devoted to slanging his boss, in carefully chosen, selective but definitely vitriolic terms, reaching his most outright condemnation with the reference to crowbars. No, I couldn't imagine quite, at that state of my experience, how crowbars could ever be necessary in calving a poor beast, but there and then, I, with all the confidence of the inexperienced, vowed that there would never be a time when I would need to use such force. Never! Never!

But times change, and the passing years have a habit of making us swallow our words, as we realise how much we still don't know. Jimmy's reference to crowbars came vividly back to me some years later. I was in bed, tucked up with hot water bottles, having alternated that previous day between penicillin pills, throat lozenges, and a cough medicine bottle. I had 'flu, and none of your forty-eight-hour varieties either! In fact, as I lay sweating it out, it came to me that maybe I should have made my will; but since my Life Insurance was already being used as cover for the cost of my partnership in the Practice of Davidson and Cameron, there didn't seem much point. I would either have to get better, or as seemed more likely, quietly decease, and hope there would be enough somewhere for the funeral. While in this cheerful frame of mind, the phone rang.

"Yes" I croaked, hoping it would be a wrong number, a forlorn hope at one in the morning.

"Parkhurst, Higher Shelfin, here. Is that the vetnary?" enquired a voice.

"Yes" I croaked again.

"Is that you, Mr Cameron?" queried the voice doubtfully.

"Yes" I repeated. It seemed my laryngeal mechanism had got a bit jammed somehow; probably stuck up with cough bottle.

"We've a cow bad to calve. She's been at it for hours now and nothing's happening. Can you come?"

"Sure you aren't hurrying her?" I gasped, my larynx springing into action at the thought of leaving this warm bed.

"No, calf's coming alright, but it's very big" said Mr Parkhurst.

I groaned. Bernard, who had succeeded Kenneth in the Practice after he departed for Kenya was not yet a partner, and was, in any case, away visiting his parents for the weekend. I groaned again.

"What's that? I can't hear you proper like. Seems to be a bad line."

"I'm on my way" I assured him, and crawled slowly out of bed.

It was only when I staggered out to the car, I realised how weak I was. My muscles ached all over, my legs had been replaced by jelly, and the wind and rain that cold January night cut right through to the bone. Mr Parkhurst was a first class farmer, one who knew his onions, who seldom if ever panicked, and if he said the cow was 'bad to calve', I was sure he would be right. He was also a very particular farmer, set a high standard, and expected the same, I did not think he would readily overlook failure, and I groaned again. Who'd be a vet?

The fine modern cowshed was warm after the night air, warm and aromatic with that lovely mixture of smells that pervades a byre — hay, silage, cattle cake, the animals themselves. A smell that always made it feel good to be a vet, working with living things. But not that night; the magic failed to work its spell, for I couldn't get over my own wretchedness, and the shivers were coming continuously as I struggled into my calving coat. Soaping the arm — at least the bucket of water was warm, I examined the patient. Farmer Parkhurst was quite right; the calf was coming normally; it was also large, very large, and big, roomy and strong as the Friesian was, she was not going to deliver this calf unaided. I got the calving chains on and tried a bit of traction. I had about as much strength as a new born kitten!

"Can you give a bit of pull here?"

"I can't" said Mr Pankhurst, "I'm only a week out of hospital after a hernia. But Andrew can lend a hand." I said I was sorry about his op, groaned inwardly and looked at Andrew. Andrew was a big lad, but only fifteen. Andrew and I pulled on the chains, the cow bellowed and strained, but the calf came not an inch!

"All we need is a strong pull here. Can you get any helpers?" I asked.

"Not at this time of night" he replied, shaking his head.

"Then we're in trouble," I said. "This calf is going to take some shifting; you daren't pull, I've got the flu and that leaves one fit man, Andrew!"

(Here let me insert an explanation. I have frequently noticed a look of horror come over a face of the layman when describing a calving. I have seen the word 'barbaric' forming in each mind, as they think of maybe six men pulling on ropes or calving chains to deliver a calf. In defence of the veterinary profession *vis à vis* the medical, I would explain that the vet cannot, as with a human mother, arrange a half ton cow in the optimum position for delivery; the calf may weigh anything up to a hundredweight; almost invariably the cow lies down on her side and the vet has perforce to lie on his side, stomach or even back, and with an arm that numbs rapidly, try to manipulate the calf. All this by the way of explanation of what's to come! If someone says, 'The obvious answer is a Caesarean Section', I can only reply that in those days we were not so expert in cattle, or so ready to whip out a knife, and at two o' clock on a winter morning, a Caesar with no assistance available, was just not on.)

I looked around our company. What could we do? To wait for morning and more muscle power was to have an exhausted mother and probably a dead calf. There was no drug that could safely be given to increase these contractions. That cow had already given all she'd got, and even our brief attempts to assist her had visibly tired her. It had to be . . . I could think of nothing else. It was a case for crowbars, of a sort. I explained to Mr P and Andrew what I felt would need to be done. Father looked about as happy as I was feeling, which was wretched with a capital W.

"But is it safe?" asked the owner.

"No," I had to reply, "but while I've never done it, it has been done and unless you can produce six strong men, we haven't a hope of delivering that calf. Come on, Mr Parkhurst," I said with an attempt at flippancy I was far from feeling, "if you and I were fit, we'd not be beaten, but we're just a couple of crocks tonight."

"Reckon you're right at that" he agreed with a hint of a smile. I had never actually known him to let himself go and laugh, his dour, deadpan countenance always masking his feelings. You never knew where you were with this man, except out, I was sure, if you failed.

"Now then, Andrew" I explained to the son, "you're the important one here tonight. Do exactly as I say. When I say 'stop', you stop at once. When I say 'steady', I mean an inch at a time. Can you handle it?"

There was a flicker of eagerness on the boy's face, but he immediately got rid of it. I thought as I looked from father to son I had seldom seen such a pair of dour Devonians. I don't know why, but they reminded me of Scrooge, at the beginning of Dicken's *Christmas Carol,* only they were more full and fair of face. I suppose my subconscious was recalling to me the reluctance of all the Parkhursts to pay their bills, or maybe I was delirious! 'Stop dreaming', I chided myself, 'and get on with it'.

"Well then, lad, let's have it" I said.

Soon a roar was heard as the tractor was started, the byre door flung open to admit a blast of freezing air and choking diesel fumes as the boy reversed his mechanical steed right up to the door, and in it. The door was wide, the cow was right opposite it, which saved a bit of shifting around, and operation 'broken vow' was about to commence. The leg calving chains were fixed together to the tractor tow bar, and when I repeated "an inch at a time, mind you" young Andrew nodded and did just that, while I, with my hand inside the cow, felt for progress and tried to guide the direction of pull. I felt the legs budge, and move up into position, yelled 'Stop', and at once the tractor stopped.

"Now for the tricky bit, the head," I shouted over the tractor's roar. As with the legs, now the head chain alone was linked to the drawbar, and I nodded. I glanced at Mr Pankhurst and thought he'd be back in hospital shortly at this rate, for his chin was almost tripping him. To say he didn't like it was just fractionally an understatement! But Andrew was inching forward, and I soon had other things on my mind as I tried to guide the calf's head into the mouth of the uterus and up into the vagina. It was coming, a minute fraction at a time. The cow, poor beast, bellowed, as the pain really gripped her, and now that the head was coming, she strained with might and main. Feverishly I tried to assist the extra large forehead or poll into the passage and as finally all was in position bellowed "Whoa, there!" Fortunately, young Andrew got the gist of what 'whoa' meant, and stopped dead. I really took my hat off to that fifteen-year-old lad. He drove that tractor like a seasoned expert, literally, as I had asked, inch by inch. We were well on the way now; another pull on the legs, then the final pull on the head, until to the immense relief of the cow, its owner and its midwife, the calf's head was free, its eyes blinking at me, its tongue sticking out the side of its mouth, its whole attitude, I thought, one of disgust and outrage at the indignity of the whole affair, as it smelt the diesel fumes and felt the icy blast coming in the door, I'm sure it said, "What a dickens of a way to arrive — and what a place, noisy, smelly, wet!" In short, it felt as I had felt when I left my hot water bottles, that life would be a far better thing if one could stay in this warm bed. But it wasn't going to get the chance now. Having come so far, the battle was won, and the tractor-friesian combination soon did the rest and the calf came with a rush, hitting me with such force in the stomach as I tried to catch it, that I was deposited unceremoniously on the seat of my pants in the dung channel. But what did that matter, I was pretty wet by now anyway, what did anything matter, we'd done it! We had an enormous bull calf — looking to my wearied eyes already half grown, and there now followed a period of mutual congratulations. The cow, which astonishingly, had remained standing throughout all that traction, was, already, as with all mothers, putting the pain of the past behind her as she licked her large son; and old man Parkhurst was actually congratulating me — I couldn't believe it — while I, my hand inside the cow to make sure there was no damage, said, "Well done, Andrew! Great driving, lad!" at which the boy forgetting for a moment the code of the Parkhursts, actually smiled.

As I made my weary way home, I reflected on the events just past. I shuddered to think what might have happened if the driver's foot had slipped on the clutch, but otherwise I was not too morose at having broken one of my self-imposed commands A 'never' had gone for a burton, but in retrospect it seemed to me that a steady controlled pull had been much more effective, and quicker, than six pairs of hands tugging at ropes.

Jimmy's boss had known what he was about when he used a crowbar, calving ropes attached, as a lever, no doubt against the concrete lip of the dung channel.

Flu or not, I was out early next day, fearful lest something had overtaken my patient but I needn't have worried. She was lying down, chewing the cud, having evidently had a hearty breakfast, which was more than I'd had. Parkhurst senior was with me, and as he looked at the beast and at me, he observed "She's looking better than you are, Mr Cameron!" I thought wryly that wouldn't be hard. Clearly we need worry no more about the patient. In fact, my only concern now was what farmer Parkhurst would deduct from the calving fee, for diesel and use of tractor!

The trouble with one 'never' going down the drain is that others are sure to follow. It's a bit like an alcoholic; the first drink is one too many and opens the floodgates. Accompanied by two students, one a lad from Nigeria, and the other a Scot, I was right out at the fringe of the Practice on the moor. Here several veterinary practices met, all roughly the same distance from home, so, in each case, notes would be compared between the various farmers as to how their vet did the job. One of my moorland clients was called Hockridge, and a rougher establishment would be hard to imagine. It was really a ranch he ran out on the moor, his buildings filthy and primitive even by Devon standards. What the dwelling house was like inside, I cannot say, for I was never in it. Since Hockridge was a bachelor and only washed about every three days, and shaved maybe once a fortnight, I could well imagine what his house was like. The reason for the visit was the annual tuberculin test, and I anticipated a long drawn-out affair, for Hockridge's young stock roamed freely three hundred and sixty three days of the year, the other two days being when they came in for the TB test. They were as wild as mountain deer, and this year, having heard that he had added some twenty Galloways to his stock, I knew there would be high jinks, for even your half domesticated Galloway can 'kick a fly off your bunnet'. We heard them before we saw them; a series of bellows, whistles, shouts and curses floated over the moor to us; and rounding a bend I saw Hockridge, some of his pals, and neighbours, most of them mounted on ponies, with much hallooing from the riders, guiding a motley collection of steers and heifers, of many colours and breeds, towards a temporary paddock he had made composed of five-bar gates tied together. This was the corral, but as to it being OK remained to be seen. All that was certain was that we had a fight on our hands. The idea was that one by one, the animals would be driven into a homemade crush, which at the front was simply a gate, and behind a plank of wood which was lowered into place when the animal had entered. There was no yoke for the neck, and the crush side from which I had to operate was just a few planks, the other side being the gable end of the cowshed.

As the two students and I dressed for the fray, the astonished Scots lad said "I've never seen anything as slaphappy as this" while the Nigerian observed. "It is rather primitive, is it not?" They had come to 'see practice' in its various forms, with pictures in their minds gleaned from the latest text books on hygiene and animal husbandry, of up to date crushes, gathering and shedding pens, a concrete yeard which could be hosed afterwards, and a little niche for the vet beside the crush, where in safety and some degree of comfort, he could do his job. Instead before them stretched a sea of sweating bovine backs, kicking and plunging about, while outside the stockade a group of men with sticks and curses sought to prevent the beasts leaning on their home made restraining wall. Since the two lads were going to assist me with finding the ear mark and noting down the identification individually, they realised that they had to enter the arena. Over the wall we went, and I heard one of them mutter, "Now I know what the Christians felt like facing the Roman lions." Still in one piece, but having accumulated a few kicks and much dirt on our various personages, we reached our point of operations.

"Let's try and do the Galloways first while they are still packed in," I bellowed at Hockridge, who nodded. But between the concept of any great plan and its fulfilment, there is many a snag. The only way to get a beast into the crush was for one of the men to go into the bunch to take its tail, and with the assistance of others, manhandle it to where we awaited it. The more manhandling that went on inside, the more the beasts pressed on the restraining five-bar gates; the result was that those helpers outside cursed those inside, while these sweating, dung covered figures cursed back. Since most of the words were in broad Devonian — and some of them new to me — with the snorts and roars all around, fortunately all was not understood by my two lads, the Nigerian merely observing "I think they are swearing quite a lot?" We did get some Galloways tested, till there was an interruption in the flow, for one black beast simply took off like a rocket, almost straight up in the air and jumped, the gates. In ten seconds flat it was over the hill and out of sight. The guardians of the gates were divided in their opinion. Some mounted ponies to recapture the fugitive, while the rest bawled at them to come back. But the damage was done, for in no time at all the rest of the beasts had cottoned on, pressed against the gates and were off. Soon the only actors in the drama to be seen were one vet, two students, and a few tested bullocks which had passed through into the farm courtyard. We sat down to wait, and eventually the cowboys and their scattered herd came back. They had all but reached the pen when the same Galloway steer kicked upwards again like an Olympic high jumper and was off at a fast rate of knots.

"Let it go," I bawled, "and bring the rest."

It would have taken John Wayne, James Stewart with maybe some help from the Magnificent Seven, provided it was on one of their top form days, to get that one back.

"What will you do?" enquired the Scots student.

"Nothing" I replied. "They'll never get that one."

"But what if it should have TB and infect the rest?" enquired the dark lad. "Then that will maybe teach Farmer Hockridge to get a proper pen" I replied.

Thus another 'never' went out the window, never to leave a job incomplete. Eventually, wearily, we got the last beast tested, and we headed for the nearest tap to remove some of the dirt. It was then that Hockridge played his ace, informing me there was a bullock bad to calve in the shippen, whither he led us, opened the door and stood back. I gaped, then said,

"How long has she been like this?"

"Reckon about two days since she started like."

Lying in front of us, on a bed of filth, was a heifer, having its first calf. It was lying on its side, but stretched full out, so that its chain – (incongrously the one secure beast was chained) was all but throttling it. the heifer was far through, and protruding from it were the head and fore limbs of its calf. Two days! From the smell it was more like two weeks. This was a typical piece of Hockridge neglect. I whirled on him.

"Why did you not call us before?" to which he replied, again typically,

"Reckoned since you was comin' anyways, might as well wait and get the visit paid by the government, like."

I thought of the lecturer who had told us we would find we might have to educate some of our clients. I wonder where he would have begun with Hockridge.

"Look," I said, "there's one of three things we can do here. One, shoot the cow. Two, an embryotomy and cut the calf up into bits, or three, try to calve it. I'd suggest to shoot her would be a kindness."

"Nor, she be out of a good 'un an' I'd like to save her" he answered.

Clearly this was to be his milk cow since every other hooved creature was out on the moor.

"Right then!" I glared at him "plenty of hot water, soap, towel, and quickly"

"Aint no hot water in house."

"Then boil some, plenty"

We waited, already tired, dirty, dishevelled. There was no offer of tea. We were out in the wilds. I looked at the two students, both silent, both experiencing for the first time how crude sometimes their future calling could be.

"You know" I said with an attempt at cheerfulness, "the first vet I saw practice with used to say 'you may not see much practice, but you will see life'. You've been in my lady's chamber to treat her darling little King Charles Spaniel; now you're getting about as rough a glimpse of practice as you could imagine, and you're going to be seeing worse yet before we leave."

Eventually Hockridge came back, with two buckets of warm water. We all washed in one, I sent him for his tractor, told him what we were going to do, then pumped the contents of the other bucket now containing liberal quantities of antiseptic and soap into the cow's uterus, and we began. Hockridge wasn't as good a driver as young Andrew Parkhurst had been, but he wasn't bad. The calf came a bit. We paused while more water was fetched for lubrication purposes, because all the uterine fluid had long gone from that little heifer. I reckoned she'd had about enough pain, she was past helping us with contractions, so gave a spinal injection which would take away most of the suffering. Eventually one foul calf was removed, the uterus pumped out with more antiseptic, and while one student inserted pessaries, the other gave her penicillin. I left him half a dozen bottles of Protein Hydrolysate to put some nourishment into the poor creature. Then, telling Hockridge I would be back tomorrow to see her, we were off. His mouth actually fell open when I said I was coming. The government wouldn't pay for that visit, nor for the calving. He opened his mouth to say something, but it was lost as I revved the car, and drove away. My two students were very quiet on the way home. I knew what they were thinking. First it was thankfulness that they would be off on the morrow and therefore not need to attend another trip to the moorman and his bullocks, to read the results of the test, in three days time. The other thought was of the horror they had seen, and of the tales they would tell to incredulous fellow students.

"Tractors. He actually uses tractors for a calving!"

In fact, I never needed to use a tractor again, but I had not quite done with sacrificing my sacred vows, and I was glad the students had gone by then, though sorry they did not see Hockridge's heifer, for it recovered, astonishingly, and he paid a whopping bill! That was the only way I knew to educate this client.

My last 'never' to disappear left me with a red face. Jim Glover, whose shop was just across from our surgery, breezed in one tea time, and said, "Alec. Could you spare a minute to look at my old bitch? There's something not right about her."

I nipped over the way and saw Jim's whippet, which was wandering about aimlessly, her back slightly arched. I took temperature and noticed there was a slight uterine discharge. Then I palpated her abdomen, and asked Jim if she'd ever had pups. Her abdomen was certainly enlarged a bit.

"No."

"When was she last in season?"

"I can't remember; ages ago; she's so old I think she's stopped."

"Well, Jim," I said quite confidently, "she's got a condition called pyometra, very common in maiden bitches. Her womb is swollen, but not too big, some discharge is coming away. It might mean a hysterectomy, but we'll try some tablets first, at her age."

"Right, Alec." said Jim, and came for the tablets.

The next morning at nine a.m., Jim walked in again in his usual jovial manner and reported.

"Alec. I thought you'd like to know that the whippet had a pup through the night. Will she still need that operation, do you think?"

"Er, no Jim . . . I think the womb will be OK now." I heard an echo from out the years from the old Vet College:

'When you are asked by an examiner for the causes of enlargement of the abdomen in a bitch, along with enlarged liver, enlarged spleen, dropsy, pyometra and the rest, never forget the commonest cause of all, pregnancy'.

I had mentally noted that, chalked up a 'never forget' in my mind, and lo, after these years I'd forgotten. Bang had gone another 'never'.

Surprises Of A Caesar

TEN

I came out of the shop, turned left, and started to make my way back to the surgery. I'd been to the barber's shop for a much needed haircut, for what with lambings, calvings, tuberculin tests and all the rush of the spring work, I'd had little time for any short back and sides. However a glance in the mirror that morning had startled me to the point of realising that if I didn't have it done soon, I'd either need to go round the various hairdressers and ask for an estimate, or let somebody have a go with sheep shears. I had an operation scheduled for four o'clock, but until then was free, so after our post-lunch conference and time of fellowship, I'd left Bernard, my new partner, to cope with afternoon consulting time and any subsequent calls, and wandered along to my hairdresser. Barber's shops are great places for brushing up on the local news, so it was with my knowledge much increased and thatch much diminished that I started back along the street. For a vet or for that matter a doctor to walk along the main street of a small town is fatal, for it always seems on these walkabouts that half the population have been waiting for that very opportunity and from all corners converge to engage in conversation about the weather, the football team, the new vicar, all part of the softening up process before coming to the nub of the matter, some free advice about their pets. I had listened to a sad story of a goldfish, a positively harrowing tale of a cat's encounter with a terrier and subsequent injuries, and had just been hailed for the third time with a "Hello, Mr Cameron; the very man I wanted to see." I was pinned to a shop window by a large individual whom I didn't know from Adam, but who evidently knew me, and with an arm spread out on the window front on either side of me was making escape difficult. I tried to follow a complicated story delivered in a loud voice, in broad Devonshire, about some kind of fits his dog took, "only it isn't really a fit, if you know what I mean." I think we were at the point in the story where the dog was lying twitching on the kitchen floor, when I became aware that I wasn't hearing my captor any more. His mouth kept opening and closing, but not a word came to me. For one nasty moment I thought I'd gone stone deaf, till I realised that I couldn't make him out because of the greatly increased background noises of engines revving, cars tooting, and drivers shouting, a din that was increasing in volume by the minute. I wondered what was causing the traffic jam, and incurring the travelling public's wrath till a vague uneasiness took possession of me, and ducking under my warder's arm with a "Better bring him along to the surgery, Mr . . . er', I took off and hared for our premises, passing on the way a policeman heading for the heart of the storm, which, as I had feared, was the footpath and main street outside our surgery.

These things, as everyone knows, are, of course, all a matter of cause and effect. The initial cause in this instance was that outside our door was parked Bernard's car, a perfectly proper and safe place to leave it. However in front of Bernard's Ford was a client's Land Rover, while in front of that again was a car and trailer with my four o'clock patient arriving. Opposite the three cars was parked a butcher's van, thus considerably narrowing the space through which other vehicles could proceed, but all would have been well had not a large touring coach tried to negotiate the gap, thought better of it, and just sat there, waiting for something to happen. Around this convoy of cars and so on, quite a little crowd was gathering, including many of the bus tourists, watching a farmer emerge from our front door propelling a sheep, followed by Bernard with a snowy white lamb tucked under each arm. The situation was further confused by my four o'clock farmer trying to direct his sheep *in* the door, while the onlookers watched with great interest, even clicking cameras, convinced that this was one of the tourist attractions of Devon. Had it not been that the Easter weekend was early this year, there would not have been so many cars and coaches about. Had not my client arrived with his sheep at the very moment another was departing with sheep and lambs, there would have been nothing to see, the coach would probably have managed to squeeze through, and there would have been no crowd of spectators. Or yet again, if the client of the first part — he whose lambs Bernard was depositing in the Land Rover beside their bleating mother — had phoned to make an appointment, this clash of comings and goings could have been averted, but being one of the easy going Tuckers, he had just, typically, arrived un-announced. Or pursuing our quest for the cause of chaos even further, had we not, as a partnership acquired something of a reputation for our sheep work, and particularly our Caesarean operations, nobody would have been there at all. As observed earlier, the whole schemozzle was simple really, when you came to think of it. The cause? A departing Caesar patient had met up with an arriving one, and together with two white lambs gathered a crowd and stopped a coach. The effect! Bedlam, a queue of cars all along the street, hooters going full blast, drivers ditto, police striding to the scene, and myself galloping into the surgery and arriving in a state of near collapse. Surprising what such a little thing could cause, but then the surprises of a Caesar were many and varied. In this instance order was quickly restored by the policeman (who fortunately was our close friend Johnny) simply driving Bernard's car up a side street opposite us, which let out the Land Rover, enabled the coach to drive on and the whole log jam to drift by.

Many vets had been doing the odd Caesar for years, but Kenneth had pioneered it in our area, the thing had been talked about and we had farmers arriving from many miles away for "the Major's operation" because their own vet didn't do it or believe in it. These men would pay cash for services rendered, and depart, remaining true to their own man for everything else. Kenneth was now practising in his native Kenya, but like Elijah's mantle of old descending on the young prophet, his reputation had passed to Bernard and me, and each year our Caesars grew in number. So the second surprising thing about the Caesar was the number we carried out, sometimes six a day, plus, of course, all our other spring work, and sheep would arrive in vans, the boot of a car or its back seat with the cushions removed, and occasionally in the luxury of a trailer to itself. We did Caesars for a variety of very good reasons, for example, where a very large lamb was just too big for a little hogg having her first lambing; or where there was a prolapse of the vagina, a common occurrence which rendered normal lambing difficult, if not brutal. Principally, though, we did Caesars in such volume because of a condition known as Ringwomb, and surprise of surprises, there wasn't any such condition, said the pundits. When Kenneth had first written to *The Veterinary Record* of the condition, he had been answered in strong terms by one of the best known vets in the country, who firmly declared that after many years in practice, he had never come across "this so-called Ringwomb", and suggested that if the sheep were left alone, they would lamb normally. He had said, in effect that Kenneth was rushing his fences, and his "Ringwomb" was merely a stage maybe twenty-four hours before full term and a normal birth. Letters had flowed in week after week taking sides in the debate, and suggesting all manner of remedies, most of which we'd tried without success. What we described as Ringwomb was a condition where a ewe came into labour normally, at full term, but where the os, or mouth of the uterus simply did not open, or open enough, to allow steerage way for the oncoming lamb. Examination of these ewes revealed a hard ring, the os, either completely closed or only slightly open, and no matter how long we'd left the ewe, the condition had persisted, and I'd seen ewes in labour for days, and die with the womb still closed, with the "ring" remaining firm. We'd thought it was a hormone deficiency but none of the oestrogens or sex hormones had proved successful. Someone had reported success with spinal anaesthesia, the idea being, I suppose, that this removed pain and allowed relaxation of the muscles, but it hadn't worked for us. Since "Hoare's *Veterinary Therapeutics*" informed us that "in functional constriction of the cervix uteri, extract of Belladonna freely applied might overcome the spasm and allow delivery to take place" we'd tried Belladonna, with little result. In fact, short of "eye of newt, skin of frog, web of spider and cow parsley gathered at dead of night, the whole to be compounded and mixed when the moon was full", we'd had a go at most things. So in the end Kenneth had started doing Caesars, and all we knew, despite the pundits, was that for a condition that apparently didn't exist, we saw an astonishingly large amount of it in Devon, in any breed of sheep, but principally the native Devon Closewools. By this operation, each year, we were saving the lives of very many ewes and lambs. It had almost become a kind of status symbol with the farming community, with farmers comparing notes at the weekly markets about how many "of them thar operations us's 'ad". I rather fancied that the ewes who'd had it were themselves a bit uppish with their girlfriends who'd lambed normally, and probably showed off their operation scar to the wondering gaze of the common throng.

The whole phenomenon of the increase in Caesarean sections was surprising, but it would never have taken place, if it had not made sound economic sense, and that this was a fact was due to Kenneth's business acumen, his skill and his character. To convince a farmer, be he Devonian or Dalesman, Lancastrian or Lincolnshire, from Caithness in the north east to Cornwall in the south west, you had to show that he was making money or saving money. This Kenneth did. Considering the time and skill involved, his charges were low; compared to human medicine, they were ludicrous. For a successful Caesar with live lambs and a live mother afterwards, he charged three guineas. If the lambs were born dead but the ewe survived, to breed another year or be fattened for slaughter, it cost two guineas. If the whole thing was a dead loss, the charge would be about £1, which barely covered cost of drugs, anaesthetic, nylon, catgut etc. Since a mother and two lambs was valued at £20, clearly there was profit in it. Even if the lambs were dead, at two guineas saving the ewe was still saving brass. If there was a risk of total loss, well, there would be that anyway to leave her alone, slaughter in that state at most bringing £2. Clearly, reasoned the farming community, there was money in it, and the news caused a stirring of interest akin to a miniature gold rush in men who would never previously have dreamed of taking a mere sheep to a vet.

Major Kenneth Davidson was a superb surgeon, his big, beefy hands being remarkably swift, dexterous and in full control of his task. Compared to him I was at first a ham-fisted bungler, but I learned much from watching and assisting him at work. Perhaps I never matched him, for he was a born surgeon, while I was a vet who did surgery out of necessity, but preferred diagnosis and medical treatment to knife work, yet in time apparently it was said "that Scottish Vetnary be alright, nigh as good's Major", while Bernard, having seen much practice with us as a student, and then succeeeding Kenneth in the Practice, was accepted from the beginning as being well trained. At first everything was carried out on the farm, sometimes on the kitchen table, more often on bales of straw in a draughty barn by the light of a Tilly lamp, or in an even more exposed corner of a hayshed where the lambing pens were sited. In those early days the op was carried out under general anaesthetic, using Chloral Hydrate intravenously. While results were encouraging, losses were heavier than we wanted, for with dirt or spider's webs festooning the walls of the shed and straw getting into the wound, a wide selection of bugs abounded to cause sepsis. Also with a drug like Chloral Hydrate, the lambs were born anaesthetised, and as they were often weakly in the early days before farmers were educated to send for us in time, they didn't come out of the anaesthetic. Results improved markedly when we had the patient brought into our surgery where we had light, warm water in abundance, aseptic conditions and all drugs and instruments to hand. They further improved — dramatically — when we did it all under local anaesthetic, so that the lambs were bleating within minutes of being delivered, and provided the mother with an incentive to recover. In time we rarely lost a ewe, and as the ewes were brought to us increasingly early as the years passed, death in the lambs was also cut to negligible proportions. A further incentive for bringing the sheep to us was that the scale of charges mentioned could operate with no visit or call out fee being necessary "and missus could do shopping or 'ave a hair do, like, wile yow be 'aving 'er belly cut".

If the profit motive and the Major's surgical skill were two important factors in the surprise soaring of Caesar statistics, there was a third factor no less important. They knew Kenneth Davidson was to be trusted. Some shared, some admired, some laughed at his unashamed Christian principles (" 'ee be verry religious, like"), all recognised and respected his sincerity, and even those who never looked near church or chapel (and most Devon farmers worshipped periodically) acknowledged that "the Major be a good man, a right good un; you can trust ee".

But the surprises of a Caesar did not end with its popularity and growth, its acceptance by the farming community or the scepticism of many critics in the profession. Day by day, things happened, the folklore increased and my four o'clock appointment that day was no exception. Mrs Drury, our extremely efficient secretary and general assistant had asked if her younger sister, who planned to be a nurse, could come and see an op. The client that day, farmer Hawkins of Pilton Grove, was having his first case, so he had arrived with his two strapping sons to see the job, while Johnny, our friendly "bobby", having cleared the High Street, thought he might relax briefly and view the proceedings. We also had a student seeing practice with us, as we invariably had in the spring. To complete the party, Jim Glover, our ebullient butcher across the road, was there. Jim had quite a history. He was a real Casanova and a plausible rogue until recently, just sitting in a church he had been converted — gone religious, they said — and it showed to the extent that he now stayed with his own wife instead of somebody else's, came home sober and paid his debts, all to the great astonishment of his former associates. Jim had taken to coming in regularly for a chat, so his presence that afternoon meant we had quite an audience for the theatre. Now, at this point in the proceedings, I think I should warn, as television announcers do from time to time, "that in what follows there might be some scenes that would upset certain viewers", so if you are one of the faint hearted, you might be as well to skip a couple of pages!

The ewe, in the midst of all this concourse having been ushered into the operations room, and the spectators having positioned themselves around, I did what was the first step, soaped up my arm and examined her *per vaginam* to ascertain if she did, in fact, require surgery, or if the lamb could be delivered in normal fashion. This examination is not painful, but uncomfortable, just as the patient tenses himself, grips tightly the arms of the chair and fears the worst when the dentist says "Open wide", and on tapping the offending molar produces a strangled groan, so the ewe in question gave a slight grunt. There was an almighty clatter, and I looked round to see the would be nurse out cold. I hadn't done a thing; no knife had gleamed in the overhanging arc lamp; no blood had dripped to the ground, so I thought the girl's reaction boded ill for her nursing career. (In fact she did, in time become an excellent nurse). Mrs Drury, with perhaps just the suggestion of a flush colouring her cheeks, whether of embarrassment, sisterly concern or sisterly condemnation I know not, supervised the carrying of the body into our waiting room cum office where it was laid on a couch to recover eventually. Bernard was to be at the desk writing for a time before going out on a case, and he promised to stay till the girl came round and make sure she didn't stagger with deathly countenance out the door or rush screaming up the street, so all trooped back to the theatre.

I hadn't liked what I'd felt. The cervix of the uterus was tightly closed alright, but it felt dry, and there was a distinct aroma as I withdrew my hand, which was not Chanel No.5.

"You've got a dead lamb or lambs here, Mr Hawkins. This operation won't be easy, which is a pity, since it's your first. You could get a couple of pounds for her if you sent her into the slaughter house as a casualty, and with dead lambs, there's a fair chance of losing her if I operate. It's up to you! What do you want?"

"What would you advise?" He was a well spoken, well educated man, by no means poor, perhaps socially a cut above most of our clients, and maybe a trifle superior in manner.

"Well, she's a young ewe, and since ninety per cent of Caesars lamb normally next time, it might be worth the risk, but it will be trickier than usual. You must decide. Surely she must have been showing signs of lambing for some time?"

"Yes, she's been paddling about a bit for a few days, but nothing to show. We're here now anyway, so go ahead," a statement which I'm sure he was soon to regret. I think curiosity more than anything decided him. Neighbours had seen a Caesar, he hadn't.

So the ewe was lifted on to the table, on her back, hind legs lightly restrained by tapes, while the farmer stood at the sheep's head and held the forelegs. Then the team swung into the established routine, Mrs Drury on one side of the patient, myself the other. It's always difficult for a narrator to decide how much detail should be put into his narrative, but just in case any reader finds himself on some lonely island with a pregnant ewe requiring assistance, or in a little colony of survivors following destruction on a massive scale, it might be as well to sketch in the main steps! First the soft wool of the sheep's under belly is plucked, then the remainder soaped and shaved, and swabbed with antiseptic. Using a very short, fine needle, the skin is anaesthetised, then the muscles beneath, and finally with a longer needle, right down to the peritoneum. All the sheep should feel is the first prick, and that was so in the case in question. Next the operation cloths were clipped in position, leaving only the area for incision visible. I was conscious of six pairs of eyes watching closely, not counting Mrs D. and self. Preliminaries over, we were ready to commence. Mrs D. clapped the scalpel into my hand from our tray of sterilised instruments, and with one bold stroke the skin was incised. The sheep never felt a thing, but judging from the indrawn breaths I heard, others did, particularly when blood welled up, to be immediately swabbed by my assistant, allowing a clear view of the little bleeding vessels which were clamped, but not before we lost one of our spectators. With a muttered, "Alec, I couldn't do that for a pension," our butcher was off. Evidently Jim didn't go in for black puddings or a wee drop of blood wouldn't have worried him! Next the muscles were cut, then carefully, the shining sheet of the peritoneum, looking for all the world like fine plastic. A loop of bowel popped up into the wound, which it had no right to do, and it was speedily put in its place. There beneath me was the uterus, and gently one horn of its V shape was brought through the incision, to the exterior. A healthy uterus with a living lamb in it was always, to me, a thing of beauty, and normally I thrilled at this moment, seeing there the wonderfully soft yet strong organ the Creator had designed, with its intricate array of blood vessels to feed the developing embyro and supply its every need. But not today! This uterus was far from a pretty sight. It was doughy to the touch, puffy, oedematous and a dirty greyish colour instead of a healthy pink. I was vaguely aware of a voice behind me saying rather faintly "I'd better be off before the sergeant comes looking for me" I cut into the horn of the exposed womb, and at that point one of the strapping six-foot Hawkins boys departed, muttering, "It's getting a bit hot in here" He looked a trifle grey, I thought. I don't know about the heat in the room, but there was certainly a stench. "Paddling about for a few days", farmer Hawkins had said. That lamb smelt as if it had been dead for weeks, and as I removed it and threw it into the lamb basket, with no pretence, or excuse, son number two departed at the double, for the door. Then reaching round to the other horn of the V, I removed a second lamb, also putrid. Farmer Hawkins, whose forebears had no doubt sailed the seas with the men of Devon under Raleigh, Drake, Frobisher and the original Hawkins, now felt a sudden concern as to the well being of his family. "I'd better see these boys are alright" he explained as he hurriedly left us. It was like the ten little niggers; soon there'd be none.

The Vet student had taken Farmer Hawkins' place at the sheep's head. I thought him strangely silent, and glancing up, saw beads of sweat on a pale forehead. I was sweating too, but for a different reason, for that unhealthy uterus was the very dickens to suture, the stitches kept tearing away. It was hard work.

"Perhaps you'd just check on Mrs Drury's sister and our clients,' I suggested to the lad. It was his first Caesar and he couldn't have picked a worse one; it was decidedly nasty, with the smell of decay heavy in the air. Now Mrs Drury and I were left alone. Fortunately the sheep was lying still, but I knew she'd leap to its head if it struggled. I knew she would not leave the room; I'd be more likely to yield first.

"Not very nice, Mrs Dru, is it! It'll be touch and go with this one."

"One of the worst we've had," was all she said, snipping away at catgut as I completed the second row of inversion sutures in the uterus, and tucked it back inside the abdomen. The rest was routine – nylon continuous sutures for peritoneum, then muscles, and finally my favourite mattress stitch for the skin. Then the whole area was thoroughly cleansed, and dusted with sulphonamide. Without my asking, she handed the loaded syringe of Penicillin (the farmer would give the ewe an injection each day for a week), and asked "Phenergan?" "Yes, the first danger here will be shock." She knew my drill and drugs of choice. "Some pituitrin, too, I think. It's a risk, but the sooner she's pushing out that muck, the better. I only hope the sutures hold."

So it was done, the sheep lifted down, a very exhausted, ill sheep, and as I removed my gown and started scrubbing away the smell of death from my hands, my assistant was already at work disinfecting the table, gathering and cleaning instruments, and putting them into the steriliser with fresh operation cloths and swabs. You never knew when they would be needed again. Feeling a bit fresher, I sallied forth to find the departed spectators, and saw a horrible sight. The two Hawkins sons were sitting on the stairs leading to the upstairs flat, and they were green! It wasn't clear whether they were at the stage of sickness where they feared they would die, or the next stage where they feared they would not die. Father was leaning against the outer door, and though pale, he at least looked human. Our student was OK and making animated conversation with Mrs Drury's sister, still seemingly happy to lie on the couch. She got short shrift from her older sister.

"You still here? It's time you got up from there, and did some work. Come and help me clean up next door." That was enough. The sister was better and out the door, hot foot for home. Mrs Drury smiled, "I thought that would get her up."

The ewe was gently carried out to its trailer, followed by its green and white owners. I gave father some words of instruction as to follow up procedure and he was gone. The ewe recovered and so did all the humans casualties.

It was just as well Mrs Drury had sterilised everything, for at 8.00 p.m. that night, Humphrey Yeo of Wayside, probably our biggest sheep farmer, phoned to say he was on his way with two for Caesars. I groaned, for I was on duty that night. Our student had been invited out for a meal and Mrs Drury did not work in the evenings. As it was a bit late to get baby sitters, Janet and I picked up our two sleeping infants, aged three and one, and putting Ian, number two into a carry cot, and carrying Neil, number one, we headed for the surgery and were there to await our patients. The carry cot was planked down on a bench with its one-year-old blissfully asleep, while Neil, yawning prodigiously, sat swinging his legs from the same bench. He couldn't sleep; he had a job to do. So, with my wife assisting, we did two more Caesars. We worked well together, and she knew the routine by now — swab, swab, clamp, hand this, hand that. Now the lambs are delivered, twins, and three year old Neil leaps to his task. His is the job of clearing the nose and mouth of mucous, rubbing the lambs' chests with straw to dry them and get the breathing going. If not successful, operations are suspended, while father does mouth to mouth respiration, and in forty five minutes the whole task is over, and one ewe and Neil's two lambs are carried out to the trailer, lambs born as hundreds around the area had been born, lives saved in the fashion that Julius Caesar, Queen Elizabeth II and countless others had been delivered. Another forty five minutes and we had another little ewe with a very large lamb, a Caesar having been performed in this case because the lamb's horns were so far developed, they were preventing passage through the vagina, a quite common occurrence in the Exmoor Horn hogg. These two had been sheer delights to perform, and one felt a sense of achievement, seeing the happy mothers, healthy lambs and satisfied farmer depart into the night, and providing a needed corrective after the seventy minutes struggle with death that afternoon. Well, the day was over, and as we gathered our instruments together, I could steal a kiss from my present assistant, something that could not be done with the other, for either she or Janet, and probably both, would have up and dotted me one. Yes, there was something to be said for a husband-wife partnership, not to mention early training for the family.

On the stroke of 10.00 p.m., we entered our living room, just as the phone was ringing. It was Alf Spicer.

"Mr Cameron, uz' got a sheep right bad to lamb; uz hears tell as how you'm got an operation that can save the lamb; be that right?"

"That's right, Alf, bring it in."

Normally I didn't do Caesars after 10.00 p.m., reasoning they could wait till morning, but it was just that time now, our student was back, and I had him volunteer to come and assist. Out for tea indeed when other folk were working. Where was the dedication in young vets nowadays! So the children were deposited in their beds once more, and after a cup of tea, Ian the student and I set out for positively the last Caesar of the day, leaving instructions with Janet that if anyone called, there was the Black Death in the town, or the veterinary had suspected Rabies — anything to stall till morning. We delivered Alf's Border Leicester ewe of triplets, to his immense delight. I think he thought the operation was responsible for manufacturing an extra lamb. He was happy, and Ian was happy for he had seen a good Caesar, and he'd done his first suturing and injections. Me, I was asleep two minutes after hitting the pillow, a sure sign of the Black Death!

Our chronicle of Caesars would not be complete without one more reference. Caesars were not confined to sheep. In fact Caesars were becoming so numerous that I felt Bristacombe was becoming more Roman than British. I did a few in cattle, once in a sow, which was rather like squeezing one's Christmas presents out of the Christmas stocking, one by one. I did a few in cats and of course, next most common to sheep in dogs. One of these was a valuable Yorkshire Terrier. By now Mrs Drury had left us to be simply a wife and mother, and our current secretary was a lass called Anne Brooks, who'd had thoughts of being a nurse, but instead became an animal nurse and our general factotum. She was a bonny girl who'd been in Sunday School when first I knew her. She was a first class assistant and had just proved it yet again in the little Yorky's Caesar. Mother was alright, but we were having considerable trouble getting her offspring going, since they had been born anaesthetised. I remember Anne and I were down on our knees beside mother and young working like mad on them when Bernard walked in. I glanced up and saw him pause as if he'd been struck. Looking at mother and pups, I said,

"Lovely sight, isn't it, Bernard?"

"Beautiful" he replied, looking at Anne.

"You feel you just want to cuddle them" said Anne as she caressed a pup.

"Rather"

"We're having a job getting them going. Could you lend a hand?"

There was no response. Bernard had a dazed look about him.

"Bernard!" I thundered, would you mind getting down here and work on saving these pups?"

"Eh?"

"These pups, Bernard, artificial respiration!"

"Oh, er, rather, I'm sure that's the right thing to do"

"Well – give us a hand", I thundered

He was on his knees in a flash, his face wreathed in smiles as he knelt beside her. After a time, I said.

"I think I can safely leave you two to cope now."

"Rather!" said Bernard, "I mean, we'll manage."

And so they have, as man and wife, for many years. Yes, a Caesar can produce many surprises, like target practice for Cupid, whose arrow, fired over a Yorkshire Terrier and its puppies, unerringly found its mark that golden day.

The Good, The Bad and The Ugly

ELEVEN

I was looking forward to the day. I had a full round to occupy me, and none of the cases struck terror into the heart, so far as I could see. I had no colts to cut, whole herds to dehorn or cows to calve. It promised to be a day of relaxed working, meandering through the Devon countryside instead of the usual rush. Furthermore I had a new little Austin van to break in, and after my original antiquated Morris van, followed on with two post-war, utilitarian Ford Populars, this was the best car I had yet owned, and the thrill of its newness had not yet worn off. Moreover I was to be travelling in some gorgeous countryside, away up on the high plateau above the sea which here and there far below cut into the land, forming coves which were very much in demand for holiday homes. The cases then were easy, the day perfect, and to add cream to the cake, my first call was to a new client. What more could a country vet desire?

As I drove down to "Hillcroft", I thought this might be alright for an olde worlde, summer time only residence, but as a permanent home it left a lot to be desired. I had been to it once before when the former owner had possessed it, and I remembered initially thinking it was the place the writer of the song "Let the rest of the world go by" must have had in mind. It was, as the song described, "a sweet little nest somewhere in the west", it was undoubtedly "a place known to God alone", for it could only be seen from directly above. The entrance was un-marked, just a gate into a field, along which one drove till motor transport could proceed no further, for it was as if one had suddenly come to the edge of the world. From there, far below, down the steep hillside, "Hillcroft" could be seen. It comprised a thatched cottage and a few farm buildings, several with their roofs falling in. If you didn't need running water, electricity, easy access or even a standard toilet, then "Hillcroft" might be alright, but as a place to farm and earn a living, it was tough going. The new owners had spotted me descending the hill, carrying what I thought I might need. They had asked me to come and inspect their livestock, give it all the once over, and advise them on a few points, and they welcomed me like some long lost uncle bearing tidings of good fortune. I thought it likely I was the first human being they had seen for some time. I was ushered into the sitting room and there regaled with coffee right away.

"You must excuse us not being very straight and tidy, but we haven't had time to get all the things we want, and well" . . . she paused . . . "we thought it more important to get some animals than a lot of furniture." I thought they both, Mr and Mrs Robens, looked ridiculously young, the dew of innocence still upon them, and somehow very vulnerable. They were recently married, their furniture was sparse and sale room, and since I knew all about that, I had a kind of fellow feeling and couldn't help but warm to their eager, fresh enthusiasm and general goodwill to all mankind.

"We only moved in last week. In fact it may not seem like it, but we were just married on Mayday." It was then 20 May, so I asked them how they were settling in.

"Alright," said the young husband, "but we've only seen two people since we arrived, and, well, coming from London, we're finding it a bit strange"

"Never mind" I tried to console them, "you'll get to know a few folks in time. Mind you, you're going to slog pretty hard for a while to get this farm into shape. It has been neglected for years."

"We know that," the young fellow nodded, "that's how we were able to buy it, it was so much cheaper than anything else on the market."

"Well, I wish you success" I said, reading between the lines and realising that they had probably sunk every penny they had, and a whacking overdraft or mortgage besides, into their dream home. "How did you come to get in touch with me, and how can I help you?"

"That's easy," piped up the young wife. "We asked the postman the first time he came. He's one of the two people who've been down . . . well, we asked the postman about vets, and he told us different names, but he said you were a Scotsman, and we know how good Scots engineers and doctors are. Besides, well, the name Croft sounded Scottish and we thought that was a sign we should ask you to be our vet. But you're, well; you're different than we thought."

"Sorry to disappoint you" I grinned. "Tell me, what did you think?"

"We thought you might be older, and be big and broad, and maybe even wear a kilt."

"A kilt in Devon?" I laughed "with the breezes whipping in from the Channel. As for the rest, well, I'm big and lean instead."

'Oh, but we're not at all disappointed" she rushed on, "we like you and I'm sure you will be very good."

"That remains to be seen. Thanks for the coffee, now for some work. What do you want me to do?"

"We want you to look at all our animals and see if they are healthy,and . . . well, we want you to tell us which of our cows are going to have a calf, and when to send for the . . . man that brings the bull." She blushed.

"You mean the Artifical Inseminator, AI for short. Right, we'll see the cows first."

"We don't know very much, but I've been studying this book (he waved a slim volume entitled *Farming Made Easy*, and we listen to 'The Archers'."

"My hat," I thought, "innocents abroad!"

"But before you do anything, we, well, we . . . how much do you charge and how soon do we, well, have to pay you. We could give you something today but it might not be enough"

That was the first time anybody had offered me money before I'd done a job, I thought. I liked them all the more!

"We send out our statements monthly, but let's forget about payment for a while until we see how you are getting on. If you need advice, you can ring me any time if you think I can help. We don't charge for phone advice" I smiled.

I could see the young fellow sigh as if a great weight had been taken from his shoulders concerning payment, and with that we headed in procession to their little cowshed, Mr clutching *Farming Made Easy*, and Mrs a large blank notebook and pencil. In the cowshed, which was the only building, apart from the dwelling house, whose roof was intact, were eight Channel Islanders, a mixture of Guernsey and Jersey. I looked them over. They'd had somebody honest buy that group for them, or else 'The Archers' or the omniscient book were better than I thought. They looked excellent beasts and I said so. I had to inspect them one by one, it seemed, so, though clearly they were in the pink of condition, for the sake of doing something, I took all their pulses and temperatures, which were duly noted in the wife's large book under the appropriate name of the animal. Then I had a quick listen at eight chests, felt eight udders, and eight dewy noses.

"Sound in wind and limb" I pronounced cheerfully. "Now for some P.D's. Could you possibly bring me a bucket of water, soap and a towel?"

"Certainly" said Mr Robens, and departed at the double

"He'll soon draw some from the well" explained the wife.

I couldn't believe it, "You really have to get water from a well?" I asked incredulously.

"For the present, yes. We plan to collect rain water in barrels, and when we can afford it, we're going to install a pump. It's all very exciting."

As I looked at her flushed young face, and saw the eagerness of this city bred couple, my faith in mankind was restored somewhat. The age of the pioneer was not quite past, and I hoped they would make out, and weather the first hard few years. By now the water had arrived, and I soaped and lathered my arm, and inserted it in the rectum of the first cow, conscious that every move I made was being closely studied. From cow one to cow two, and I was proceeding with number three when Mrs Robens asked,

"Why are you doing that?"

"I want to be able to tell you which cows are in calf, which are not, and how far on the pregnant ones are."

Her face cleared. "Oh, I see, it's just like an enema before an operation you are doing"

"Pardon?" I queried, not following the drift of her thought.

"I had an operation once, and I had an enema before it, but your way is much quicker, and not so messy!" I stared in bewilderment, as she queried

"But why do they need an enema before a pregnancy test?"

"I'm not really giving them an enema, Mrs Robens, it's just that you can't put your arm in a cow's rectum without getting it dirty!"

That settled, I turned again to the patiently waiting number three. I was busy palpating the uterus, when the voice came back at me again.

"But why do you need to, well, do that, and get your arm dirty. What's it for?"

"To find out if it's in calf or not. You can mark the first two down as not in calf."

I could see two puzzled faces staring at me. Very slowly Mrs Robens laid down her book. I could not think what I'd said or done, but clearly their faith in Scots vets in general and this one in particular was shaken.

"But . . . but . . . you're in the wrong place" she expostulated, while her husband blushed crimson. Then she went on, doubtfully "Or are cows different from people?"

I could see I had been taking too much for granted. They couldn't have heard the episode from 'The Archers' dealing with pregnancy tests. I really had to turn away from these two intent young faces to avoid doubling up in mirth. I gulped a few times, and then explained.

"The only way I can tell how far on in calf any cow may be, is to examine the womb through the rectal wall. I don't go through it," I hastened to add, before they conjured up pictures of holes poked through rectal walls. "The womb lies below the rectum and, like feeling through stiff paper, I can examine it and tell roughly how far on a pregnancy is. I can't really tell below ten weeks though some vets claim they can, but after that, I can give a fair estimate. Mind you, it's not by any means 100 per cent accurate, but it's a reasonable guide."

They still looked suspicious that I was either doing irreparable damage to their cows, or having them on, so I picked up Mrs Robens book and pencil, and proceeded to draw the relative positions of rectum and uterus. I then turned back to the long suffering cow three and said "Put this one down at about fourteen weeks. You can work out the approximate date of calving later."

So we proceeded along the line. Four were in calf, the furthest on being seven months. From the cowshed we proceeded to a ruinous shed in which reposed two large white sows. I didn't bother with temperatures and so on there. They were clearly as right as rain, and equally clearly very heavy in pig. Next we cursorily inspected the sheep — six ewes — which they had carefully penned for my arrival. I looked at their feet and mouths. They were old ewes, but they might get a couple of breeding seasons from them. I explained about foot rot, about innoculations for a variety of diseases in sheep and lambs and promised to speak to Bill Haley along the road, to see if they could run their ewes with his ram. I thought a ram with only six wives would feel distinctly cheated and grossly insulted, when all his pals had about ten times that number. I was just turning away from the sheep pen, when I recalled.

"Oh, yes, a word about Pine"

"We've got it" said the wife enthusiastically.

"Eh?" I said. "Who told you about Pine?"

"Oh, everybody knows about Pine and what it does" she exulted. I couldn't see anything to be so chirpy about in having Pine, and felt that somehow our lines were crossed again.

"Show me the Pine?" I demanded, peering more closely at the sheep.

"It's in the house. We keep it in the kitchen"

"In the kitchen?"

"Yes, I've got six of it"

"Six, in the kitchen! Isn't it a bit crowded?"

"Well, the kitchen is rather small, but they only take up a little corner on a shelf," she said, as if that made everything clear.

"I think we must be talking about different things," I suggested. "Pine to me is a disease — really a deficiency . . . in sheep. What is it to you?"

"Oh, I thought you meant the disinfectant which was recommended to us as fine and strong."

That settled, I proceeded to explain that Pine in sheep was a disease where the sheep simply pined or wasted away, and it was the result of a defiency of cobalt in the bloodstream, which deficiency in turn came from the ground. I went on the explain you could dress the ground, which was not always easy, nor wholly satisfactory, and the better way, certainly for them with six sheep was to give the sheep, individually, a supply of cobalt.

"It's not absolutely certain that it is cobalt alone that is missing, since it has been shown that iron also, if deficient, can cause the condition. There's very little Pine in Devon, but it occurs along this plateau. I've some pellets in the car. They're called bullets in this case, so if you come up along with me, Mr Robens, I'll let you have a supply. You can also borrow my gun for shooting them over the sheeps' throats, which might save you a scratch or two. Oh, by the way, Pine also occurs in cattle, so I'd dose them as well."

Mrs Robens had been busy scribbling all this down, obviously as an appendix for *Farming Made Easy*. I could imagine them both at night, side by side on the couch, swotting it all up.

"Now come and meet Jeremy," said the little woman. "He's in the orchard."

The only Jeremy I knew about was the local MP, but this Jeremy was a donkey.

"We inherited him with the farm," burbled Mrs R, "and well, we thought he would be very useful for pulling the milk up to the hill top on some kind of sledge, when our little tractor sticks"

I duly admired Jeremy, and reflected that either his former owner was an ardent Liberal, and called his donkey after his MP, or else he was of another Party, and had meant a donkey's name as a constant insult to the Liberals.

I thought by now I had seen everything and said I'd better be on my way, but they insisted I come and drink more coffee and talk about their general strategy. While the coffee was preparing, Mr Robens and I talked, with Mrs R hopping through from the kitchen frequently to hear the discussion.

"I think you've made a good beginning," I said, sincerely, "but you will have to decide whether you are going to specialise or diversify."

"Oh! Ah!" exclaimed the two in unison. I reflected that an awful lot must be missing from their text book and 'The Archers'!

"What I mean is that on a small farm, you have either to choose one thing, and gear all your planning to that — say, your Channel Islanders, or you can decide to have several different means of income. In your position, and on this farm where your only crops will be grass and hay, I'd say, diversify. Don't put all your eggs in one basket. I'd go right away, and repair the roof of that old barn, and get some hens in there in deep litter, and when you can afford it, I'd buy one or two beef animals, young beasts, which you can fatten up. That would give you milk, beef, eggs and pig weaners to sell, so you will always have the till ticking over."

I leapt to my feet.

"I really must be on my way," and accompanied by the young fellow, and cheered on my way by fervent thanks from his wife, I reached the car, gave him the mineral bullets, gun, and was off, with my ego considerably boosted, for they had hung on every word I'd said, whereas in Ayrshire I was more often than not told by the farmer what he wanted, like issuing instructions to the plumber to fix a new washer on a tap.

My next call was to another "townie" couple, who had been clients for several years now. I stopped the car at the top of their road as I always did, and gazed at one of the loveliest little bays I know, Forest Bay. At the foot the sea, surging ceaselessly in to the shore, met the forest whose feet were almost in the waves, and whose trees covered all the visible land around, presenting a scene of great beauty and an atmosphere of timelessness. I felt I must get a photograph for that day the sea was a deep, deep blue, contrasting with the softer blue of the sky, and the various shades of green of the forest. At the foot, on a little knoll above the beach, stood the old Manor House, looking, as always, perfect in that setting, as if it had grown up naturally with the trees. Only one thing marred the scene. Just above the tree line, and indeed cutting into the forest itself, was a great gash of turned up earth, and a strip completely devoid of vegetation. Here stood a pig farm, a large one now, owned and run by the Ingraville's, the tenants of the Manor House. I nosed the car down towards the piggery, saw no one about it, so procceded on down to the house. I remembered my first visit there, and my introduction to Mr Ingraville, clearly not his original name for he was Polish and had been a cavalry officer when the Nazis invaded his homeland. His wife, well, I don't know what she had been, though an actress was hinted at, and certainly I never saw so much make up on one face, layers of it, scrapeable with a knife! The other member of the Ingraville entourage was Cleopatra, a pet pig who ran about the house like a dog. They were charming, yet I always got the feeling that the whole thing was a great charade.

Today's call should be easy, for they wanted to discuss scouring in their piglets, and how we could prevent it. I rang the bell, and walked in to the lovely old house, which now had a distinctly aromatic odour of pig about it, and to my surprise, instead of the normal gushing welcome, was met by an obviously angry female face, and a distinctly morose male one. Clearly there had been conflict. A poor, lean, rather shifty eyed and distinctly odoriforous man emerged nervously twisting his cap in his hands. I recognised him as their pig man.

"Ah, here's the vet; we'll see now if you're telling the truth" thundered Madam Ingraville. "Come, Leopold," she called over her shoulder, and her husband duly trotted to her side. "You come too, Walters," thundered the Prima Donna, and all three leapt into their Land Rover – well, the lady rather flopped in, having no longer a leaping figure. Like a little dog, I followed on in my Austin, wondering what calamitous event had occurred. I thought probably a pig had lost a tooth, or something similar, remembering how they had called me out over twenty miles one evening to see a pig with a cut ear, the cut proving so minute that all it needed was a dab of vaseline. But I was wrong, in this instance, for there, lying in the yard, at the foot of a wall, was their boar, the father of the herd, and he would father no more pigs. He was very dead. I looked at the body; nothing was very obvious externally.

"Has he been ill?" I queried.

"No, he has not" came the raging reply, "he has been killed, by him" and she pointed dramatically at the wretched Walters. Lady MacBeth couldn't have done it better. Mr Ingraville meantime was spluttering in Polish. Just to make it clear, he ended with an explosive "Blast you, you murderer!"

"I tell you, I did nothing, sir. I just found him lying here" said poor Walters.

"Pschaw – a likely story. He was quite alright an hour ago" said Mrs I.

"We've seen you kick the boar, you wretched assass ... assass ... killer" came Mr I on cue with his line. It was a rather nasty situation, and I was going to have to arbitrate, to be the detective who was to ferret out the truth. So from a Veterinary Surgeon come to discuss scouring pigs, I was changed in a moment to the Pathologist in a homicide ... or rather a pigicide. I hadn't come prepared to do a PM, but I had a few scalpels in my bag, so got to work. I found the cause of death too, to my great surprise and relief, though I doubted if it was going to help to restore normal relations and general bonhomie between the warring factions. The boar had bled to death, from an internal haemorrhage in the abdomen. It could conceivably have been a kick, it could have been a fall. There was no trace I could see of an aneurism, and I was pretty sure in my own mind that somebody or something had landed the poor old boar a hefty thump. I explained this to the watching threesome, and immediately Mrs Ingraville went into her pointing routine, with quite a long speech, the gist of which was that they would sue Walters for damages, and he was to be gone and never darken their pighouse door again. The wretched man, as pale as a sheet, protested his innocence once more, turned on his heel and went. He was back in two ticks, having forgotten his bicycle and lunch tin.

"He shan't get away with this. We will definitely prosecute," said my lady. I pointed out that no one, certainly not I could say for certain a kick had done this and I lightheartedly pointed out that there were no boot nails embedded in the skin, or traces of shoe leather on the abdominal area! Perhaps, I said, they should consult carefully with their lawyer before they embarked on a voyage with a somewhat suspect chart. I was invited down to the Manor, but since they were both seething, and seemed likely to be so for some time, and having no particular desire to witness the dash of a Cavalry Officer, nor listen to the soliloquys of a tragic queen, I left.

Near the Bay of the last incident, at the mouth of a little river, stands a large, imposing country house, which is owned and run by the Church of England as a retreat, a conference centre, a refuge of peace, a haven to which come those in need of instruction, or rest and renewal of body, mind and spirit. Attached to it was a farm, with, among other things, a herd of Guernseys. In fact the whole set up bore some resemblance to a Kibbutz. Kenneth, who had taken me on as partner was himself a lay reader of the Church of England, and on the committee of the Centre, so we offered our professional services free, only drugs supplied being charged. I started off very suspicious of the whole thing. It was not that my Scottish upbringing made me resent giving anything free — it was more my Presbyterian background that made me then suspicous of anything non Presbyterian. If the RC Church was on the road to perdition, then the Anglican Church, especially the High Church, wasn't far behind! But that Centre opened my eyes, for there I met numbers of people, clergy and laity, who were always jumping up and down in their liturgy, who burnt candles, even incense, and who bowed to the altar — all things that were utterly alien to me, and yet among those folks, so very different from me in the expression of their faith, were men and women who were truly saintly. Not a halo round the head kind of saintliness, not a sickly or weak thing. It was as if these people, from every walk of life had learned a great secret, discovered a truth long sought, and found abundant wealth. They were gentle folks, and in contact with them, some of the sharp corners of my square Presbyterian position, were smoothed over.

The person I saw most was Ursula. Bernard could never get her name right, and called her Hiroshima. Ursula was in charge of the cattle, and was not unlike her Guernseys, a sort of golden glow surrounding her, as if a light was burning within. But she was far from other worldly, was an expert with cattle, and slim little thing, though she was, could tackle heavy tasks. She also had probably the cleanest, most sterile cowshed and dairy in Devon. The task for the day was simply to wash out a cow, that is to insert a metal catheter into the womb, and pump in some antiseptic solution, to clear up the lingering metritis or inflammation of the womb. But veterinary practice is full of surprises, and one often hears the words, "Oh, when you're here anyway, would you look at such and such?" The "such and such" on this occasion was a cow with an enormous lump, about the dimension of a size three football.

It was one of those cases that looked much worse than it was, though I don't suppose the bearer of the lump would have agreed. The lump was on the chest wall, just behind the shoulder, and was in fact, an abscess, probably caused by a horn poke from another cow. This one was ripe for the knife, so having obtained an old bucket from Ursula, and advising her to stand well back and hold her nose, it was lanced, to let an enormous quantity of pus drain into the bucket. The hole was made big enough to allow complete drainage, and before I had finished, Ursula was busy with the disinfectant in her cowshed. No form of poison had a chance with that girl around!

By now, my gastric juices were straining at their leash to get at some food, so having duly supplied this, at a cafê I went on. I had an appointment with an RSPCA Inspector at 2.30 pm. I met him at the farm, which I didn't know . . . it wasn't one of mine, for that would have complicated matters. There we inspected three dogs, all collies, while their surly owner looked on in silence. They were in a deplorable condition, and made my temper rise. All were thin to the point of emaciation and two had deep toxic, weeping wounds, which hadn't happened yesterday! The third was an old dog, partially blind, its eyes covered over with matter, and its body a mass of bedsores. I saw the little shed which was their home, with its earthen, foul, stinking floor . . . no wonder!

"Why did you not have these wounds treated, and what caused them?" I queried.

"Reckon they wus caused by them barbed wire fences. I did put some tar on them like, an' left it to nature. She be the best healer."

Stockholm tar treatment, once, and leave it to nature! Mind you, he was a wild man, and probably carried out his philosophy on himself, but he was for the high jump this time. The RSPCA were definitely pushing this case, and I was there merely to be in a position of "an expert witness" in court. The dogs were taken into the Society's care, pending a decision as to their future. It was an ugly business. These dogs had served him well as sheep-dogs, but like all too many hill farmers' dogs . . . even sometimes shepherds' dogs . . . they were merely flung some food and shut in a dark corner. Yet, I'm certain, with the loyalty of their kind, they would have defended him with their lives.

The next call wouldn't take long, I thought. Further along to the next village, and now at the furthest point of the Practice, perhaps twenty-eight miles from home, I had simply to give a dog its Distemper innoculation. I found the house, with difficulty, an upstairs flat. I thought I was back with the dogs again for that room stank of a mixture of cooking, stale tobacco smoke, spirits and just plain dirt. A figure rose from a couch as I entered, having been conducted upstairs by the landlady from down below. She had simply, and without apology, thrown open the door.

"Mr Leighton-Jones?" I asked.

"Flight Lt. Leighton-Jones, old boy" came the correction.

The room was very dim, the curtains drawn, and as he switched on the light, I saw a figure, swaying somewhat, clutching glass in one hand and cigarette in the other; what instantly drew my eyes was his face. I had seen burned faces before; but none quite so dreadful as this one, which looked as if the surgeon doing the skin-grafting was tackling his first case.

"I'm sorry," I said, "I didn't know you were in the RAF."

"Not any more, old chap . . . Not any more . ., hic . . . when you're no more use to them, you're O-U-T . . . out . . . damn them."

"Were you fighter or bomber command?" I queried.

"Fighter . . . old Spitfires . . . I was one of The Few . . . as they called us, till I bought this" he said, lifting his chin to reveal even more scarring on his neck. "A Messerschmitt 109 got me on my tail. Pretty, isn't it . . . Well, say something, damn you!" and he thrust his face close to mine. He reeked of gin, and his eyes had the bloodshot look of the heavy drinker. I drew back involuntarily, and said simply "I'm very sorry."

"Sorry! That's all we get now, sorry, sorry, sorry. What good's sorry? Can that cure you, give you a new face, huh? What woman would look at you with a face like that" he pointed, "and it's sex that makes the world go round."

"I'd always heard it was love" I said.

"Love!" He spat out. "No such thing, only sex!"

"Were you married when you were shot down?" I queried

"Still am. Got a wife somewhere, but no job, no prospects . . . and this!"

I was about to ask where his wife was, but he forestalled me, "I left her. Can't ask a woman to live with this." Again he thrust his face into mine. "But I get by; there's compensations," holding up the bottle, "and others," he winked incongruously. I thought it was time I did what I'd come to do, so said.

"You asked us to innoculate a puppy. Where is he, or is it she?"

"It's a bitch, and a blasted good one, so don't you go messing it up with your innoculations" He opened a door to reveal a bedroom, with a female form recumbent on the bed, out cold, and from the room came bounding a lovely Irish Setter.

"Trouble with women is they can't hold their drink," he muttered. The dog was all over him, licking his hand, pulling at his jacket, licking that scarred face. I found the scene in those sordid surroundings at one and the same time indescribably ugly and infinitely moving.

The injection was soon over, and the dog, after an initial yelp, bounced and rolled all over the place.

"She really is a beauty," I enthused. Setters were among my favourites.

"Course she is, didn't I tell you? Now I suppose you want paid?"

"If you care to, or we'll send a bill."

"No, get it over with. I'll give you a cheque," which after a bit of searching for his book, he did.

He got up and lurched towards me, and grasped my jacket lapels. He had a point to make, it seemed, and I was his prisoner.

"By the way, what do they call you . . . vet . . . vet . . . vetnary surgeon, what were you with in the last show, eh? Bet it was something safe like the Pay Corps, or no," he paused and laughed as at some huge joke, "it would be the Medical Corps. Half of that lot were blasted vets, I always said."

I told him I had been too young to join up at the outbreak of war, and by the time I was age, it was well on the way to being won, and as a vet student, I was deferred. He sneered, gave me the full flavour of his aromatic breath, and muttered, clutching my lapels firmly. "Knew what you were doing, eh, didn't you?"

I counted to ten, laid down my case, disengaged myself from his clutch and said.

"Flight Lt, it so happened I wanted to be a vet. I am truly sorry for what you have suffered," I held up my hand, "though I know you don't want pity. We all in Britain owe you fellows a tremendous lot, and we know it. But I didn't think any Battle of Britain pilot would let any Nazi fighter down him for life. If you're not a phoney, get up and fight, sir, and as for love, just look into your dog's eyes. Maybe somewhere there's another pair of eyes that still look like that, for you. Good day to you.' I left him open mouthed, swaying on his feet. It was unfair, I thought as I left, that I, who had suffered nothing should preach at someone who'd been through the hell men make of their world. I consoled myself with the thought of that Irish Setter to whom its master was the fairest thing on earth.

I turned the car's face towards home with a taste in my mouth, thinking of the callousness of that shepherd towards his dogs, and the senselessness of war that could produce scars that reached right down into a man's very spirit. Yes, an ugly afternoon, and it was not quite finished for I had one call to make still.

Mr Pike would probably have come bottom of my list of favourite clients. He was an incomer from the north, though the locals would soon overlook that, but he was a swaggering, coarse braggart of a man who knew all the answers, and proceeded to show it by making an unholy mess of what had been a good farm. If I'd been asked whether I'd like to spend time on a desert island with Mr Pike or a rattlesnake, it would have been a close vote. Rumour had it that he was now in queer street financially, and he owed us quite a bit. I was going to his farm to treat a cow, but I knew I'd have to talk about his account, and this I always detested. As I pulled into his yard, he was bellowing at a lad carrying a bucket and he wasn't choosing his words as he let him, one of his sons know what he thought of him. He greeted me with a glare and a nod, and strode towards his byre, with me following. Not a word was spoken till he stopped at an Ayrshire cow, gave her a slap and growled,

"Felon . . . a bad un."

I examined the cow's udder, having learned that felon was one of the many names for Mastitis. One of the cows quarters was as hard as a board, a summer mastitis due to a bug named Corynebacterium pyogenes.

"When did she calve?" I asked

"Bout a week ago."

"And I bet she had this when she calved."

He glared at me, and muttered "Aye."

"What have you done for her?"

"Stripped out a lot o' muck — stinkin' it were, put in some o' your penicillin and rubbed her bag with mustard."

I nodded and said.

"I'm afraid, Mr Pike, it wouldn't matter what you did, you wouldn't clear that. She's lost that quarter. It's called summer mastitis, what she's got. She picked it up when she was dry, and unless the beast is really ill with it, you wouldn't notice it. What we recommend is when you're drying off a cow at the end of a lactation, you fill the udder with penicillin, then seal off the teats with something like collodion. It isn't 100 per cent but it's as good as we know . . . that, and innoculation against it, which isn't 100 per cent either. I'm afraid there's nothing I can do for that quarter, but she can go through life on three wheels."

"Typical of you fellows; nowt I can do for it, then a whackin' great account."

"Uh . . . huh . . . Well, about your account, Mr Pike, we haven't had a penny for three years. I'm afraid I'll need to ask you to let us have something on account now."

His face cleared like a summer storm passing. In as far as it was possible for Pike to become all sweetness and light, he did. He even attempted a smile, but since it was so long since he'd used the smiling muscles, it came out as a kind of twisted leer.

"I know, Mr Cameron, but things have been hard lately, but I'll let you have it within a fortnight." I looked at him suspiciously, but short of digging in my heels and saying "Pay now," I didn't see what I could do, so left it at that. He even shut the car door for me as I got in and signalled goodbye. I should have been warned!

So the car's face was turned homeward. It had not been a hard day; in fact in terms of visits done or difficult cases, it had been a very easy round. But in types of visit, the day had progressed from the sunshine start with these two innocent pioneers and the visit to Ursula and her Guernseys, to the encounters with the Ingravilles and Pike, and the unpleasantness of the cruelty case and the representative of the RAF . . . ex. In retrospect the day had deteriorated from good, to bad, and to ugly, and as if in keeping with my mood as I drove home, I saw great black clouds massing out over the Channel. We were in for a downpour, how quickly a day can change, and one's moods and emotions. I reflected that this had, in fact, been a day typical of veterinary practice — and of life. Oh well, just time for a bite of food before evening surgery.

In practice, each case history is either a complete story, or a continuing saga. For the most part, that day of the good, bad and ugly, as I had mentally dubbed it, was a serial story, and produced repercussions which shook our Practice, and affected several lives. Take the ugly. The hill farmer was tried for his cruelty, had the book thrown at him, his old dog put to sleep — a kindness that, and his other two found worthier masters. My other dog client, the Flt Lt. — well, his cheque bounced and enquiring for him one week later, I found he had gone, taking his Setter with him. I wondered, was it just possible he was looking again for eyes that had once shone with love for him, and maybe could again? Or was it, as seemed most likely, a drift to some other flat, some other companion, and daily dependence on the bottle? I would never know.

Pike did a moonlight flitting two weeks after my visit, taking stock and possessions with him, and only leaving his debts and no forwarding address. The Ingravilles fought their case against their pigman, but largely because I could not categorically say that death had come from a kick, but merely that the injury *could have* come from such a blow, they lost. In Scotland I reckon it would have been "Not Proven". Costs were awarded against them, and some weeks later, Mr Ingraville was declared bankrupt, with his sole assets being one shotgun, the majority of his possessions meantime having been safely passed to his wife's name. I never saw them, nor Pike again, nor their money. It was a real blow to the solar plexus to lose two large amounts, and there was a certain amount of wailing and gnashing of teeth as we sought to meet our monthly drug bills, for we were, at the time, in one of many financial recessions we've experienced since 1945.

Hiroshima — or rather Ursula, continued in her own competent way, while the Robens — well! I was wakened one morning about 6.30 by the insistent ringing of the phone. Milk Fever, I thought, as I reached for it. The voice at the other end was plaintive, not to say accusing even, and the gist of the message was that the cow I had said was seven months in calf, had been due by her calculations to calve that night, and, well, they had sat up all night, and it hadn't calved. I groaned and smiled at one and the same time, which is not as easy as it sounds, and explained.

" Mrs Robens, I told you that our tests were not 100 per cent accurate, certainly not to days, and even if they were, cows, like people can be ten days before or after nine months and that is still normal." Quite a speech for the time of day, I thought! The client wasn't satisfied, and asked

"But how will we know if she's calving?" I groaned again, this time without the smile.

"Where is the cow?" I asked.

"In its shed."

"Is it standing with its back arched, or paddling about uncomfortably on its feet, is it groaning, grunting or making any other noise and has it any water or other discharge coming away?" — A ten second lecture on calving.

"Well — no,"

"What is she doing?"

"Lying down and chewing her cud."

"Then lassie, you go and do the same — well, lie down anyway!"

The little woman phoned a week later at a respectable time, and breathless with excitement informed me that Belinda had calved, everything was fine, but, well, they had missed it, for having kept watch for a week, exhausted, they'd gone to bed that night.

"And she did it all herself, Mr Cameron? Isn't nature wonderful?"

"It surely is" I agreed. Well, animal nature anyway. I wasn't so sure about the human variety, but I hoped that this refreshing twosome would be spared the harsher side of things for a time, and the morning dew of their innocence would linger awhile. It helped to offset the Pikes of this world!

Monkey Tricks

TWELVE

I had done it! I had actually bowled an off break. The first time I'd been a bit doubtful, thinking maybe the ball had hit a bit of dirt or something, but two in a row surely couldnt be luck. I saw myself as the Jim Laker of our Monday night team; far better to use the head, and by sheer skill trap a batsman than rush up with a full head of steam as was my wont, and find my fastest ball despatched for four. So in a state approaching bliss, I prepared to bowl a third spinner in the portion of yard at the kennels ideal for such practice, when Janet's voice summoned me back to reality. I remember there was a note of urgency in it that perfect late summer evening as she called.

"Visit, darling. Mr Trevelyan is on the phone and he seems very upset. He wants to speak to you."

So with a sigh, I threw down the ball, dreams of glory banished for the moment as I picked up the phone.

"Alex? (In Devon they always sounded the x in my name instead of the more usual Scots abbreviation of Alec). "This is Charlie Trevelyan"

He sounded strained, not at all the usual cheerful greeting of our local Zoo owner and administrator, whose TV appearances with some of his pets had endeared him to millions of children. He went on, "You know that escaped monkey . . ." His voice actually broke. "Could you come up right away? I'd appreciate it."

"Why, sure, Charlie, but what's up?"

"Look, I'd rather not talk on the phone; I'll see you soon."

I went to my car in some perplexity. What could have upset Charlie so?

I had seen him fight his way through some pretty tough times, and overcome many disappointments as he sought to establish his zoo, until it became, I believe, the biggest private one in Britain. I knew all about the escaped monkey too — who didn't? The saga had begun several weeks back when Charlie, well pleased with life for it had been a profitable season at the zoo, walked out after breakfast for his morning rounds. Suddenly he was pulled up dead in his tracks. There were monkeys on the roof and the realisation hit him that the only person who kept monkeys hereabouts was himself. He bellowed "Irene" and his head girl came at the gallop. She was a bonny, blonde, gentle girl, passionately fond of animals and expert with them.

"Irene! There's monkeys on the roof!"

"I know, Mr Trevelyan, I was just coming to tell you. It's the Dead End Kids." Breathing fire and slaughter, Charlie and his head girl headed for the "Dead End Kids" enclosure, Charlie roaring, "Who did it? Who let them out?"

In fact he found that the crafty "kids" had let themselves out. The lock of the enclosure had become corroded with the sea air, and the rest the monkeys did for themselves. The "kids" were Rhesus monkeys, one of the smallest, most common, most popular and certainly most mischievous of all the macaques. Many a visitor had required placating after an arm had reached out and removed his spectacles, pulled his child's hair or stolen an ice lolly. The daily cleaning of their pen was a comedy turn, for invariably one of the bunch would steal a mop or throw a bucket of water over the attendant — and now eight of these bundles of trouble were free amid an unsuspecting public, only one of their number remaining blissfully asleep through it all, and no doubt cursing herself later about all the fun she'd missed. Three were recaptured that day, leaving five at large, in the midst of the holiday season! Of course the police had to be notified, the local paper gave wide coverage to the 'great escape', and the media kept the world at large informed of developments. Anyone seeing the escapees was asked to contact the zoo, and for days it was inundated with calls, not one of which proved accurate. It seemed as if every dog or cat crossing a road had become a Rhesus monkey, and 'sightings' were reported far and near. After three days a further three were captured just a mile from their home, leaving two still 'gone away'. A lady in the town found herself confronted with one of them in her hall one day. The monkey fled upstairs and went into the bathroom, whereupon the lady shut the door on it and phoned the zoo. Charlie and Irene arrived with net and box and opened the bathroom door in time to see the monkey coolly unlatch the window and escape. However, its freedom was shortlived as it was caught the same day in the garden shed of the same house. One more left to catch, but that one was to cause many heart flutterings, and become a legend. Never had Bristacombe gained so much publicity, rivalling for a time Loch Ness and its famous beast! Stories abounded of the antics of this Rhesus, some no doubt apocryphal, but others with a grain of truth in them for he was at large for weeks, enjoying to the full his freedom in this best of all worlds, and living it up as only a Rhesus can!

A courting couple seated on a park bench had heard a rustle in a rhododendron bush behind them, imagined they had a peeping Tom, and while the girl remained demurely on the seat, her gallant swain had edged his way into the bush to come face to face with a character from a Tarzan film. Which of them was more startled is hard to say. Both gave a yowl, both leapt in the air as did the waiting maiden, and while the monkey made his escape via the trees around, the gallant lover emerged with blanched countenance and leapt on the bench beside his girl where they clutched one another tightly — till the ridiculous nature of their pose struck them and they headed for the girl's home. Their story now grew to indicate that the brave young blade had saved his girl from attack and driven off what was possibly a gorilla!

Most sightings of the creature had been in one area of the town just up from our surgery, a couple of streets of terrace type houses some four storeys high. The monkey of course found plentiful scraps of food in dustbins, but in houses so perfectly endowed with drain pipes, the Rhesus soon found it easy to obtain tastier bites. One little girl went to the kitchen on some errand in time to see the rear end of the creature disappearing through the tiny top window. Her parents had refused to believe her story and impressed upon her the advisability of always telling the truth. Another woman, a guest house owner, having seen her guests to bed was enjoying the luxury of a long soak in her bath when she got the feeling that she was no longer alone, and sure enough, there at the window was a wrinkled face and two beady eyes beholding her with interest, three storeys up. Whether the monkey was male or female she knew not, but causing a miniature tidal wave she had leapt for a bath towel, with a yell that startled all her guests. I liked the story of the little lad who had gone into the kitchen to find the monkey sitting on the table eating a banana. He rushed to the living room and announced

"There's a monkey on the table" to be told not to be ridiculous. Shortly afterwards the mother had cause to go to the kitchen, and the crash of her fainting on the floor fetched her husband at the double. The monkey had by now escaped. "I told you there was a monkey here" junior protested, and earned himself a hearty clout on the ear as if he somehow had been the cause of the mother's condition. There was a state of unease around Montpelier Terrace and adjacent streets, but all efforts by Charlie and his staff to capture the errant one had been in vain. By the time they reached a 'sighting', the 'Dead End Kid' was probably in another kitchen, and the uneasiness grew. A warm well fed monkey was probably harmless, but this one had been at large for weeks now, the nights were getting chill, and who could say what might happen. There was one final happening, the truth of which I cannot verify, but it's a good story, and there must have been some truth in it. It concerned Billy Biddlecome. Now the town of Bristacombe had few real drunks, but Billy was one of them, a regular soak, unless his wife kept him under restraint. On this occasion he was on his own, his wife staying the night at South Molton with her mother, so Billy had a night out with the boys. Returning late, he fell into bed, placing the remains of a bottle of Scotch on the bedside table for night-time emergencies. Wakening in the middle of the night, just as dawn was streaking the sky with pink fingers, Billy had felt in need of a thirst quencher. He reached out a hand and failed to make contact with a bottle. He groped about, muttering to himself, until he became aware of other mutterings in the room. His bleary eyes searched the room in vain till finally he beheld, in the dim light, a hairy creature clutching a bottle and observing him from the top of the wardrobe. Billy stared in sheer mortal terror, his eyes, it may be presumed growing larger by the minute, (though of course no one was present to confirm this) till in the grip of the horrors he dived under the bedclothes where he remained until his wife found him at 11.00 am that day. The veracity of this story could not be confirmed since Mrs B could make nothing of her husband's utterances, Billy himself was convinced he had progressed beyond pink elephants to hairy monsters, and the monkey wasn't telling. The only certainty was that a half bottle of whisky was found on the wardrobe top and Billy never touched another drink the rest of the year. But while the monkey might have wrought some moral benefits on the like of Billy Biddlecombe, it was clear that something had to be done, and soon, for the physical safety of others, particularly children in their prams. Nowadays, of course, a knock out dart would presumably have been fired at the fugitive, but they were unknown then, and his daylight appearances were so fleeting, that he eluded every effort at capture.

That was the state of the saga of the Bristacombe monkey when I got into my car that night and drove the mile up to the zoo. Charlie was waiting for me at the gate, very agitated indeed. He grasped my arm and filled me in with a rush of words.

"We got a phone call tonight saying the Rhesus was on a roof. He had been down on to the terrace and stolen a baby's bottle from its pram. Everybody was up in arms, so I knew what had to be!"

Charlie went on to tell me how he had spotted the errant one on the roof, took careful aim with his .22 rifle, steadying himself with his arm on a wall. He mustn't miss; at all costs he mustn't only wound for then the monkey would have been really dangerous. It must have been a terrible moment for Charlie, for if ever a man loved animals, had patience with them, and made allowances for them, it was this man. He didn't miss! The little animal came cascading down the roof and its reluctant executioner had to turn away, his hands over his ears, so as not to hear the thud of its fall. I was still mystified as to why I had been called by the time I reached Charlie's living room, though desperately sorry for him. There lay the little creature beside the sack into which it had been thrown after its death. I looked at it in pity, and with interest. I had often read in western epics of some bad lad having a hole neatly drilled between his eyes. Here I witnessed it for the first time; the hole was exactly that. I looked again

"Charlie! He's still alive!"

I looked round at the poor man, who could only nod. Tears were coursing down his cheeks.

"Yes, Alex!" at last he managed to say. "I want you to save him."

I examined the monkey; it was deeply unconscious; a superficial examination failed to detect any broken ribs, but only an X Ray would show that, and who knew what internal injuries there might be — besides a bullet through the brain.

I took Charlie, made him sit down on a couch, and sat beside him. "Now look, Charlie! You know I'm just about as fond of animals as you are but it would take a brain surgeon to save him, and there are no vet brain surgeons. Besides, no human surgeon would attempt anything without sophisticated tests and possibly the nearest place might be London. The only reason I can think of that he's not dead is that at the angle you shot him the bullet must have travelled upwards and missed any vital centre — but Charlie, there's only one hole. The bullet is still in there. I can't save him."

"Well, will you let him take his chance as long as he doesn't suffer?" he pleaded. Who could refuse?

"Alright, we'll have a go, but you know, boy, that the chances are about 1000 to one." Charlie nodded.

I gave the little creature clinging so tenuously to life a shot of morphine, sufficent to ensure he would remain unconscious, sat with the Trevelyans for a time and watched my patient. The breathing was coming easy and regular, not laboured. I was satisfied he would be out for the night.

Next morning early the phone rang. The message was not unexpected.

"Alex, he's gone; we sat up with him; he didn't suffer."

I hesitated; it's not easy to tell an animal lover this.

"It's best, Charlie, best for him and for you." Then, trying desperately to find some word to cheer I said. "Remember what the poet said?"

"One crowded hour of glorious life is worth an age without a name."

He'd had his hour. He had known for a time, the glory of freedom.

To Die Or Let Live

THIRTEEN

Leaving the car in the private parking space of 'The Willows', I quietly opened the fine wrought iron gate, which, like everything at 'The Willows', betokened excellent taste and the money to indulge it. I climbed the first few steps that led to the garden path, as I had done often before, but today, before proceeding any further, I paused, and sat down on the garden wall. It was quiet there, and I felt badly in need of a few moments by myself, to control my emotions, before proceeding to the next case. Glancing over my shoulder, I could just see the roof of the house, with behind and towering above it, the rocky knoll at whose feet it nestled, and so, safe in the knowledge that my presence was as yet un-detected, I gave myself up to the luxury of a rest and reflection. It was a glorious summer day, and in the garden behind me, bees droned and buzzed, blackbirds sang, sparrows chirruped and chaffinches chattered. In front and far below me were the glorious and much photographed sands of Mortecombe, stretching three miles into the distance, the far end barely visible in the heat haze of that blazing August day. On the sands, as always on such a day, were hundreds of people, but so vast was the beach and its attendant dunes that there seemed plenty of space for everyone. I could see little figures dotted everywhere, soaking up the sun and acquiring a West Country tan (you could always tell the newcomers by their white faces) but also up and down the beach many football or cricket matches were in progress. Mostly it was cricket, for at that time a Test Match was on many miles away, and from dozens of radios the voices of John Arlott or Brian Johnston, would be giving a ball by ball commentary of the fight for the

Ashes, inspiring the beach contestants to emulate, or identify with a Compton or Cowdrey, a Statham or Laker. In the sea figures leapt and plunged, and I'm sure shouted and screamed, but up here all the noises of men were drowned by the crash and thunder of the ocean, whose majestic, foaming, curling breakers plunged beachwards, bearing surfers on their backs or swamping rubber dinghies. Over all stretched an azure sky, merging blue grey with the sea at the distant horizon. It was a typical summer scene of joy, gladness, relaxation or the thrill of adventure, yet I felt none of these today as I watched, for I could not forget Silver, and as if my thought had been their cue, at that moment a line of ponies came over the brow of the gently sloping hill which formed a perfect backcloth for the long expanse of golden sand, washed ceaselessly by the dying foam of the waves as the great green combers reared far out to launch themselves futilely at the shore. Silver should have been along with these ponies. Two weeks ago he had been with them, someone on his back, probably a child experiencing the thrill of a first riding lesson, for Silver was quiet, gentle, trustworthy, ideal for beginners. Just two streets away from 'The Willows', Silver was dying in the loose box where I'd left him.

It had been perhaps ten days ago that John Wilkinson, owner of the stables, had called me. Silver had been brought in with the other ponies, to be groomed and made ready for another day's toil over the dunes, and up the hill and fields beyond. But something was clearly wrong with the little grey pony that morning. He walked stiffly, dragging behind the others, and stood in his box listless, head down, pained looking. Silver had a temperature and I set out to find why.

"He was alright yesterday, and when we put them out to grass last night" said his owner, as I proceeded to listen to his chest with my stethoscope. His lungs were clear, though his respirations were faster than normal. He had no nasal discharge, no obvious abscesses, just that stiff, don't want to move look. What was it? I'd run my hands over neck, back and limbs — nothing. It was only when I ducked under his head at the feeding trough that I'd found it, and as soon as I touched his brisket (the pad of muscle and fat at the front of the chest), he'd whinnied and reared. The wound there was not big, but already it was a dirty, almost black colour. I didn't like it, for I knew what had casued that wound, or was at any rate ninety-nine per cent certain: an adder. Every summer we had adder bites. Every summer I'd treated cattle, sheep but principally dogs, and all had recovered uneventfully. I'd never seen one in a horse before, and by the look of it that wound had happened the night before, probably just after he'd been turned out to grass, and lain down for a roll, and delicious scratching of the back to get all the itchiness and stiffness out of him. He must have lain on the snake, for the viper seldom bites unless molested. This was one of the many occasions when I wished that our patient could talk, just to be sure of the details. So here we had a bite, or from the look of it, several bites some fifteen hours ago, a long time for the venom to be circulating in the bloodstream. I'd cut open the black, diseased area, drained out the discharge already puffing out the whole brisket, washed and syringed with antiseptic, and used antibiotics both locally and parenterally, plus a few other drugs which had always sufficed before. We did not stock snake venom antidote; in fact it was doubtful if there was a hospital then in the whole area which had any, but I'd never found it necessary before. Every day, sometimes twice a day, I'd seen Silver. He'd had every drug I could think of, and also those suggested by the vet I'd called to give a second opinion. The stable girls had bathed, cleaned and poulticed that wound which daily grew bigger. They'd stayed on in the evenings to talk to the little pony, sponged down his fevered, sweating body, worked on him ceaselessly and caressed him lovingly. We fought very hard, and so did Silver, but it was a losing battle, as in an incredibly short time the whole brisket — skin, fat, muscle just rotted away and sloughed off. Today Silver was down. He could not get up and he would never get up. I had not injected him today for there was no point; the battle was lost. I'd merely stroked the little beast's neck, pulled his mane and said, "You've fought hard, boy, but we must take you away from all this pain now." But I couldn't! As I looked at those trusting, soulful, brown eyes, I couldn't do it! I chickened out! Somebody else must do it. I think John Wilkinson understood when he saw me rise from the little animal. He hadn't questioned it when I asked him to phone the RSPCA Inspector and get him to come with his humane killer. Even now the Inspector would be on his way; perhaps already he'd arrived and soon there would be a merciful release. I blamed myself for not finishing the job, and puzzled again if there was more I could have done; one always did. These moments communing with nature didn't take away the disappointment, but they brought some healing and put things in perspective. The tides would still ebb and flow, birds would still sing, and up in these dunes a few adders would still lurk for the unwary.

But I must go on, up to the villa, one of several in that lofty place. The gardens must have been a blaze of glory, but they were passed un-noticed that afternoon. I rang the front door bell and Miss Plumtree and a horde of dogs answered the call. I knew that there were, in fact eight dogs, all Cocker Spaniels. I wasn't too clear about the number of Plumtree sisters. There were three I'd met at their fine house with its magnificent view, while others were vaguely alluded to, but the number of dogs was always eight. The sisters were anything from fifty to seventy-five years old. It was impossible to say, for they dressed, wore their hair, and conversed in a way that was pure "Victoriana". The furniture of the house, and the jungle of pot plants in every room all spoke of a bygone age. Clearly the sisters had been well endowed by father Plumtree, long since deceased, but despite their wealth, they always seemed to me rather forlorn, left behind like driftwood on the beach when the tide has ebbed, and a little bemused by this strange, modern world. They were called Emily, Letitia and Victoria, and in the way they fluttered around, fussed, became flustered, yet always remained completely courteous, I thought I could see Miss Marple, Agatha Christie's famous crime detector, with the kindly manner but air of bewilderment. Well, not all of the sisters. Victoria was the exception and Victoria was addressing me now, "You will take tea?" she queried, though really it was more a command than an enquiry. One always 'took tea' with the Plumtrees. With others you had tea, drank tea, or enjoyed a cuppa. At 'The Willows' one 'took tea'.

"And how are you, Mr Cameron?" enquired Miss Letitia.

"Very well, thank you."

"And Mrs Cameron, and your two dear little boys?"

"Thriving, thank you."

"How is your garden?" ventured Miss Emily timidly. She was clearly lowest in the peck order of the Plumtree girls, and though they employed a gardener, Miss Emily was never happier than when out there. It was her great love in life, and I thought likely her place of escape from older sister Victoria. She had been well named. I'm certain that papa Plumtree, on first beholding this latest arrival, had taken one look at the square jaw, wide forehead with furrow even then on the infant brow, and had pronounced unhesitatingly "Victoria".

"Oh well, my garden is nothing compared to yours," I answered Miss Emily, "but it's coming on."

By now afternoon tea had arrived, brought by some minion from the kitchen, and I knew from the past that polite conversation was the order of the day till this afternoon ritual had been observed. It was positively infra-dig to discuss the purpose of one's visit till 'tea had been taken'.

"Isn't this a terrible world we're living in?" asked Letitia.

Thinking of Silver, I agreed heartily "Terrible."

"These strikes — I'd sack the lot of them" pronounced Victoria.

"Oh, ah ... yes" I grunted, picturing the toughest shop steward quailing before this redoubtable lady.

"And that man Attlee. It beats me how dear Winston can possibly stand him," she went on. I am a strictly non political animal, certainly in public, but I was moved to say,

"Oh, I don't know, Miss Plumtree. He did a lot during the war and he and Mr Churchill seemed to work well together then."

"But he's such a little man," (with a distinct nuance on "little") "and as for the rest of his gang . . . " She left it unsaid but I had a picture of Messrs Wilson, Dalton and Bevan with masks on their faces, and bags marked "Swag" on their backs. I hastily changed the subject.

"These are lovely scones, Miss Plumtree, who's the baking expert?"

"Our Mrs Buxton does most of it, but these are actually Emily's." Little Emily looked, abashed, embarrassed but also pleased. I fancy nobody ever took notice of poor Miss Emily. The meal proceeded to its leisurely close, the trays were removed, then Miss Victoria leaned back to issue the order of the day.

"It's little Rupert. We want you to take him away and put him to sleep" I gasped! "But he's only a baby. It's only months since I gave him his Distemper innoculation." I looked at Rupert lying peacefully on a couch.

"What on earth's wrong with him?"

"His ears are too long for a Cocker; they get in his food and this will certainly lead to ear canker. Also he's had one or two little cysts between his toes. I'm afraid he's from a weakly strain."

"But, Miss Plumtree, ear Canker and interdigital cysts are nothing, and can be easily treated. You can't put a dog down for that." Attempting to be flippant, I added "It's like putting Mr Attlee down because he's too small!"

"And a very good thing too!" Clearly I'd said the wrong thing. She went on, "But it's a totally different matter. Rupert is our dog and our responsibility. Mr Attlee is a man, and can presumably look after himself, or have a wife to do it for him." I was seething. Over the past year or two I'd destroyed two or three dogs for no very good reason, but this was getting ridiculous, indeed criminal. Long ears! These dogs were highly pedigreed, the sisters were apparently genuinely fond of them, and presumably vice versa. I had protested before and been over-ruled and informed that if I would not do it, they'd get Mr Dick. That gentleman kept a pet shop, and I knew he used strychnine for his destructions. I couldn't have that.

"Look, Miss Plumtree," I argued, "Rupert has his whole life before him. If you find him . . . ah . . . imperfect, I could easily find him a very good home."

"No, Mr Cameron, we wouldn't dream of him going to someone else and not knowing if he was happy. I'm a Christian Scientist and know that our little doggies have a better life waiting for them on the other side. My sisters and I have talked it over" (I knew who'd done the talking!) "and have decided this is much the best thing, best for Rupert. If you cannot do it, I'm sure Mr Dick will."

It was blackmail. At least with my method, the dog didn't know a thing. With strychnine it was agony, if only briefly. It was also monstrous that these old ladies who'd lived a completely sheltered existence, never having to move out into the wider world to earn a living, should decide for a trusting animal, whether to die or let live. Suddenly as I looked at them, they seemed rather sinister and terrible, no longer the Miss Marple detective, but the murderers. But then, if you believe that a canine Valhalla was just around the corner, I suppose you could sleep not only with a clear conscience, but with a smile of bliss. Did Christian Scientists believe that? I must check up.

So Rupert accompanied me to the car. I knew in a few weeks I would be summoned to Epivax his successor, and keep up the required number of eight. The little black dog frisked and frolicked all the way to the surgery, eagerly studying the passing scene. With our specially concentrated Euthatal, all he knew was the prick of a needle, in five seconds blissful sleep. In thirty seconds he was dead. The sentence to die and not live had been passed and carried out. I felt a bit sick. There was another dog tied up in our back premises, also a spaniel, but this time a large dun and white one, with brown splotches on her, and the most gentle face and tender eyes you ever saw.

"What's that one in for, Mrs Drury?" I asked.

"To be put down."

"What! Why?"

"I'm not sure why. She's not young, she has a small mammary tumour, but I think they just got tired of her."

"Who were her owners?"

"I didn't know them. They were strangers to me, just paid cash and left."

"Well, Mrs Dru . . . I'm not doing it. I'll take her home."

So the dog became part of the Cameron household. The name Lass seemed to suit her, and she soon readily answered to it, and proved herself to be a lovely, quiet, soft creature, gentle with the children, beloved by them, and the most obedient member of the family! The tumour was tiny, benign, harmless. One day I'd remove it, but there was no hurry, and she most certainly enjoyed her remaining time.

At 9.00 pm that evening the phone rang. Janet and I looked at the clock, then at each other, and both said "Parkhurst". This was his regular time for ringing. Though very well off, he was always after free advice, almost weekly.

"Bristacombe 250, Mr Cameron speaking."

"Good evening, Mr Cameron! Parkhurst, Shirwell Ford here."

"Good evening, Mr Parkhurst," I glanced wearily at Janet. We had the whole ritual to go through every time, like at 'The Willows', but without the scones!

"Fine weather we're having, Mr Cameron."

"It certainly is."

"Perhaps a trifle dry for the root crops, wouldn't you say?"

"Perhaps."

"I expect you have a lot of visitors about in town."

"Thousands of them."

"You'll be kept busy, then."

"Yes."

"Oh, Mr Cameron," . . . now we were getting to the request, though he always managed to make it sound like an afterthought or intrusion into our polite conversation. "I wonder if you could just slip over tonight and do a little job for us. Sister has an old cat she thinks it would be better to put to sleep."

"Why? Is it ill, or in pain?"

"No, just old. It's hair has got a bit matted and it smells rather."

"I'm sorry. I won't be over tonight, Mr Parkhurst."

"You won't?"

"No."

"Why is that?"

"Well, Mr Parkhurst, my partner's on holiday, it's been a long hard day, it is not an urgent case, and can very well wait till morning."

Steel in his voice now! "Sister would like it done tonight."

"Well, now, if that's so, if you care to jump in your car and bring it here, I'll oblige, though matted hair is common in old cats and can be cut off or combed out. Besides, I was on your farm just the other day, and no mention was made of it then. Surely it hasn't grown old in a matter of days?"

Long pause . . . I guessed what was coming . . . Still very polite . . . "Oh, Mr Cameron, brother and I were talking one night and we thought it might be an advantage to have two veterinary surgeons, from different Practices. If you don't feel you can come tonight, I might have to ring someone else."

He'd come this blackmail once before and insisted I come out quite late one evening to see a lame ram, which he admitted had been lame for nearly a week, but would definitely need treating that evening. Not wanting to antagonise a client, I had successively bitten my lip, gnashed my teeth, frothed at the mouth and gone. But not tonight. I'd had enough killing for one day. So, equally politely I replied.

"Well, now, Mr Parkhurst, that might be a very good idea and then you could ring your other vet alternate Fridays for advice. Yes, a good idea! But if you do decide you still want my services, you can give me a ring in the morning or bring the cat in tomorrow, for it's getting a bit late to come now tonight. Good night to you!"

I slammed down the phone in great glee. I'd wanted to do that for a long time to old Parkhurst . . . the man who paid his bills to us once a year and then asked for discount . . . the man who kept his bills to a minimum by regular free phone advice . . . the farmer who usually didn't want you to call unless you were passing anyway, so that he wouldn't have to pay a visit fee, but who expected instant service when he clapped his hands. Yes, I'd enjoyed that. There was a lot unregenerate in me yet!

Parkhurst was at the surgery next morning, cat basket in hand, and a jar of cream as a peace offering in the other. I looked at the old cat. Its hair was matted, but that didn't matter, being merely an indication that it couldn't clean itself properly any more. But it was thin to the point of emaciation, if had few teeth left, its head was down. Life held nothing for it now. The decision to die or let live was in this case, easy, and the carrying out of the decision painless, indeed a kindness. The old man departed with his now empty basket, and for the first time I felt sorry for him. He had plenty of money, an excellent farm, first class herds of sheep and cattle. He was a man respected for his knowledge of the local breeds, and a judge at local Shows — in short, a successful man, yet somehow as he limped towards his car that morning, an empty cat basket in his hand, he seemed curiously forlorn, even somehow vulnerable.

Perhaps this curious experience was but fancy, as unreal as dreams that fade in the full light of day . . . Maybe it was, for me, in an odd sort of way, future events casting their shadows before them, but somehow, just momentarily,

I pictured Parkhurst, an old man in a hospital bed, with no close family of his own, and respected as he was, a man with few real friends. I wondered, would there be for him, as for the cat, a merciful release?

Maybe these were the first musings of what experiences would come to me, in years ahead; I cannot say. As a vet, I took hundreds of lives; I had a licence to kill, yet I never enjoyed it, and would certainly never wish such a weight to be put on any man in relation to human life. In some cases, I have to confess, at the time I would more cheerfully have taken the owner's life — as with Miss Victoria Plumtree — when a trusting animal was just put out of the way for no good reason. But for others, like Silver and the cat, I knew that, repugnant though it was, to hasten death was an act of mercy and kindness.

I have since then, over many years, almost weekly, stood beside a bed and watched someone fight a brave, but losing battle, and I've pondered deeply. It is my view that in such cases, assuming everything is being done to ease the patient's suffering, to take life would be, very often, to deprive a husband or wife of experiences and moments that are very precious, and forged only in the fires of suffering, shared together. But there are other cases where I've wondered! I have gone into an enormous ward of geriatric patients, the beds close together, scarcely allowing passage between them, beds containing people who have lost all awareness of surroundings, and all control of their actions; I have seen folks lose all dignity, privacy, individuality, and become increasingly distressing for their loved ones to behold week by week. Cabbages! That's how society has labelled such poor beings. I know all the arguments against any form of euthanasia, at any time, and respect deeply the views of all who hold them. I have the highest regard for the sanctity of human life, and a deep love of old folks. As a minister of the Gospel, I have no doubts of the reality of "that other world", nor of our basic belief that man is an eternal spirit. I know all the questions regarding any form of euthanasia — I give no answers. I only know that many times I've come away from a scene of extreme weakness or debility, and with indignation and concern have said to myself, "I wouldn't treat a dog like that!" I have, conscious, oh so conscious of my own helplessness, wondered what He, who was and is far from helpless, and whose hands in Galilee were tender to soothe and to save, would do in our day, in a ward of folks weary, longing, sighing, yes and asking to be released to "go Home" — and I've heard an echo as of old, saying, "Blessed are the merciful — for they shall obtain mercy."

Instant Results

FOURTEEN

The buzzer in the telephone switchboard was going as I went in the surgery door. Extension two. That was from our house. Mrs Drury, that model of all the virtues in a vet's secretary-cum assistant-cum- anaesthetist-cum-bookkeeper-cum-receptionist was already coping.

"I'll give him the message, Mrs Cameron."

She answered my raised eyebrows.

"Your wife on the phone. Just after you left, a call came in from Hopkins, The Grange. A cow with a Stroke."

"A Stroke, eh?" I pondered. "Know who these folk are, Mrs Dru?"

"No, Mr Cameron, they're new clients; a small farm out Fardley way. Mrs Cameron said they sounded very upset on the phone."

I glanced at the other case list for the day so far. There would be plenty more before night, so I initialled those I was off to, leaving Bernard to pick the rest. Fardley was one of these little out of the way places that abound in Devon and are part of its charm. I felt my spirits rise as I drove along and a song came to my lips (one of our students "seeing practice" had once reported to his wife in wonderment, "he sings as he drives") It was a gorgeous May morning, fields were greening up with early summer freshness, trees were bursting into leaf, birds were skimming merrily in front of the little Austin Van as she cruised along these famous sunken Devon lanes. They weren't really sunken. It was simply that generations of farmers had built a dyke, then covered it with earth, and on top planted a hedge, thus making high walls which were excellent windbreaks from the cold nor-easterlies or wet westerlies, for sheep and out wintered cattle.

They were the high hedges that had driven my old teacher Sandy Gray to distraction on his honeymoon years ago in Devon when he snorted "Glorious Devon, if you could see anything over these hedges". It was glorious Devon that morning, with the high banks a mass of yellow primroses. Yes, it was good to be alive, to be free, to be a country vet on such a day, so why not sing a stave or two! I had been through Fardley before, a tiny hamlet tucked away off the main roads, just a cluster of houses and little farms jutting out any old how and a sign marked "Post Office" pointing vaguely in the direction of a little thatched house. Roses were already in bloom on the walls, lupins and paeonies making splashes of colour in the borders as I walked up the path and entered. I had apparently been observed, for there behind a tiny counter was a little old lady with rosy cheeks, eyes creased with wrinkles which I suspected had been produced more by smiles than tears, and a gentleness and serenity about her. She greeted me with a hearty "good morning" and equally heartily I agreed it was and asked if she could direct me to The Grange. She looked at me over her spectacles and queried

"Oh, you'll be the Veterinary! Now would you be Mr Cameron or the young vet?" I said I was both; both Mr Cameron and young.

"Yes, you do look young" she said a little doubtfully "I thought you must be the assistant" She went on "you'll have come about Grizelda?"

"Grizelda? Who might she be?"

"She's Mr and Mrs Hopkin's Guernsey cow — a darling creature, as gentle as a lamb, and so are the Hopkins'. We're all Chapel, you know" she added, as if somehow this explained everything. I nodded "Me too," not to be outdone. (I had early discovered that so far as the Christian Religion went, in England you were either Church or Chapel, the latter designation covering Baptist, Methodist, Congregational, Independent Missions, Pentecostal and a few others) She was a delightful little body, twittering like a perky chaffinch, but finally she recalled I had asked for directions.

"You just go over the ford and take the first lane on the left and that's The Grange. I do hope you can help Grizelda."

So I left my little pippin of a Postal Officer and thought there was bound to be customer satisfaction there at all times. I found 'The Grange', left the car in the lane, and pushed open a gate to be greeted by a huge man and a tiny little woman, who had been awaiting my coming with anxiety.

"Good morning to you" I called. "And to you, sir" they replied with olde worlde charm — I almost expected the lady to curtsey.

"You found us alright, then" boomed the man in a voice that reminded me of a stop on the organ marked Basso Profundo.

"Yes, I found you." I explained that the lady in the Post Office had directed me.

"That would be Miss Browne with an E at the end" explained the little wife. "She's Chapel like us; we're mostly Chapel hereabouts; it's Grizelda" she added. I wasn't sure whether that lady was also Chapel, but thought it was about time I saw her. But first Mr Hopkins had to explain.

"We've mostly had Mr Warman before. (Warman was the opposition, a deadly and not always very ethical rival.) But you're just as near and we heard you were Scottish, and the Scottish were very good with cattle!" I thought, wryly, that we used to get a great name for stealing English cattle, but hoped I would live up to their expectations. A cow with a Stroke could be anything from a cerebral haemorrhage to a tumour on the brain. Eventually I was allowed to see Grizelda, little Mrs Hopkins bounding on in front and throwing open the door of a loose box. In one corner was a calf some twenty-four hours old, while on a deep bed of spotlessly clean straw lay Grizelda, deeply unconscious. I tested her eye and ear reflexes, took her temperature and pulse, my every move being watched intently. I felt I must go through the motions and justify their faith in Scots vets — but one glance would have told the most raw recruit to the veterinary profession, even if he hadn't the initial advantage of a Scots pedigree, what was what. I had been astonished since coming to Devon at the many who had not seen a condition that was a daily occurrence back in Ayrshire and in most dairying districts of Britian.

"Never had owt like this before" boomed Mr H, as if divining my thoughts.

"Can you do anything?" earnestly entreated his little wife.

"Yes, Mrs Hopkins, I think I can soon put Grizelda right. Could you just bring me a bucket of water, not too hot, soap and a towel?" She departed at the double while I got out my flutter valve, calcium bottles, tin of needles, bottle of iodine and a swab. Then, having put one of the calcium bottles in the bucket to bring the contents to about blood heat, I clipped the hair over about an inch of mammary vein, swabbed with iodine, and said to my client, "Now! I hope a spot of blood doesn't worry you?"

"Nay, lad" boomed farmer Hopkins, "seen plenty of that in the first war."

"Right then, you hold that," I said, giving him the calcium bottle with flutter valve attachment to hold, preparatory to gravity feed into the bloodstream. "When I tell you, turn the bottle upside down and let me have the end of the tube."

I stuck the large bore needle into the mammary vein, and out spurted some rich dark blood. I called for the tube, when there was an almighty crash, and I turned to see a client flat out on the floor, and the calcium pouring from the tube (miraculously the bottle hadn't broken), while blood still flowed from Grizelda. My assistant who had seen plenty of blood had, like not a few others, fainted. His wife was hovering over him so I hovered over my patient, inserted the nozzle into the needle and soon the life-giving calcium was gurgling merrily into Grizelda. One bottle in, I turned to the human casualty, suggested to his wife (who was buzzing around like an agitated humming bird) that she get her husband a cup of water, and also mop his brow with a cold cloth to bring him round. I didn't know if that would help, but a glance assured me he would be OK and it gave her something to do. Then the second bottle of Calcium Borogluconate was injected subcutaneously and in about fifteen minutes Grizelda was sitting up, looking around her, as was Mr Hopkins. It was a close thing who would recover first but Mr H made it by a short head. He gazed at his Guernsey in wonderment, Mrs H. looked at her man in concern, both looked at me and said "It's a miracle; you've given us back our Grizelda," and with that the lady of the hour lurched to her feet unsteadily and headed for her calf, giving tongue from one corner, while farmer Hopkins on equally rubbery legs, staggered up from the other. They were like two punch drunk boxers who'd had about enough. Little Mrs H. was ecstatic, and hopped about betwixt one and the other, enthusing, "My sir, it's just like the Bible, Lazarus being raised from the dead, or being born over again."

I didn't know whether she was referring to her husband or Grizelda, though I agreed it was a good description. Over the inevitable cup of tea which this time I waited to drink to make sure the old man was alright (one was offered tea virtually every call in North Devon), I explained the phenomenon to them.

"Your cow had Milk Fever, Mr Hopkins. In the old days they thought it was a germ in the milk that caused it, so it got the name, and they used to inject a weak solution of iodine into the udder, mighty uncomfortable, but now and then it saved a cow's life. It was certainly better than the older cure of whisky, which never yet saved a cow with Milk Fever, but I suppose by the time the cow had had a drink, the farmer and vet a few each, they were all past caring anyway when the poor beast died. By and by somebody on the Continent found that you didn't need iodine, that water would do, then somebody again found to pump the udder up with air was even better. But all these were shots in the dark. When they worked it was simply because they stopped the udder producing milk which allowed the level of calcium in the cow's blood to rise again, but of course the udder was often ruined. Then in the 1930s, a Scots Vet" (I had to get in a plug and keep up their regard for our ability) "took blood tests from 100 cows suffering from Milk Fever. In every case the blood calcium level was too low, so what we do now is simply inject Calcium. Mind you," I went on with utter sincerity, "I've seen this hundreds of times and it still seems like a conjuring trick, a miracle really. Your cow would have died by this afternoon without treatment, but as you saw, within half an hour, she was up on her feet. I know of hardly anything in all medicine quite so dramatic as this."

Mrs Hopkins murmured "Once I was blind, now I see."

I nodded, bade them good day, and to vociferous thanks went out to the car. I arrived there at the same time as Miss Browne with an E at her end.

"Oh, Mr Vetinary," she gasped, "I'm glad you're still here. Your office phoned me to say would you please call at the Rectory. The Rector, dear man, had called up to say that he had a bullock, gone quite mad — 'Maze as a brish' were his words, and could you go right away?"

This was another new client so I enquired where the Rectory might be. They proceeded to direct me, one booming and two twittering voices, with much arm waving and correcting one another. Finally, Mr Hopkins, now quite recovered said "Look ee here, surr; it be nigh about a mile and a halv over by. I'll show ee," in his anxiety lapsing into his rich Devon accent which I loved, while Mrs H, with a different anxiety, that for her huge man, announced "If you go, Perce, I go too" So his name was Percival, I mused. She went on, "you might come over all queer like again." I wasn't sure if the little lady was more concerned about his physical well being or the possible spiritual taint of hob nobbing with Church, but anyway they both piled into the little van, while Miss Browne waved us "Goodbye" — also with an E. After sundry wrong turns, for Perce and his missus had different ideas about right and left hands, eventually I pulled up in front of an old, large, rambling house, with quite a few outbuildings apparent beyond. We were met by a wild looking figure striding rapidly towards us. He had an elbow sticking out of an old jersey, his hair was dishevelled, and his clerical collar was only fastened at one end, so that the other stuck out in front like a direction finder.

"Quite extraordinary!" he announced. (He certainly was) "Oh, hello, Mrs Hopkins-Percival, good day to you" he said, proceeding to raise a hat, then finding there was none there, he tried to fasten his clerical collar to its retaining stud and appear presentable. I gazed fascinated as the collar end came away again with a ping. The poor man grabbed it in one hand and me in the other.

"Look here, Mr . . . er . . . er Cameron. I put a call through to my own vet, Mr Darnaway" (I didn't mind him; he was a cheerful old chap, and co-operative rather than the vindictive Warman) "but he is out on a case, then I telephoned you to discover you were actually here in Fardley. It seemed quite providential, but whether you can do anything, I doubt. The poor animal seems stark, raving mad." *Ping* went his collar yet again as he tried in vain to fasten it with one hand.

"Is it a cow, or a bull or a young beast?" I queried.

"It's a two year old heifer," he explained as he led me to his shippen – his recalcitrant collar pinging merrily as he led me on.

"See, in here" he whispered, lest the mad beast would hear us, and he peeped in the top half of a stable type door, "Quite, quite gone," he said, pointing to his head. It wasn't clear whether he meant himself or his heifer, it being a moot point which was looking the wilder, but I gave him the benefit of the doubt. "Have you ever seen anything like that before?" he demanded.

"Yes, a few times, but this ones a beaut!"

"Really." He paused and further exclaimed "extraordinary," as if it was beyond the realms of understanding that there should be so many mad bovines in the world. Then he asked, rather piteously, poor man, "Can anything be done?"

"Mr Cameron just brought our Grizelda back from the dead, Rector," said little Mrs Hopkins. "I'm sure he'll put you right too."

I looked at her quizzically and wondered if she was having a wee theological dig, then decided that at that moment I really was her hero. I explained to the distraught cleric;

"Your heifer has Staggers, Rector."

"Good gracious!" he exploded "who has been giving her alcohol?"

I really couldn't restrain myself any longer. Here were two staunch Chapel goers looking suspiciously and wonderingly at one distraught High Churchman, dressed in rags and half a clerical collar, while from the shippen came thumps and bellows reminiscent of a Malemute Saloon when the boys had come to town and were whooping it up – and all this in quiet little Fardley. I recovered and apologised for my unseemly mirth, and said, "No, no, Rector. Alcohol has nothing to do with it. Staggers is variously called Stomach Staggers, Mad Staggers, Grass Staggers, but really it is a hypomagnesaemia." I was rather maliciously pleased with that. I bet when it came to quoting Atistotle, he could beat me to a frazzle, but clearly hypomagnesaemia had him beat. He looked bewildered, so I hastily went on. "A magnesium deficiency. It affects the brain, can and often does kill an animal, but if we can get some magnesium into her, we might pull her round, provided there is no brain damage. The difficulty will be holding her steady, for it must go directly into the blood stream, into a vein, in an acute case like this."

I nipped through the door and was soon out again, as she charged me, a characteristic of the condition. It seemed a hopeless proposition to get in there and restrain her without loss of life or limb. I looked around.

"Is there any other way I can get in?" I enquired.

"Only from the hayloft above."

"Then, Vicar . . . ah . . . Rector, if you have a rope handy we'll prepare for a heavenly visitation." He looked at me doubtfully. Did I seem too flippant, I wondered, so hastily went on to explain.

"We have no hope unless we can restrain that heifer somehow, and what better way than from above. Now, I'll go up into the hayloft and drop a noose over her head. When she charges, she'll pull the slip knot tight, and it's up to you and Mr Hopkins here to get in there beside her and secure her by that rope to a post, stanchion, anything. It'll be hot work . . . maybe you should take your collar off. So the pinging collar ceased to ping, but there followed an equally mad fifteen minutes. Several times I had the dangling noose almost over the beast but always she dodged. Finally I suggested the Rector call to her over the stable type door and from the loft immediately above when she headed for the door, I would try to lassoo her. Thankfully, it worked, the rope pulled tight and out of my hands, but the big burly farmer and the lean, rangy Churchman were in there like a flash, grabbing the trailing end of the rope and securing it round a post. I swung down from my lofty abode to lend a hand. That heifer struggled like mad. I tied another rope round her horns, gradually releasing the lassoo which by now was all but throttling her.

"Now, Rector, you pray that I can hit this jugular vein pretty soon, and that the magnesium will be in time to work, but I warn you, it can also kill sometimes. Mr Hopkins, I suggest you look the other way. I wasn't so expert with jugular as mammary veins, having trained on Ayrshires, where the mammary vein was about an inch in diameter. However, third jab, I got it, and once again the flutter valve routine was repeated, but this time, much more slowly, watching the respiratory rate with care. The beast quietened a bit, its flutterings beneath us lessening.

"Now for some Chloral Hydrate to quieten her a bit more, then a spare supply of magnesium under the skin, and I think you'll find, I hope anyway, that the combination of Church, Chapel and Infidel Scots Presbyterian has worked wonders."

"Amen to that" came from a perspiring parson. The young beast was quivering but little now; the madness had gone. We guided her into a loose box where for the rest of the day she could be watched, but I was pretty sure she'd be OK now.

"Do come in and have a wash," invited the Rector, I followed, so did the Hopkins, and in the next ten minutes we gave ouselves over to some hearty and very necessary ablutions. Presently Perce Hopkins boomed, "You know, Rector, I reckon that ther yiffer was jus like the man in the Scriptures as was allus cuttin himself with knives, or like that thar Gardenin swine."

"Indeed you're right, Mr Hopkins, though I think it was Gardarene — an instant cure, a miracle — and from above too," he smiled.

He really looked quite a different man without his collar. He apologised that his wife was out and so he could not offer us tea.

"Will you have a little refreshment?" he enquired. "I can soon get that." I thanked him, no — I didn't indulge. The Hopkins shook their heads resolutely.

"Well, I think I will," said the man of God, "as the Scriptures also say — 'Take a little wine for thy stomach's sake and often infirmities', And he did. By the size of the noggin, his stomach was pretty bad or his infirmities very frequent!

I dropped off Perce and Mrs H, and went on my way, well satisfied. That was one of the joys of being a vet, I thought; you saw an immediate result for your work. Two animals rescued from death in quiet little Fardley that morning, thanks to the knowledge of medical science and a modicum of skill in the operator. So different from the poor old Rector, I thought. Apart from his glebe-land which he farmed as part of his living, what results could he show? The thoughts passed idly through my mind, with no realisation then that I would often return to these very questions in my next vocation — but more of that anon.

I've quite often noticed how you've seldom been near a place, and then you seem never to be away from it. So it was for a time with the little community of Fardley. Two weeks after their Milk Fever, the Hopkins had milk trouble again. This time it was reported that a sow named Jemima had farrowed a litter of fourteen and had no milk. Could I come? I grabbed that one for myself before Bernard could volunteer, for we both especially loved that district of the Practice. As the Austin headed once more for The Grange, I thought ahead, as vets do, to what was likely to await us. Almost certainly this was Agalactia, which simply means, of course, no milk. Again, as with Milk Fever, it is a misnomer. In fact, the sow delivers her piglets, and nature provides her with a requisite number of teats and milk enough to feed her hungry brood — but something has gone wrong with the mechanism. There's a spanner in the works, an infinitessimal fault, but with disastrous results. The "let down hormone", as it is called, produced by the tiny pituitary gland in the brain, triggers off the mechanism — releases the trapdoor, if you like — to let the milk flow. Without that hormone functioning, the udders can be bursting with milk to the sow's acute discomfort and the piglets' utter despair, yet not a single drop will come, and the piglets will starve to death.

Two pictures always came to my mind when I thought of this condition. One was of a lecturer we had, a bumptious Englishman — though I'm sure the two facts were coincidental! A man given somewhat to exaggeration. He had a habit of speaking out of the side of his mouth, so that the words were squeezed out seemingly reluctantly, giving a peculiar timbre to his utterances. In describing this condition he said to us — "You stick the needle in, then jump back quickly, or you'll get your trousers splashed with milk!" I had never seen that quite happen, though I had seen some pretty prompt responses. The other memory was of my student days, visiting with my old boss a farm near Barr, in Ayrshire. There that evening, two sows had farrowed, one with twenty-one piglets, and the other fifteen, and neither had any milk. I'm sure it was some kind of productivity record matched only by the volume of despair that permeated the place as we arrived. In the mother of twenty-one, the injection of pituitrin worked like a charm, and all was well, except that queues were forming for the available teats. But in she of the fifteen, no amount of the hormone availed. The drug had no effect, as sometimes happened. Clearly in these instances there was some other unknown factor, but that farmer's wife set too and bottle reared fourteen of these fifteen pigs, getting up every few hours day and night to do so, and in fact winning a prize at a local

Farming Show with one of them. I vaguely wondered, as I journeyed onward, if Perce or Mrs Hopkins would do that, if need be; I rather thought they would.

I was received with open arms. It's marvellous what an initial success does for a vet with a new client — and was led immediately to Jemima's abode. She was one of two sows (the other being introduced as June,) on this little farm where they had something of everything but generally found the summer B and B visitors their best source of income. I looked at Jemima and her squealing, hungry, piglets, told Perce to shut his eyes again, jabbed Jemima behind the ear, the easiest place to pierce a sow's needle bending hide, told him he could look now, and at his expectant glance said "Now we wait a little. How's Grizelda?" They took me to the little one acre orchard where she was grazing, whistled her up to the gate, and the gentle creature stood there, placidly chewing the cud and regarding me with her big brown eyes as I stroked her head. Mrs Hopkins twittered,

"Here's Mr Cameron, Grizel — he saved your life, you know," Grizel chewed on. Life was good now, why think of the past. The reunion over, we looked at mother and piglets. I knew before we reached the pen all was well. No longer was there the squeal of hungry piglets, but instead that lovely deep baritone grunt of a sow suckling its young, while from each little knob came a contented sucking note, like a line of bell ringers pulling their rope in turn.

"Well I do declare," said Mrs Hopkins, "if I didn't know you for a Chapel goer I would say you were a wizard. Do you never fail, Mr Cameron?"

"Often," I said, "you just haven't found me out yet!"

I was presented with a jar of Devon clotted cream for Mrs Cameron, and pressed to take the service in their little Methodist Chapel some time. I promised I would, with pleasure, and I meant it. They were the salt of the earth, these simple, straight, homely folks. I thought I'd have a quick call at the Rectory. I was met by the Rector in full clerical attire just off to a Diocesan meeting. "Would you have a quick look at a lamb?" he asked. "It's a late one" he explained and is all crippled and poorly." I looked at the pathetic wee beast and gave him a rapid synopsis.

"Joint ill, for certain — infection through the navel at birth, localisation and swelling in the joints, either will die or won't thrive — unless you're prepared to spend something on it and a lot of time with it, and even then, I can't promise." He said he would try. He was a kindly soul, and he knew what it was to have frequent infirmities himself! So I gave the lamb a massive dose of serum, left him a bottle of penicillin with orders to inject daily, poultice or otherwise heat treat the joints, and make sure it got its full milk ration from the ewe. It took time, but it worked. Three weeks later when I was out visiting Miss Browne's cat, which had ear canker, I called at the Rectory and saw my patient, now virtually whole, if fractionally stiff, but putting on weight, and doing — that word beloved by shepherds and so descriptive. Doing! I congratulated the Rector on his patience and perseverance.

"You know," he said, "I've been thinking of your visits. The first one was dramatic, exciting, a quick and visible result, all over in no time and a beast made whole. This lamb has taken weeks of treatment and coaxing, but it's whole now too. I think I've been learning a lesson. Before I used to scoff at the sudden convert — the Billy Graham approach — for it wasn't mine, but your curing that heifer from its madness made me see things *can* happen in an instant. But probably most of my work is like treating that lamb. Others" — he paused, searching for the right words — "maybe find wholeness, that's what the Greek for salvation is, you know (he twinkled at my ignorance) slowly, bit by bit. But the end result is the same, and the Person treating them, the source of healing, the same."

He knew more than Aristotle, did that gentle soul. After years in the ministry, I've good cause to remember his words. One fold, one shepherd, but many ways to both. A sudden finding Him in a blaze of noontide heat, or a slow progression, following and finding maybe as the evening shadows fall. But both are equally real experiences of the Shepherd, by His sheep.

Variety Pack

FIFTEEN

"Bernard, what's a coypu?" I asked as I put down the phone.

"Haven't a clue" came his prompt reply.

"I think it's like a rat, only bigger," said Anne. We both looked at her in admiration, not only because she was easy on the eye, but regularly our secretary would surprise us with the scope of her knowledge. Two weeks ago she'd put us right on an ocelot.

"Charlie in trouble again, then?" asked Bernard.

"Well, his coypu is. It doesn't sound very much and if it's only a kind of rat, I reckon I can manage. If it had been these black bears, Bernard, I'd have remembered a calving in the middle or Exmoor! Besides, there are a few things he would like me to see, so I'll get a free conducted tour of the zoo — maybe if I'm in luck I'll get a choc-ice going in!"

It was a glorious warm, early summer afternoon, just the kind of sleepy day for a leisurely zoological expedition — plus a choc-ice. Bernard hadn't a lot on his plate, so I didn't feel too bad on this occasion at exerting my prerogative as senior partner in selecting my cases.

Charlie Trevelyan and I had three things in common. We were both fond of animals — actually he was animal daft and an F.Z.S. We both earned our living from animals; and we were both perpetually hard up, since his Zoo and my Practice were still both at the "ploughing money back to reap the benefits later stage." The one big difference was that he was acquainted with a far greater variety of the animal kingdom than I was and was liable to appear in his car, in public or on television with almost anything, and in recent years I, who had been trained on horses, cows, sheep, pigs, dogs (including cats) and a little bit on poultry had been in total ignorance till I found Charlie thrusting them at me "for my expert diagnosis and treatment" when I didn't even know what a coypu was! Needless to say in many of my cases I had been singularly unsuccessful, not always because of the rarity of the species, but from one of two very good reasons, always assuming, that is, that I was a moderately competent vet. My lack of success sprang firstly from the fact that in those days there was no literature whatsoever on diseases, diagnosis, drugs of choice, let alone dosage, for the exotic creatures at Charlie's zoo, and there were probably at most four experts on such animals in the whole UK to whom hapless vets like me could turn to for advice. Black's *Veterinary Dictionary* has nothing to say on the restraint of a hippopotamus, nor can Hoare's *Veterinary Therapeutics* advise me on the dosage of digitalis, or any other drug, for a goatimundi. So literature being nil tended to cut down success rates. The second reason for my high failure rate was almost as old as creation, and I imagine plagues present day practioners as of yore, for it concerns a law as ancient as time, as immutable now as when beasts first walked our planet: that the weakest goes to the wall. So animals, even in captivity, would often mask symptoms of illness from their fellow creatures and from man, till they could hide them no more, and by then, from the vet's point of view, it was too late. Case after case could be quoted to illustrate this law of the wild.

I remembered being gripped by Charlie at the gate one day and rushed to the puma's cage. I knew a puma was a mountain lion, and was therefore a member of the cat family, but my life hitherto had been completely puma free, and as Charlie hustled me cagewards that day, I felt the doom had come upon me. I was in mortal terror of either disgracing myself by fleeing, gibbering with terror from the cage, or in not making it to the door before the puma had sampled me! As it happened, I needn't have worried, for I could see as we reached his cage that the puma was breathing his last. I reached for the Adrenaline bottle, but before any stimulant could be given, our patient had gone, his final gesture being a despairing lunge with one paw at us, the ancient foe. I looked at that great cat lying there, and if there was a sense of relief in my heart, there was also a feeling of great pity. He was beautiful, so sleek and graceful, even in death. I suppose he had been happy there — he had certainly been well cared for — but every sinew of his legs, his powerful hip and shoulder muscles, his proud eye now unseeing, had been designed for him to wander the high uplands of his homelands and he had died, far away, in a cage.

"There didn't seem a thing wrong with him till yesterday when he was a bit off colour, and then today he wouldn't eat at all" said Charlie.

"Sure?" I queried. "Certain sure" – and you can't be surer than that in Devon. "Let's see then, Charlie, what killed him."

I carried out a post mortem there in his cage, the great cat's body still warm, and almost at once found the trouble. You couldn't miss it. A massive great fur ball about the size of a cricket ball and compacted together almost as hard, was lodged in his small intestine. All cats lick themselves, all cats get small fur balls, but usually so small that they are passed without the owner ever knowing of their existence. I had certainly, on occasions, treated cats for the condition, and all had recovered uneventfully, for all had shown symptoms in time. Never had I lost one. Truly the law of the wild seemed to be "thou shalt show no weakness". For this and all the intestine around was massively inflamed and even gangrenous. That fur ball had been growing for weeks, as more and more fur bound itself round the initial small nucleus, and in his last days, with the gut completely blocked, the pain must have been intense, yet the puma had borne it without visible sign.

"Poor lilol' thing" Charlie was sighing. "He must have suffered with that." "He sure did," I agreed. We both somehow felt humbled and somehow better men for having witnessed what one creature of the wild could endure. Charlie stroked the soft coat of this, one of his prize exhibits, but in that moment Charlie was not thinking of the cost, but of a friend lost. That was the great thing about Charlie; always he was full of new plans, new schemes, further extensions. Costs were prohibitive, money was tight, but these animals were more than money earners. They were his charge, his concern, his friends. His enthusiasm was boundless and infectious. He had earned his Fellowship of the Zoological Society.

Today it was a coypu, not a puma. I found that it *was* a kind of rat, to be exact a South American aquatic rodent. There wasn't much wrong with it, though I let Charlie do the handling. It had a skin condition of sorts, for which I prescribed a shampoo of sorts, to be followed by a cream. The beauty of many skin conditions is that they are delightfully vague, and even for the experts, treatment is often a case of trial and error. The coypu dealt with, Charlie conducted me on a tour; he had time on his hands; he wanted to show me new additions and get some advice, and since I also had time I was content to wander round the whole zoo. Almost every cage, every enclosure brought back memories of battles won or lost, and everywhere were creatures I had seen before and treated for injury or disease. First we went to the aviaries, where Charlie had about the best and biggest collection of birds in Britain at the time — hundreds of them. The over-riding impressions when you entered were of colour and sound. It seemed as if some artist had been busy and made merry with every known colour. Bright reds were equalled by vivid greens; softer orange matched gentler pink, while pastel shades abounded. Over all was the chatter of sound; screeching of parrots, the call of the mynah bird, the soft intimate murmurs of dozens of pairs of budgerigars — macaws, chaffinches, cockatoos, canaries, dozens of species, the noise inside augmented from time to time by the quacking of muscovy ducks outside, the scream of a peacock or the hissing of a goose. It was here, in the aviaries, that I'd had my greatest failures. These birds, I soon found, are very subject to nose, throat and chest infections. I kept peering suspiciously for psittacosis, but it was always straightforward chills, croups, bronchitis or pneumonias, and naturally I had used, where I thought it necessary, penicillin. I might as well have given potassium cyanide. For what reason I know not till this hour, penicillin was fatal to my avian patients. So we switched to Chloromycetin, a broad spectrum antibiotic, and it was as dramatically successful as penicillin had been seemingly lethal. We loitered long in the aviaries; you could have spent an afternoon there. Then we moved outside to the children's corner. There I spotted, amid its friends a kangaroo, whose leg, one of the little front ones, I had once encased in plaster. Ducks waddled about, bantams proudly strutted, lambs lay in the sun. There too were my two goats. When I had first seen them in their own paddock they had resembled two bundles of old rags borne by thin sticks of legs. A faeces sample had revealed a quite astonishing concentration of round worms. So they had been dosed a few times, their pen moved, the ground ploughed up in their "goat sick" paddock. Now they were sleek, and growing fatter weekly on children's titbits. We came to the enclosure of the "Dead End Kids" whose exploits are recorded elsewhere. Opposite it the ostrich was out taking the air, his head turning like a periscope on top of his long neck.

"Remember him?" grinned Charlie.

"I surely do," I smiled back.

I could afford to smile now but there had been few grins around when first our paths had crossed. It had been almost my first visit to the zoo, a Sunday afternoon. Word reached me via the minister's wife as I taught my Sunday School class of eight and nine-year-olds, that I was to phone home as soon as class was over, and then proceed to the zoo to stitch the ostrich's neck. Immediately my class volunteered to accompany me *en masse,* but since that wasn't on, one lad, Barclay Beer, now a pillar of the Church of England, for some reason was selected. Probably he had just got in first. Lesson over, Barclay and I proceeded to the surgery, from where I phoned home, merely to have the message confirmed, with the addition to take plenty of thread for it was quite a big cut. Thread indeed — I'd have a word with Charlie about my suture materials. I filled a tray with needles, nylon, forceps, scissors, and all the necessities, as I thought, for suturing an ostrich's neck. What I badly omitted to take was a hammer! We arrived at the zoo, my nine-year-old assistant proudly carrying the inevitable black bag, while I carried the tray. Barclay swung the bag at the gate meaningfully, to show he was with the vet, like showing your ticket in some soccer battleground to show you are one of the combatants. Charlie was waiting for us at the ostrich pen. Since it was Sunday, all his assistants were off duty. I walked in and stopped dead. "Quite a big cut" was a conservative description. In fact at first sight it seemed to me it was all cut and no whole. Closer inspection showed that the ostrich had ripped its neck from top to bottom, exactly like a zip becoming undone. Apparently a protruding nail had been the cause. I looked at my patient in bewilderment, and probably it showed for Charlie reassured me that "all I had to watch was his feet". I glanced down; I believed him; the ostrich's feet were bigger than my size 11's, and equipped with useful looking nails on the end of each toe. I then looked up, and realised what big birds ostriches were. I had never been this close to one before and it towered above me. I had been well instructed on how to cast or otherwise restrain horses weighing a ton, bulls weighing about fifteen hundredweight, and had proved these methods reliable many times in practice, but nobody had ever told me how to restrain this bundle of feathers weighing but a fraction of my horse or bull.

"Anaesthetic" I thought, "but what?" I had never tried any form of general anaesthesia on birds before, and didn't think I ought to practise on the biggest of them. So, with more confidence than I was feeling, I announced, "I'll spray the edges of the wound with this to take some of the pain away" and proceeded to scoosh half a container of ethyl chloride on the ostrich. Now the great thing about ethyl chloride is you can see where it is for a layer of frost forms, but its drawback, as with all local anaesthetics, is that it only freezes the surface. To get deeper, I'd need to inject all round that wound, and somehow I didn't think that the best way to get acquainted with Mr Ostrich — besides I was sure I detected a definite twitch in the feet as though he was flexing the muscles preparatory to having a go. After a moment I approached the patient, whose neck looked as if it had recently been removed from a deep freeze.

"There's a good boy — good boy — good boy — atch, you brute" as a foot whistled past me. So we tried again, stroking the back, getting nearer to the neck, when to my delight the ostrich suddenly sat down.

"Now's our chance, Charlie; quick, let me have that water and disinfectant" The ostrich continued to sit, as I cleaned the wound as best I could. Then for good measure I gave him another nozzle full of ethyl chloride, stuck the needle in to begin the stitching, and in a twinkling that pen was the scene of furious action. At the first jab of the needle, the bird took off, with me after it, my junior assistant headed for the door, and Charlie ran around the pen. Since its dimensions were not large, there was a limit to where you could go, and for a time it looked as if I was chasing the ostrich, hanging grimly to my needle, and the ostrich was chasing Charlie. We went round and round in this merry fashion for some time, when lo — just as suddenly as before, the beast sat down. I think this sudden sitting movement must be a characteristic of ostriches, probably to get their heads down out of sight in the long grass when the feather hunters are spotted on the horizon! Charlie said — "I'll sit on his back and hold him down." The first part of his statement was absolutely spot on for Charlie sat on the ostrich's back, but the second part of the prediction was way out, for at the touch of my needle, the ostrich got up again, Barclay headed for the door once more and the whole mad circus act went on again, me pursuing the ostrich, hanging on by a needle while Charlie galloped merrily round on its back! Something would have to be done, but what?

"Get a sack" I suggested. Charlie obliged, that is, once he had leapt or fallen from his mount. "Now when he sits down again, put that over his head. It's just too bad if some dirt drops in the wound, but at least I'll maybe be able to creep up on him without being seen and get a start made."

In time, the ostrich did its celebrated flop, was blindfolded, and while I emptied the remains of my ethyl chloride spray on the wound, I commanded my assistant-acting-unpaid to return with the suture tray, which he did with the greatest reluctance and a murmured "Oh, Mummy, Daddy . . ." over and over again like some African incantation.

Feeling like a seamstress who had just completed a particularly long stitching stint, I inserted the last suture, packed the wound around with sulphonamide powder, and with Barclay safely out the door, whipped the sack off the head. The ostrich sat on, seemingly now at peace with the world, while Charlie and I wearily made our way from its pen.

"It should be alright, I think, but you understand I've never stitched an ostrich before, so I'll look up for a couple of days to see how the wound's healing. Meantime, Charlie, for Pete's sake get a hammer and knock that nail in so that it doesn't un-zip itself again. Come to think of it, a wee tap on the crown with a hammer might have let us get the job done more quickly. I'll remember to bring one for general anaesthetic purposes next time!"

We departed for, I felt, a well earned tea, while Barclay went happily home with two ostrich feathers and many a tale to tell. The wound healed perfectly, and the scar went unnoticed in the flabbiness of ostrich skin neck. As for Charlie, I don't believe he ever knocked that nail in, or else another sprang out, for some two years later, the creature repeated the process. I didn't see it that time; I reckoned Bernard needed to gain experience!

"We had some fun that day" chuckled Charlie, as we moved on our tour, coming next to the lion cages where resided Mary and Butch. Mary had recently had another litter of cubs.

"That makes forty-six now, a European record," said Charlie with great pride. I liked Mary, and recalled how once we had treated her for Milk fever (calcium deficiency), but thought that the strain of perpetual motherhood was now beginning to show, and maybe they should stop. They had no more cubs. We talked of a previous litter, named Shem, Ham and Japheth. I don't recall which of these sons of Noah had the abscess in his ear, but I well remember the struggle to net and treat one large lion cub. Next we passed by the black bears cage, my step quickening at that point for I knew what Charlie was going to ask and he did, "Don't you think their claws are a bit long?" I peered at them.

"No, I wouldn't say so. Bit longer maybe than in the wild but nothing to worry about."

Charlie had brought up the subject of clipping bears' claws before and I had always side-stepped it, for in these pre knock-out dart days I didn't much fancy a wrestling match with his bears, roping the legs one at a time, pulling them up to the bars, and clipping the claws. I could understand his anxiety, for he was sensitive to complaints from the public, and these every zoo attendant knows well. Charlie paused in his stride, as if divining my thoughts

"You know, I think the only reason some people come here is to find fault." That was condemnation indeed, coming from Charlie, who was the most benign of men, in my experience seldom saying anything about anyone unless it was good, and to the credit of his brother man (or person!). We paused a moment by the chimps, little thinking then that Bernard and he would spend a whole night trying to re-capture one which had escaped and point blank refused to re-enter its cage. We had come again to the main entrance gates, where, in his enclosure, a healthy, fat sea-lion was taking a cool dip. Again we paused, and memory took us back.

"Do you remember?" Charlie began. "Fine" I replied.

The sea-lion was being sick, had lost weight, was listless, and generally off colour. Since sea-lions were again an un-named species at College, I contacted Oliver Jones, the famour London Zoo vet, who tried for years to breed from the giant panda at his zoo. But if he was unsuccessful in that venture, he was successful in many others, and a mine of information for the uninformed like me.

"Has he recently lost his mate?" he at once asked when I gave him the sea-lion's symptoms. I'm sure I held the phone away from my ear and looked at it in wonderment. This man was hot stuff!

"As a matter of fact he has, but how did you guess and what's the condition?"

"Almost certainly an ulcer — peptic or possibly duodenal. I've seen it a few times here after one of our sea-lions has lost its mate. Only answer is a new mate; he's pining, anxious, typical syndrome"

I had reported the expert opinion to Charlie. That particular type of sea-lion was about £300 at the time, and Charlie, I imagine, had already over-spent on other species.

"I can't possibly afford a new mate just now. Can you try something?" So we had. We'd put the ailing creature on to vitamin B, given him the usual Bismuth, Kaolin type of white stomach mixture, and tried tastier morsels of a finer fish. In fact we gave him pretty well the standard treatment for a peptic ulcer in humans, at that time, vit B, stomach mixture, lighter diet and he'd responded, started to pick up, stopped pining, and in a short time been his usual sleek self again.

"You know" I said to Charlie, "peptic and duodenal ulcers are very common in people; as a matter of fact I had the beginnings of one myself a couple of years back. I've sometimes wondered if Oliver Jones' cure is what we need. What do you think, Charlie?"

He looked at me blankly. "How do you mean, Alex?"

"New mate was what the man said," I grinned.

He roared with laughter, slapped me on the back, said "come and have a choc-ice (I thought he was never going to offer) and sit over here."

"Over here" was a seat that gave us a most magnificent view right over

Bristacombe harbour, and away across the channel to Wales. The sea was deep, deep, blue that day, with lighter patches here and there and ever changing patterns as light clouds scurried overhead, colours I've always associated with the sea off the north Devon coast. Around us the trees were in full leaf, the scent of blossom was in the air, and the bird song of our native species as they flitted among the trees merged perfectly with the sounds coming from the variety pack behind us. We both fell silent and just let all this loveliness wash over us. Then Charlie said

"The world looks very beautiful
And full of joy to me;"

"Indeed it does, very lovely" I agreed.

"I used to play that hymn, Alex. I was a Church organist at one time."

"Well, now, Charlie, that I didn't know. So was I; or rather I should say I played a Church organ. Got me £80 a year and helped to put me through College."

"What Church would that be, now?"

"Oh, a wee country church — Church of Scotland" I said

"Mine was country too, but C of E. But Alex, when you look at a view like that, what do denominations matter. You just want to sing together, in harmony, in praise to the Almighty. You know, Alex, we can learn a lot from the animals. Look how many there are living in harmony, some of them natural enemies too. It can be done. Did you know that I had, as the Bible says, 'the lion lying down with the lamb'. They were called Leo and Persil. Word got around about them, natural enemies being great pals, of course they were both young, you understand. Anyway, I was asked to take them and any other animal to a service for animals in St Paul's, Covent Garden. Canon May took it. Went again the next year and took a monkey and Jill, an African grey parrot. She disgraced me. The Canon was a big man — weighed about eighteen stone. He had to stop for several rests going up the pulpit stairs to get his breath. When he finally made it Jill shouted "Cor!" The Canon, the verger and the congregation exploded. Later in the Service the Canon stopped to mop his brow and up pipes Jill with 'There's a pretty boy!' It was a good address about being kind to God's creatures, and what we would learn from them, but I was on edge with my wretched parrot. She kept butting in. When Canon May said 'let us consider the king of the beasts', up she pipes with 'Pretty poll'. But the Canon took it all in good part. He was a fine man, gone now."

So we sat on, seemingly reluctant to take our eyes from the view before us or shatter the peace that wrapped us round that day. I felt I would be content to live in this glorious country overlooking the Bristol Channel and tend animals there all my days, but it has been decreed otherwise. Bernard remains in practice. But there is no zoo on the hill to visit. For the zoo, with its variety pack, where Virginia McKenna filmed, where Johnny Morris and other notables visited and where tens of thousands found pleasure is no more. The view remains, enjoyed by the visitors to, and dwellers in the Holiday Centre there. But Charlie is still busy in the town park with a miniature zoo, still proving that a variety pack can co-exist, content and in harmony, in this best of all worlds entrusted to us by God.

The Monkey On My Back

SIXTEEN

We moved into Moorton's old, large, but homely Manse a month after I had preached for the Charge. It was a house that seemed to say "welcome" as soon as you crossed the threshold. Many generations of ministers had lived there, going back three hundred years to the first, who had been ejected from this very house by a dozen dragoons, on the order of the Bishop, for King Charles the Second, like his father and grandfather, was determined to be head of the Kirk of Scotland, and impose episcopacy. After all, he reasoned, he ruled by divine right . . . but Scotland's people worshipped a higher divine . . . and, so many, like Moorton's first minister, were forced from their homes and church buildings, to shelter in caves, and worship behind a dyke, with their guards posted to warn of any approaching Redcoats . . . The guards who later were to form the Cameronian Regiment. I prowled around the house, and with my love of history, felt a tremendous privilege to be in this place, so steeped in the lore of the ages. I wondered in which room the minister, with amazing courtesy and forgiveness, had treated his captors to a meal, and prayed for them . . . amazing grace indeed!

The last painters and plumbers had moved out, the furniture was in place, the boys had surveyed the passing scene already from the branches of every one of the fifty climbable trees in the garden, trees dotted still with the remains of rooks' nests. I had walked round and round the acre of ground, or rather wilderness, and tried to picture it laid out in strawberry beds, vegetable plots, and rose gardens, just as it had been, we understood, forty years before. A series of ministers, who, though excellent in other respects, had clearly not been gardeners, had allowed nature to take over, and nature had, with samples of every known weed. All that remained of the fine walled garden was the wall . . . and a patch of rhubarb. But, for our coming, farmers had already been in, ploughed the whole garden up, and cut the grass, my love of gardens, like so much else, having somehow filtered through the grapevine. I should have been content. After three years of preparation, I should have been glad that I had reached the culmination of it all, that in one day's time I would be ordained, and begin this new life for which I'd been trained. The kids were thrilled by it all, Janet loved her kitchen, we were well satisfied with our new home, and had already received so much kindness. I should have been very pleased by it all, but I was wretched. I still had the monkey on my back. He had been there since ever I'd left Devon.

That monkey had clung to me, chattered in my ear, and generally made life troublesome for me every single day since I'd given up practice. Many times he'd told me I was a fool. A herd of cattle in a field on a winter morning, their breath rising in clouds in the frosty air — and I was back calving cows or treating milk fevers and a host of other conditions, out in the open air. Even more nostalgic was each spring with the shrill call of lambs and the deeper bleat of the ewes in many a field, and my fingers would start to itch, for perhaps above all I'd loved the lambing season, never ceasing to marvel at the annual miracle of new life, and the unfading wonder of delivering a lamb, saving a life, and seeing a contented mother nuzzle her lamb, and how, on its shaky legs, with unerring, inborn accuracy, the lamb would head straight for food. Driving past fields of lambs was the hardest thing of all, but even a cat curled up on a sunlit window ledge, or a couple of dogs romping in a park, stirred the memory. Animals I loved, treating them had been not only my livelihood, but my life, and fool that I was, I'd given it up! Idiot, the monkey continually chattered in my ear! Then there was the financial side. After years of building, the Practice was really taking off, and when I could look forward to taking on another one or two colleagues, being the senior, and being comfortably off, I'd given it up. Madman! said the monkey. I couldn't argue about it. From a secure future with our own house, a spare car for my wife, and a considerable income, I was going into a "tied" house, an uncertain life, for congregations could be fickle and easily tire of their minister, all for a low salary for which most churches expected the wife to serve as well as her husband. What had I done! By every human standard the whole thing was sheer lunacy, and my decision would result in years to come in my family being denied many things they would otherwise have had.

Again, the monkey whispered "You are throwing away five hard years of study in a course infinitely more difficult than theology, years for which your parents sacrificed much to put you through." That too, was undeniable. My mother had kept hens, ducks, geese, turkeys — sold eggs — and every Christmas, fowls for the table, when the whole family, and two old friends would sit around in a cold outhouse, the air thick with feathers and down, as we plucked hundreds of birds, all to educate my brothers and I. Now, said the monkey, that sacrifice has all been in vain. I had thrown it all away for a vet, medical or dentistry course was not equivalent, said the University, to an M.A. of half the length of the vet course, so at the end of the Divinity training, despite doing a B.D. course, there was nothing awarded, and one was doomed to remain an oddity, a freak, a minister with no apparent ministerial qualifications, forever a vet in the vestry! So the monkey had nagged at me day after day. Now, in these last days, the monkey had changed species, had grown horns and a forked tail, and the demon doubt was seen in his true colours, and having a real go at me, as I sat in the study, head in hands.

"If you were a son of mine, I'd advise you against this change," said old farmer Conibear, and he was a wise man. "You're a passable preacher but you're a good vet."

"How can you possibly leave sunny Devon and its kind folk, and go back to cold, wet Scotland," another had asked, and added "you'll live to regret this."

"You'll get more bites and scratches from people than ever my old cat gave you," said Miss Inglewood, and very likely this would be so.

So blow after blow thudded in. I was on the ropes, punch drunk, and old Nick was fairly hammering in the uppercuts, straight lefts, and thumps to the solar plexus. But was it really old Nick? Was it not just plain common sense? Humanly speaking — from a family or financial point of view, there was no possible way I could justify this daftness. My actions hadn't been rational. Why had I done it then? Was it some kind of wish fulfilment of my father, who had wanted to be a minister, and was a far more worthy man than I was? It had just not been possible for him, for his mother had died when he was young, he was the youngest of a fairly large family, there were no university grants, and in the post war years of depression, wages had been low. There was no way he could realise his wish — so he had taken any job he could get, and become a railwayman. Moreover, he would never even see his eldest son as a minister, for he had been snatched away in his fifties, just before my course commenced. I was far from clear about all the why's and wherefore's of my move. In the cold light of day they didn't seem to make much sense, nor could they be explained to others. I just knew, that willy-nilly, I seemed to have been gradually propelled along this path. Kenneth, as a lay preacher, had inveigled me into it, and this had grown and increased till I was preaching every second Sunday in one or other of Devon's many little Methodist, Congregational or Baptist Chapels. I'd always been keen on youngsters, and involved in different kinds of youth work. I had been taught to believe, and proved to my own satisfaction that it was true, that life's surest foundation was a sound Christian faith.

"But why did you become a minister?" Francis Gay of the *Sunday Post* had asked me on the phone. How could you cram all the forces at work, the issues involved, into a short, snappy answer on a telephone, to an unknown voice at the other end? I'd answered something like this:—

"In North Devon, with its many small farms, the vet was treated very much like the family doctor, so you came to know your clients well, not just as clients, but in many cases, as friends. Your advice was asked on all kinds of things, quite apart from their animals. As time went by, I came to see in this life there are really only two kinds of people — not Scots and English; rich or poor; Labour or Conservative; black or white, but those who had this strange, intangible thing we call faith, and those who hadn't. The former might not be in Church every Sunday, but it seemed to me, as an outsider looking in, that this faith was very real, something that worked, an anchor that held them in life's storms. Those without it appeared to me to be poor in comparison, and not only had no anchor, but had missed the boat! So eventually, I, who never in my life had thought of becoming, or wanted to become a minister, eventually felt that this 'faith thing' worked, and that I should try to share it with others." That statement, I suppose, about summed it up. It had been a call, like Masefield's *Sea Fever*, "A wild call, a clear call, that may not be denied." I had repeatedly, over several years, heard this voice say, "This is the way; walk ye in it."

I had felt that my conscience would never let me rest again unless I at least tried the door, so I had written to Tom Allan, just about the best known minister in Scotland at the time, asking his advice, and how a vet went about becoming a minister. Busy man though he was, he'd replied, and passed my request to the powers that be, and secretly hoping that the doors wouldn't open or that I would be classed unsuitable, I'd gone on step by step. The Old Testament had a record of men who had been reluctant prophets, who'd been called against their wish, almost. I was no prophet, but I understood now how they had felt, for one by one the doors opened before me. I was accepted, and felt as if I'd been taken by the scruff of the neck and thrust into this whole thing. We'd had various signs . . . at any rate they were to us . . . along the way, directing us on. I say "we", for from the beginning it was a joint venture. It had to be, and I recalled how I had come home from surgery one evening, feeling I must really broach the question of giving up the Practice to Janet, and before I could speak she'd said, "I think, my dear, it's time you were seriously thinking of the ministry!" I'd gasped! Was this telepathy, ESP, or was it something higher? As for sacrifice, Janet had always emphasised that she'd married Alexander Cameron, not a vet or a minister — but the man — bless her!

So I wrestled in my study that day. The voice whispered, "There's still time to turn back!"

If I'd been a swearing man, I would have said "Go to hell!", and even if arguably, this might not have been accurate geographically, it would certainly have been scriptural and sound theologically concerning the wretched creature on my back. I just groaned aloud, and held my drooping head.

"Now, now" came the voice in soft, soothing tones. "Stop worrying and fussing. You're just being prudent. You can do far more for the Christian cause as a layman than in a dog collar. What's happened is simply the concern any person brought up in a good devout Christian home would have for helping others, and telling others about your God, well . . . you've just let it go to your head a bit. Besides, as a vet you would have more money to give away to charities, churches and missions. Pull out now!"

The arguments were subtle — the battle hard — but Gethsemane cannot be avoided. Tomorrow night one of the questions at ordination would be "Are not zeal for the glory of God, love for the Lord Jesus Christ, and a desire for the salvation of men, so far as you know your own heart, your great motives and chief inducements to enter into the office of the Holy Ministry?" No man can answer that without a clutch at the throat, and great heart searching. It's a question that cannot be ducked or glossed over.

So, when the family were in bed, and the noises of the world were hushed, like King George VI on the night before his Coronation slipping into Westminster Abbey to be alone, I went quickly and alone into Moorton's lovely old Kirk, and there in the silence faced up to that question. All around me were the influences of the past. The very hush of that place seemed to carry an echo of many voices, of men and women to whom this house of prayer was the dearest spot on earth. The soil of this parish, more than any other in Scotland, had been stained by the blood of the martyrs for whom zeal for the glory of God had been life's chief end. In the quietness of that darkening building, which tomorrow would ring with songs of praise, came to me, it seemed, whispers of the past, from those for whom love for Christ, and concern for their fellows, had indeed been the chief motives for entering the ministry. I thought of all they had given up, security, family life, even life itself in some cases . . . and then I thought of One who had given up everything, coming from Heaven's glory to Earth's gloom, out of His vast love. By comparison, I was not giving up anything, and there, in the deepening hush of that ancient Church, the monkey at last jumped off my back – the devilish taunts ceased, at least for a time.

I knew I was no great shakes. I was certainly no plaster saint, and aware of a fair old number of faults and failings, but I believed that truly it was love for Him, for others, and zeal for God's glory that had brought me here. Others might understandably laugh, or criticise. I would doubtless falter many times still, but in that precious moment I knew I was where He wanted me to be. That meant everything, and on the following night, in an atmosphere that was very special, and in a service that was unforgettable, the people of Moorton and I plighted our troth to one another and to God. If I had now, as the lovely old phrase put it, "the care of souls", I had also around me many souls that cared. The marriage was complete. The monkey was shut up in his cage, at least for a while!

"Welcome"

SEVENTEEN

"I regret to have to tell you that your new minister is not the man you think he is. In fact he has a past — quite a past — he's been in trouble with the police."

The congregation was silenced. There were gasps here and there and the looks we had been getting all evening hardened into stares. What was this? On the platform Jimmy licked his lips. He was enjoying himself in anticipation of further revelations. Jimmy Duncanson and I had gone through Trinity College together, and since he had been in agriculture, there was a common bond between us. We were more or less on the same theological wavelength; we were both married with a family; we normally sat together at lectures and had endured many a weary hour side by side both doodling on our note-pads when the lectures were especially dry . . . and now the blighter was spilling the beans on his closest friend!

"Yes — with the police" he repeated. "John Stevens, your minister and I were driving along Bath Street one afternoon when we saw these three big fellows laying into one wee fellow. The odds didn't seem fair, so we stopped the car with a screech, and leaped out. The fight was taking place on the steps leading up to a terrace house where the big fellows had the wee chap down. Alec was first up the steps and wondering which big fellow to tackle, with us close behind him, when one of the big men said,

"Police! Dial 999 for help and give us a hand" We stood and stared, not quite sure what to do. The wee man was fighting like mad, throwing the big fellows about, but before we could join in the battle, a police car came roaring up, out piled some bobbies, and eventually the little chap was handcuffed. It seems he was a wanted criminal, actually had a gun on him, and the three policemen, off duty and in plain clothes, had recognised him, tackled him . . . and we had been going to help a criminal!"

The company in the Church Hall relaxed. Their new man was maybe alright after all . . . as far as the police were concerned anyway.

The welcome social was in full swing. The tables had been groaning under their weight of food, with the kind of spread that only a country congregation supplies . . . scones, pancakes, sausage rolls, sandwiches and cakes of every conceivable variety. Tables were arranged all round the hall, and on the platform was the top table, where the minister and his wife, their friends and all the various speakers were seated. Our four little sons were tucked up in bed, cared for by a baby-sitter, but we were on public view, being eyed, in kindly fashion, of course, by everyone in the hall. What would this new man be like? A vet . . . well, at least he was different . . . but could a vet make a minister? Janet was undergoing equal scrutiny, for a minister's wife was at least as important as her man. We were trying to be on our best behaviour, but I had already disgraced myself. In front of me was a plate of huge meringues, I had picked one up, bitten into it, and it had more or less exploded on my face, covering me from ear to ear in a sticky mess . . . a plastered minister!

The night before in all the solemnity of a Presbyterian Ordination, I had taken my vows in the hush of Moorton's lovely old Kirk . . . a service whose atmosphere lives with me to this day. But the following night was for socialising, for presentations to various people who had helped during the short vacancy, and for a mutual "getting to know you" by minister, his lady, and the congregation of Moorton. It was also a time for revelations about the Camerons by their friends, and words of advice fron senior colleagues.

"You will find your new minister a grand preacher" (praise I certainly didn't deserve) said Revd Andrew Eastham, the Interim Moderator or acting minister during the vacancy.

"He's up to date, modern, but not too way out, not like the man who was always trying new gimmicks to get his congregation's attention. One Sunday he instructed the Beadle to be up in the Church loft at the sermon, and when the text was announced, to throw down one of the pigeons which roosted there. The preacher announced his text: 'Oh for the wings of a dove and I would fly away and be at rest!' . . . but nothing happened. So he repeated it, twice, the second time bellowing out the words. At last the trapdoor opened and the Beadle's face appeared.

'Minister!' he shouted, "the cat's been up and ate the doos! Wull I throw doon the cat' " (Loud laughter).

Andrew went on, "He's not a blood and thunder preacher either, like the man who every week pounded the backboard and gave his people what for. One Sunday he was preaching on the Day of Judgement: 'There shall be wailing and gnashing of teeth,' he thundered, when from the back seat there piped up a man without a tooth in his head.

'Fit happens tae them wi nae teef?' he enquired.

The minister glared, then announced

'Teeth will be provided!'"

(More laughter as the company pictured rows of teeth sitting in jars just waiting to be gnashed).

Then Rev Andrew paid a lovely tribute to my father and mother who had latterly been members of his Church. I was glad of his words, for I knew this was a hard night for my widowed mother. Before the Social, she had said, with tears in her eyes, "If only father could have been here. He would have been so proud."

Andrew gave place to Revd George Meek, after a duet by the two sisters Agnes and Mary Black. George had helped during the vacany too, and he spoke up and said how glad he was that the new minister had a young family, for there was nothing like a family for making a man humble and keeping his feet on the ground, and he went on to tell of a certain family who were sitting in the Manse pew one Sunday when, to his horror, the minister noticed one of his boys plunking paper pellets at the congregation in the middle of the sermon. The Manse pew was the front row of the gallery, so he had a good view, had the boy, of most of the congregation. In full flow the minister stopped his oration and glared at his son. The wee fellow was not one whit abashed, but merely waved at his Dad in the pulpit and called out "That's alright Dad! You go on preaching and I'll go on wakening them up."

(More laughter and glances at the minister)

"But," went on George, "remember your minister is also a husband and father. He has to give time to his family, and don't expect Mrs Cameron to be at everybody's beck and call all the time. She will do her part, have no fear, but she has her hands full with four wee laddies. Give them time to settle in."

I was very glad of George's words, for in the few brief days we had been in the Manse, Janet had already been asked to be President of The Woman's Guild, President of the Mothers' Circle, and take over as Girl Guide

Captain. It seemed the Mothers' Circle were in dire straits for "the President has a wee boy now, and you can't expect her to carry on!" I had decided to put my foot down right at the start, and pointed out that my wife had *four* wee boys to look after, that she would do her share in church life, but one organisation at a time. I don't know if I was too popular, but I was determined to clarify things right from the beginning, and hit this curious notion that many folks have that because she is the Lady of the Manse, it is somehow her duty to do everything that is asked of her.

George then went on to give me some advice. "Despite what some folks think about ministers only working on a Sunday, you will find the ministry every bit as demanding as your vet life. You must learn to take a day off . . . go fishing, or take up golf. That's a good way to get you out, away from your parish, and get rid of a lot of frustration. You will no doubt find one of your elders who will take you with him to a golf course. When I was a young minister, I used to play with my senior elder, who was almost a scratch golfer. I was just a beginner, and as the elder won every hole, I got more and more discouraged and embarrassed. To cheer me up with his way of it, the old man said to me 'Never mind, Mr Meek, one day you will have the job burying of me'

That was no help, for I pointed out to him that even then it would be his hole."

George paused to let the laughter die down, then went on

"Mind you, you've got to be careful golf doesn't get a hold on you. A certain minister's Manse was right beside a fine golf course, he was a keen golfer, and one glorious summer Sunday, he was up early, and went out to have a look at the course. It was deserted, and he was sorely tempted to have a few holes before anybody was about. He was tempted and he fell! It so happened two angels were watching the scene, one a new recruit, the other an old, experienced angel. The young angel was shocked.

'Look at that' he said, 'a minister playing on the Lord's day. You'll have to punish him.'

'I will' said the venerable seraph.

The minister teed up at a short hole, swung the club sweetly, the ball soared in a perfect arc; landed on the green, bounced twice and went in the hole. A hole in one! He was overjoyed. He'd never had an ace before. The young angel was puzzled.

'I thought you were going to punish him?' he queried. The old angel smiled a sweet smile and replied,

'I have! He'll never be able to tell a soul about it'"

(More laughter... the company was thoroughly relaxed now.)

So the evening wore on with song and story, presentations to various people and to us. I thought, as I looked out at the assembled vast throng, I had seldom seen a happier bunch of people, and thought also what a lot of nonsense was talked about Kirk functions being wet, wishy washy, goody goody, drab, boring affairs. I had listened to some fine speeches ... sure, some of the jokes were old, but all were good and wholesome ... I had enjoyed some excellent singing and music ... and as I looked out from the platform at a host of happy, smiling faces of young and old, I felt a warm glow inside me.

These were my people. This was my little flock. No doubt there would be difficulties from time to time, perhaps criticism at times, but that night there had been a resounding "welcome" from one and all. We were wedded together, one family in the service of God and His Church. That strange creature, a vet in the vestry, had been accepted.

A World Of Their Own

EIGHTEEN

I sat at my desk in the Manse, remembering my days as a vet. I had so many memories.

"Is it alright for you, John, if I pick you up about seven tonight, and you can maybe take me round some of your district?" I asked on the phone one morning.

"Fine, man" replied John. He had been in farming and we had mutual acquaintances so there was no reticence or reserve between us as can exist, indeed often has to exist, between a minister and his people, for a variety of good reasons. From past knowledge, John and I were free and easy together. I was gradually getting to know my flock, being conducted by each elder and introduced to his complement of maybe twenty to twenty-five families. John was elder in the Waterfoot area of Moorton.

"I'll take you to so and so"— John reeled off a few names, "and we'll end at Low Blackpark. Man, be prepared for a shock; you never saw anything like that. They live in a world of their own out there, prehistoric!" John rang off, chuckling.

"A world of their own, prehistoric" The description had a familiar ring about it. My mind went back ten years as I sat at my desk musing. Ken had used that very description when first he sent me to the Tucker's farm at Keystones in a fold of the north Devon hills.

"Expect anything, and be ready for anything," he said. It sounded intriguing, even slightly sinister.

I duly arrived at Keystones, after driving down a rough track which vaguely meandered across a few fields. I was a bit late, which I didn't like for a first visit but COD 330, my ancient Morris Van had played up again that morning. New cars were virtually unobtainable in these post war years, and old ones that were only fit for pensioning off were still in use, and commanding high prices. COD had been paid Cash on Delivery alright, but it lived up to its title in other ways too. It was a proper COD indeed! That morning it had refused to budge; I had swung the starting handle till my hands were raw, and finally, not for the first time, had to be towed to get her started, hence the delay. I thought as I approached it that the farm had a pleasant enough setting, sitting as it did in the cleft of a hill overlooking the blue waters of the Bristol Channel far below. It would be exposed in winter, no doubt, but this was a fine spring morning of soft winds and scudding clouds. The good earth was just having its last short snooze before awakening in the glory of spring's new life. There weren't many buildings about the farm, and the dwelling house looked very bleak and bare with its slate covered exterior. No neat gardens and palatial barns, silos and all the rest that there had been in my native Ayrshire, but I had got used to this by now in Devon.

I noticed as I pulled up, conveniently leaving "Coddy" on a hill for an easy start that there were five ponies tied to a rail and five characters lounging on the wall beside them. I couldn't spot John Wayne among them, but otherwise it was a perfect "Western" set. I looked carefully and could not spot any guns, but I had been warned to expect anything, so you never knew. After all this was the family to which Basil belonged, a cousin of the present lot. Everybody knew Basil. He was none too clean, generally had a drip at the end of his nose, and was only ninety per cent or maybe less, as the local saying had it. He attended a tiny independent Chapel near one of the other Tucker farms, and on one occasion was out with the pastor for a day's shooting. Suddenly Basil's twelve-bore blasted off, the shot so "adjacent" to his companion that he leapt heavenwards like a startled grouse.

"What — what did you do that for, Basil?" he demanded. Basil didn't believe in using two words if one would do, and merely grunted "magpie — bad luck!"

"But your shot wasn't anywhere near it" said the petrified parson.

"No matter; fire anywhere breaks the bad luck" explained Basil patiently.

"Well, look here, don't do that again for you nearly blew me away."

I knew Basil quite well. He was a friendly soul, but was the plaything of anyone who wanted a laugh on the receiving end of much hurtful hilarity, the butt of many a 100 per cent, consciously superior mind. He had a grasp of life's basic realities and was happy with what he had. Despite the innate superstition of many country folk he had still a real piety, a sincere, if simple faith, and a heart of love for all mankind as big as his large, craggy frame. I also knew his cousin Donald who was a different kettle of fish, a rogue of the first degree who would have cheated his granny, and who did cheat many, but generally managed to steer clear of the law. He was, physically, all angles; a lean individual with sloping shoulders and long arms and a nose and chin which seemed almost to meet. He never smiled, and communicated with snorts, grunts and sly looks. He kept sheep, anybody's he could annexe, and when his flock was not grazing on the sides of the road, it was in somebody else's fields, for Donald was sorely troubled with bad fences round his own fields, and never had time to mend the gaps, for he had other nefarious pursuits which kept him busy. Thus he eked out a farily comfortable existence with a life of busy idleness. Donald had a collie dog which followed him everywhere, a wall eyed creature which he kicked, beat and continually abused, and yet which would have given its life for this unworthy object.

But Basil and Donald were not in the welcome committee of five whom I took to be the sons of old farmer Tucker, gathered here for the occasion at the parent farm of Keystones. They came from the other Tucker strongholds of Brindacott, Buttersby and a few others, which were farmed by the various sons, all bachelors, and who had as their cooks and housekeepers their sisters. There seemed to be a happy haphazardness about their methods, for I was to discover you never quite knew which son would be where, nor which sister would be the resident cook for that period. As I walked down the little hill towards the reception committee, I became aware of five feminine forms gathered in the porch of the farmhouse, eager, it seemed, to catch a glimpse of the new "vetinary". I smiled towards them and gave them a hearty "good morning", whereupon they disappeared like rabbits down a burrow. I wondered if I had sprouted horns since morning or if they were all bereft of the gift of speech, but it transpired they were all so shy, retiring and modest beyond belief, that a strange man addressing them before they had been properly introduced was enough to send them scuttling for safety. I tried the men, shouting as I approached, "Good morning! Sorry I'm a bit late but the old car wouldn't start."

"Aar!" they responded, continuing to prop up the wall.

I sidled up to my five cowpunchers very deliberately, in my size eleven wellington boots, I had my own "colts" plainly visible, belted over my long black waterproof coat and carried high on the hips for instant action, each gun loaded with twenty shots — in one Avian Tuberculin and in the other Mammalian. I had come to do the annual Tuberculin Test.

"I'm Mr Cameron, the new Vet; you know; the Major's partner"

"Us knows" grunted one, while they continued to stare in an off hand fashion.

There followed a long pause. The conversation was distinctly languishing, so I ventured "Nice day?"

"Aar!" said the previous speaker, evidently the talkative Tucker.

"Ar — I mean er, can we make a start? We've quite a few beasts to do"

"Reckon us'd better wait till vather comes" said the speaker of the house. Now I'm by nature a friendly soul, and what with females disappearing as soon as I hove in sight, and four males who had yet to open their mouths but who continued to scrutinise me closely, I found it all a bit un-nerving. I felt it only wanted Basil to appear waving a gun to send me scuttling for the car, but I tried again.

"I don't think we've met; I'm Cameron — " I was interrupted.

"So ee jus zaid" confirmed the spokesman. He was sharp!

"Yes, but I haven't met any of you. Who's the oldest?"

The brother who talked was about seventeen, and he introduced himself as Kingsley, and he nodded to the others, who were respectively Ivor, Bernard, Cyril and baby Arthur, aged about fourteen.

"Do ee like it here en?" asked Kingsley, providing a positive rush of conversation. "Love it" I said.

"Aar" they nodded, with the obvious assumption that nobody could fail to like it. "Hyer comes vather now; us'll get started." nodded Kingsley to the old man slowly climbing the hill towards us. I noticed the loungers pulled themselves erect at the advent of father. I shook hands with the old boy who gave a few "aah; aars" in my general direction, which I took to mean welcome. "Vather" had only one eye, but I thought it was not unfriendly, with maybe even a twinkle in its blue depths.

"Where do ee want to start then?" asked Kingsley

"What about the cows, then you can let them out for a bite. I've kept them long enough with being late"

"Oh, no matter; us had nothin' much to do, like" which I was to find was an excellent summary of the Tucker philosophy. They would have been absolutely at home with a West Highland crofter for whom "there was always tomorrow", but who's to say that their outlook on life was not the most comfortable?

So we started with the cows, tied up in the murky dark shippen or byre. I clipped the neck hair, injected the tuberculin, while Arthur was despatched for a torch, a rag and some meths so that we could clean the ears of the beasts and read the numbers tattoed there. I soon found that Ivor, the oldest and quietest, was also the most responsible, but even so, on this occasion I thought I had better mark up the book myself. The cattle were a scrubby lot, badly wintered, but having them tethered to a stanchion was half the battle and they were soon done and turned loose. I noticed that they took their time on the way to the bite of pasture, in keeping with the leisurely outlook of their owners.

"Now where?" I asked.

"The bull, I reckon" said Kingsley. I was conscious in the casual way he said it, and in the eager looks young Arthur was darting at me — he had not learned to present a deadpan countenance on every occasion yet — that this was a test case for the new vet. Now I am not braver than the next man, and have my own particular fears and phobias, but fear of bulls was not one of them. Respect for them, yes; care in handling, by all means, but not fear. Besides, having dealt with Ayrshire bulls, the most treacherous of any breed, I had found the Ruby Reds as the North Devon breed was called locally, docile big creatures up till now.

"One of you come in with me, and stand behind me till I inject him, then when I grab his ring, get that ear number."

So, accompanied by Kingsley, I braved the bull in his loose box, gently rubbed his back, and then with a couple of quick jabs had the tuberculin in his neck. I was conscious when I rejoined the others that I had clearly passed some kind of test. It was only later, much later, that I learned my nice quiet beast had more than once had a go at a Tucker, and generally they approached him with pitchforks at the ready.

"Where now?" I asked.

"The yiffers and steers, us reckons" said Cyril, finding tongue.

I was conducted to a smallish shed, which housed the yiffers and steers. Never up to that point in time had I seen anything like it — a world of their own indeed, for in that confined space some thirty-five to forty young beasts were milling around, treading in what had once been straw bedding, but was now many feet deep, indeed half way up to the roof. To stand erect in places was for me impossible. There was no ring, stanchion, crush or any other means of restraint such as all the best veterinary books had described. But the Tuckers had their method, and it was sheer mayhem. I noticed "vather" wisely retire outside, and all of a sudden we were at a rodeo. Keystones Farm, I thought, was well named, for never outside the silver screen had I seen anything quite so like the Keystone Cops, as followed now. Here we were right back to the slapstick, custard pie days, only when I opened my mouth to speak, what hit me slap on the face was anything but custard. This had hurtled in my direction as a direct result of Kingsley with a "Ya-hoo" leaping on to a Yiffer — or it might have been a steer's back. It was impossible to determine, for the only light in the place came from two slits in the wall. It was true, there was a large hole for a window, but this was completely boarded over, and once a year, when these beasts were turned out to graze, the board came down, and the residual dung forked out into the yard. Again I thought of my veterinary hygiene books and how they had emphasised the need of proper ventilation extolling louvre windows and the like. I stood there, my face covered in mud of a particularly repugnant flavour, and watched as Kinglsey rode his animal round and round till it collapsed under him. That was the signal for me to dash in, guns at the ready. The animal was then marked with a piece of marking crayon — a keel mark — to show it had been done. To find out ear numbers was hopeless; that would have to wait for three days hence, when if any reactors showed, we would be compelled to scrub through layers of dirt to find the tattoo.

Soon the shed was a maelstrom of steaming, sweating beasts, flying dollops of dung, as the Tucker boys made whoopee and rode their beasts to a standstill. It was at this point that I discovered they could in fact all speak, and that Arthur, presumably to show his manhood, had learned an oath or two. So the battle progressed. Perhaps you have, like me, watched these saloon fights without which no good western epic is complete, and wondered how the contenders could pick themselves up again and again, and head back into the mêlée. I saw it all happen that day, until, covered in mud from head to toe, and with rivers of sweat coursing down my back, I decided to join in the fun. As a yiffer/steer passed me at a trot, I grabbed hold of it, one hand on a horn, other hand grasping nostrils, and with a heave, as I had often seen my old boss in Scotland do, I threw it to the ground, put a knee on its jaw and jabbed in approximately the approved areas — when lo, there was a great calm. It was just as if in the middle of the aforementioned saloon fight, somebody had suddenly said "Whoa there", or the James brothers had walked in, and everybody paused, chairs ready to crash on an opponents skull, fist drawn back for the right uppercut, or bottle about to be hurtled at the large mirror which all good saloons seem to require — presumably so that a bottle can be thrown at them. It was something like that, and I was conscious the whooping had ceased and I was being closely scrutinised by five pairs of eyes.

"Darn me, but oi nivver saw that done before" said Kingsley. "How was it you did it?" So I showed them again, picking the smallest animal I could see, and in that moment I knew I was accepted as an equal, a true, fully paid up member of the Tucker brotherhood. From henceforward over the years our relationship was grand. I could say anything to them, and they would take it, and by golly they said plenty to me in return.

I don't know how long it took me to test these few bullocks — a whole morning easily, when normally, with animals properly housed and restrained I would reckon to get through around two hundred. I only know that eventually the torture was over, and I fought my way through the steaming mass of bodies, human and bovine, all covered in dung, ninety per cent proof, and reached fresh air and father, who surveyed us as we came out with a few expressive "aars and uurs" I was absolutely limp and glad to avail myself of the offer of a wash in the house, having first divested myself of my black, now greenish brown coat, and scrubbed my wellingtons. Various maidens fled before me as I was conducted into the kitchen, where with a dollop of hard soap and cold water I did my best to look human again. As I was clearing the soap from my eyes, I became aware of a large form standing in front of me, proferring me a jam jar containing some of Devon's famed clotted cream. Having seen the state of hygiene that prevailed in the Tucker establishment, I was a bit doubtful about taking it, at least until I was sure the cows were T.B. free. But I could hardly refuse, so took it in the spirit with which it was offered — and lived to tell this tale! I also looked with great interest at the figure in front of me, Mrs Tucker, she was a large, raw boned woman whom you could hardly now call beautiful, yet she undoubtedly had a presence, a bearing, and I had no doubt that her will was law at Keystones and beyond in the other Tucker outposts, an influence and power that was all the more real because it did not seem to require enforcing; it was just somehow accepted. If father was respected, mother, I was sure, was loved.

That was my first contact with this family who lived in a world of their own. There were to be many others. I thought of some of them as I sat at my desk remembering. I remembered a number of gymkhanas, where I was honorary vet in attendance. Well did I recall how the landed gentry would come from miles around, plus the horsey types who did the circuits, of how they had to pass under my measuring rod to be eligible for the under fourteen hands class, and how young ladies whose accents you could cut with a knife, you know, would stretch out ponies that were patently too big, to try to squeeze them in, and of the unladylike retorts I received when I excluded them. I particularly remember Kingsley Tucker on an old grey mare, a working pony, riding bareback over the jumps, and beating the young Harvey Smiths and David Broomes of the day. He was a magnificent horseman, and just seemed part of his mount as they flowed over the fences. I recalled too how a postman friend had gone one cold winter day to deliver the Keystones mail, and had been astonished to find the front door open, and a tree trunk sticking out. He followed it in over the stone floor of the living room, and found to his astonishment that the other end of the tree was actually blazing in the huge old fireplace, and every so often, some muscular Tuckers, would slide it in a bit further, all to save them sawing it up. I dare say they managed to get the door shut by night. The odd thing was that they seemed to prosper. They never seemed in a hurry, but, apart from gymkhanas locally, they had little interest outside their work. I don't know if the sons were paid wages or simply given their keep, but "vor zertain zure" they made money, acquired more land, and even bought a town house, where the young ones occasionally lived, and had to acquire two television sets, for they could seldom agree on which programme to watch. For a time they broke out into a positive rash of spending, and reminded me of story currently going the rounds of a farmer who came in from Exmoor and plonked a biscuit tin on the bank counter, instructing the teller to check it, for there was £1000 there. The teller unfolded the crumpled mass, laboriously ploughed his way through it and said "£999, sir." The farmer maintained there was £1000 and insisted it be recounted. Still it came to £999, whereupon the farmer's wife said "Dang me, Erb, us's brought the wrong tin." Thus were the Tuckers, wild, untameable, unpredictable, rough and ready, yet intensely loyal to their friends, sympathetic to any friend in need. I suppose that they were the stuff that the old pioneering families were made of, and they had the same piety and godliness, despite their rough ways. This was not a natural thing for them, but acquired from mother, who, quite late in life had found a real, personal faith, an anchor to hold her in life's storms, and longed that each of her children should find that same sure anchorage. If ever there was an example of the power of a mother's influence and a mother's prayers, it was demonstrated here. Orthodox Christians they could never be, and being Tuckers, some favoured the Baptist Church, others the Church of England, a few the Plymouth Brethren, and one or two a little independent mission right on the crown of a windswept plateau, where he who had almost met an untimely demise from Basil's shotgun, exerted a considerable ministry among these pioneering families of the wild uplands. I knew them well; I remember them with considerable affection, even though their world was not mine, but a world of their own.

As I picked up John my elder, I wondered what surprises awaited me in "prehistoric" Blackpark. After several calls at other homes, we eventually turned the car up the farm road to the two Blackparks, the first of which was our objective. I like to know a bit about the folks I am going to visit, if possible, but beyond telling me that there were two brothers Baird, Davie in his eighties and John a mere stripling of seventy odd, that they resisted change, holding out against milking machines for cattle for years on the grounds that if the Almighty had intended beasts to be milked by machine, He would have seen fit to provide tubes on the teats, and that only that year had John finally, to keep the peace with his son and maybe to provide an interest to keep him out of trouble for he was "a wild loon", allowed a tractor on the place.

"They will like be sitting one on each side of the fire, puffing their pipes and going 'poop, poop' (here John imitated a spitting sound and action). Man, it's amazing the distance they can get. They'll maybe have a bottle between them too, sitting on the table. Have a look at one of its legs; it's gey near scratched richt through wi' the cats."

The car swung into the yard, a typical old style Ayrshire steading with the house forming one end and the farm buildings two sides of a square, of which the entrance was the final part.

"Look in there" said John, clutching my sleeve. "Leave your lights on?"

I obeyed and beheld a most ancient Morris with canvas hood, and beside it a modern, large Rover. On both hens were roosting.

"John drove that old car for near thirty years," I was informed. "He would just come out, chase the hens oot, gie the seat a bit dicht wi' his sleeve, an' away to the market. He's only had the Rover about a year an' he's been in the ditch wi' it three times already, blind drunk, but aye blaming it on this new fangled machine. I think the auld car kent its way hame by itsel'."

This then was my background knowledge of the Baird brothers, who as John the elder had predicted were indeed sitting on either side of the fire, with their feet up, and their pipes drawing nicely. I only got one glimpse of their amazing prowess as they spat towards the fire, but on the strength of that one demonstration, I should say, Davie, the older brother, was the champion, after all he'd been longer at it! John introduced me as the new minister, and they received me with courtesy and gravity, ushering me to a chair. All the chairs were ancient straight back wooden models. I glanced surreptitiously around me, and John Baird's eyes spotted mine alighting on the table.

"My grandfather made that" he announced, and sure enough there was one leg very much thinner than the rest, with a cat even at that moment sharpening its claws on it. The room was bare, carpetless, with, of course a stone floor. The fireplace was ancient, enormous, like many I had seen in Devon when first I went there. Beside the fireplace sat a huge, three-legged pot, a bit like a witch's cauldron, I imagined, and various other iron kettles and pots, which when required were hung on the hooks or "swees" over the fire. John had been known to bemoan the fact that you couldn't buy three-legged pots any more and it was hard to get a blacksmith to repair one. The only other items of furniture or equipment in this large bare room, were a large dresser, with plates arranged along it in approved ancient fashion, and a very old sink. All this was taken in while the brothers Baird were taking me in. John was officially a Church member, appeared generally at "the sacrament", and was "very generous, putting £5 in the plate", an elder had informed me. Davie had no Church connection, but in that rural parish, I tried to visit everybody, regardless of persuasion or none. We were one community, and the Church in a very real way was at the heart of it.

I noticed that Davie had been reading a book, while John had the *Glasgow Herald* stretched out around him — no gutter press for them! I was just wondering where to begin when John took the first of me and asked, "What do you think of Free Trade?"

I was astounded, and I'm sure showed it. What I thought about it was nil, for I only remembered it as a phrase in a history book but I didn't dare show my ignorance, and soon John was in full flow about the respective policies of Gladstone and Disraeli, Lloyd George, the Irish question, bringing us up to date and castigating the iniquities of the present government. At some point in this monologue, Davie shuffled off to bed. Presumably he had heard it all before! I nodded and grunted, and realised that here before me in these primitive surroundings was a man of considerable knowledge and no mean intellect. Then, while John my elder and myself just listened, John Baird turned his attention to the Kirk. He had been a great sermon taster in his youth, and could tell me the "heads of the sermon" that James Black had once preached.

"Man " he said, "in these days the preacher took you by the scruff of the neck and dangled you over the pit o' Hell, till you could smell your clathes singein' and decided you would do onythin' to get oot o' landin' there."

I was mightily impressed by this armchair theologian. I ventured to ask if he'd been at Moorton Kirk lately and he fixed me with his eye and said, "I've heard you."

Clearly my preaching, which some thought too evangelical, was milk and water to John Baird compared to the "real preachers they had long syne". Then John turned to his schooling in the tiny one teacher school at Waterfoot. What an amazing "dominie" had been there, for I knew from the records that from that little country school had come two doctors, three lawyers, half a dozen Ministers, an MP and a New Zealand Cabinet Minister, and these country loons like John, who had stayed on as a farmer where his father had farmed before him, yet whose knowledge, grasp of world affairs, and homespun philosophy were the fruits of seed sown by that lone schoolmaster in one tiny out of the way hamlet. Now and then as he talked, John's sense of humour would shine through, and I realised, what others had already told me, how in the old Waterfoot discussion group he had been such a livewire and doughty debater. But the night was drawing on . . .

"You'll put up a prayer afore ye go, meenister?" asked John.

I did, as was my wont, but after the flow of eloquence I'd heard, my words seemed poor, stumbling things. So we departed for the car, with John's solemn "Good night to you both" speeding our departure.

"Well, what do you think?" asked John the elder as we got into the car.

"I think you might have warned me to swot up my history!" I grinned. "What a man! How long has he been a widower?" I enquired.

"Man, he's no a widower. His wife and family live in a wee hoose in the village. They've never lived wi' John. It seems his folks thought he was marrying beneath himself, and they wouldna' have the wife aboot the place. He looks in to see them whiles! (Since there were six of a family, that presumably meant he had called at least six times, I calculated) "But they hardly ever see each other now, never go out anywhere, though one of the lassies keeps hoose for him and the youngest boy works at the farm. John's a clever man, but a gey lonely yin. His regular companion noo is the bottle!"

I dropped my elder at his house, and slowly made my way Manse-wards, trying to remember those lines about "the tragedy of might have been".

As it happened, I was called back to Low Blackpark a few months later.

Davie was ill and sinking fast, and could I call. I found the kitchen shining, a few rugs on the floor, and a bright young woman busy at the sink. It seemed one of John's sons had moved in with his wife to look after the old men. I was taken upstairs to see Davie. He lay in a poor little room, a room that seemed crammed full of books, but Davie was beyond where I could reach him. Unconscious, his mind was roaming in distant places, probably back to the days of youth, when life had been uncomplicated, untarnished, and full of hope of all that was to be. I sat in that dark room for a time with the dying man, silent in prayer as I commended his soul, so soon to fly away, to its Maker. I buried him a few days later, and afterwards visited John, all alone again, for he had fallen out with his son, and they had left him. There was little I could do for him either that day, for by his elbow was one empty and one half empty bottle. I knew John would not lack the "solace" of John Barleycorn, for the Bairds were worth tens of thousands, their own earnings augmented by a legacy from a brother who had made good overseas.

I mused long before the study fire that night on my two "prehistoric" families. One ill educated, ignorant even, the other well educated, knowledgeable. The one close knit as a family, the other fragmented. The Tuckers with their simple piety and code of living, John Baird with his considerable theological and philosophical knowledge. I thought of them long, and as I went to bed I had a picture of an old man facing the years, with only a bottle for his companion.

There was no doubt in my mind which family had won, in this race of life.

Each In Its Season

NINETEEN

A certain Bishop, years ago, was travelling on holiday in the Scottish Highlands, journeying on one of these trains that give the passengers their money's worth. It stopped at every station, and at many more places as well, where passengers still got on or off, or where a loaf of bread, or a leg of pork, and in one case a wee pig, were handed over to folks waiting beside the line. At one such halt, in the middle of nowhere, a shepherd accompanied by his dogs, joined the Bishop in his compartment. The shepherd was a friendly soul, and was seen deep in conversation with his companion, who, being on holiday, was disguised as a normal layman, and might have been anybody. After a time it became clear to the Bish that his companion was puzzled as to who, or what he could be, so he remarked

"You know, I'm in the same line of business as yourself. I've got a flock too!"

"Iss that so new?" replied the 'herd, "and how many sheep would you be haffing in your hirsel?"

"About half a million" replied the Bishop without batting an eyelid.

The shepherd was greatly astonished.

"Haff a million! Haff a million! Whateffer do you do at the lambing time?"

While not possessing gaiters or other quite comparable clerical attire to the Bishop, I too had my little flock at Moorton. We didn't have anything quite the equivalent in season or in busy-ness to the lambing season of my vet days (a period in my former life I miss to this day) but nonetheless, there were particular seasons in the life of one's flock, and in the yearly round.

There was, for example, the wedding season. This tended to be split into two distinct parts . . . in spring before 1 April, or in the early autumn. In the innocence of my early days, I assumed that spring weddings were due to the romance of that season "when a young man's fancy lightly turns to thoughts of love". The autumn I presumed to be a practical time of year in a farming community when the harvest was safely gathered for another year. My sentimental notions were speedily shattered to learn that romance or expediency had nothing whatever to do with it, but simply that these, then, were the times of year when maximum rebate of income tax could be reclaimed by a married man, and I was astonished to learn of a city colleague who actually married ten couples on the optimum Saturday of spring. How sadly do our dreams depart!

The Manse doorbell rang, and there, looking somewhat apprehensive, stood George Reid and Betty Thomson with their attendants. They had come for a rehearsal of their wedding of the next day . . . a quite unnecessary proceeding, for we had already been through the whole service and subsequent reception festivities, on several occasions. But couples . . . or more correctly, brides, like to savour the whole great day to the full, and in advance . . . Bridegrooms sometimes give more the impression of a double dose of doom! I led the way to the study and at the door paused and asked, "Sure you want to go through with this? I don't advise it."

They looked at me, completely taken aback, glanced at each other, then Betty stammered

"What do you mean, Mr Cameron?"

"Let's go for a wee walk" I said, and even more mystified, they followed me in bemused fashion across to the adjoining Church and its old burial ground. We paused at a particular, ancient gravestone.

"Read that!" I said,

Betty read aloud,

"In memory of John Calderwood, Farmer, Clanfin, died 1856 aged 51; his brother Robert Calderwood, Farmer, Craigneuk, died 1863 aged 55 and William Calderwood, Farmer, Meadowside, died 1864, aged 62."

Betty's eyes travelled to the bottom of the gravestone, where she read the one brief line

"And their respective wives"

"That's marriage, Betty" I pronounced solemnly, "the wives are not worth a mention!"

They looked at me uncertainly. "This vet-minister was surely a queer fellow", I could see them think, but at last they saw the twinkle in my eye, laughed heartily, and the ice was broken. It was a much more relaxed group that then filed into church for the rehearsal, which went smoothly enough, and in the course of which I emphasised to the attendants that when it came to the Blessing, only the couple knelt on the stool. After all, it was the couple's day . . . besides, the stool only accommodated two.

Their great day dawned fair, the guests assembled, the bride joined her groom before the table, the first hymn was sung, then as the ceremony proceeded, the door opened, and a man clutching a handkerchief passed right behind the wedding group, and handed the handkerchief with a few whispered words, to the person at the end of the pew which held the bridegroom's family . . . parents, brothers, sisters. The hankie was passed from hand to hand with the same few words of explanation, while I, somewhat curious as to this wedding version of "pass the parcel", continued with the words of the service. Eventually the handkerchief reached the bridegroom's father who was right at the end of the row, next to the wall, and he took the proffered hankie, and casually put it to his mouth. His teeth had arrived! Judging by his slick, wristy action, I would say it was not the first time he had carried out this public procedure with his molars, managing somehow, with splendid camouflage, to get them right way up in his mouth.

We came to the vows.

"Do you, George, take this woman, Betty, to be your wedded wife, and do you promise to be to her a loving, faithful and dutiful husband till God shall separate you by death?"

George thought a moment while I peered at him and nodded, indicating his turn had come. I thought I'd need to kick him, but finally he nodded and murmured "I do"

"Do you, Betty, take this man George to be your wedded husband . . ."

I paused to take a breath, and the bride immediately, cheerfully chirruped "I do."

I completed my question, and the girl again made her affirmation, surely making clear to her bemused Bridegroom her undying fealty!! But the look he gave her tended to suggest,

"Trust you to use four words when two would do!"

Then came the moment for the couple to kneel in that most lovely part of the service where the Aaronic blessing, the oldest in the Bible, is bestowed on the new man and wife. The trouble was George's younger brother, the best man, tried to get on the stool beside them. Had he succeeded poor Betty would have been tipped off the other end, but he didn't quite succeed, being elbowed in the ribs by George who advised him in a stage whisper, and with real brotherly love, to "Get up, you fool!" Ministers are supposed to keep going despite snags, and not betray their feelings overmuch, but at times, as with George and Betty's nuptials, it can be somewhat difficult. However, despite the hitches another marriage was solemnised . . . if that's the right description on this occasion, and the wedding party departed for their reception. Each week over the wedding season saw its marriage, and each one was different, and for the couple and their guests, special, and for me, moving, as two young people set out on the adventure of sharing everything on life's journey.

But spring was not only the wedding season. It saw the start of the wandering season.

"Daddy, there's an old gentleman at the door wanting to see you" announced Neil one day. Aged nine, and gravely courteous; everyone to Neil, was a "gentleman".

"He's a poor, poor, poor old man wif no coat" added David the tender-hearted, aged four.

"I expect he's a tramp!" pronounced number two son, Ian, from a not inconsiderable experience of tramps in his seven years.

"Twamp! Man! Old!" added baby Alan, thumping his spoon in his high-chair, while the dog, Bruce, who made Alan his special charge, wagged his stump of a tail in agreement.

The boys were all correct. He was an "old gentleman" . . . he had no coat . . . he was undeniably a tramp, one of the many "gentlemen of the road" who called at the Manse from time to time. Our present caller peered up at me from beneath a downcast countenance, and asked, "Are you the minister . . . him that was the vet?" What difference the vet title made, I'm not clear, unless the caller thought vet-ministers had more ready cash than ordinary ones, but I acknowledged I was the minister.

"Well, you see, Father . . . er Reverend . . . I've been walking frae Liverpool wi' just some lifts, to get tae Glesca' tae see ma auld mither. She's in a gey bad way, and I wondered if you could help me."

I pondered a moment. He was probably an old rascal and I was a ready "touch", but maybe, just maybe his story was true, Glasgow was not far away, and we were, as Christians to "be not forgetful to entertain strangers unawares."

"I dare say we can manage a bus fare" I responded, handing over half a crown.

"You widna' hae a cup o' tea? I hivna ett since yesterday."

"Come in and we'll give you something"

"That's rale kind o' ye"

Janet gave him bacon and eggs while the boys looked on with big eyes and the dog with suspicious ones. He told us his name was Willie McCafferty . . . told us again his mother was very poorly and not expected to last long . . . confessed as he leaned back in the chair picking his teeth that he had not been a very good son, and had not seen his old mother for five years . . . recounted almost with tears what a mess he had made of his life but would like to make a fresh start, and could I give him a book to help him. Much moved I gave him one of Professor Barclay's *Daily Study Bible* books . . . and another half crown, and eventually he left.

A month later he called again, wondering if I could help him with something as he was on his way to Birmingham to look for work.

"How's your mother?" I asked.

He looked completely blank, then muttered

"Oh . . . ah . . . she's a' richt"

He got another five shillings, called down blessings upon us, and left.

Throughout the summer various other wanderers called seeking help, and with the most harrowing stories of ill fortune. It seemed some poor souls had never really had a chance in life, so the half crowns and cups of tea were regularly dispensed. One suggested he could do with the kind of coat I had on, and while I remembered the bit in the New Testament about those with two coats giving to those with none, I really only possessed the one coat. By the late autumn the wedding season was almost over, and so was the wandering season, or so I thought until one incident.

Returning from a visit to my mother one cold, wet, dark evening, we found the fire almost out, and while the family took off coats I headed for our huge coal house, once a stable, to get an arm-ful of logs. There was no light in the place, but even in the pitch dark, I knew my way to the pile of wood. As I groped warily to the corner where the fuel lay, I stepped on something softish, squelchy, something that was firm yet yielding. I thought of a sack with straw in it, perhaps. I picked up some logs, but as I reached the door, it dawned on me there was nothing like that in our coal house. I felt the hairs on the back of my neck stand up as the realisation came

"That was a body!"

I dumped the logs in the fire, grabbed a torch and the poker (I am in most ways a pretty traditional being!), and leaving Janet and the family standing at the back door of the Manse as re-inforcements, headed, trembling, back to the coal house. It was a body right enough, so yelling for Janet to phone for the police, I advanced, poker at the ready, and demanding to know what the body thought it was doing lying there! There was no reply . . . and I feared the worst . . . but eventually there was a stirring in the corner. Now there had been a couple of burglaries in the parish in the past week, and convinced I was facing a desperado, I kept my distance and shouted

"Come out of there! Don't you dare move!"

How he was to do this (I had now ascertained the "body" was male) he clearly didn't know, so compromised by sitting up on the pile of logs where he had been lying, and in the light of the torch, I recognised Willie McCafferty. He seemed placid enough, and so, feeling somewhat sheepish at my over reaction, I invited him into the house.

"What were you doing in there?" I demanded.

"Och, I came to see if you could help me, but when there was naebody in, I just went for a sleep till you came back."

Feeling sorry for the poor, shauchly creature now, I put the kettle on to give him a cup of tea, which he had just started when the village Constable, plus a colleague from the neighbouring town, burst on the scene, demanding

"Have you got him?"

"I've got him, Jimmy, but I think maybe I've wasted your time. He's a tramp kind of body called Willie McCafferty, and he's been here before, but when I stepped on him in the pitch black of the coal house, I have to admit I got a fright."

"He'll likely be the burglar" said the policeman, coming, with his colleague, into the kitchen where sat out wanderer.

"What's your name?" demanded P.C.McCluskey

"Hugh Murphy" replied our "guest". I gaped!

"What were you doing here?" shouted the Bobby. I thought he was about as excited as I was, but I suppose, if you have had two robberies in a week in a district where a forgotten Dog-Licence was about the only regular crime you might be excused for getting a bit uptight.

The tramp protested he had been doing nothing, only waiting to see the minister.

"Some story!" snorted the officer of the law.

I didn't know how the KGB went about these things, but I thought our two large men in blue were pretty impressive in their interrogation. There was no brutality, far from it, but under their rapid barrage of questions, I'd have confessed to anything! Eventually Willie McCafferty, alias Hugh Murphy, was led off to the Police Station. Next morning, a finger print expert arrived, dusted our doors and windows, finding his "dabs" on our kitchen window where our tramp had tried to force an entry, but alas for the Police, the prints did not match those at the burgled Coal Merchants' or Post Office. The prisoner appeared in court, and to my relief, was let off with a stern warning. I didn't like the idea of having landed a man in jail for sleeping on a pile of logs. It seemed that Willie McCafferty, alias Hugh Murphy was really a Daniel Hodges, with a record for vagrancy, another for never having worked in his life, and possessed of no mother in Glasgow.

My faith in mankind was somewhat shaken, and no matter how I looked at it, I had to admit my attempt at reform or conversion had not been a notable success!

The wanderers kept coming each season, but the supply of half crowns gradually dried up. I also took steps to obey the scriptural command when seeking logs

"Let there be light!"

"The Wud You've Got"

TWENTY

In my early months as a minister, I spent long hours in the study, not only preparing for meetings, Sunday School, Bible Class, Youth Fellowship and the Sunday sermons, but just thinking, planning, and examining my ministry. Early on I came to the conclusion . . . which has remained with me . . . that I was not a committee type of man. I could cope with the Sunday congregations, I loved visiting people, young, middle aged and old, in their homes, but when it came to Session meetings and the like, I was uptight beforehand, and drained afterwards. I was abundantly blessed in my wife in a host of ways, and on committee nights she was a tower of strength with her quiet support and understanding.

I came out of a Kirk Session meeting one night early in my stay at Moorton very upset. Things had not gone well. Elders had argued, decisions had been deferred, work I wanted to see begun had not been agreed upon. In short I felt it was a mess. As we left the meeting room, Duncan the Treasurer came up to me and said

"Dinna worry, Mr Cameron! Things will work oot. I ken you're anxious to see things done, but you canna change folk; you've got to work wi' the wud you've got."

Duncan was a joiner, he knew all about wud (wood), and I sat long at the dying study fire that night thinking of his words. In many ways I was blessed in the kind of wood I had to work with. There was Duncan himself, strong, determined, a prodigious worker, and as long as he felt a thing was right, quick to get on with it. There was dear little Andrew Phillips, my Session Clerk, of all things a pawnbroker to trade in Glasgow, but a saint with a beaming face, a gentle, kind, loving, understanding man with whom

I shared many of my dreams and problems. He had been twenty years in Moorton but was still regarded as an "incomer". Not long before my coming, an old lady of eighty-two had died, and Andrew, speaking to one of the locals had said,

"Well! That will be one of your oldest Moortonites gone now!" He was answered with withering scorn.

"She wisna a Moortonite! She was twa year auld when she came here"

There was the other Andrew, Andrew Crombie the Beadle, an old soldier who had faked his age to join up as one of the early volunteers in the Great War . . . A man who lived for his Church, kept it shining, and was in every sense the "minister's man".

I had two stalwart supporters in Jimmy Aitchison and Maxwell Watson, who, like me, felt that changes were necessary if the Church was to thrive, and in their enthusiastic way, supported me to the hilt. Great men! There were the two senior elders, Robert Murchison, in his nineties, but in church every Sunday, and John Brown, a lovely man with a wonderful family, all thirled to the Kirk, and supporting the minister in anything he might try. There was my own elder, Jimmy Rodgerson, quiet, understanding, loyal, true. My thoughts turned to my two golfing partners, Tom McMichael, a retired policeman, and Ian Bryce, the local vet and a good friend. Then there were farmers like Jimmy Gibson with his quaint, old fashioned ways and pawky sense of humour . . . Jim Shankland and Jim Grant who were great practical helps, and ploughed and worked the enormous Manse garden every year.

As I thought round them all, and many others, I came to the conclusion that I was really a lucky man in my office bearers, and maybe my dissatisfaction at times was entirely my own fault of trying to rush change. Andrew Eastham had said to me,

"Always remember . . . quick in the town, but slow in the country. Take your folk along with you and hasten slowly."

I concluded that night that he was right, that there wasn't much wrong with the wood, only the man trying to work it, and I should leave things to evolve slowly, and just do my weekly work. For there was plenty of that, as varied as ever my vet's life had been.

"Mr Cameron! Can you come right away" said the agitated voice on the telephone. "Mrs McMinn has tried to commit suicide in the butcher's shop."

The oddest thought came into my mind . . . "what an appropriate place for the deed!", but aloud I replied "I'm on my way."

We had no resident doctor in the village, most of the men were away at work, so I imagine they felt a vet/minister was the best person available. I had visited the McMinn home twice. They were the poorest family in the parish, and although they had never been in a church in their lives, I tried to visit every home, regardless of religious persuasion or none. The first time I called they were breaking up the sideboard to fuel the fire, for they had no coal. The second time the house was in darkness and I had to nip up to the Manse for an electric bulb before I could see them. Well . . . not completely in darkness . . . in the corner was a light, the television set, just about their only piece of furniture . . . a sad commentary on the times if one was looking for a sermon.

Mrs McMinn was bleeding from the wrists, but not too badly; she had a dazed look on her face and clearly did not know where she was or what had happened. We dressed the wrists, bundled her into my car, and I headed for the nearest town and the first doctor I could find. His examination was brief.

"Drive straight on to the mental hospital" he said. It was a harrowing journey of fifteen miles as I fearfully watched that she would not throw herself out of the car. In fact she did try to commit suicide on the way, but at last, to my great relief, we reached the hospital and I handed her over to proper medical care.

She had a stay of a few weeks, and returned, apparently sound in body and mind once more, but to the same dreadful, housing conditions, large unemployed family, and abject poverty. I could help a little financially, but do little to really alter their situation, but at least I could show concern and that the Church did care.

I met him by accident when I went over to the Church one afternoon. Young he was, and clearly greatly upset, with tears streaming down his cheeks. I didn't know him, and asked if I could help. He said he didn't think so, as he had already spoken to his own minister about his domestic problem, but he wanted to sit in the quietness of a church and pray, and ours was the only one in the area that was always open. In fact I'd had to fight hard in the Kirk Session to have the Church kept open, for we had many visitors who wanted to see our old, historic building, but the elders were afraid of vandalism. (In fact we never did have any act of vandalism commited over the years . . . only once during the night having the building broken into and our Property Fund box, which had little in it, stolen. A clean thief he was, for he had then proceeded to wash his hands in the Vestry wash hand basin.)

My young visitor just wanted to do what many have done, call for higher help in a domestic situation that had got beyond him. He came again and again and I like to think that he at least found peace there. I was reminded of the old man who used to go into a large city church every day and just sit there. One day the minister asked him what he did each day. The old man smiled and said,

"I look at Him, and He looks at me."

That's real prayer!

"You've got a visitor," my wife informed me when I came home at tea time from a round of visits. "He's been here for two hours," and the poor girl had been plying him with cups of coffee and conversation till I would return.

He proved to be an alcoholic, called Jim, who had just happened to get off the bus at Moorton, he didn't really know why, and made his way to the Manse to look for help. He didn't want money, just somebody who could maybe help with his wasted life. For it was wasted; he was jobless; his marriage had broken up; he had a wife and four children somewhere who couldn't put up with his drinking any longer. He had a prison record for violence, had been "dried out" innumerable times in mental hospitals, but was now a broken, beaten wreck of a human being, scarcely able to eat, only drink, even meths. He had been employed in the family business of monumental sculptors, had served in the war with distinction and been a Sergeant Major, but after years of sponging off his parents, had finally been thrown out of the business. Now he was a wanderer, a poor ruin of what had been an intelligent man, a skilled worker, and in the early days a good son, husband and father. What could we do?

We kept plying him with coffee, and discovering he once could play table tennis, I phoned Jimmy Aitchison, and willing soul that he was, he came round and we played with Jim till he was weary, and ready to sleep. I didn't feel like risking him in the house with my wife and four wee bairns, but felt we must help somehow, so we gave him a bed in our caravan, and there he stayed. He was almost a full time job in the early days when he had "the shakes" and the craving was strong in him, but he kept off the bottle. In time we found him a job on a farm and I recall his tremendous joy when he was able to send his first wage to his wife. The weeks passed, and the months. Once he crept off to the pub and I pursued him, and literally dashed the glass from his hand. I thought he was going to strike me, but he came home quietly. So the time went on—six months without that fatal first drink for the alcoholic. He ate with us, the boys accepted Jim as one of the family and gradually a normal human being arose from the wreck that had been. Janet was absolutely marvellous in the way she treated him, and cared for him, and one evening he said (though he was older than Janet).

"Mrs Cameron! I wish you were my mammy."

It was pathetic, but moving, and we felt we were doing what Christ would have us do. Indeed, nuisance that he was at times, we had grown really fond of Jim. Then we went off on holiday, the "crutch" was removed, and we came back to find Jim had broken out, assaulted a policeman, and was in prison.

We tried again, and again, sometimes winning, sometimes losing, but finally Jim moved on in his wandering, out of our orbit, leaving behind in us a sense of failure, but a little consolation in that we had tried, and for a short time he had been a human being again.

Jim is but one of many alcoholics I've tried to deal with over the years, usually with little success, and the tragedy is that many of them deep down are very likeable people. But it has coloured my thinking and actions. I accept that many finer Christians than me enjoy a drink, and in no way do I stand in judgement on folks who like a glass with friends and can control their drinking. Often I've been misunderstood, laughed at or downright condemned because I don't drink . . . but Jim and his like, and a string of broken marriages caused by the bottle always come to mind . . . and I feel . . . who knows . . . that maybe I or some youngster watching me at a wedding or some other social occasion could become another Jim . . . and I've always felt, with deep compassion for these poor souls, "There but for the grace of God go I."

I was given an extra task for six months — to be chaplain to a large geriatric hospital some distance away, until another man nearer at hand could be appointed. I visited every week, moving among the beds of old folk, some completely helpless, some just weak and weary, some mindless. On Sunday evenings some of the Choir and Youth Fellowship would come with me and we would take a little service in two of the wards.

One day visiting I came across a new patient, much fitter than most.

"How are you?" I asked.

"Fine, thank you, who are you?" she replied.

"I'm the Chaplain"

"But *who* are you?"

"Oh, my name's Cameron and I'm from Moorton"

"Hah! so you're Cameron! I've no time for you" she went on in a very correct, indeed very affected voice.

Now I don't like affectation, and while I'd often had my leg pulled about being a vet turned minister, and suspected that must be the reason for this madam's condemnation of me, for the first time I felt my hackles rise, and thought, in rather unchristian fashion, "You old besom! Lying there condemning somebody you don't know" But I managed a smile and asked why she had no time for me. I was right in my conjecture.

"Vet — minister — can't make up your mind, can you? A man is one thing or another and shouldn't change boats in mid-stream"

"Oh, I don't know," I said. "I have the best possible example for doing what I did."

"What do you mean?" she queried.

"Well, our Lord was a working carpenter to the age of thirty before He became a wandering preacher."

She shot up in bed and looked at me as if seeing me for the first time.

"You know, I never thought of that" she exclaimed in surprise, and from then on she couldn't have been nicer!

I discovered there had not been a communion service for sixteen years in the hospital, so decided to hold one. I have never known an occasion like it. My faithful elders Jimmy Aitchison and Maxwell Watson came with me to assist. We asked no questions, whether Protestant or Catholic, whether Church member or not. Whoever wished communion (and that was nearly everybody) was given it.

It was a moving occasion of great peace, and quite different from the more formal celebrations in Church. Many of the patients had to have the Cup held for them. Somehow, I felt in its simplicity, it had been like the Upper Room where it all began. We left one old Highland woman of ninety-four, almost blind, singing softly to herself in Gaelic, "I to the hills will lift mine eyes." For a short time she had been transported to the hills of home, and communion seasons she had known there in happier days of youth, and another old dear, well advanced in years, at the end exclaimed to me with shining eyes.

"*He* was here. *He* really was!"

An unforgettable experience of . . . as our fathers called it . . . "the Real Presence."

"I hear you're a minister now" said Leslie in the train one day. I replied that was so.

"Man, I thought you had more sense!" he said. "A quarter of a vet's salary, nothing but criticism, and tell me, what good has Christianity ever done for the world?"

Leslie had been at school with me, was brainy, and now a lecturer at University. We had a rare old discussion for there's nothing I like better than getting the jacket off, so to speak, and getting down to basics. I told him the first hospital of which there was any record, the first home for the blind, the first free dispensary had all been founded by Christians, and surely that was some good Christianity had done in the world. I might have told him, though only thought of it afterwards, that in various ways the work of caring was still going on. I should have told him about our "battle" and my honourable scars.

The week before had been Christian Aid week and with ten other ministers and priests, of varying ages, shapes and sizes, I had taken the field to play against the Stirlingshire Police at football. They seemed giants compared to our little, shaughly, bowly legged team, but feeling like Christian martyrs facing the lions, we performed in the arena, a large football field surrounded by a very big crowd, carrying banners of "Come away the clergy," and cheering our every effort. I don't know if they were pro-Christian, but they were certainly anti-police! My first encounter with the police centre half knocked me half across the park, and it looked as if we would be slaughtered. But as time went on, it was obvious we had some hidden talents. Our goalkeeper was performing heroics, though sorely troubled with his bonnet falling off . . . two of the young priests had a fair turn of speed . . . our right half, a rugby player, was sailing in with great gusto, and the inside trio (total age 120) were showing an ancient craftiness which produced goals. Yes . . . we actually won, the police took it in good part . . . and though I had skinned knees and aching muscles for weeks afterwards, it was all in a good cause and some needy people across the world benefited from the large sum collected.

In the early summer of my first year at Moorton, we had a similar encounter when the men of the Church took on the Youth Fellowship at football, and all the village turned out to see the minister in shorts! After a stern battle, which the lads took seriously and the men did not, and with some help from the referee, one of the stars of a big First Division team, we gained a creditable draw — and the Kirk was shown as a place where people really could enjoy themseves.

Every week I visited one of our village schools and the very large Academy in the town, to conduct the school assembly and take R.E. in some classes. I particularly liked the wee one-teacher school at Waterfoot. What a welcome I always received! There was wee Jeannie anxious to show me her handwork . . . Sarah proudly pushing into my hand a painting which might have been anything but which you agree is like a cow . . . and Billy telling you in his gruff voice that the mare had a foal last night. Eventually we would get down to the short service, or the story for the day. They liked the stories best and were full of questions. Come to think of it . . . the Master teacher had lots of questions for his stories too.

There are many learned people in places of authority who would close the little country schools. I emphatically disagree with them or the contention that the children get a better education in a larger school. Of course so much depends on the teacher, but from that little school at Waterfoot, as I've mentioned elsewhere, in the lifetime of one schoolmaster, came doctors, a lawyer, several ministers, an MP and a Cabinet Minister of New Zealand. In addition, and perhaps more important each child was taught well, given a love of poetry and taught to use words, so that in later years they formed their own debating society. Farm children, all of them, and taught by a wise teacher on their own wave-length — like the schoolmistress in one school who was trying to teach the doctrine of the Trinity a mighty difficult subject.

"Imagine, Angus," she said to one boy, "you have three sheep at home. Call one Father, one Son, and one the Holy Ghost. They are all the same, but yet all different."

A few days later she was revising the lesson.

"How many persons in the Trinity?" she asked.

"Twa, Miss" said Angus.

"Oh, Angus, do you not remember me telling you about the three sheep?"

"Aye, Miss, I ken, but you see the Holy Ghost chokit on a turnip and he's deid."

Unassailable logic, if not theologically sound!

The lesson over, on each visit, I would be seen off by the whole school, with waves and cheers. Yes, I like the wee schoolies!

I had come to Tom Longmuir's farm one April day on just a routine visit. It happened to be milking time in their dairy herd, and as was my custom, I had a walk up to the byre before going to the house. I loved the sight and smell of the cattle, something I miss to this day. Tom was nowhere to be seen, but I found his teenage son busy with the milking.

"Faither's in the hay shed" he informed me. "He's busy trying to lamb a yow."

I made my way to the hay shed, which was divided by bales into partitions, with in each little section a ewe and lambs. I found Tom down on his knees with his hand inside a ewe. He greeted me with enthusiasm, and a measure of relief.

"Just the man I need!" he said. "I've got a right corker here and I'm beat with it."

"I'll have a feel, Tom, but I'm a bit rusty. It's a few years since I lambed a ewe."

So I got down on my knees, after having taken my jacket off and thoroughly soaped my arm. It was a big lamb with the head well back, and not too much room in the ewe. I've been blessed with a long arm, fairly slim pair of hands, and I was able to reach the head, but couldn't bring it round into the correct position.

"Tom, could you get me some fresh warm water, put some Dettol in it, and three bits of binder cord."

The years had rolled back, and I felt I was doing what I had done many, many times, and loving it again. The water and cords were fetched, I gave them a good swill in the antiseptic water, then proceeded to put one on each of the lamb's fore legs. I then pushed them back to make a little more space, and after some difficulty managed to get the third cord through the lamb's mouth and round its head. Then, with my hand still inside the ewe's womb, I said to Tom.

"Now pull on that rope, but not too hard" and as Tom did as I had asked, I managed to guide the lamb's head round.

"Now the leg ropes, Tom" and up came the legs into position. It was now a simple matter of traction, and in a short time we had a big lamb lying on the straw, spluttering its way into the world. Tom busily rubbed it down with a wisp of hay, but the ewe was already round at her lamb, licking it dry, and "talking" in that lovely, deep throaty way to its new born lamb. It felt good . . . and it looked good to see the instant reward for a few minutes' work, a live lamb and an undamaged ewe.

"Meenister! I'm right grateful to ye" said Tom, "and while you're here, maybe you would take a look at a beast. She's off her grub, doon in her milk, so there's something no richt."

So we headed for the byre, and I had a look at his cow. I had no thermometer, but checked her pulse and respirations, which were normal. I had a listen at her rumen, the big first stomach, and while it was a bit sluggish, it was still churning over. But I was certain what her trouble was, for while up at her foreleg taking the pulse, the smell of acetone came to me strongly.

"She's got acetonaemia, Tom, or as maybe you would say she's stawed. You better get Ian Bryce out here to give her a bottle of glucose, or a shot of insulin, or whatever he uses."

I, of course, didn't possess any of these remedies, and I was already feeling guilty at doing a fellow vet out of a job. Tom Longmuir looked at me long and earnestly, then his face broke into a big grin.

"Man, you're a handy fellow to hiv for a meenister. If you canna cure a beast, you can aye say a wee prayer ower it!"

I smiled too, but didn't say anything, but thought back to the many times, in the middle of a hard calving, when, like many vets, I'm sure, I had indeed breathed a prayer.

We finally got to the farmhouse, saw Mrs Longmuir, had a cup of tea and a chat, then I went on my way, feeling that maybe a vet/minister had his uses. The Longmuirs, though by no means regular church goers, were in their pew the following Sunday. "Ah well," I thought, there's many a way to get folk to the Kirk!

Christmas Eve; surely the most magical, happiest night in the year! Moorton was silent under a December moon, the roofs of the little cottages glistening from the touch of frosty fingers, the windows bright with the twinkle of fairy lights.

Eight o'clock found the carollers assembled at the Church Eventide Home, about fifty of them . . . mostly young, but augmented by some seniors like Jimmy Aitchison and Joe Gibson, the Cub Master, and a tower of strength in the background of any Church activity. Carols ancient and modern were sung with great gusto, if not always in the right key. Then out into the streets, feet crunching on the snow-clad roads, breath steaming in the frosty air, faces aglow in the light of lanterns carried by the excited youngsters. Up and down the village we went, sped on our way by shouts of "Happy Christmas!," and singing of the *Good King Wenceslas* and the *Child born to be King.* Into the "big hoose" where a party was in progress, but where they stopped to listen and smile, and where the collecting cans were generously filled. At Mary Clanachan's house *Child in a Manger* was very appropriate, for a babe had been born that week. Outside old

Andrew's home we sang very softly (even the grunters in the company muting their bass notes) for Andrew, all knew, had not long for this world. "*Sleep in Heavenly peace*" we sang to the old man, like a benediction at the end of a long life.

Then into Mrs Beaton's house, all fifty squeezing into her little living room, for lemonade and shortbread were laid on for the singers, and the heat of the room was welcome. Then on again, youngsters skipping on ahead, collectors rattling on doors, voices becoming a bit cracked in the night air, complaints of "we're ower high," grins for pyjama clad bairns peeping from behind curtains, waiting for Santa to come with his exciting bundles, and finally the Pub. Would we go in? Why not? Jimmy and I did, to the great consternation of some of the customers who tried to hide behind their pints from the august presence of the minister. But they all stumped up for charity.

Finally the Manse, a heat at the fires blazing in every room, hot soup and sausage rolls prepared by Janet, the Manse boys hopping about in excitement at this invasion. A final rousing sing around the piano, then the climax of it all . . . the Watch-Night Service, carol singers in jeans, wellingtons and Rangers scarves augmenting the great crowd assembled for this Service with its unique atmosphere. A great peace seemed to wrap us all around as we heard again the wondrous story of the child laid in a manger, and felt ourselves one with shepherds, wise men and angels as we brought our worship, and at midnight sang that loveliest of all carols, "*Still the Night.*"

Only one night in the life of our little community, but a night of nights, when hope was abroad in the world, and in every heart the feeling of goodwill to all men, because of the One who came to bring His peace to every longing soul.

There was one man in our little community I visited every week, Davie. His wife helped at the Manse one morning a week, and when I ran her home, I would stay and have a chat with Davie, and we both cherished these talks. He had few visitors, and was pleased to see me, and I always learned something from this good, God fearing man.

Davie had been a shepherd, and a good one, but long before retiring age he had to give up his work because of a bad heart. His flock was now composed of statuettes of sheep on the mantelpiece, photographs of prize tups he had bred, and a few hens which his faithful collie had to content himself now by rounding up. He made crooks as a hobby, and I will always cherish the two he gave Janet and I just before he died. For Davie has come down from his last hill, and gone Home to the great sheepfold where all kinds of breeds gather at the last.

I will always remember these talks we had, and in particular one story he told me. As a young lad he was apprenticed to an older shepherd up in the hills of Ayrshire. One night there was a tremendous blizzard of snow, and the old man felt he would have to go out and bring down as many of his sheep as he could to the safety of the lower ground. But before he went, he had his moment of communion with his God. He took down from the wall his fiddle, and slowly, meditatively, like a prayer played "Nearer, my God to Thee, even though it be a cross that raiseth me." Then out into the violent storm he went, refusing to let the lad Davie go with him. The old shepherd saved many sheep that night, but he himself did not return. In the morning a search party found his body in a snow drift, his faithful dog beside him. The good shepherd had given his life for his sheep.

Davie never forgot that experience, and grew up to be a man like his old teacher. He and his wife were a happy, cheerful couple, but Davie sorely missed his flock, and I like to think our "cracks" round the fire about sheep and shepherding, pulpy kidney, lamb dysentery, dipping, clipping, lambing and all the rest gave him an interest week by week.

We laid him to rest on a wild stormy day, having sung his hymn in Church. A good man had gone to his reward. The shepherd was Home from the hill.

So the weeks and months passed at Moorton, each week bringing its joys and sorrows, and as I thought around my flock of a night, I was well content with my task in life — and with "the wud I'd got."

"The Cure For All Ills"

TWENTY ONE

Written on the heart (or at least a bit of paper) of every vet's wife, housekeeper, receptionist or anyone trusted with the taking of a message is a List marked Very Urgent, Urgent or Can Wait. While it is almost certain that in the minds of all animal owners each case comes into the Very Urgent category, in fact there are comparatively few which can truthfully so be described. Bloat, Choke, Staggers, some calvings, lambings, foalings, farrowings etc and the list is almost exhausted. But there is one other condition which may well appear, and indeed be ringed around. It is known by a variety of names — Urticaria, Hives, Blaines or Nettle Rash and it is so listed for a different reason.

"If ever you are called to a case of Urticaria" said our old Prof, "drive like blazes or the beast will be better before you get there!"

The symptoms of this condition, particularly in cattle, can be startling, even alarming, and since it is of such rarity that most farmers come across it but once in a life-time, almost all rush at once for the phone. Young Derek Hocking of High Deane was typical as he begged me to come with all possible speed.

"Ur vace be swollen somethin' terrible, ur eyes is near shut, an' she's blowin' like the dickens"

I smiled to myself and said I would see her in an hour.

"An 'our!" wailed Derek "Can't ee cum quicker like? I tells ee its 'orrible an' I reckon if her head keeps growin' like it is, ur brains will zoon be comin' out 'er ears!"

It was a graphic description and a pretty gruesome thought;

"Derek, this looks far worse than it is but don't worry, I'll come right out. Anyway, you know fine that Friesians have no brains, so her ears are safe" I, an Ayrshire fan, was always ribbing him about his Friesians.

I had intended to do another call on the way, but often, in practice, you have to "treat the client" as much or more than the animal, so I was with him in ten minutes.

The case was exactly as had been so vividly described, face swollen, eyes puffed up, lips sticking out, and a hang-dog expression.

"I don't know what you call it here, Derek, but the technical term is Urticaria. She's allergic to something. Have you changed your cattle cake lately or something?"

I wasn't treating it too seriously for it simply isn't a serious condition. Untreated, it will disappear in twenty-four to thirty-six hours; with a shot of some anti-histamine drug, a bit less. As I talked with Derek and his father, purely from habit I was going through the routine of temperature taking, pulse, respiratory rate, and the general look of the cow. The temperature was 105°F (normal for cow is 101–102°F). "Must have forgoten to shake the mercury down" I thought, gave the thermometer a vigorous shake, and still one minute later came up with 105°F. Cows with Urticaria had a normal temperature. Taking the pulse up at the radial artery of the fore leg, I was able to kill two birds with one stone, for at the same time I could count her respirations. Pulse was eighty (normal around fifty) while her respirations at thirty were about twice as fast as normal. There was something more than Urticaria here. I looked at her — "always study the way a beast looks and the expression on its face" — the voice of old Geordie Dykes, our Prof, came back to me. We had thought it amusing then, even ridiculous, as my medical friends do still, but I had found old Geordie knew more than we gave him credit for, perhaps being put off a bit because every lecture was sprinkled liberally with his experiences in the trenches of World War 1. Yes, this cow looked ill with an anxious expression. The normal Urticaria expression was embarrassment, like a woman being caught with her curlers in at tea-time!

The Hockings, senior and junior, were studying me as I studied their cow. "Us hasn't changed our veedin' like; only thing I can think is it was the red drink."

"Red drink?" I pounced. "Why did you give her that and when?" Veterinary diagnosis is a bit like a jig saw, putting together the pieces that you can pick up from patient and owner, and putting them together till all fits, or even like a detective drawing clues from unwilling witnesses. Sherlock Holmes, if he hadn't been so taken up with his wretched fiddle could have been a first class vet, as a lucrative sideline from his other work!

"Us drenched hur last night for she was dowie, like, off her grub, an' hur milk was down."

"Well, ten to one, your Red Drink caused the Urticaria, something in it she was allergic to. I'll give her a jag which will soon put that right, but that swollen face was putting us off on the wrong scent. We've got a sick cow here."

Out came the stethoscope, and right away I could here the squeaks, whistles and gurgles that signified Broncho-pneumonia. I thought I could also hear the "creaking leather" associated with pleurisy diagnosis.

"Pneumonia, Mr Hocking" I said to the old man as I gave the cow a jab of penicillin. "Her milk will go right down. Put a rug on her, or stitch some sacks together and put them over her for some heat, and I'll see her tomorrow. Why on earth you keep giving this red drink beats me, for it doesn't help pneumonia, and I don't know what it does help except constipation. Do you know what's in that drink? Epsom salts — ninety per cent — plus some ginger and a bit of colouring! Wouldn't be surprised if some of it didn't go down the wrong way last night and make the pneumonia worse."

I was laying it on. Derek was a good and progressive young farmer, but his father was of the old school to whom So and So's Red Drink took second place only to the Bible for reliability, and authority. After all, "if vather and grandvather had used it for their cattle, why not us," was the attitude, but I thought if it got about that the Red Drink which adorned every shippen in the shire was shown to be just a waste of money, and maybe even dangerous, I'd have done some good. But the old man wasn't giving in so easily. I suppose he must have felt as if I was blaspheming his gods. He fetched a packet.

"Read that" he stabbed triumphantly at the well known label. Probably he hadn't his specs! I read it.

"A proven remedy for all chills, fevers, pneumonia, stoppage of the bowel, founder of the feet, rheumatic pains and swollen joints, a purifier of the blood and the perfect remedy for almost all conditions in horses and cattle."

"See?" said the old man "didn't I tell ee?" He spat eloquently.

"But read on, go on" he urged. So I obliged and read aloud the quote from Mr A.G. of Wiltshire who'd used the drink for thirty years, and never needed a vet (probably he kept hens, I thought). Mr W.C. (that at least was appropriate) declared that his father and grandfather had never been without it. My mind boggled at what ¾lb of Epsom salts would do for father and grandfather – but assumed it meant their stock.

"They can't all be wrong" said the old boy, poking me on the chest.

"Cures sunstroke – also excellent for frost bite" I muttered.

"What's that, speak up!" said old man Hocking.

"Twas nothing; I was only recalling a cartoon I saw once" I assured him. "Look, Mr Hocking, look what your Red Drink has done here. If Derek hadn't phoned me, you'd probably have given her another dose, and that would have killed her one way or another" The alternative methods possible were messy even to imagine! "If you want to have a stomach mixture or a laxative by you, for that's all your drink is, O.K. – or better still come to my surgery and I'll give you some powder at half the price – but if you had pneumonia would you take Epsom Salts to cure it?"

I'd said more than enough regarding the folly of trusting in patent medicines and using them indiscriminately, yet I knew almost every farmer in my Practice bought these by the dozen from the purveyors of quack remedies. Faith, I thought, is a fine thing, but blind faith can sometimes be utter folly.

As I drove on to my next case I recalled my old boss who had made up his own cattle stomach mixture, called it 1001 and sold it in considerable quantities, as a stomach mixture. It was an excellent prescription, and as an assistant it was some time before he let me make up any of the mixture, and swore me to keep secret its contents. I remembered too the old vet who used to retire to an inner room there to make up some of his own special brews, safe from his assistants' questing eyes. But these, handed out for specific conditions, by vets, were very different from the mass of Tonic Draughts, Blood Conditioners, All-in-One-Mixtures, Three-in-One Powders, Red Drinks, Black Drinks and for all I knew Tartan Drinks sold by the purveyors of cure-all ills, and often sold as such, and bought in vast quantities by the farming community. For the most part, the sales reps of the various firms were friendly men, had a living to earn, but beyond a basic knowledge of the ways of the country made no claim as experts. Much more serious was one man, representative of a very well known pharmaceutical firm, a household name, which dealt both with vets and sold certain products over the counter to farmers. Kenneth had trusted John Pusey, and given him large orders, and even now, most of our vaccines, sera and antibiotics came from his firm, and presumably he gained considerable commission. John hung about the markets, was well known to the farming community, and had established a sound foothold with at least some veterinary practices. But I had, from various little bits of information, a suspicion that the same man was running with the hares and hunting with the hounds, and not very long after Kenneth departed to practise in his native Kenya, and I took on Bernard as partner, events moved rapidly to a climax and produced a showdown. John had been going into a certain farm one day, one of our clients, and noticed from his car a cow which had Bloat, or was "tinged up", distended with gas. Now this is a common condition, can be caused by a variety of factors, and on occasion can be cured by some reliable Bloat remedy — on occasion! John told the farmer about his cow, persuaded him he didn't need a vet, and forthwith sold him a couple of dozen "Bloat Cures" and told the farmer to pour one over the cow's throat. This he maintained, would scatter the gas, and all would be well. Who needs vets? Some hours later I got a panic call — a re-direction from my wife from one farm, to go at once to the other, for the "beast was like to burst". Well trained as she was, she had told them to try to keep the cow on the move, not allow it to lie down, or very likely it would burst. (In fact the condition must be absolute agony for the beast, as the gas builds up in the rumen and eventually the stomach wall does, like a punctured balloon, burst. Mercifully, usually the pressure through the abdominal wall has caused such interference with breathing and the heart circulation, that the animal may be unconscious or dead before the explosion) In the case in question, I was just in time. I had to "stick" the cow immediately, pushing a trocar and canula right through the stomach wall. The trocar is a sharp pointed stiletto, which fits closely inside a hollow tube, the canula, and once the poor beast has been stabbed, and the trocar removed, the gas comes bubbling out of the canula. Needless to say, this is only done when deemed absolutely necessary, and barbaric though it sounds, the instant relief to the cow is immense. I then rounded on the farmer, and good client or not, asked him what he had been playing at, what had kept him, and a few other things beside. He was a decent sort, a good, and intelligent farmer, yet he had believed the Bloat cure would do all, since John Pusey said so. By now I was calming down a bit, so grinned at him and said,

"Put not your trust in princes, even if called John Pusey" Had to get in a dig! "Now let's see, Mr Zeale, if we can find what caused that gas to form."

"Reckon it was just the young clover" said Mr Zeale.

"And I reckon not. Feel that. Put your hand on your cow's throat."

"A lump, what is it, well, dang me, I bet it's one of the last of the winter's turnips we scattered this morning to the milk cows" He was right. Tympany or Bloat can be caused by various things, including young, succulent clover, but it can also arise mechanically when the cow which burps every half minute or so without ever a "pardon me" just can't do it, because of a turnip or potato stuck there, thus preventing those hearty rumbles as the cow's cud and gas comes up. There are two ways of removing a turnip, by putting your arm over the cows throat and bringing it up, provided you've still got an arm left, or by passing a long tube or probang and pushing it onwards down the gullet into the stomach. This is by no means as easy as it sounds, and many a probang has punctured many a gullet wall. However that night one of the many implements and instruments the vet has to possess for only one specialised function, did what it was made for, and within moments of the turnip hitting the stomach wall, we were enveloped in an aura of gas as the cow made up for lost time and regurgitated with considerable rapidity. I knew that the next bloat at the Zeale farm would bring me a prompt call. Actions that night had spoken, as they mostly do in practice, a heap louder than words.

The next day I phoned John Pusey, and asked him which college he had attended. He laughed,

"The best of all, the college of experience, lad."

"So you reckon you know it all, John?"

"Well, not all, Alec" more guarded now "what's biting you?"

"You are, John. You took upon yourself to advise a client of mine yesterday what was wrong with his cow, without even seeing the beast, except from your car. You told him he needed no vet. That cow, John, is going about this morning with a hole in its side and its very lucky to be going about at all. We've been good clients to you and your firm in the past, man, and you have your job to do, but John, if you ever try to do mine again, and advise on individual cases, so help me your headquarters will hear about it!"

He managed to say he was sorry and it wouldn't happen again before I hung up. Within a few days, I was out on the fringes of the moor investigating the deaths of lambs. I did a P.M. on two typical cases of Pulpy Kidney.

"How many have you lost?" I asked the young farmer, who was a very new client, and not yet well known to me.

"Reckon about two dozen" he said "Yus, someways about a dozen before we asks Mr Pusey to look in, and 'bout the same since."

"Mr Pusey?" I questioned. "He was here because you asked him?"

"That's right. Folks reckons he knows more about sheep than any vetinary" the young fellow replied rather hesitantly.

"And why have you not called him again? I expect he gave you something."

"Oh, aye, he cuts open the lambs, bit like you, likes, only he was quicker, maybe, said it was worms, and gave us stuff to dose them all, and that would do the trick." He looked up aggressively "But missus reckoned we ought to give you a chance."

I ought to have been grateful to "the missus" for her consideration, but I swallowed hard a few times and said

"Look, John Pusey is not a vet. He knows a fair bit, I admit, the same way as a car salesman knows a bit about cars, but he isn't a mechanic."

I could see I wasn't getting through, so said, bluntly,

"Look, if your wife was at death's door, would you ask the chemist to call or the doctor?" "The doctor, I reckons."

"You sure would unless you happened to be trying to get rid of your wife." I hoped I wasn't giving him any ideas!

"Well, do you know that John Pusey isn't even a trained chemist, yet when he said 'worms', you believed him, spent pounds on his mixtures, and you've lost another dozen lambs?"

"Well, you always reckons to lose a few, like, an' I just thought the worm drenches hadn't had time to work."

"Well, they are your lambs, and, and you can do as you please, but I'm telling you they are dying of Pulpy Kidney, which is so common, that nearly everybody injects them when they're born and its near enough 100 per cent effective. Sure, there's a few worms about them, but you'll find that in almost any sheep you open, and I don't say but what John's drenches mightn't help later. But if you like, I'll send one of these lambs up to the Ministry Laboratory. It won't cost you anything, and that will tell us for certain."

He thought that would be a good idea, or rather his wife did. She had joined us half way through my talk, and clearly was much more progressive than her husband. The lamb went off, the report came back a few days later, confirming the diagnosis, and I gave him the necessary amount of serum and vaccine, telling him to come to me at the beginning of next year's lambing and I would fix him up with what was needed. I wasn't back at that farm for a year, and then it was simply to do their annual Tuberculin Test.

"Had any trouble with lambs this year?" I asked as we went round his few cows.

"No" he assured me, "us had Mr Pusey here and he fixed us up with same stuff you gave us last year. He really knows a lot, does Mr Pusey."

He knows which side his bread's buttered on, I thought. He had cashed in on my work, and sold this young chap all the vaccine and serum he needed, and it was more expensive, I knew, than the brand we used. But I kept quiet. You can't win, when the Pusey's of this world knew all the answers and can cure all ills.

In the meantime I'd written to his firm, as I'd warned him, complaining of his interference and unethical behaviour. We got a letter of apology and presumably he got a rocket, so for a time at least, he had to walk more carefully.

Of course, this faith in a person or product is far from being confined to Veterinary Medicine. Give a "cure-all ill" enough TV advertising, and the public is crying out for it. There is plenty of "quackery" about, and I find a deal of "ersatz religion" too. It comes in all kinds of packages, attractively labelled. There's the fellow who believes an hour on Sunday is his weekly insurance payment to the Almighty to protect him from life's troubles, or reckons an attendance at communion and maybe Christmas is all that's needed to keep his Santa Claus kind of God happy, and ensure similar Santa Claus type benefits. I've seen dozens of this persuasion over the years. Then there's the person who has latched on to a new faith, and here, in a twinkling, has found the remedy he has long sought, and zealously seeks to bring others into his sect for there alone is the truth.

I recall two instances of this at Moorton. One day two young fellows came to the Manse door, and asked if they could see the Church. I showed them round, telling them something of its storied past. Then they rounded on me for the real purpose of their visit. They had, some months before, become Mormons, and were now, with all the freshness and keenness of the new convert, seeking to set my feet on the right path.

"Do you prepare your addresses?" one enquired.

"I do," and quoted the old saying about sermon preparation being ten per cent inspiration and 90 per cent perspiration. They shook their head sadly.

"You don't believe in preparation?" I asked.

"Certainly not," enthused one. "I just go into the Church and say what the Holy Spirit puts into my mouth there and then."

I was naughty enough to ask if the Holy Spirit could only guide in a church and not in a study and recalled a man who had gone into his pulpit and waited for the Spirit to speak.

"I'm sure he did" said one of the youngsters with an emphatic nod.

"He surely did; he asked why the preacher hadn't thought about what to say before he dared to stand up to preach to others."

Now there is much to praise in Mormonism. Who can but be impressed by the upright lives, the morality, the tithing of their income by such well known figures as golfers Billy Casper and Johnny Miller so that their Church gets a tenth of their earnings? Who can but admire the crusading fervour of young students and others who give one or two years of their lives, without pay, as missionaries. But if there is much to admire in the Mormon ethic, and a great deal in their singing, youth approach and shining sincerity that is very attractive, I cannot accept that the teachings of their founder Joseph Smith and his famous successor Brigham Young are the truth, the whole truth and nothing but the truth. As I thought earlier of the Hockings and their Red Drink, faith is an admirable thing, blind faith can sometimes be the most utter folly. So we agreed to differ as the two young men and I bade goodbye. I was well used to being put in my place, and my feet set right, for each Friday in the village a meeting for children was held which sought to correct the errors of the Church as perpetuated by me and my fellow clergymen week by week. For to the originator of this meeting there were few, if any truly Christian ministers. He was a member of the Plymouth Brethren and ministers were anathema, blind leaders of the blind. Now I have a number of friends in the Brethren, and it is but right to say not all hold this view, clergy-wise. Equally I freely admitted that a university education in Divinity does not necessarily make a Christian. If a Divinity training was a must for the practice of Christian living, then Jesus was a non starter. What I did believe was that to an already committed Christian, a college or university training was an aid in their future ministry. I had often chuckled over the story of the old minister who died and went to his Heavenly reward, where, to his surprise, he was asked to get in the queue at the pearly gates. he was somewhat put out, that he, after forty-five years of service in the one parish should have to wait his turn – and not even a back number of *Punch* or *Country Life* to hold his interest. His chagrin turned to wrath when a stunning young blonde swept past him and was at once admitted. He demanded an explanation, to be told by the recording angel, "That young lady passed her driving test but one week ago, but in that week she put the fear of God in more than you did in forty-five years."

The fear of God – that was the theme at the children's meetings in the village hall. I went along once or twice to show interest, but my presence was manifestly ignored. There were choruses, quizzes, sweets for prizes, all of which we had in our Sunday School. Then the twenty of so youngsters from about four upwards sat through a long address where the book was freely pounded, and a bar of chocolate given to the one who had sat most quietly. We sent one of our lads, David, along, feeling we ought to support, and not discourage, any good endeavour. In time, he started quizzing us about death, and where he would go, or we would go, afterwards. He was five years old at the time. Then his nightmares started. So I went along to the children's meeting the next week, and heard these kids in the talk told repeatedly that if "they did not accept Jesus tonight, they might be knocked down by a bus crossing the road, or take some deadly disease before next Friday, and they would go to Hell." The fear of God indeed in kids aged four to eleven! Our lad stopped going, the nightmares ceased, and so far as I am aware has grown up to hold a strong, sure, and reasoned faith. Shortly after my Friday tirade, I happened to be visiting a family in the village, the only Brethren family in the parish. They welcomed me graciously, then the wife proceeded to say what a fine thing it was that somebody was doing something for the young people (I thought it should have been *to* them) each week. I thought of all our Sunday School classes, our devoted teachers, our youth clubs, three football teams for the young, Church based, and other work, but only nodded. I was saddened that this version of the Gospel was being propagated, that children were being told to take this Red Drink, for it, and it alone, was the cure of all ills. I once asked one of our Sunday School youngsters, aged about ten, why she went to the meeting, and was promptly told "to get a bar of chocolate." "I thought that about summed it up."

Just A Bit Of Sport

TWENTY TWO

"I hear John Pearson has got himself into trouble," one of the Moorton elders said to me one Sunday after morning service.

"In what way?" I queried.

"Gambling! Mind you, it's his wife and bairn I'm sorry for."

I was sorry for Mary Pearson too, but also for John. I was also absolutely astonished, for although they lived some distance from Moorton, they belonged there originally, John was a regular in our Church, and I had always thought him a steady sort of fellow and knew he was a good husband and father. His parents were in Church nearly every Sunday, and I knew they would be deeply disturbed. So I went to visit John and Mary, and found Mary alone with their little girl in their small, pre-fab house. I was shocked at Mary's appearance; she was normally a plump girl, but she had lost weight; her usually round, smiling face was furrowed with hurt and worry; she looked haggard, and just drew herself along in a hopeless fashion.

I found it difficult to talk, and also did not want to seem to be intruding in their private affairs, but clearly Mary was at her wit's end and very badly needed to share her load with someone.

"It began, Mr Cameron, with just the odd bob on a horse. Then the bobs became pounds, and it got more and more until the whole wage was gone every week. We're hundreds of pounds in debt and the Electricity Board are threatening to prosecute us. We owe so much to different folks — the grocer, the milkman, the rent — that John's wage is being confiscated before he gets it to pay off these debts."

"And how are you living, lass?"

"Oh, John's folks and mine are helping, and we get by, but I don't know where it's going to end. It's like some terrible disease that's got hold of him – and it all began with just a bit of sport, with his way of it."

"You know, Mary, I can hardly believe this of John. He's always seemed such a sensible fellow that I find it hard to understand that he could let it get a hold of him like that."

Mary sat silent for a while, then quite sudenly burst into tears – great sobs that came from deep inside her and wracked her whole body. I let her cry uninterrupted for a time, for there can be a healing in tears, but I also felt terribly helpless and not a little angry that anyone should cause his wife such misery. After a time the poor woman pulled herself together and apologised "for making such a scene". She gathered the little girl to her, who had been looking on, completely mystified, and crying with her mother.

"It's like some drug that he's hooked on, Mr Cameron, and I can't see how we're ever going to get out of the mess."

"He needs help, Mary. Have you thought of Gamblers Anonymous?"

"Funny you should say that, Mr Cameron! He's going up to Glasgow tomorrow with some man to a meeting of that, and I'm hoping and praying that it can help, but it seems to me it will take a miracle to save us from the awful trouble we're in . . . him and his sport."

"Well, lass, miracles still happen. We must go on praying for one."

And there and then we did, in simple words that came from the heart.

"Mary, don't be offended, but we have a wee fund in the Church which I can use to give to anybody I think needs help. It isn't very much but it will at least keep you in food for a few weeks, and nobody but me knows who gets the money."

So I left a little bit with the poor girl which she promptly hid in a tin "where John won't be able to find it." I left her, promising to look back, and as I looked at her drawn face, feeling a cold fury about the whole unholy business.

On the drive home the words "just for sport" kept going through my mind like a chorus, and I found my thoughts drifting back to a scene from Bristacombe and my vet days.

It began when three dogs met late one evening. One was a wild, half trained Alsatian cross that came from a tinker encampment; the second was a farm Collie, a well trained, faithful animal which brought the cattle in for milking twice a day and was gentle in its handling of sheep. It slept in a barn, and could come and go as it pleased. The third was a Corgi, the pet of a little girl, which had been turned out for its evening run and normally just played round about their country cottage before coming in for the night. The three dogs met up on the High Road between Bristacombe and Mortecombe, frolicked along the road together, playing the canine version of "tig", and in their joyous abandon getting further and further from their respective homes. By and by they came to a field, and in that field were some interesting, woolly creatures. Tired of their game, they went over the dyke to investigate these other animals, which broke before them and ran for their lives. This was better sport and soon the chase was on, just a bit of sport, but in time a chase wasn't enough. It would be more exciting to catch these woolly bundles . . . and so it began . . .!

Early next morning I had a phone call from Geoff Gascoigne. Geoff was a young farmer, struggling to get going, heavily overdrawn at the bank but determined he would make a go of his small, upland farm. Geoff was not only a client, but a friend, and he had shared his problems and his hopes with me. That morning there was a catch in his voice as he pleaded,

"Alec, can you come out right away. I've had dogs among my lambing ewes. I tell you it's like a battle-field out here."

I bumped my way in the old van up his farm road, the roughest and most twisting in the whole Practice, and found Geoff standing in the yard, his shoulders slumped, his whole attitude one of utter hoplessness and despair. Behind him was a trailer piled high with the bodies of dead and dying sheep.

"There's twenty-seven of them, Alec, almost half my flock" said Geoff. "See if there's anything you can do for them."

I moved among that pile of suffering sheep. I had never seen anything so terrible before. Their wounds were horrific . . . throats torn open . . . legs hanging off . . . abdomens ripped open . . . and there was a feeling of utter helplessness in me as I went from sheep to sheep . . . injecting penicillin here . . . stitching wounds there . . . and sometimes with the humane killer bringing a merciful release to the remains of what had once been a sheep.

"It'll take a miracle for us to survive this, Alec. We were counting on their lambs to keep the Bank Manager happy and give us a breathing space."

We moved from the sickening scene out to the field where the slaughter had taken place. The remainder of his sixty ewes were huddled together in a corner, stunned, shocked, terrified, and exhausted. As we walked up the field, I spotted something white lying in the bottom corner.

"There's one you've missed, Geoff," I said, and we headed towards it.

"It's Snowy!" exclaimed Geoff. "She was young Billy's pet lamb last year. She's just a hogg. Poor lil ol' thing . . . she must have been hunted into that corner and couldn't get out."

The little hogg was far through, lying with its neck stretched out and a dreadful gash in its throat. Somehow that little hogg, trapped there by three dogs, unable to escape or fight back, brought the obscenity of the whole dirty business home to us even more than the pile of bodies. As I looked at the little animal, I realised to my complete astonishment that she was also in labour, and before our wondering eyes she gave birth to a tiny little lamb, with the last of her strength. We pulled the lamb around to her head, but her eyes were already glazing in death. Yet somehow, in a strange way, this lamb from his dying hogg seemed to lift the young farmer somewhat.

"She's given us her lamb" muttered Geoff. "Imagine that! With her dying breath. I've never seen anything like it. You know I think Snowy has been trying to tell me something . . . a life from the dead, in a way."

He knelt beside the dead mother and its little lamb, already struggling to get on its feet, and as he stroked the dead little creature the tears flowed down his cheeks, and he kept saying over and over again

"Dear li'l Snowy! Dear li'l Snowy!"

Then his head came up, he got to his feet, squared his shoulders and said

"I'll struggle on, and Alec . . . I'll win through!"

When we got back to the farmyard, after having inspected his other ewes, we found the police had arrived, a Sergeant and a young Constable. They looked at the heap of bodies on the trailer and the Constable was promptly sick. The Sergeant was white too, but with anger.

"This is damnable" he said through clenched teeth. "I've seen sheep worrying before, but never anything as bad as this. I know it won't help you, Mr Gascoigne, but we'll get these dogs."

Well, they got two of them. The culprits had been spotted by a farm worker on his way to the early morning milking, and he gave a good description of them. That afternoon the police came into our surgery, followed by a farmer with a Collie, and a couple with a little girl carrying a Corgi. The father was highly indignant at the very suggestion that their dog would ever harm a sheep.

"Look at her! Can you imagine her ever hunting anything?"

"We'll soon see, sir." I retorted.

I had little sympathy after the scenes in the farmyard that morning. Both dogs were given a shot of Apomorhine, which immediately made them violently sick, and the vomit was composed of masses of wool and strips of flesh. They were undoubtedly guilty, condemned from their own mouths, and the penalty for sheep worriers carried out there and then, after the owners had been removed to the waiting room, where the police were explaining this was the law and that "once a worrier, always a worrier." It was hard, particularly for the little girl, and the policeman's statement may seem a sweeping assertion, but in my experience it is correct. I never liked taking life, but felt as I gave the two dogs the specially prepared strong anaesthetic that they were having a painless death, something very different from what they had inflicted on little Snowy and the other ewes. The Alsatian cross was never found, the tinkers having moved on, so the chief culprit did, in fact, escape, to cause further killing elsewhere, when it felt like a little bit of sport.

For Geoff it was a struggle, but somehow the lesson of little Snowy had seemed a sign of hope to him. Her lamb was reared, the Bank Manager proved sympathetic, and Geoff fought on and won through, moving some years later to a bigger farm.

I called to see Mary Pearson from time to time, and she told me that so far as she knew John was not gambling, and that "the meetings in Glasgow seemed to be helping". Then one evening John came to see me at the Manse. As I showed him into the study, he gripped my arm and said,

"Mr Cameron, you see the biggest fool in creation here, – but I've learned my lesson. I haven't had a penny on a horse for three months and its all thanks to G.A. I'd like you to come up with me to a meeting and see what they're doing up there."

So it was arranged, and John and I drove up to the hall in Glasgow one evening where Gamblers' Anonymous met in one room, the wives in another. Mary was not with us, having their little girl to look after, and perhaps still a bit sceptical. I had my eyes opened that night as I saw and heard speaker after speaker tell their story. They were from every conceivable background – a company director, the manager of a large furniture shop – from well dressed men right down to the latest recruit that night who was practically in rags, had been sleeping rough, and pleaded with someone to go from GA to the night shelter where he, and others like him, some of them also alcoholics, slept on newspapers at night. Two of the best dressed men in G.A. volunteered to go to the shelter and see what they could do, and I realised that a real sense of camaraderie and caring existed between these mutual sufferers and addicts. That night they all spoke of the mess thay had made of their lives, and as I heard stories of stealing, embezzling, furniture being sold, houses being re-possessed, marriages breaking up, my thoughts flashed again to that scene in Geoff Gascoigne's yard and the heap of casualties there, all in the name of a bit of sport.

I don't know that I would have cared to bare my soul in public as these men did, but clearly there was strength in this mutual sharing and fellowship, and encouragement for the new boys in seeing one of their number get his two-year badge, two years without a bet. Each man had a book, a book that was for whatever religion, a kind of prayer book. I drove home with John, having greatly enlarged my experience and modified some of my views, and thinking of One who in His life on earth had compassion for the outcasts and dregs of society, and all who had made ruin of their lives.

Some months later I happened to be at a Youth Fellowship meeting in a church hall where the speakers were two men from Gamblers Anonymous. One of the two was John, a different John, a man able to look the world in the eye again. He was a man trusted once more by his employers, a man clearing his debts, who had not gambled for many months. He wouldn't say he was cured, for an addict would seldom say that, but he had been addiction free for a good period of time. He told me privately after the meeting, with a thrill in his voice, that in some months time he was to become a father again.

Clearly the marriage was saved. Life was good again. We had had our miracle.

With Dignity And Daring

TWENTY THREE

"How are you today, Mr Mackenzie?"

"I canna complain."

He had silicosis, making every breath an effort; he had a failing heart and kidney complications so that fluid gathered in his legs and lungs; when he wasn't in bed, he was in his chair by the fireside; he was completely limited to the four walls of a room, the outside world but a view from the window; he knew he would never be better. Yet always his reply was "I canna complain," and he meant it. It wasn't bravado or an attempt at some kind of stoic philosophy, a shrug of the shoulders that indicated you had to just somehow put up with it all, and it certainly wasn't a wish in the slightest degree to be thought gallant. He really didn't and wouldn't complain for he genuinely reckoned he had many blessings to count. Not an old man in years, he was aged far past his years by suffering and weakness, yet for him, his wife beside him, his family's regular visits to their Dad, the warmth of a coal fire, a drink of cool water, clouds scudding across the sky, a storehouse of happy memories, the dawn chorus of the birds heralding a new day after a night of suffering . . . All these were glorious things that outweighed in the balance of life the weakness and struggle that were his constant companions.

I often visited John Mackenzie, for ministers were supposed to bring comfort and cheer to the suffering, yet as we talked, he was the one who did the cheering, and I would leave his house humbled, and ashamed that a twinge of rheumatism had me moaning and sighing all over the place.

The time came for him to go into hospital to give a temporary boost to his tired heart, and ease a little his laboured breathing. He was a sick, weak man scarcely able to lift a hand, but what a welcome he gave me in his hospital room!

"I'm awful glad to see you, Mr Cameron. Sit doon and tell me the news. Whit's fresh at Moorton?"

"Nothing much except the wind — it was fresh enough when I left."

He laughed at my feeble joke as if I'd said something clever, and our talk ranged far and wide, every sentence he uttered punctuated by long pauses while he gulped in air. Here was a man who walked close to God, so it was as natural as talking to John, to talk with John to his Father and commit home, family and future ino His safe hands. John was content to leave it all there. But before I left, he asked,

"Would you do something for me?"

"Surely."

"Would you go into the room next door and talk to the man there. He's frae America an' hasn'a many visitors. He's got a lot o' money but I doot he hasna' muckle else."

John's summing up of his hospital neighbour was about right. I realised this after five minutes, during which the American gave me a rapid picture of himself painted in glorious technicolour. He was a Scot, really, who had gone to the States as a young man, and now returned to his birth-place to retire. He told me of his many financial deals, about some of his clever dodges, the people in high places he knew, his success with women, including three American wives and now a Scottish one. He was able, he told me, "to beat the hide off" anything or anyone that stood in his way. A big man physically, he was big, it seemed, no matter how he looked at himself.

"Good of you to look in, Padre, but there's not a lot wrong with me, and I'm gonna ask the chief guy here to tell me straight from the shoulder what it is, so that I can get outa this place."

Now and then I tried to get a word in, but he kept going like a tape-recorder on his favourite theme, himself. Yes, a big man, I thought; in the phrase we had used as boys, "a big blaw" (boaster).

"Would you like me to ask a blessing?" I enquired.

"Come again, Padre?"

"Will we have a word of prayer together?" I asked hesitantly. He was amused . . . hilariously so.

"Suit yourself, Padre" he chuckled.

In prayer I felt I was talking into a void. There was no sense of a Presence here, like there had been next door.

"I'll see you next week" I said, and made my departure, glad to breathe some fresh air again.

A week went by and I saw John again. He was a little better, but greatly disturbed.

"I wish you'd see what you can do for the Yank. He's in an awful state, puir man!"

He was indeed. Huddled down in the bed, his large frame seemed to have shrunk, and his eyes had a tortured look. He was mouthing curses at doctors, nurses, padres, his wife and the world in general. It really was a very terrible picture. It seemed he had insisted on the truth, and got it. He had advanced, inoperable lung cancer, and a life expectancy of perhaps a few months. I felt deeply sorry for him, for who can say how any one of us would react to such news, yet I felt somewhat nauseated too. The man next door had lived with death as his companion for a long time, and he knew there was not long to go, but John had a Companion stronger than death. This poor creature seemed to have no companion, no friend to share, not a soul, for he had turned against the one in life nearest to him, his wife. For the first time in his life he was in a situation where all his money, power, clever-dick dealings and important acquaintances were as nothing, and he couldn't cope. It was a desolate scene. The room seemed cold and empty, and I felt very, very helpless.

"Is there anything I can do?" I asked.

"You can go to Hell . . . you, and all your kind!"

He was, I felt as I finally left, already in his own private Hell. I could only say

"I'll be around next week, if you would like to see me."

On the drive home, I thought of the two scenes, the two adjoining rooms. In the one was dignity, in the other desolation, and I recalled others like John I'd known, who had this same, strong anchor in life, who knew the calm in the eye of the hurricane. This was one of the things that had made me a minister, noting over the years in different lives the tremendous difference faith made. Incidents of the past came drifting back to me, odd, seemingly unrelated things, and strangely, I remembered Lulu. Lulu was one of Charlie Trevelyan's chimpanzees, a gentle beast who was a favourite with all visitors to his Zoo, and with millions of children through his appearances with her on "Blue Peter" and other TV programmes. I remembered well his call one evening:

"Alex? Could you come up and see Lulu? I don't like the look of her."

Neither did I when I walked into his house and saw the chimp. She was huddled in an armchair by the fire, and with her outstretched arms gripping the sides of the chair, and her wrinkled face resting on a cushion, she looked like a wise old grandmother watching over her family. I examined her, with a sinking heart.

"I don't know what it is, Charlie, but she's dying"

"Never! Are you sure, Alex?"

"As certain as it's ever possible to be. How long has she been like this?"

"We've noticed her getting a bit thin" said Charlie, "Maybe a fortnight ago we first suspected there was something, but only today did she just want to stay in her house. We brought her in here to watch her."

The law of the wild again, I thought . . . Never show weakness till it can no longer be hidden, for the weakest go to the wall.

"Charlie, I wish I could do something, but I'm afraid it's far too late. I honestly don't know what she's got, but since monkeys are very susceptible to TB, we'll give her a big shot of streptomycin and hope for the best."

Lulu watched me with her sad eyes as I opened my case, and scarcely moved as I injected her. She was far through, but suffering in silence, with a strange dignity about her.

She died in the night. A post mortem showed that she had indeed tuberculosis, was riddled with it more than any animal I'd seen. Yet she had borne it with the quiet gallantry of wild things, doing at the Zoo her job of making people happy and smiling, right to the end. Contact with the vet at the Zoo where she had lived till about twelve months previously revealed that they had lost many of their chimps with TB, the human strain, and the outbreak had been traced to some filthy character spitting at the animals. (Thereafter zoos found it necessary to put glass fronts on their monkey cages.) Lulu had clearly been infected then, all those months ago, and the disease had spread till her whole body was affected, and no one knew . . . no fuss, no refusal to work, no complaints, dignified to the end.

Human beings are not creatures of instinct like wild animals. They are logical, thinking beings, able to reason, knowing the end of a thing, and thus knowing fear or apprehension. John Mackenzie had a similar dignity to Lulu, but he had something more, much more. He had lived with disease and weakness for years, and as a thinking, reasoning human being, had recognised death as it slowly came towards him. Yet in it all was faith. Here was a man who *dared* to believe, for faith has to dare. There was no repining in him. Rather, it seemed to me as the months passed the dignity of his bearing became more marked, and as the shadows gathered round him, serenity and calm seemed to enfold him. A few months after his hospitalisation. I saw him for the last time on earth, in his own home. He smiled and said, as matter of factly as if it was only a trip up the street,

"I'm going Home, Mr Cameron. It's no' far noo,"

"Don't talk like that, John!" his wife protested.

John just smiled, gripped my hand and asked,

"Will you put up a prayer?"

There were tears in my heart that I daren't show in my eyes, yet a great peace too as we spoke, so naturally, to the One who is always near, and who said,

"In my Father's house are many dwelling places. If it were not so, I would have told you."

John said "Thank you, Mr Cameron," then in a lower voice . . . "You'll help mother, I know."

I nodded and left him. In these moments, this humble man had shown not only dignity, but daring . . . The daring of great souls in every age who have looked beyond life here to hereafter, and known that just as surely as the sun would set here, it would rise on the other side. Known that over in the far horizons of eternity, there would still be oneness with friends on earth, and with the great Friend.

I never saw the American again. He had moved to another hospital well beyond my orbit. There was a chaplain there, I knew. I could but hope that the sick man would somehow come to terms with himself, find the peace John knew, and even in weakness be able to say, however hesitantly,

> "Let me no more my comfort draw,
> From my frail hold on Thee;
> In this alone rejoice with awe,
> Thy mighty grasp of me."

The Greatest Thing In The World

TWENTY FOUR

"You must make time in your ministry to read, to study, to keep up to date with the latest thought and developments."

So we had often been told by our Professors at Divinity College and University, and while I suppose they were right, I was finding it mighty hard to do, for two reasons. Firstly, there just wasn't time in a busy church in one's work, like visiting one's people, the sorrowing and suffering. True, they had said, make time, but my life seemed too full to do even that. The second reason was that, after a veterinary course of five years very hard study . . . *very* hard study . . . and having just completed another three years studying for the ministry, less difficult, but still demanding, I felt I had done enough concentrated reading for a lifetime. Of course I dipped into books, but mainly to help in preparing talks and sermons, and I confess it seemed a luxury just to read with no particular end product in view.

One book, however, that I did study early on was Henry Drummond's *The Greatest Thing in the World*, and it set me thinking. I agreed with the famous professor about the greatest thing in the world . . . love, for I had frequently seen it in action in my ministry, as well as in my vet life.

I recalled an incident at Hill Barton in dear old Devon. Hill Barton came about bottom of my list of favourite farms, not because of the farmer, Fred Bowden, for he was a decent young chap and good farmer, but the farm was perched on top of a hill, and there was no road to it. You drove up a track as far as you could, and then walked the rest of the way over several fields. I was re-directed by our secretary on to it one day via a phone call to another farm I was visiting, without any information about the kind of animal I was to see, let alone what was wrong with it. It made life a bit difficult for I didn't know what drugs or instruments I might need, and at Hill Barton you couldn't just go out to the car and collect whatever you required, you had to trudge back over these fields to your car a long way off.

So on that bleak, cold, wet early April day before I left the car, I checked my two cases . . . yes . . . I had most of the regular drugs and tools of the trade there. But to make sure I stuffed the pockets of my old black waterproof coat with more bottles, draped a stomach tube round my neck and set off, wondering, not for the first time who would be a vet as the rain poured down and soon was running down my neck and stinging my eyes in the driving wind. I did some more wondering when I got near the farm and it seemed to me that half of Devon was gathered there. I suppose, to be more accurate, there were about ten people huddled on the side of a little hill just down from the farm buildings, all looking at a cow stuck in the middle of a bog. It was up to its belly in the water, and there was a rope round its horns with which the assembled company had been trying to pull it to safety. A tractor was parked nearby, with the ground at the edge of the morass churned up where its wheels had just spun on the boggy, sodden ground. Everybody looked at me expectantly, and I did yet more wondering. What did they think one solitary individual could do where all that man power and machine power had failed?

"How did she get in there, Fred?" I asked the young farmer, as if it mattered, but I had to say something. He just shrugged his shoulders and said,

"Don't know. Hur calved yesterday, like, but she seemed a' right this mornin' and was turned out to get a bit of grass. Us found her there at milkin' time this afternoon."

"Calved yesterday, eh? Could have a touch of Milk Fever on her then."

So I plunged into the bog, sinking over the tops of my wellingtons and had a look at the cow, a big Shorthorn cross. Temperature was down, pulse slow and lazy, chilled, I thought in that perishing swamp. I gave her a bottle of calcium into the bloodstream, and another mixed calcium, magnesium and phosphorus subcutaneously.

"Now we wait a little." I shouted to the crowd of spectators. It was mighty cold waiting in that marsh, almost up to the knees in water and with the rain still sweeping down. Calcium intravenously usually worked in about fifteen minutes, but it seemed to make little difference that day. I pricked the cow with a needle, rubbed the base of its tail between two sticks, poured some water into its ear — old fashioned tricks to try to stimulate a stubborn animal. But nothing worked, and it looked as if nothing would work. The cow's head was down, its chin resting in the peaty water. It had given up trying, and was doomed.

"Have you a horse?" I shouted to young Fred.

"Aye, us 'as" he shouted back.

"Well, bring it Fred, and we'll see what it can do."

So a big cart horse was brought, the rope from the cows horns attached to its harness, and the horse led forward. At least that was the idea — but after a few yards to take up the slack of the rope, the horse also stuck. It staggered and plunged, but its feet kept slipping in the mud and the cow stayed as it was. What on earth could we try next?

Then far back in my mind a little bell tinkled, advice an old farmer had given me, yet really very obvious. I called to the young farmer to go up to the farm and bring down something. He looked at me with surprise, but did as I asked, and eventually he came back carrying the something, something quite small, with four legs, but which was giving tongue in a high pitched voice and since it didn't like the rain much, doing plenty of shouting. It was, of course, the cow's calf, which after the fashion of dairy herds, had been removed from the mother at birth. Fred Bowden stood on the edge of the swamp holding the struggling calf . . . and almost at once the cow pricked up it ears. It gazed at the bank, and at its calf. It was then the miracle happened. The cow gave an almighty sprackle, heave and splash and pulled itself out of that clinging, cloying muddy water. In no time it was clear, and nosing and licking its calf. We all looked on in wonderment and thankfulness. What brute force, ten men, a tractor and a horse, and scientific know-how in the shape of a vet's treatment had all failed to do, love did . . . the love of a cow for its calf.

I sat back in my study chair and thought . . . that's it . . . that's my main function as a minister . . . to speak of and show love . . . not just the love of a cow for its young . . . but a greater love, the love of God. Because it was love that sent His son into the world to teach, to heal, to show compassion for all, yes, and to go the whole way to a Cross and give Himself for all mankind. Was there ever such a love, one that embraces all, good and bad, saint and sinner? And the glory of our faith: love incarnate conquering death, and showing the power and extent of His love that not even the last great enemy could defeat.

'For God *so* loved . . . He gave His son.' "Never forget that *so*," said a famous conductor to the choir about to sing Stainer's *Crucifixion*, "for it says it all."

"Now abideth faith, hope, love, these three, but the greatest of these is love" wrote St Paul.

Aye . . . the greatest thing in the world indeed, as Henry Drummond had said in his book, and I felt very humble, but also proud, that somehow the great Father had entrusted me who had tried to heal animals because I loved them (and will to my dying day), with the message of His matchless love, and so led a vet to the vestry.

Poultry in the Pulpit

ALEXANDER CAMERON

To My Family
Neil, Ian, David, Alan
and grandson Ross;
and to the wider family of the
congregations to whom I have
been privileged to minister.

CONTENTS

Prologue

ONE

'Mr Cameron – can you tummle your wulkies?' asked young Stewart.
'Can I do what, Stewart?'
'Tummle your wulkies – look, like this' and he proceeded to do several somersaults.
'Oh, I see, Stewart. We called it tumlin' the cran at Glenafton where I was a boy, but I could never do it.'
'What! Never?'
'Eh, no . . . I think it's something about not liking to be upside down.'
'My, you're queer. I doot you were feart,' he concluded.
Our lawns at Kilmarton were ideal for all sorts of games among our three lads, Neil, seven, Ian, five and young David, two. Almost every day in summer they were joined by the McPherson youngsters and sometimes their cousin Hugh, who lived in nearby Dunlop. the McPhersons had a family of boys, like us, Mure, Alastair, Ian, Stewart, just fractionally older than our brood. Bill McPherson was congregational minister at Kilmarton and he and Sheena were among our closest friends, then and now, and since their garden was small, their laddies came down to our wide expanse and played traditional games like hide-and-seek, cowboys, football and games of their own devising among the many bushes and trees on the lawns. They were attired in a variety of gear from trousers, braces and big boots to shorts and bare feet.
In July of 1961 we had an addition to the family when baby Alan arrived, just months after Bill and Sheena had another boy,

little Graham. Not many days after she returned from hospital, Janet was up in our bedroom attending to the new babe when she happened to glance out of the window which overlooked the lawns. Right at the window grew a beautiful gean tree, and Janet was petrified to see that one end of a rope had been slung over a branch and the other end was tied round David's midriff. His face was as red as a beetroot and he looked fit to burst as he fought back the tears while all the rest of the gang were hauling him up off the ground. The game had been cowboys, and David was being lynched! Janet gave a yell, hammered on the window, and with a thump David fell to the ground as the lynch mob realised the victim's mother was not too happy about the proceedings!

I had been preaching in the Laigh Kirk, Kilmarton, ever since I started my divinity studies at Glasgow Trinity. The weekly pulpit supply fee was a great help, and since the much-loved minister Andrew Hastie had died, the great, enormous but gracious manse had been empty, as negotiations dragged on and on for two years to unite the Laigh with the former United Presbyterian Kirk, Cairns. Eventually the Kirk Session of the Laigh suggested we live in the manse, and if I was willing to take the Bible Class, perhaps start a Youth Fellowship, do some visiting and take some funerals, as well as preach weekly, they would be willing to pay me practically a minister's full salary. This was truly manna from Heaven, for most of my share of the Bristacombe practice had gone to provide a home for my mother, my father having died just before I gave up practice, and mother finding herself in that cursed thing, a tied house. It was even more welcome manna with the addition to our family as money was in short supply. Nevertheless, looking back over the three years of study at Trinity with no kind of grant to assist, it was nothing short of marvellous at times the way we were provided for financially. It was hard work, of course, studying daily in Glasgow, preparing weekly sermons and practically running a Church, but the experience was invaluable, and our time at Kilmarton was a wonderful one for my first Charge at Moorton, the neighbouring parish, where, as recorded in my previous book, *Vet in the Vestry*, I was eventually appointed minister, succeeding the Revd Bruce Young who had been a great help to me at Kilmarton. It is customary to present a new minister with robes in his first Charge, but I had been given Andrew Hastie's practically new gowns by his sister, and I have been proud to wear them all my ministry.

Bill and Sheena were not spared their little lad, Graham, for long, as tragedy overtook him. When just a little fellow of two, Sheena found her little boy hanging on a nail in the wall at their back door, where, as he tried to climb the wall, his jersey had caught and been pulled round his neck. We mourned with, and for our friends, as did the whole of Kilmarton, in a so simple, yet tragic death. In time Bill left the Congregational Church and joined the Church of Scotland, maintaining a fine ministry in several places, particularly in the Gorbals where he saw a brand new Church built. In time he went to the quiet of the country until his recent retirement, a faithful ministry despite a life time of ill health and an artificial leg, both the result of his years in a Japanese prison camp where he, astonishingly, and despite his suffering, heard and obeyed the call to the ministry.

Looking back to these years at Kilmarton, two quite opposite events stick in my mind. One was crawling and weeding in the strawberry patch and listening on our portable radio to England thumping Scotland to the tune of nine goals, and poor Haffey the goalkeeper bearing the brunt of the nation's disgust. I am sure I pulled out more strawberries than weeds that day as the goals rattled in!

The other event was my first experience of the strange ways God guides. I had been visiting a very ill man called Mr Stewart and though he always treated me with respect, he also held me at arm's length. I just could not get close to him. One day I set out to do a few visits at one end of the town and found myself to my utter amazement outside his door in a totally different direction. I was astonished to find myself there that day. I just seemed to have been carried and set down there, but I went in, and for the first time got close to Mr Stewart. He was no more ill than usual, but he wanted to talk – and talk about life's basic things – so we did. We read the Psalm 23, had a word of prayer and I left, leaving a man who had clearly found peace of heart and mind. The next day when I got back from Trinity, I received a message to rush to Ballochmyle Hospital as Mr Stewart, quite suddenly, had become worse and could not last long. I hurried as fast as I could, but was too late. I grieved with his wife, and yet marvelled too. We had not had any indication the day before when mysteriously I had been led to his home that this would be his last day on earth, but the great Father had known, and brought, even though at the very end, peace and calm to a wearied and troubled soul.

Many times since, such things have happened, as with all ministers, but I first saw the marvellous and mysterious ways God works in Kilmarton. All my two and a half years there were clearly a preparation for Moorton, where this story begins, the vet back in the vestry, with many a look back to my days among pigs, pets, ponies and all the animal kingdom, and some comparisons with the life of a parson.

Thems as knows best

TWO

'Hello' said a female voice over the phone, 'I'm looking for a brain.'

'Have you lost one then?' I was tempted to ask, but instead said the rather flat, but certainly puzzled, 'Beg pardon?'

'I suppose it does sound a bit queer, right enough' she went on, 'I'd better start at the beginning.'

'That might help,' I agreed.

'My name's Helen Boyd and I'm Secretary of the Kilmaurs and District Young Farmer's Club. We have our first meeting of the new session two weeks tonight and it's to be a Brains Trust. We have three brains lined up . . .' I laughed 'Queer picture. Are they sitting on a shelf?'

She laughed too, but went on, 'We need a fourth brain and when I read about you in the paper, I thought 'the very man.'

'You certainly didn't read that I had a brain . . . maybe the Trust might be nearer it,' I suggested.

'You are Mr Cameron, the new minister of Moorton?'

'That's true . . . very new . . . two days to be exact.'

'You were a real vet and you are a minister?'

'That's true too.'

'Well, there you are then! The very man! I don't know what brains ministers need, I suppose they just get their sermons out of books, but I know vets have to think a fair bit, I mean animals can't talk and all that, and I thought "kill two birds with one stone" . . . he can answer the animal questions and the holy ones . . . not that we're too holy in the

Young Farmers' she added a bit doubtfully. 'Say you'll come . . . please!'

I laughed again and replied, 'Who could resist such a plea? OK. Where do you meet and when?'

So the details were settled and I was lined up for my first outside engagement almost before the furniture had settled properly in the Manse. I didn't know it then, but it was to prove the first of hundreds of requests, over the years, to give a talk, a slide show or be on a panel.

I duly turned up for the Brains Trust, found a surprisingly large crowd assembled, met Helen Boyd the brain researcher and also met my fellow 'brains' – a pig breeder, a traveller for sheep dip, a lady apparently famous for her biting wit and campaign for Woman's Lib . . . and me, the total unknown of the company. The President of the Club was in the Chair and I was mightily impressed by the way he handled the whole evening, as I nearly always have been at YFCs up and down the country over the years. They could teach many of their seniors a thing or two about the conduct of a public meeting.

The questions had been handed in beforehand, and they varied from how to get blackcurrant jelly to set (about which I knew nothing) to the subsidy for hill cattle (where I knew little more). There were, however, many on animal diseases and a surprising number on Church affairs, and invariably the young Chairman would turn to me on such occasions and say 'now we'll ask the man who knows best' or 'now for the expert'. After ten years as a vet I did not class myself as an expert, but I had learned a bit, and with two weeks in the ministry I did not consider myself anything in that field, but somehow got through the questions, which, among others, included:

'How can we prevent staggers . . . in cattle,' added the Chairman amid laughter.

'How do you treat Orf in sheep?'

'What really causes Braxy?'

'Why can't ministers be more human?'

'What's the purpose of a Bishop's get up?'

'How can the Church attract young people?' How I wished I knew an answer to that last one as I looked out at these bright young faces!

The night flew past and I found I had thoroughly enjoyed myself. I do not know if much was learned from my answers, but, clearly, in their eyes, I was, for the night, in my departments, the expert. Later, as I wrote up my diary for the day, my mind kept turning to the Chairman's words . . . 'the man who knows best', and I thought back to how I had been so classified on numbers of occasions in our vet practice at Bristacombe, and before the dying study fire, I drifted off on the wings of memory.

I was puzzled, on two counts. First of all, I wondered why I was there at all. I had passed the sprawling farm buildings of Meadway several times, knew the tenants were called Price, and with a dairy herd that size they must need a vet regularly. I had never before been called, therefore, they had another vet. I did not mind a bit. The practice was growing steadily and from what I had heard of the Price brothers, I reckoned I was better off without them. Why then had they called me out that cold January night to calve a cow?

With my calving coat on, arms scrubbed up and right arm inside the cow's uterus as far as I could reach, I was even more puzzled. What on earth had we here? I looked round the stony faces of the reception committee, three of them, standing watching me in complete silence. I thought they looked a bit like the three brass monkeys, 'Hear no evil, speak no evil, see no evil', only much more villainous than the monkeys! I came out of the cow, took off my calving coat, stripped to the waist to gain a few extra inches, and re-inserted my arm. She was an old Friesian and very deep, and despite my six foot, one and a half inches, I felt I could do with a leg up to get far enough in. I could trace two front legs, but where was the head? I checked – yes – they were front legs, not rear, it was not a breech presentation. I had seen a calf with two heads, one with six legs, but never one with no head – and then I felt the loose flap of skin and the sharp edge of bone. I paused and thought a bit, then withdrew my arm, went to the bucket of water, carefully cleaned my arms and body, then dressed slowly and deliberately. I had my jacket on and was reaching for my coat when one of the surly crew shouted, 'Where the devil are you going?'

I smiled a mirthless smile and retorted as coolly as I could.

'You're right about the Devil, but he's not going . . . He's been here already and I don't like his work or fancy his company!' Quite a speech, I thought, 'So I'm off home,' I added.

'What do you mean?' piped up brother Bill. The other was Joe.

'Look, Mr Price, I don't like being made a fool of and I'm not in the habit of clearing up other people's messes. I'm going home for these very good reasons.

One, I am not your vet. Two, you never told me somebody had been at this cow before me, and three, whoever it was should be hung, drawn and quartered, but the most I can do is report him or you to the RSPCA. In my years as a vet I've never before examined a cow and found a headless calf inside, the head cut off a living calf and the skin and jagged edges of bone stuffed back in, and you hadn't the guts or common decency to tell me. The person who did this is a devil alright, for as well as killing the calf, he's probably condemned this cow to death.

Finally, I'm not going to have it said you had Cameron, the vet, out to one of your cows and he killed it. Good night to you. I'll send you my bill in due course,' and I headed for the door. I was flaming mad.

But Joe Price reached the door before me, looking sheepish. When I heard his feet behind me, I half expected him to clobber me, but he was all remorse or seemed to be. At any rate he was barring my exit.

'Look, Mr Cameron, us's done wrong in not tellin' 'ee like, but Sam Godber's a dab 'and at calvins, like, an' us thought he would manage but it bate 'im.'

'So you're Sam Godber!' I glared at the third man present, a swarthy, unshaven, thick-necked individual, not unlike the Devil, I imagined. 'I've heard of you and seen some of your work and taken the blame already for two cows you killed.'

He stepped towards me, mouthing curses, and looking ugly. There's one in every parish, somebody reckoned to be a dab hand 'when cows are bad to calve'. He thrust his unshaven face close to mine. I kind of hoped he would hit me, for I was livid and spoiling to do something. I'm afraid I would have found it hard to turn the other cheek that night.

'I never killed no cows no-how,' he muttered.

I looked through him; in fact, in retrospect, I thought my performance was worth an Oscar! Now he became more abusive still.

'Look, sonny,' he sneered, 'I've calved more cows than you've ever touched an' I reckon I've forgotten more than all that thar book learnin' they gives you at college.' This was quite a speech for him, though actually it was somewhat longer than reported for every other word was an obscenity. I listened to his tirade and thought of two cows I'd seen, one with metritis (inflamation of the womb) and the other with a ruptured womb. I knew what some of the farming community had said . . . 'we had Sam Godber, an' he calved them a'right, but vet lost them after.' It was always the vet's fault, said thems as knows best.

'Well then, in that case, Mr Godber, since you know it all, and certainly more than me, I suggest you go ahead and finish this calving you started.'

He really had no answer to that, except more curses. By now the other Price brother was beside me, pawing at my arm.

'Please, Mr Cameron; Sam's done 'is best, like, but this thar's a job for thems as knows best. (I was exalted in status, I thought.) We can't leave the poor beast like that.'

'Then send for your own vet,' I snapped. 'Why didn't you anyway?'

'We didn't reckon Mr Warman 'ad take it too well, like, to us 'avin 'ad a go.' I bet he wouldn't. He'd have sworn at them for five minutes probably, without repeating himself, and then told them to send for the knacker. 'We knew you was a bit of a preacher, like, an' we thought you'd take more kind to it, do you see?' Probably what they really meant was 'he's a soft mark', for I confess I wasn't feeling very Christian just then, but I don't suppose Christ was the picture of gentleness when He took a whip to the rogues in His Father's house.

I looked at the two Price brothers, and the man Godber, tough nuts all of them. Then I glanced at the poor beast. Whatever else I was, Christian or no, I was supposed to relieve suffering.

'Alright,' I said, 'I'll do what I can on two conditions. First, that if this cow dies, you'll say you called the vet too late, and second, that Mr Godber, who reckons he knows it all anyway, clears out.'

This was rubbing it in a bit, but I was hanged if I was going to have a critic looking on, a sort of back seat driver, and equally determined I was going to give no secrets away to this fellow who badly wanted teaching a lesson. They hesitated, and the two Prices looked at Godber.

'A'right, I knows when I'm not wanted. I'll go.' 'Swine,' he snarled as he passed me. I did not mind. I had been called worse.

It was no easy task delivering that headless torso. Clearly the calf had been coming head first with fore legs back, and unable to repeal the head or advance the legs to the normal chin on legs position, Godber had cut a living calf's head off, and pushed the stump inside. Then, with the vaginal wall swollen, oedematous and lacerated, he had taken fright and advised getting the vet. I got my calving chains on the forelegs. I used special chains rather than ropes, for they were stronger, easier to grip, less liable to lacerate the vaginal wall and more easily sterilised. Then I managed to put another chain round the flap of loose neck skin, more or less enclosing the jagged ends of the calf's neck bones. Then masses of lubrication was pumped into the womb and vagina, and while the brothers pulled on the leg chains as directed, I shielded the vaginal wall as best I could with one hand over the neck stump, and slowly advanced it with the neck chain. Then with the stump and legs outside, it was just a question of pulling. It was a big calf, but it could have been saved. 'And it was a heifer too,' murmured Joe. For the first time that night I began to feel a twinge of pity for any human present. I cleaned the cow there and then (removed the afterbirth), inserted some pessaries, gave a whacking dose of penicillin and intimated I would be back for the next two days to give more injections. She did fine, and I gained half a client. They evidently did not like to leave their own vet, but they were genuinely grateful, and came to us for some cases.

Godber? He went on acting as midwife. I sometimes think it takes about as long in remote country districts to counter this kind of quackery, as it did Mary Slessor to checkmate the witch doctors of Calabar, for in the minds of very many, it is only the likes of Godber with no book learning, but plenty of experience, 'as knows best'.

Frank Fowler was also reckoned to be in the ranks of 'thems as knows best', but he was a different kettle of fish from Godber. Nature had endowed him with a small, narrow hand – or rather two of them – infinite patience and considerable know-how in the ways of sheep. Every lambing season, if the farmer was beaten, the first line of approach was usually the wife or daughter, smaller hands again. If they were beaten, you sent for Frank. He was good, there was no doubt about it. But sheep were valuable at that time in the early 1950s, a ewe with twins was potentially £20 anyway, so it was worth considering having a vet, at the very most two guineas a time, possibly less, and that was all the ewe would fetch for slaughter, again possibly less. So one triumphant day I was summoned to a case where Frank was stuck. He was there to watch proceedings, plus a few neighbours. Frank would never 'bad use' a ewe, but if two or three hands have been there before yours, the uterine fluids are usually dried up, the ewe exhausted, and perhaps a lamb or lambs dead. The audience that day, with the exception of the farmer, probably hoped for a failure. What could this Scotsman do that their own Frank could not? What, indeed, that Scotsman was wondering himself?

I examined the ewe, trying to look assured and confident before this audience, and for that first case I was in luck. All I could feel was a multitude of legs, and no heads. I knew Frank would never be guilty of a

Godber decapitation, so I patiently worked away, sorting out what were back and fore legs. The two essentials of lambing are undoubtedly patience and gentleness, and in multiple births, it can sometimes take time to get everything in position. Now the great disadvantage of spectators at a lambing is that they cannot see a thing, at any rate what the vet is doing inside. I got a pair of hind legs, eased them up gently, and felt the lamb come – a breech presentation. I grunted 'this one will be dead' and I was proved an accurate prophet, which greatly enhanced my standing with the spectators, but I knew fine that a breech that had been so long in the delivery as this one had, would be dead, the lamb had suffocated. Then to appreciative murmurs I brought out two smaller lambs, normal front presentation. The heads had been twisted right back and their legs tangled with the big breech lamb, but no matter, the ewe had live twins, and as she nuzzled her lambs and 'talked' to them in that lovely throaty way, I reckoned that her satisfaction and mine about matched.

I have always enjoyed lambings and constantly marvelled at this new, young life. To me lambs were the loveliest of all new born creatures, certainly far and away beating babies, though no mother would agree with that. Every lambing produced in me a sense of wonder and of achievement, even though the emotion was tempered with the knowledge that in a few short months that little bundle of life would end up on a plate with mint sauce. I always marvelled too at how quickly both mother and offspring were on their feet after the birth. I remember getting into trouble with my mother-in-law after Ian, our second son's birth. He arrived during the lambing season, and though not seeing his birth, that being frowned upon by the medical profession then, I was at the nursing home shortly afterwards. Having duly admired my new son, I kissed my wife and said, 'Why are you still lying there? When are you getting up?' She spotted the twinkle in my eye, but her mother did not, and she rounded on me and retorted, 'Up? Up? Oh, you big cruel brute. She's just given you a lovely son and you expect her to be up already. Ach, men!'

'Oh, I don't know,' I replied. 'I lambed a ewe at Martincombe just half an hour ago, and it'll be half way up Hangman Hill by now!'

I would not have been human at the lambing I've described to feel no gratification, succeeding where others had failed, but after all I was only doing my job. It was just a week later that I had an even greater sense of achievement. I was actually summoned by Frank Fowler himself to his own farm, to deliver a lamb. It could not have been easy for a man almost twice my age to admit that others knew best, but he did. I knew this was bound to be a corker, for Frank would never have summoned me to the very shrine of the sheep kingdom unless it was an exceptionally difficult case.

'Big lamb, head back,' was all Frank said. Around the straw lay his ropes and bits of fine cord. beside the ewe was a bottle of green oils, that famous remedy favoured by shepherds for all ills and an excellent lubricant. I was not too confident this time, as I looked at that Devon Closewool ewe lying with its neck stretched out, exhausted. But I had one secret weapon Frank had not and I used it that night. A lamb, as a calf, is normally born with front feet first, and head resting on them. It is impossible to deliver a lamb if the head is not coming with the feet, and perhaps the most common difficulty, especially if the lamb is big or the ewe small, is for the ewe, as it strains in labour to advance the forelegs, instead of the head sliding into the passage with them and pushed forwards with each contraction, because of the tightness is pushed backwards until it is turned right round in a looking-over-the-shoulder position.

That was the problem with Frank's ewe, and his lambing cords told me he had been trying, in traditional manner, to get a cord over the lower jaw, or even round the neck, to bring up the head. So I did not, after a quick examination, even try with cords, but produced my secret weapon. I saw Frank's eyes on me as I took it out of the steriliser. This was something new to him. It was, in fact, a blunt eye hook, with a long handle, available at that time, and just recently available, only to vets. It had to be used with considerable care. So, repelling the legs, I manipulated my hook into the bony eye socket, and as the ewe strained, ever so slowly I managed to bring the head round, until with a jerk it was in the correct position, following the legs. I unhooked my new toy before Frank could see what I had used it for, and then, by pulling the legs only, the lamb was delivered, alive, and with eye undamaged.

As I cleaned up, I could see Frank minutely examining my weapon. 'Could you get me one of these?' he asked.

'Sorry, Frank, they're only available to vets. It's a dangerous toy, you know!'

'I can see that, but you know I'd be careful.'

'I don't doubt it, Frank. I know you're good, none better round here at lambing a ewe. But once you had one, every Tom, Dick and Harry would be after one, and can you imagine the suffering that could be caused? Besides,' I grinned at him, 'I've got to earn a living too, you know.'

'I dare say you're right,' he replied, though clearly disappointed. 'The likes of this is best handled by thems as knows best.'

Of all the branches of the animal kingdom, none, like the equine, is so afflicted with experts, self-pronounced, or raised to the status of thems as knows best by a reputation, or sheer brass neck, developed over the years. The wide boys, the fly guys, the know-alls abound in the horsey world, especially in that of the competition or thoroughbred fraternity. We had only a few work horses left in Devon, but everybody kept at least one pony on his farm. Many had hunters, and there was the odd thoroughbred that had not made the grade. Horses went the rounds, and in their life-time might have a variety of owners, and here and there a seller would find a vet ignorant enough, genuinely deceived, or very occasionally unscrupulous enough to pass an animal as sound, when in fact it was not. It was my experience too, that for all the camaraderie that existed on the surface between horse breeders, there were plenty ready to pull a fast one. I liked the story of the horse dealer, who, having had a Christian unbringing, would always conclude a deal with a quotation from Holy Writ. On one occasion he had been guilty of a piece of sharp practice, having passed off an old broken-winded nag to an ignorant buyer, as sound in wind and limb. Coming in the house, gleefully pocketing the cheque, he was rebuked by his wife for what he had done, to which he replied readily, if quoting somewhat incorrectly, 'he was a stranger and I took him in.'

I knew that Fred Boothby was of this breed. He was the horsiest type for miles around, kept a few ponies, and what he lacked in farming skill, or willingness to work, he made up by his horse-dealing. It was therefore, with no great enthusiasm that I looked forward to my visit one afternoon to his farm of Greystones. He had recently bought a pony and wanted me to vet it, since he was somewhat suspicious of it. There had been a time clause in the bargain that if any fault was found within a week, the seller would take it back, or give a price reduction.

The uneven yard of Greystones seemed filled with horses and attendant males or females as I drove in. All the clever jacks were there, including, I noticed, Donald Tucker, his pointed chin and nose seeming to meet as ever, and his eyes always appearing to look past you. There had evidently been considerable discussion, debate and argument about this latest piece of horse-flesh to arrive at Greystones, and I realised at an early stage that my judgement was keenly awaited; maybe they had even been wagering on it, the 'sounds' and 'unsounds' being about equal in numbers. Now I was no horse expert, as I admit elsewhere, always feeling more at home with cattle, sheep or pigs, but I had been fortunate enough to grow up in the country, work on farms where horses were still the norm and a tractor a luxury, and I had seen practice in a part of the country famous for its breeding of Clydesdales. Even in my assistantship years at Mochrum, I suppose I treated a horse every second or third day. True, these had almost entirely been work horses, but the diseases and defects were the same in their loftier kin of the hunting field and the turf, so I had obtained rather more experience than the average general practitioner today.

I looked at Fred Boothby's pony. It was a handsome chestnut, with a bold carriage of the head, a lovely arched neck, and long flowing mane and tail. He had paid a pound or two for that, I reckoned, and clearly this was his hope to clean up some winnings at coming gymkhanas and country meets.

'That yer hoss is a rale topper, I reckon,' announced Donald Tucker in a rare moment of speech. Usually he just communicated with grunts, nods and sly looks. His remark was greeted enthusiastically by many present, but others, including, I noticed, Fred Boothby himself, were silent. I did not like the man much, but he knew a horse. I had his daughter trot it up and down, then walk it, and suddenly make it break into a trot. Then I had it ridden round and round in circles. It seemed sound, yet there was just a suggestion of stiffness now and then, even a stumble on occasion. Then I examined him limb by limb, sounded his lungs, tested heart-beat and pulse, felt for any scars. I was sure there was a something but what? Suddenly I recalled an old Clydesdale I had seen as an assistant.

'Is he stiff when you take him out first thing?' Boothby nodded.

'And does it gradually wear off as he gets going?' Again he nodded. There were comments from various sources.

'Oi be stiff, like, mornings mesulf,' said one old codger.

'But it don't wear off you, Bert,' retorted a wag.

I went over the horse again minutely, running my fingers up and down his legs, feeling the joints, tendon sheaths, looking at the feet, until at last I got it.

'Your horse has a ringbone, what they call a high ringbone, Fred.' I beckoned him over.

'Feel the pastern joint in that near foreleg.' He obeyed, followed by Donald Tucker who was adamant there was nothing amiss with 'this 'ere hoss.'

'Danged if I can feel anythin' there,' announced Donald.

'Shut up, Donald,' said Boothby. 'Vet's right, 'tis swollen there for sure.' He looked at me somewhat belligerently as if I had done the dirty on him and demanded 'What do we do then?'

'Oh, I can treat it for you alright, but you'll never have a winner here. The swelling might go away for a bit, but almost certainly will come back. I should think that whoever sold you this horse knew what was what, for a ringbone could easily be missed in the first week.'

Half the company were looking at me suspiciously, as if I had put the ringbone there, but one or two, Boothby included, were looking with some respect, and I heard him speak of vets as 'thems as knows best'.

So I was moving in a mixed society. The Prices had said that of me, now Boothby, none of whom I would have trusted with a shilling. But Frank Fowler had said it too, and as I sat at the now dead study fire, I recalled the young President that night had also used more or less the same phrase. I felt a trifle smug, until I remembered that folk like Godber were so addressed too. Oh well, at least I was one of the élite!

The rock whence ye are hewn

THREE

The Church at Moorton was old, built in 1643 during the Covenanting struggles of the 17th Century, cruciform in shape, whitewashed, with distinctive features like its crow step gables, an outside staircase to one of the galleries, sentry boxes at the gates where in the days of the body snatchers elders had stood guard at nights to guard the new graves, and where the office bearers still greet the flock on a Sunday. Beside the gates were two table-like erections for the offering and I used to feel it was typical of the caricature of the canny Scot. You had to pay at the gate before even reaching the Church doors! There was an outside bell-rope where the Beadle, Andrew Crombie, tolled the bell to summon the worshippers, protected on wet days by someone with an umbrella. Fastened to the outside of one wall was a metal collar, the jougs, where evil-doers in days gone by had been punished for such crimes, according to our old records, as

> 'Bleaching washing on the Sabbath day'
> 'Cursing, swearing and fighting with ye mother-in-law'
> 'Calling an Elder a slavery loon'
> 'Telling the Minister it was a black day he came to Moorton'.

This last entry encouraged me no end, for the first minister, William Guthrie, was a saint, a preacher of great power whom folks walked twenty miles to hear. Moreover he was a kind, caring man who had presence about him, so that whether fishing for brown trout in the Moorton Burn, or black sinners in the parish, he always seemed to have his Lord by his side. He was a man much loved, a moderate man, a gentle man in hard, cruel days, but even he was expelled from his Church by order of the Bishop for preaching freedom of the faith and the one Head of the Church, no earthly monarch like Charles II or James II, but the King of Glory. I used to think that if such a man had, at least, one local critic, then it was to be expected I would have plenty more.

Inside the Church was beautiful in its simplicity, with its fine wood which positively shone, dusted and polished daily and lovingly by Andrew. The pulpit was central, on which there was a sand-glass like a large egg timer, which Andrew solemnly turned as the sermon commenced each Sunday. Every eye in the building following him up and down the steps. Only when the deed was done, I discovered, did the folks settle down to listen to the sermon, the shape of the Church making the congregation seem like a large family gathered around. I never preached the glass to its end, but one day when I was elsewhere, a visiting lady missionary did. Our boys did not know whether to be pleased or disappointed that Dad's record had gone to 'yon wifey that preached the glass dry.'

Surrounding the Church was the old graveyard, and since the Manse was just across the road, I thought that at night when the trees were rustling and the owls hooting, it would be somewhat eerie. Graveyard stories there were in plenty, like the one where a man the worse of drink, taking a shortcut one Saturday night fell into a newly dug grave waiting for a funeral on the Monday. He could not get out, and eventually fell asleep. At 6.00 am the next morning, a dairyman taking the same shortcut heard moans and groans coming from the bowels of the earth. He went over to investigate, saw the shivering and now sober figure at the bottom and demanded, 'Whit's wrang wi ye, making a' that noise.'

'Oh, I'm awful cauld,' came the response.

'Nae wonder,' said the dairyman, 'you've kicked a' the dirt aff ye!'

There was another story, a definitely authentic one, of a Beadle who was going down the path of a Borders Church to light the coal fire in the boiler early one Sunday morning, when a voice called him from under one of the six-legged, flat-top gravestones. Another roisterer had evidently sought shelter there the night before. The Beadle was whistling as he walked when the voice from the dark, and apparently from the tomb hailed him, 'Man, John, is it that time already?'

The terrified Beadle did not wait to enquire but fled for his life.

The tale was often told me of how one night in Moorton the Church bell had started to ring. The folks shivering in their houses were afraid to investigate, convinced it was a warning of some kind or the Devil himself. Eventually one brave spirit did go to the Church and in the darkness could just make out a white figure with horns and a tail tolling the bell. He fled, and reported his findings, whereupon everyone was convinced it was indeed 'Auld Nick' himself. Only with daylight did the population head for the Churchyard where they found a white cow with the bell rope tied to its tail. Clearly some joker had enjoyed the night of his life.

But our graveyard was in no way 'spooky'. Indeed it had a calm atmosphere, as if those there, after life's fitful fever, slept well, and many nights I walked through it, savouring its tranquillity. It was a famous graveyard, for it had many headstones to Covenanting martyrs, sixteen in all, more than any other Church in Scotland.

Best known was Captain John Paton, farmer, elder of Moorton Kirk, and soldier of fortune under the great Swede, Gustavus Adolphus. He had a farm in the parish, and just a few miles from it was the Covenanters' cave, where many a time he, or some other hunted man found refuge. Early in my ministry, I visited the cave and climbed up into it. It was a poor place, cold, damp, big enough for maybe three men, but in its position a secure hiding place for many of the men of the Covenant when Scotland was divided between those who fought for religious liberty and those who took the part of the King as he sought to impose his will, his form of worship and Church government, and especially his Kingship of the Kirk. So for fifty long years the struggle for freedom of the faith was waged, claiming many lives, and leaving in its wake memorials all over lowland Scotland to those who gave their lives for what they held dear. Religious freedom came finally with the accession of William of Orange in 1688.

As an old man Paton was captured, tried and condemned to death. A petition was raised on his behalf, he was pardoned by the King, but legend has it that the Bishop kept back the news till after Paton's execution in Edinburgh's Grassmarket, with the story that the pardon had arrived too late. Paton handed his wife his Bible from the scaffold, and symbolically it ends with the words from Revelation 12, the last few chapters being missing,

'They overcame by the blood of the Lamb and by the word of their testimony, and they loved not their lives unto death'.

This faith and courage was the motivating force of these men and women, and their gallant struggles 'the rock whence we are hewn' in Scotland's Kirk today.

North of the village was the moor from which it took its name. It is quiet on the moor today. There you can lie on a clump of heather and watch the bog myrtle wave in the breeze, see a hare lope over the hill, hear the plaintive call of the curlew and perhaps the bark of a fox. It was not always so peaceful, for often the moor would resound to shouts, to the cries of hunted men and the thunder of galloping horses, for right on the top of the moor is the farm of Lochgoin, where in the killing times of the late 17th Century many a fugitive found refuge. The tenants of the farm were the Howie family who had come to Scotland in the 12th Century for religious freedom. Often the farm was raided by dragoons, the cattle driven off, the buildings set alight, but no Covenanter was ever caught there.

On the Tope, (the top of the hill) stands a large monument to John Howie who in his *Scots Worthies* and other books told the story of these days. The monument is to him, but indeed to all the men of the Covenant, and for years, like Moorton's little Kirk and Kirkyard, had been a place of pilgrimage for those interested in Scotland's storied past and keen to learn more of that rock from which Scotland has been hewn. They came by busload and car to see, to listen to talks I early found I was expected to give, and to photograph the graves of the martyrs.

One day, Duncan, my treasurer, a local Councillor and no mean historian, came to me in a state of considerable anxiety. He launched straight in.

'Tom Howie's been offered £2000 by an American for the relics. We canna let them go oot o' the parish! Whit can we dae?'

So we talked about it at length, decided we would form a Trust and somehow try to raise £2000, a considerable sum in those days. We got Tom (the last of the Howies of Lochgoin) to agree to hold his hand and give us a chance to buy the relics of Moorton – flag, drum, Paton's Bible and sword and many others. We enlisted Sandy Paton, a descendant of the famous Covenanter, and feeling very small, the three of us proceeded to launch appeals the length and breadth of the land. Quite early we had a great boost when Lord Rowallan, former Governor of Tasmania and Chief Scout, and landlord of Lochgoin, expressed an interest, and was promptly voted Chairman of the Trust. Gradually money came in until one glorious day we had the total. Then, on an even more glorious day and in a magnificent gesture, Lord Rowallan said he would gift Lochgoin to the Trust, and have as tenants old Tom Howie's daughter and her husband at a modest rent, provided they made over one room of the little whitewashed farm in its ring of trees, as a museum room.

I was asked to produce booklets about Moorton's Covenanters, and on a shining July Sunday, with a detachment of the Cameronians on guard, (the regiment that rose from the Covenanters and took their name from Richard Cameron, the young Lion of the Covenant and who had stood guard at many a Conventicle in the hills) on that Sunday we held a never-to-be-forgotten Service, followed by a Conventicle at Lochgoin. The Captain of the Cameronians posted his men, then marched smartly up to me on my pulpit (a farm trailer) and announced in the words his forerunners had used many times

> 'Reverend Sir! The pickets are posted, there is no enemy in sight; the Service may proceed.'

The Revd Ronald Falconer, BBC Director of Religious Broadcasting led in prayer, we sang the old Psalms with a precentor as our forebears had on many hills, then Dr Stewart Mechie, my old history lecturer from Trinity, gave the address, on, of course, 'the Rock whence ye are hewn'. There followed a moving ceremony as Lord Rowallan handed over the Title Deeds of Lochgoin to Duncan as Secretary of the Trust. As the sun beat down on the assembled vast throng of 600, and in the blue distance 'Paddy's milestone' rose out of an azure sea, as the soldiers marched the boundaries and the sheep and curlews called, I felt, as others there, that we were making our own little bit of history. Ronnie Falconer evidently felt the same and said, 'We must repeat this next year, for television.'

But by the next year the Cameronians had been disbanded in the government's re-organisation of the various regiments, and instead I was asked to do a week's television talks on the Covenanters and the Cameronians, something that was achieved in much fear and trembling, as is recounted elsewhere.

Lord Rowallan and the faithful Duncan are long gone, Sandy Paton more recently, and I am the only survivor of the original trustees, but others have come forward. Lochgoin is visited by hundreds each year from all round the world, and Moorton's lovely little Kirk sits secure and solid amid its surrounding gravestones, slumbering the years away as the men of the Covenant slumber, waiting for the day of Resurrection.

Robert Louis Stevenson captured it perfectly when he wrote,

> Blows the wind today, and the sun and rain are flying
> Blows the wind on the moor today, and now
> Where above the graves of the martyrs the whaups are crying,
> My heart remembers how!

Sporting on the green

FOUR

'Howzat!' came the stentorian voice of Neil, our eldest son. 'You're out! That ball was hitting the middle stump if your big leg hadn't been in the road.'

'No . . . a'm no oot,' retorted Ronald the batsman.

'You was LWB,' said David, aged five.

'It's no' LWB, you dopey,' corrected young Billy, who bore the nickname of Miggermite, 'it's ebberwubbleyou.'

'Och, you be quate, loon. Fit div' you ken,' said the batsman, sticking to his guns.

'Definitely out,' pronounced Trevor.

'Come on, Donian,' said Ian the wicketkeeper, 'the ball was hitting the wickets.'

'Naw, it wisna.'

'Him zoot,' piped up baby Alan, aged three pointing, and determined not to be left out of things.

I sighed. The voices, getting louder by the minute, came floating in my open study window as I tried to concentrate on a sermon, no easy task when our lads and half the village were sporting on the green.

'LWB,' reiterated young David.

'Och, you gommerel, fit div you ken,' replied Aberdonian Ronald. 'It's LBW but it's no LWB – och, you ken fit a mean.'

I knew what would shortly happen, and sure enough it did. David Ferguson the policeman's son, and captain of the batting side, shouted above the increasing din.

'Get your daddy to decide!'

The cricket nearly always deteriorated into an argument and nearly always I was called on to mediate. I did not mind that particular night for it was a glorious summer evening, the sermon had stuck, and I thought I would rather be in the midst of a cheerful mêlée than scratching my head over my notes. So out I wandered, gravely listened to the claims and counter claims, and then with the wisdom of Solomon gave my verdict.

'A free shot at the wicket by the bowler to decide.'

That always seemed to calm the storm, and Neil duly ran up, aimed the tennis ball at the home-made stumps . . . and missed.

'That proves it,' grinned the jubilant Donian. 'I kenned I wisna oot,' and so the game continued again till Mum called young David and Alan in for bed. The others gradually drifted off home, until only three boys were left. Another Test Match was over, and a draw was a favourable result for all concerned.

We did not have what you might call a lawn as such at Moorton. There was an immense stretch of grass in front of the Manse with a large clump of trees down one side where every spring the rooks built their nests and our children tried to provoke heart attacks in their parents by their antics up these trees, hanging upside down, climbing high, or swinging on overhanging branches. We kept the grass under control and reasonably short with a rotary grass cutter and as time went by, by dint of much hard labour, the grass had almost the consistency of a proper lawn. In one corner towards the Manse, Janet built a rockery, and beyond it we had a large patch of Hybrid Tea (HT) roses, which were annually our pride and joy. There were ten dozen of them, and we knew them all by name, treating them almost like members of the family.

'I see Papa's in bloom' (Papa Meilland),

'Ena's hanging her head as usual – a shy rose', (Ena Harkness).

'What a glorious scent has Shot Silk,' and so on, round our floral family. Beyond the rose garden was a wide border stretching across the front of the Manse, just below the study window, and here too were roses of the Floribunda type. We got great pleasure from our garden, having seen it develop from a wilderness, not least the enormous walled vegetable garden which annually was ploughed and worked for us by my very willing farm elders, Jim Shankland and Jim Grant. When we first arrived, it was so wild you were in danger of being lost in it. Indeed when I first fought my way into it, I thought I might meet some former minister trying to find a way out, but over the years these two men worked wonders, so that everything was laid out neatly in beds and plots.

But our pleasure was nothing to that of our laddies. The lawn was their own private stamping ground, and the grass ideal for their football, cricket, cowboys, hide-and-seek and a variety of games of their own devising. The thing about our lawn was its versatility. It was, in rotation, Hampden Park, Lords or Wimbledon, depending on the season. Football was, however, without question number one, and regularly a host of village children would be sporting on the green with our brood of four. We had Jimmy Rodgerson, the joiner, erect a miniature set of goalposts at one side, and many a rousing battle was fought on our own 'pitch', and there Dad and the boys would play a game of their own invention called Combi – short for Combination – when the ball had to be controlled and passed in two touches, thus developing skills at an early age which were to come to fruition later on as all four developed into really first-class players, even allowing for a father's natural pride. I had promised Neil, the eldest, a shilling at Bristacombe when he could kick with his left foot as well as his right, and he practised and practised to earn his shilling until he was, in fact, genuinely two-footed. The others got the same offer, no account being taken of inflation, and they all went at it day after day to earn the coveted award.

When Test matches were on television, as has already been indicated, they became Cowdrey, Sheppard, Statham, Laker and the like, and many a stern battle was fought, though, as fervent Scots, they were never very sure whether they wanted England to win. If a batsman was proving difficult to shift, Dad, if he was around, was called on to do his fiery Fred act, when, as Trueman, I would rush up and hurl the tennis ball down. Sometimes it got near the sticks which did duty as stumps! They played and played, seemingly oblivious to the midges, which on many nights, speedily drove me indoors.

One day my elder Jimmy Aitchison came to me and said 'There's some saying you're no too parteecular who you let into your gairden to play wi' your boys.'

'What do you mean, Jimmy?' I queried.

'Catholics!'

'What about Catholics?'

'There's two o' these weans are Catholics an' they're in the Manse gairden.'

'Good!' I exploded.

'Good?'

'Good! The more youngsters are together, the less trouble and bigotry there would be in the world. I'm delighted these laddies want to play in the garden.'

Jimmy's face broke into a big grin, he slapped me on the back, and said, 'Man, I'm pleased to hear it. That's what I feel too, but you ken what some folk are like.'

'More pity them,' I responded, 'there'll be no Catholics in Heaven and no Protestants either. It won't matter there,' and the subject was closed. Roger Flynn, a wee Catholic boy, was, in fact, a close friend of Ian's and later on played regularly for our Bible Class team.

It seemed our lads had evolved their own code of conduct and behaviour and those allowed into their garden had to abide by it. This was made clear one evening when Janet was standing at the kitchen window which happened to be right at the Manse front gate. Outside the gate stood two tough wee fellows from two poor homes in the village. They watched the fun inside with envious eyes, at the same time not wanting to seem too interested, but clearly longing to join in what was going on. Eventually one said,

'Are you fur in?'

'I dinna ken; are you?'

'Och, we micht as weel.'

'Weel, mind, if you go in there you canna sweir!'

So saying, they opened the gate, prepared to cut off swears in mid-flow for the sake of getting a game. I really felt quite a paternal pride when I heard that.

Our 'lawn' was ideal for picnic teas in the summer, and Neil and Alan, forever dubbed through their lives as 'big man' and 'wee man' by others, though both are now over six feet, having summer birthdays, had birthday teas with their friends, when we erected our big, old, brown ex-army tent in case of rain in Moorton's fickle climate.

The great occasion of the year, however, was Guy Fawkes night. For weeks the boys would collect rubbish round the village and sticks from the wood and build a huge bonfire. On the great night they assembled with their special friends, each clutching his fireworks, and occasionally one of my twin brothers, Fergus or Graham and his five year old son, Hugh, would come up to join the fun. They let off their fireworks under careful supervision, then midst mounting excitement, the bonfire would be lit, and all sat round it for the feast. We sizzled sausages, roasted potatoes (and ate them half raw!) and Mum had always prepared delicacies like muffins, perkins, ginger cake and treacle toffee. Then, as the fire died down, Dad had to tell a ghost story.

One night, after a particularly creepy one, the friends of the boys all mustered together to go home *en masse*, feeling that a crowd was more security against ghoulies and sinister women in black who beckoned from the tomb and said 'Come with me, come with me'. My brother Fergus thought he would add a touch of realism, and draped in a sheet, he nipped into the old churchyard just across the way, intending to leap out at the kids as they reached the end of the wall. It seemed a good idea but something obviously miscarried for no phantom appeared. Eventually he came hirpling back, carrying his sheet, having in the dark tripped over one of the flat topped grave stones raised on its six legs, and banged his leg good and proper which is enough, of course, to discourage any sensitive ghost. On another occasion, I told a story about vampires.

'Och, that's not true,' bragged Ian to the others with great bravado. 'I don't believe in vampires,' and somewhat hesitantly, the others agreed. They did, however, just to be safe, hurry home, their walk breaking into a trot, and finally a mad gallop to reach their respective houses. I had a little luminous cross which sat on the study desk and the next morning it had disappeared. It was found eventually beside Ian's bed, that, of course being the recognised preventative for vampires. He who did not believe was taking no chances! Yes, the Manse garden saw quite a few stirring scenes.

Moorton Church, like most country churches, had to have fund-raising events from time to time, and it was decided one year to hold a Garden Fête in the Manse grounds, with various stalls in the Church hall. The fête was to be opened by Frank Beattie, captain of Kilmarnock FC, and the great attraction was Campbell Forsyth, Kilmarnock and Scotland's goalkeeper, who was to be in the boys' little goalposts, and at a penny a shot, all and sundry were to try to beat him. Our football-mad sons were in a fever of excitement at the prospect, especially Ian who supported Kilmarnock, but even little Alan, an avowed Celtic fan, condescended to allow players of another team in his garden. (Many years later, when we had left Moorton and when Ian was himself a star, having played for Aberdeen, then Kilmarnock and gained a Scottish League cap, he went back and opened the then fête).

The great day dawned fair; the village folks came in droves, and farmers and farm workers travelled in from the country. The fête was duly declared open by Frank, then there was a mad stampede by the ladies for the baking and produce stalls where some of the attendants like Kathleen Sturrock, Babs Aitchison, Jean McKinnon and many others were on duty, but from the beginning a queue of both sexes and all ages formed to try to beat Scotland's goalie. Dressed in a track suit and trainers, he leapt and dived across the goals and not a ball went past him. I had a few tries, hit it my hardest and a giant paw just plucked the ball from the air. Then Neil, aged about eleven at the time, had a go, and lo and behold scored – a *bona fide* goal too, not a put up job, the ball going in at the post. Young David also later succeeded. The various stalls were kept busy, most people had a got at the many other games in the garden where men like Harold Lambie, Tom McMichael, Jim Davidson and John Brown were calling out their wares in true showman fashion. The pony rides of Jimmy English were popular with the little ones, and a good time was had by all, the Church also benefiting with a large amount of money.

While Duncan, the treasurer, and others counted the takings Joe Gibson, John Andrews and many other willing hands cleared up. The Woman's Guild and Mothers' Circle tidied up the remains of their stalls, auctioning any left-overs. Campbell Forsyth, hot, dirty and sweating had a bath in the Manse which completed Ian's bliss and put him into his own seventh Heaven. Scotland's goalkeeper had bathed in his bath. Why, the very dirt was precious!

Thus does a little community rally round to support its Church, enjoying much fun and fellowship in the process.

In some ways our fête took me back twelve years to my first Gymkhana at Bristacombe, held annually out in the country at the curiously named village of Upper Down. I was asked to be the vet in attendance, my badge of office and free tickets for two duly arrived and eventually that day also dawned fair. All morning floats laden with cattle and sheep and Land Rovers hauling horse-boxes had been heading for the field from near and far, for many of the competitors went the rounds of the various gymkhanas. Those taking part also included a number of young, semi-professional riders who were destined to make their marks at the Horse of the Year Show and other prestigious gatherings in years to come.

One gymkhana is much like another, and I imagine most country vets have been asked to be in attendance. James Herriot in one of his books describes his hilarious adventures and gives a comprehensive picture of the proceedings.

First I had a quick walk through the marquees to see the flower arrangements, knitting, sewing and dressmaking of the women, marvelled at the enormous onions, leeks, carrots, beans and the rest, but hurried to the animal pens, for animals were my real interest. There husky men in smocks or shirt sleeves were busily engaged with brushes, curry combs, buckets of water and whitening powder, preparing their charges for the ring, in which at that moment was a parade of magnificent Clydesdale and Shire horses, their harness gleaming. Suddenly the loudspeaker crackled into life:

'Would Mr Cameron the vet go to the cattle pens?'

I collected my two black cases, having loaded my car with everything I thought I might need, and feeling ten feet tall that my name had, for the first time, been broadcast to the world, or at any rate to Upper Down! At the cattle pens a little crowd was gathered around a recently calved Shorthorn cow which was just barely standing, wobbling about on its feet. One glance gave the diagnosis – Milk Fever – so calcium was duly administered intravenously and under the skin, being careful not to leave any lumps or bumps which would have told against it in the ring. I had just put my cases away when I was again called on the tannoy to go to the dog show. There the judge said to me, 'Would you examine this dog? I don't like the look of it.' Neither did I when I saw it. There were little globules of pus in the corner of its eyes, eyes it kept half shut against the light, occasional shivers and a generally miserable appearance. In short, one very unhappy Springer Spaniel.

'There be nowt wrong wi' him oi'm zertain zure,' said the owner.

'We'll soon see, sir,' I responded in my best vet-client manner, though it was abundantly clear we had one very sick dog. I took the temperature which was well raised, listened to the stertorous breathing in the chest and gave my verdict to the owner.

'Sorry! You can't go in the Show. Your dog's got Distemper or Hard Pad (we still believed in the latter then) and the sooner you get him home and to your own vet the better.' The dog's owner had appeared a bit aggressive at first, but at the mention of Hard Pad, he blanched, and asked pathetically,

'Are you sure?'

'Certain,' and he departed with his sick pet.

'Mr Cameron to the measuring stand for ponies,' came the next call, so I went to the Secretary's tent, collected my measuring rod, and headed for the queue of ponies that had already formed. Each pony had to pass under the rod which consists of an upright pole with a horizontal bar which slides up and down the pole, the pole measures in hands, each hand being four inches.

I began badly. The first rider was a helmeted, breeched and booted young woman waving a piece of paper.

'This is a certificate from the vet at Tillietudlem testifying my horse is under fourteen hands.'

'Sorry, miss, I'm not allowed to accept any certificates. Each horse must go under the rod.'

So she stretched her horse out to its full length and I eased the cross piece down on to the withers, or highest point of the horse's body . . . but all the stretching in the world could not make that horse under fourteen hands.

'Sorry! You'll need to go up to the next class.'

'But you've *got* to accept this vet's certificate.'

'No, I haven't. You'll have to see the stewards if you're not satisfied.'

She fetched her father, a big, blustering, prosperous looking character wearing a multi-coloured waistcoat and a large scowl. We had a rare old argument while the queue got longer and more impatient, but I was determined 'they shall not pass if not eligible', and muttering threats and imprecations and waving their certificate, they eventually stumped off, the pony rearing and kicking out in my direction to show it had the same opinion of me as its owners. It took some time to measure all the entrants, and while most passed alright, the odd one had to move up a class but generally the rider took it philosophically. I had never seen so many horsey types in one group before, and it was quite an education. The locals, entering for the fun of it and with little thought of winning, took it all in good part, particularly as I was vet to many of them. It was the visitors and semi-professionals who treated this 'still wet behind the ears – Scotsman – not a proper vetnary', as one described me, with derision.

I breathed a sigh of relief when that task was done, had my tea, then went and listened to the band who were giving somewhat modified versions of Gilbert and Sullivan, tuneful if not always strictly in tune. Next came the judging of the Pets' Corner, a motley collection of dogs, cats, budgerigars, parrots, rabbits, hamsters, guinea pigs, tortoises and so on, all gathered for what was meant to be a fun event. How on earth do you compare a tortoise with a Golden Retriever, a rabbit with a parrot, I wondered? I did the best I could, though really I would like to have given them all a prize for virtually all the owners were children. If I may quote my famous colleague of the Yorkshire Dales again, this fun event got him into big trouble and produced a sparkling story. I was more fortunate. Most of the crowd clapped the winners, and I escaped in one piece.

The rest of the day was given over to the pony events and jumping, and I had to wait to the bitter end in case of accidents, for nestling in my car was a humane killer which I fervently hoped I would not have to use. The day which had started so fair had deteriorated, it being now cold and damp. Many cattle floats were taking their charges home, and to keep out of the way and to keep warm, I eventually sat in the car.

There were fun games with the ponies, like the potato race when each rider had to grab a potato from the top of a pole and drop it in a bucket, dismounting if he missed. There was a version of musical chairs, but the evening finally became concerned with the serious side of the jumps. I noticed all styles of riders, some very upright in the saddle, some very hard on their horses, tugging at reins and bit, some riding with taut reins, others with slack – but despite all the grand horse experts from miles away, the star of the show and undoubted champion was young Kingsley Tucker, one of the famous rough and ready family I described on another occasion and who were particular favourites of mine. Where other riders sat very upright in the saddle and kept tight control of the horse's head, Kingsley had no saddle, riding bareback, and crouched low over his mount's neck, he gave the horse his head so that horse and rider seemed fused into one. He raced up to each jump on his old grey pony, and again and again had a clear round, beating all the 'fancy' riders from 'away', to the mounting excitement of the home crowd. He was a natural horseman, his riding a delight to behold, and no one clapped louder than me when he was finally awarded the cup.

After I came into the ministry, of course, I lost touch with most of my former clients, and it was about thirty years later I saw Kingsley, when Janet and I were holidaying in 'Combe with Bernard and Ann. It was in Brookfield Free Church, where we had worshipped weekly all these years before. Sitting beside our life-long friends Lil and Cath, Lil whispered, 'That's Kingsley Tucker.' I was surprised to see Kingy, for Church had not been a regular part of his schedule when I knew him last, but I was also deeply concerned, for I would scarcely have recognised him. He looked an old man, was clearly very ill, pale, drawn, in pain as he slouched in the Church chair. He would, at that time, be about forty-seven. I had a few words with him at the close of the Service and he gave me a great welcome, the old Kingsley smile lighting up his face. He told me quite calmly he had cancer and it was a struggle now to get to Church.

I could not get him out of my mind, and determined to go and see him in his home, particularly as Brookfield was without a Pastor at the time. His wife welcomed me warmly and showed me into the bedroom where Kingsley lay, looking more ill than ever, but despite his weakness and the fact he was clearly a dying man, he seemed delighted to see me and eager to talk. We relived the old days and I reminded him of his success at my first Gymkhana all these years before.

'Aar – them was grand days, Mr Cameron,' he said, and for a moment he was that brilliant young rider again on his old, grey, working pony. He told me that three of the five Tucker boys were dead, all young, and he spoke quite naturally, and indeed enthusiastically of the faith he had found, and of the tremendous strength this had been to him. Beside him in bed was a well-thumbed Bible. Here was no temporary conversion, no passing thing, but a deep lasting experience, a strong anchor, that had held him in many misfortunes and I was confident it would see him through to the end.

He was on his last ride, taking the jumps one by one as cleanly as before. He was heading for the winning post in style.

I never saw him again. He died shortly afterwards, but I was confident the verdict of the Judge would be – 'Clear Round'.

Rejected

FIVE

During my three years training for the ministry, I returned to my original trade in the summer holidays, and acted as *locum tenens* for vets on holiday, for money was tight, and with a wife and family to keep, and no kind of student grant, I had to earn as much as possible. I worked in various places but three come to mind.

In Cirencester I was greeted by the vet's secretary with the words, 'Pity you weren't here last week. You would have had some fun.'

'Oh? Why was that?'

'We had a travelling circus passing through for a few days, and the boss was asked to visit, not knowing what kind of animal he had to treat. He was met by the elephant trainer who informed him that one of the elephants, the fifth in a line of six, had a large abscess on the leg which required lancing and draining and said, "She's quiet, but just watch the one next to her," and left him to get on with it.'

'Well, I like elephants – but preferably from a distance, so I'm mighty glad this was last week,' I replied.

I was then conducted to the house where I was to stay for a fortnight. It was a stately mansion belonging to a retired dentist and his wife, and my corduroys and sports jacket seemed very humble and considerably out of place in that opulent setting. Carefully minding my Ps and Qs, I got through the evening meal and subsequent conversation, but it appeared next morning I had literally put my foot in it. I was informed by one of the two elderly maids that I had omitted to leave my shoes outside the door for polishing. I looked at my scuffed old brogues, said

'Oh-ah-sorry-must have slipped my memory', as if the procedure was my usual nightly ritual. Though the owners were kind enough, meals were very formal affairs, conversation exactly correct – in fact I was miserable, the more so as the practice was very quiet and I had little to do. I remember spending hours with a book on trees in my hand, wandering the lanes, studying the various varieties in that lush, gracious part of old England. Anything to escape from the house where I had to wait impatiently for the phone to ring, and during that fortnight I became quite an expert on leaves, bark, seeds and the various varieties of trees they signified.

After a lazy two weeks for which I felt I had not earned my fee, my next port of call was Stroud in Gloucestershire. It was a busy little town and proved to be a busy practice. This was normally a two-man affair, a youngish man and an elderly semi-retired vet, and I was, of course, taking the place of the younger man for two weeks. Now I am not a good map reader (my wife is always the navigator, and an excellent one, on car journeys, except for her propensity suddenly to explore unmarked, single track roads with a gradient of about 1 in 3!) and consequently looking up farms on a strange map, in a district where I did not know a single road, was time-consuming, especially if it was an urgent case. So the old boy would regularly direct me.

'You go along the main road south to the *Beetle and Wedge*, then you swing on to a B-class road till you come to *The Fox and Grapes*. Follow that to *The Merry Huntsman*, where you take a left on to an uncharted road till you reach *The Cricketers*, where you'd better ask your way.'

It was the same each day and I got to know every pub around Stroud, of which there seemed to be a remarkable number! The old vet had the high colour of a heavy whisky drinker and each day he had a fair load aboard. He was never under the weather, however, always neatly dressed in the pre-war vet costume of breeches and matching jacket one of the many who had come through the hard times in practice between the wars, and in his day had been, I imagine, a very competent vet, with still his love for the old remedies on which I too, as an immediately post-war student, had been nurtured. The surgery had that lovely smell of our trade of *nux vom, ammon carb*, gentian, ginger and the other ingredients of the many stomach powders that were dispensed, a smell that is absent from the modern vet's dispensary. His wife told me one day, to my surprise, that her husband was a high churchman of the Church of England and always gave up whisky for Lent, which must really have been a considerable sacrifice. His other love was roses of which he had a great variety in his fine garden where he pottered away the days. The only rose I knew in those days was Peace, but he immediately snorted and said, 'Terrible rose – not one thing or another – give me whole colour. HTs all the time, and none of these blasted bi-colours and hybrids.'

If I had learned about trees at Cirencester (all of which I have forgotten), I gained a love for roses at Stroud which has stayed with me, and in our three homes since then we have always had many roses, mostly HTs, and yes, mostly whole colours. Thus are the ignorant initiated in their formative years! All in all, life in Stroud was full of colour, busy, and the time flew past, concluding with a fascinating visit to Peter Scott's bird sanctuary at Slimbridge on my way home.

But my favourite port of call was Windermere in the Lake District, where I stood in for the then vet, Mr Bell, on several occasions. These were glorious days amid the magnificent scenery. Janet and I have always loved the Highlands and this was the English equivalent. Fortunately, Janet was able to be with me some of the time. I explored lakes large and small and steep valleys, on my way to cases in a Land Rover, and grew to love the area, the only snag being the amount of visitor traffic on the roads, making it impossible to hurry to any case. While I had my share of farm cases, in the many large houses fringing the lakes or little ones perched precariously on ledges, I treated dogs and cats, and the days passed happily and smoothly enough, with no deaths or tragedies.

One day however, I was asked to collect a cat to be put to sleep in Windermere itself. I found the poor animal, which apparently had just become redundant, (the kind of euthanasia I have always hated), popped it in a cat basket, deposited it in the back of the car and set off for the surgery. It was a warm day and the Land Rover windows were open. There was a constant miaowing and scratching coming from the basket, but I drove on regardless, when suddenly a cat shot over my shoulder and out the window of the moving car. Now it is considerably humiliating to lose a patient, and although I had thought the basket escape proof, it was apparently not so for that determined feline. Mind you, if I was going to my death, I should have struggled a bit too. There was nothing for it but to go back to the owner's house, explain what had happened, and tell them if it returned, to get in touch with me. I never heard any more, so presumably the cat had gone wild or found another home, at least a better fate than that planned for it.

Just after I got back to the surgery, the police arrived with a little dog that had been run over and badly hurt. It was a terrier cross, a little mongrel – but I have a soft spot for mongrels, and of course promised I would treat it as best I could, though it appeared in a bad way. The police departed, promising on their part to try to find the owner of the dog, which was collarless, with nothing to identify it. I had nobody to assist me in the surgery at Windermere, but laid the unconscious little form gently on the table. There were many cuts and lacerations, one leg was hanging limply, its membranes were pale, so clearly it was in shock with perhaps internal haemorrhage. I carefully felt it all over, but could find no fractures except its useless rear leg, though without X-rays to assist, it is possible some ribs were gone. I injected it with various drugs to control the shock, and hopefully arrest any internal bleeding, then set to work on the visible damage.

By now he had stirred, so I put him under a light anaesthetic, set the fractured leg in plaster, and then began the long process of clipping hair, cleaning wounds, dressing with sulphanilamide powder and suturing. It took a considerable time and I realised all the while that there was a fair chance the police would not find the owner and I was spending quite a bit of Mr Bell's suppplies on an unidentified dog. But what else could be done? 'Put it down', a voice had whispered to me early – save yourself a lot of work – 'besides it might well die anyway.' I could not put a helpless creature down, condemned without at least a trial. There were no kennels at the Windermere premises, but there were some dog baskets, so laying him gently on a blanket in one, I switched on the electric fire to warm him and counteract shock, fitted up a primitive drip into a vein, and generally made him as comfortable as I could.

The surgery at Windermere was attached to the house, so all that evening I kept popping through and looking at him. He was still under the combined effects of anaesthetic and shock. No owner appeared. I got up through the night and had a look at my patient, who was now wide awake, yawning prodigiously, so I tried him with water and a little food which he did not even look at. Nor did he look at me. He was just a lost wee dog, wrapped in his own misery and loneliness.

The next day and night passed, and the next. Other patients came into the surgery, were treated and departed, their owners looking wonderingly at the little dog in his hospital bed. He was really an attractive little fellow, a little gamin, normally, I was sure, full of fun, mischief and the joy of living. Still he pointedly disdained to look at food or water, even when held under his nose or when meat was smeared on his mouth. He ignored me, taking his further injections without a movement or a murmur. Obviously a one man dog, I thought, and I was not that man. Then, on the third day the police came in to say they had found the owner and he would be looking in shortly. I was delighted and relieved. The wee dog would be going home. I was in the surgery when I heard the outer door of the waiting room open, and immediately there was a transformation. My patient came alive at the sound of recognised footsteps. He sat up in his basket, licked his lips, gave a little whimper of excitement and waited. So did I. But the steps came no further. I went out into the adjoining room and there was a big, rough looking man with a young man, obviously his son, along with him.

'You've got my dog,' he launched straight in. 'Well, you can keep him. He's nowt but a blasted nuisance, more trouble than he's worth. I don't want the beggar back.'

'But your dog trusts you, and needs you. You should have seen the way he came alive when you arrived. He's had a fair old knock, but nothing that time won't heal. You won't even have any more expense, he's pretty well patched up now.'

'I expect you think I'll pay for what you done,' he sneered. 'Well, you can think again. I never asked for no treatment. Get rid of him for he's nowt but a pest.'

I talked to him, I reasoned with him, I even pleaded with him, but to no avail. He refused even to open the door and look at his dog, and eventually stumped out. The matter was closed.

With a heavy, sinking heart, I opened the surgery door. The little dog had dragged himself from his basket despite his useless leg, and was immediately behind the door, tail thumping the floor, head erect, eyes bright.

'All would be well now, master had come and would take him home.'

But the master had come and gone, and as it heard the footsteps recede, the little dog's head went down. Why had master left him? Why? Why?

There was but one thing I could do, put the little creature down. There were no facilities in the town for keeping an injured dog. The RSPCA, I was sure, would not board such an animal with an uncertain future, as under the leadership of Mrs Gorman at Bristacombe they had done. I lifted him slowly on to the table. He did not cry or move. Life held nothing for him now, and as I gently patted the little head and smoothed the rough coat, with a heart heavier than I have seldom known, I pressed the plunger and he was gone, and oddly, like an echo from the past, I seemed to hear the words:

'Away with this man! We don't want Him! He's just a source of trouble – Crucify! Crucify! Crucify!' – even though, like the little dog, He went on loving to the last.

'Having loved His own, He loved them to the end.'

The call that costs

SIX

'Where will it be this year?' asked Tom the Polis.

'How about Majorca?' suggested Jimmy, the tattie merchant, with a grin.

'Weel, I've been workin' it oot,' says Bobby, the Car Convenor, and proceeds to elaborate on roads A class, B class and no class at all, and manages to lose us all in the process. Bobby had a wonderful gift for confusion, but was an invaluable member of our committee. As the local milkman he knew everybody in the village, and acted as the news carrier from house to house, always with his hearty laugh.

'Whit aboot tea; will it be sausage rolls or gammon salad?' asks Margaret Gibson, one of our food convenors.

'Will we go to a Kirk hall or Agnes's canteen?' queries the other food lady, Margaret Harrison.

The Guild of Friendship committee was in full swing, and while the Secretary, John Brown, tried to keep a minute, I, as Chairman, endeavoured to keep us to the point, for we all had a tendency to go off at a tangent and discuss the price of beasts at the mart, or wee Jeannie Jones' appendix. The Guild of Friendship was perhaps one of the most practical things I ever did in a sermon, when, concerned about the number of elderly folks living alone, I suggested we should form an organisation which would provide a concert and knife and fork meal every six weeks in the winter, a car outing and meal in the summer, and have a list of our younger people 'twinned' to some old person, whom they would visit regularly. It had proved to be a resounding success, and it was sometimes difficult to decide whether the organisers or the senior citizens had most pleasure from the Guild's work. It was really a heart-warming sight to see so many old folks tucking into their meal, the tongues wagging merrily, while in the background the two Margarets, aided by many others like Renée Lindsay, Margaret Berry, Nancy Murchison, Babs Aitchison and many more cooked and served the dinner. Then it was over to little Mrs Hill, who, though only a half pint in size, was a half pint of good nature and fun, and organised the concert. Equally impressive was the sight of twenty or thirty cars setting out in convoy on a summer day, their drivers giving up an afternoon and evening to provide such happiness to so many as year after year they completed a mystery tour. The minister was tucked into the middle of the procession, 'for he goes ower quick tae be in front', and in the rear car our mechanic, Jock, ready for any emergency. These committee meetings of the Guild of Friendship maybe lacked something in orderliness, but were more than compensated for by the degree of real camaraderie and fellowship. I sighed contentedly as I made for the Manse, another meeting over, blissfully unaware that the next morning's post was to bring a letter which would have far-reaching consequences, and eventually remove the close relationship with these good folks I had come to love.

When I opened the letter marked BBC, I gulped. Me to do this? I was being asked to do a TV series, linking the Covenanters to the Cameronians, with a history of both. I was honoured and flattered, of course, but also terrified, for the letter specified that there would be no autocue or other moving screen with the words printed on it, such as newsreaders and other speakers use. Furthermore the talks were to be delivered without notes, and a week's lectures were all to be recorded in one afternoon. I immediately yelled for Janet.

'Read this, lass! I could never do what they want.' She read the missive carefully and coolly, and then with a confidence in her man he certainly did not feel, she said,

'That's great, Alec. You'll do it fine.'

'But . . . but . . . no autocue to read off, and if possible, no notes! How could I remember all the details they'll want, especially crammed into one afternoon?'

'You could record it on tape, and listen to it played back again and again till it is fixed in your memory.'

'Och, you remember what happened to Andrew Eastham when he

tried that with his sermon. He was so bored he fell asleep in the middle of it.'

'One thing's certain,' I went on, 'Moorton's fairly getting on the map now. The Late Call series on STV, but they had a moving screen; the Covenanter's Trust; the Conventicle, the pages in *Life and Work* (the Church of Scotland's magazine), and now this. You would think we were St Giles or something. I never expected all this palaver.'

I sweated and worried over that BBC letter all day. Should I say 'yes'? These talks were to be considerably longer than my five minute epilogues, and would need a great deal of swotting up of the Cameronian Regimental history. I pretty well knew enough about the Covenanting side, but the story of a regiment from its foundation to its amalgamation was something different and I shivered when I thought of all the dates and names I would have to remember. However, at last it was decided, I would have a try. After all, unless I made a complete botch of the whole thing, it could only help our Covenanter Trust, our lovely wee Kirk, and maybe the gospel, so feeling as important as Cliff Michelmore or some other seasoned TV reporter, I wrote accepting the invitation.

Then followed several afternoons in the Mitchell Library swotting up history. The old library was still the same, earnest students poring over notes, business men hurriedly turning pages of works of reference, old men dosing the afternoon away over their book, and in the alcoves, young couples, mainly students, sitting together, whispering surreptitiously as they watched out for the prowling attendant who had frequently told Janet and I in the 1940s to stop talking. I wondered if they were still dubbed 'The Gestapo' by the students of the 1960s?

Having noted down reams of background material, I eventually decided I had enough and there followed the composition of it all in spare moments between my normal Church duties, usually in the 'wee sma' oors' when everyone was abed and the house silent. It had to be made into an interesting series so that folk would not switch off in the first minute, and yet do justice equally to the Covenanters and Cameronians. It was a bit like making up the various concoctions I had brewed in my vet days, putting the ingredients into a mortar, mixing and grinding them together with a pestle, and looking with interest at the end product. Having written out my script, it had to be typed in my usual dashing two finger style, and submitted to the producers for approval.

So step by step things progressed. As it neared the afternoon for recording, I was a bundle of nerves, and felt I would break down in the middle, gibbering with fright. Well, I did not do that. In fact I nearly did not get started, for when I saw the studio, my little desk and three moving cameras with cameramen sitting on them, I almost turned tail and bolted. How on earth did these stars look so cool before the cameras? Why three cameras? Oh, mother I wonder if my tie is straight? Is my hair still shed? Where's the nearest toilet?

I said a prayer, swallowed a few times and marched to my desk and my doom. I got a dab of powder on my shiny nose, looked down at my notes (I was allowed them after all but told to try not to use them, just to keep looking into a camera) and we began, voice tests, lighting adjustments, conferences between the various technicians involved, me being told to try to look relaxed (Huh!) and at last we were off. Fortunately the cameras only photographed my upper half, so my knocking knees did not show. I found it considerably difficult to concentrate on my talks with cameras advancing and retiring, lights beating down making the small studio like an oven, and all the time, as I had been urged, I had to look pleasant as if I was enjoying the whole thing. I found it a help to imagine an interested listener sitting in his armchair at home, and I talked to him. Before I knew it, the first address was over without any need for a re-take. My confidence grew somewhat. Then the second talk and still no re-take. My confidence soared. Soon I was in full flow – who's Cliff Michelmore or Richard Baker anyway – anybody can do this! Eventually all the talks were delivered and I staggered out to be congratulated by a generous producer, and with the father and mother of all my headaches from my effort of concentration, the lights and camera lenses. But it was done, hooray, praise the Lord!

I drove back slowly to the quiet of Moorton from the Glasgow studio, as limp as a wet rag, but feeling good. I knew now what Shadrach, Meshach and Abednego had felt in the burning, fiery furnace and the relief of delivery. Indeed I was inclined to think mine was an even greater miracle than that in the old Book, and suddenly it dawned on me, I was also getting paid for it.

I received numerous comments afterwards when the series went out, many asking me if I had only one tie, and what state was my shirt in at the end of a week! But the tangible result, among others, was that Moorton was now known nationwide. The numbers attending Lochgoin and visiting our old Church increased, sale of Covenanter booklets went up, we had increased requests from many quarters for visits to the

Church and lectures. But there was another side effect which gradually showed up.

I spotted them as soon as Andrew showed me up to the pulpit that Sunday in late autumn, a group of four all sitting together. 'Ah-ha,' I thought, 'a scouting party from another Church.' They had already been spotted by the congregation and were getting long looks, for in our wee country Kirk we had few Sunday visitors, especially at that time of the year, and any stranger stood out like a sore thumb. Had these folk come to steal away their minister, the congregation was clearly wondering? After the Service the itinerant four were shown into the vestry by my faithful old Beadle. 'Some people to see you, Mr Cameron. They would like a wee word with you, but I hope you dinna listen,' he whispered. The deputation was from Glasgow and they would like me to consider their Church, a fine Church, they emphasised, with a lot of young people about it and a great choir. I thanked them and said an emphatic 'No'. A few weeks later the business was repeated, this time the deputation, from another city Church, being crafty and seeking to hide by sitting separately in different parts of the Church. I was highly amused by the intense scrutiny I received for everything I said or did; one even was jotting notes in a book. The Moortonites were hardly welcoming to their visitors, treating them to hard stares and scowls. Again I said 'No'. So it went on. Groups appeared uninvited for I had applied for no other Charge, being completely content where I was. I had letters and phone calls, each it seemed, outdoing the previous one in the desirability of their Kirk. It seemed I was known and wanted, and while it was flattering, it was unsettling. We asked the boys how they would like to live in Glasgow, Aberdeen, Edinburgh or Timbuktoo to be met by emphatic negatives.

It is required of a minister that he shall stay at least five years in his first Charge. I was in my sixth year, had seen the Church grow a little as new people came into the private development on the edge of the village, some of them like John Andrews (later Session Clerk) and Colonel Bill Munro (now Secretary of the Lochgoin Trust) outstanding folk with much to offer. There were those, already elders, like Gibby Anderson whom we welcomed to our Session. The Sunday School, Bible Class and Youth Fellowship were flourishing, not only on the spiritual side, but in their respective football teams. Every boy in the village wanted to be a Cub, run magnificently by Joe Gibson and Ian Brown, and Guides and Brownies were very much alive. Our oldest two boys were performing with considerable skill in the Bible Class team, young David equally so in the Cub eleven, while baby Alan could not wait to be old enough to join in. In addition to our greatly appreciated Guild of Friendship for the elderly, we had started a Study Group. Janet was happy with her home and Women's organisations and we felt part of a warm-hearted community where people seemed to like us and where I was welcome in every home. Why shift? We were near our relatives in Ayrshire, my mother and brother Fergus in Prestwick, other brother Graham, an elder in Andrew Eastham's Church at Dunlop. Janet's parents were near at hand in Maryshall, her brother Alec and wife Helen in Ayr, and there were other relations in Mochrum, where I had started my vet career with Ian Buchan. In short, we were at home, and there we meant to stay.

Then in February, returning about 2.00 am from the induction of my friend Jimmy Duncanson to his second Charge at Methil, we found in the front porch the magazine of Aldermouth Old Church and a cutting from *The Scotsman* advertising the vacancy. Not knowing the place at all, I looked it up, out of curiosity, in the Church yearbook. It was about twice the membership of Moorton – they were getting bigger! We discovered eventually the literature had been left by Andrew and Nan Archibald, two friends with Moorton connections who now lived in Aldermouth. In fact the whole Archibald family had visited little Moorton on several occasions, for grandfather Archibald had ministered there for a long period years ago. It was clear Nan and Andrew were now dropping hints. But I did nothing about it. It was still a definite 'No'. Then a curious thing happened. This one would not go away. It niggled on in my mind. It was not the size, or the pleasant area of the Moray Firth, or an increased salary. It was, what? I could not explain it, it just jolly well would not go away, a kind of jagging in my mind by, I believe, in retrospect, God's Holy Spirit. I had a phone call from the Archibalds urging me to apply, but still I did nothing till one evening in May I came in from a Communion Service and had an over-mastering feeling that unless I got rid of this prickling, I would never be comfortable again, and somehow I felt I had to phone there and then. So I looked up the original advert, found the name and phone number of the Interim Moderator (supervising minister) and rang him.

'Er . . . hello . . . eh . . . ahem . . . my name's Cameron and you'll think this a queer kind of call, but you see, it was suggested I might be interested in Aldermouth Old. I wasn't, but it just won't go away, and I'm phoning to find out if you have now settled on a minister, as I imagine you will by this time.'

'Ah, Mr Cameron,' came the reply, 'I know your name well. We've discussed you in our meeting, and no, we haven't fixed on anyone. Would you be willing to come up and preach before the Vacancy Committee?'

Here was a shock. I had been phoning up to clear my mind and get peace again and found myself asked to preach for the place. Oh blow! What did one do? I gulped and stuttered a bit.

'Oh, I'm not sure I'm ready for that.'

'Well, why not put it to the test. I know exactly how you feel for I eventually had to leave a place I loved.' He was a wise man, was dear old John, and was destined to become a very close friend. So we talked, and eventually I agreed to preach before their committee in three weeks' time, though on the strict understanding that I was far from sure, and even if they selected me, I might still say 'No'.

'That's alright,' John replied, 'I understand. No commitment either way.'

So we travelled north, stayed overnight in Elgin, and I preached morning and evening there before the Aldermouth Vacancy Committee. We were given a five-star lunch and afterwards a tour of the parish by the kindly Archibalds, then a visit to Church and Manse. In both we gasped and looked at each other. They were built in the grand manner, magnificent buildings. The Church was immense and after little Moorton's Kirk it looked like a cathedral. But it was beautiful, with superb stained glass windows, especially one of the Last Supper which I was told was illuminated in the evening by a spot-light and looked, with its mellow colours, like an old master painting. There as a fine pipe organ and we were told of the outstanding organist, Jim McMichael who, though blind, with his wife Jean trained a choir of thirty and a Junior Choir of forty. The pulpit was central and equipped with two microphones, one for the congregation and one for deaf aids in certain pews. The font was huge, of Sicilian marble but what perhaps impressed me most was the fine old wood of the pulpit, pews and gallery, wood that was highly polished and clearly lovingly tended.

'John keeps the Church beautifully,' said Nan Archibald, 'he's the full-time Church Officer, teaches in Sunday School, keeps the grounds, arranges communion duties and I don't know what else. He and his wife

Elizabeth are in the Church working every day – a great man – a great pair.'

There was a Hall and Boys Brigade (BB) hut and when we came to the Manse, built of the same stone as the Church, we counted thirteen rooms, plus, of all things, a butler's pantry. I thought back to my boyhood in a council house and felt I was being offered a peerage!

We left on the Sunday evening for the long trip back to Moorton and after a short distance, I stopped the car, went behind a hedge and changed from my best suit to flannels and sports jacket. We had been on our best behaviour for twenty-four hours and in our best clothes, now we relaxed, and as we journeyed talked over our experience of the weekend, but despite all we had seen, and the kindness of the people we had met, we were far from certain we wanted to move from our humble wee Ayrshire Kirk. But then we had not yet been asked by the congregation of Aldermouth and deep inside me was a hope that we would not be asked, for I loved my Moorton folks and the little white-washed Kirk with its storied past. But we were asked! In a few days I had a phone call. Would I be the sole nominee, preach before the whole congregation in Aldermouth, and would I give my decision about this in four days? I was honoured; I was flattered; I was being asked to be minister of one of the largest churches in the north, for I had discovered that in addition to the 1000 plus members, there were a further 500 adherents. I should have been over the moon, but I was miserable.

There is a hackneyed old story of a Manse couple who had received such an invitation and, so the story goes, while the minister went into his study to pray for guidance, the wife was already packing. Well, it is a crafty wee tale, but it was far from like that with us. My four days deadline passed and I had to phone the Revd John and tell him I was not sure and would need longer. Night after night I walked Bruce, our Boxer dog away out into the country and looked back at the lights of the village. In that house at the top were two sisters, one with a stroke who always looked forward to my visits. Below them were Mr and Mrs Crombie, my faithful Beadle and his wife, leal, loyal, true. Along the road a little way was a woman recently widowed. I had been involved with all these folks, with almost every home in the village. How could I go and leave them all? Besides, the family were unhappy about leaving the place they knew.

'What about our Bible Class team, Dad?' said Neil.

'Yes, we can't leave that,' piped up Ian. Both were really promising footballers. David joined in,

'I'm not leaving the Cubs.' He too was in their team and an equally good wee player, and baby Alan chimed in,

'Will there be a swingy where we go?' The swingy was the play park.

A week of uncertainty, indeed rank misery, passed and I had to phone Aldermouth once more, cap in hand and say, 'I'm terribly sorry, I can't decide. I'll understand it if you're fed up with this fellow and go ahead with someone else, but we are going tomorrow on holiday with our caravan to Dornoch. We'll come via Aldermouth and I'll definitely give an answer then. If still uncertain, I'll say "No" and you can proceed with another candidate.'

Friends who knew about my invitation could not understand me. The challenge of a Church in size about three times my present, a Sunday congregation of maybe 600, a beautiful part of the country in the dry Moray Firth area, a larger stipend, a stately home – what was holding me up? I prayed and prayed for guidance. Someone said to me 'darkness about going means light about staying', but someone else said 'darkness about staying means light about going', so that was stalemate. That was still the state of affairs when we drove into Aldermouth two days later. We arrived in a thunderstorm which matched the storm within me. However, soon the sun came out, and as a family we walked up towards the Church, whose massive square tower was visible for miles, and as we walked the most wonderful peace came stealing over me, and by the time we reached the huge, majestic building and its adjacent Manse, my doubts had been laid to rest, or almost.

Our boys were thrilled, if somewhat over-awed by what they saw. There was a field next to, and belonging to, the Manse, and it had goalposts in it – their own private park for my football-mad sons. That settled it for them! In the well-tended garden was John the Beadle, who welcomed us with his quiet smile, a smile I was to get to know well in twelve marvellous years without a word of difference between us.

But that night I did something that was absolute cheek. I put down a Gideon's fleece, so to speak. I made one proviso, but told no one about it, not even Janet, only God. If even one person voted against me in their secret ballot, I would take that as a sign I was not meant to go. I was fighting against things right to the last but it seemed the Almighty was determined to show me once and for all, for it certainly could not have been my preaching, but the vote was 100 per cent 'yes'. I had no excuses left.

That call was, next to my decision to give up vet practice for the ministry, the hardest decision I have had to take in life. It was now clear that all the time my jagging, my restlessness, my pull towards the north had been the Holy Spirit at work, and sometimes the Spirit can make us profoundly uncomfortable, a call that costs. Later, the Revd John told me that the first time I had phoned all these weeks before, that night when an inner voice told me to ring then, he had actually had the Vacancy Committee with him telling him they were hopelessly split over three candidates, and not too happy with any, and my call when it came, though many would say chance or coincidence, was clearly God working in His own way.

Everything did not move smoothly after our decision, for Janet, completely out of the blue, took ill, requiring major surgery. What was to be done? Call off Aldermouth? But I had already told Moorton I was leaving in September. Have the operation and arrive in an ambulance? That was not on. Mercifully, we had an understanding surgeon who really decided it for us; he would keep my poor wife going on various medicines till we had settled in at Aldermouth, and then she would travel south for surgery.

So, bit by bit, the pieces fell into place and after some very tearful farewells to my Moorton people, we embarked on the next stage of the voyage, but comforted by a word ringing in our ears and hearts.

'Jesus Christ, *the same*, yesterday, today and forever.' The same Lord would be at Aldermouth and I remembered that He too had had a call that cost, a far more awful choice than any other human has had to face, in Gethsemane, and He had made his choice and conquered for the sake of all mankind. To compare my struggles with Gethsemane was almost blasphemy, but my, they hurt, and yet why should I be so reluctant?

I had merely been asked to change houses and Churches, and indeed move to a delightful place with wonderful, kindly poeple. It would be the same job I had done at Moorton, and in a sense as a vet, only the flock would be different.

The golden years

SEVEN

We flitted to Aldermouth one glorious September day in 1968, pulling our caravan behind us. The furniture van had beaten us to it and the men had started to unload. Our next door neighbour was also a minister, Gordon McRae, minister of the High Church, and over the years he and his wife Winnie were to become good friends. Like us, they had four children, and naturally the bairns were curious, like all children, as to their new neighbours, and Jean, the eldest, from her bedroom window overlooking our doors, gave a running commentary to the rest on the proceedings, which apparently produced several surprises for the girl.

The first things the furniture men unloaded were several tea chests and a roll of netting wire, which latter they proceeded to erect in our back garden, and from the tea chests fluttered hens and bantams. Jean called in astonishment, 'They've got hens!', which, incidentally, had laid us our tea *en route* from Moorton. Then we pulled up with our caravan, from which leapt our Boxer dog, Bruce, which, like all Boxers, looked as if his bite would be worse than his bark. From the car tumbled four boys and a somewhat stiff mum and dad, and Jean became more and more amazed, calling out, 'They've got a big fierce looking dog, and it came out of a caravan, and there are four boys.' The poor girl must have thought a tribe of tinkers was taking root just over the wall from her.

We had come a few days before I was due to start work, to allow us to get settled in. Andrew Eastham and his wife came up on the Saturday for Andrew was 'preaching me in' and introducing me to the congregation at morning service. Now Andrew had been my parents' minister, and was considerably older than me and a wise counsellor and guide in my Moorton days, and while the Easthams were a delightful couple, we held them in veneration. They had no children so our brood were warned to be on their best behaviour, and for such honoured visitors Janet had made a big effort in the house and the kitchen – best china, table beautifully spread and everything ship-shape. During the meal Mrs Eastham was admiring the crockery and cutlery when young David, aged nine, piped up, 'Mummy, are these the spoons you got with Green Shield stamps?' Collapse of parents, and great hilarity from the Easthams! We had a thoroughly happy weekend with a delightful couple, and on their departure, I felt my new ministry had truly begun, same vet, different vestry.

Now, in most ways I am a fairly traditional minister of the Kirk, some would say old-fashioned. At any rate I have always felt visiting one's flock to be important, and while I realised that in a congregation of over 1000 homes it was a very large task along with the many other duties, I was determined at least to try to get round. So week by week, on two or three evenings a week, I would go with one of the elders and be introduced to his district, while on several afternoons a week I visited the sick, sorrowing, handicapped elderly and housebound, trying to make them feel they were still very much part of the Old Parish family and the family of God. Willie Barclay had said to us at Trinity College, 'Get round your people as often as you can. You will learn so much from them, and a great deal of your preaching will come out of these visits. You mustn't be a stranger to your flock.'

Now while I am certain Dr Barclay was right, there has never yet been a minister who has, in the estimation of all his congregation measured up, like the young minister, a keen botanist, who went to his first charge. Bit by bit he got round in visitation until one day he arrived at the door of a formidable female who met him, hands on his hips, the light of battle in her eye, convinced he should have been to her long since.

'Weel, you've come,' she said in a voice singularly lacking in sweetness and light, 'if I had been some kind o' fancy puddock stool you'd have been here long since!'

But quite apart from feeling that I ought to be out and about as other duties allowed, I enjoyed this part of my work and still do, and feel my life and ministry have been greatly enriched by meeting people in their homes, particularly those walking in the golden glow of evening. So it certainly was at Aldermouth.

There was Mrs Laurie whom I first saw in the Northern Infirmary the day after she had had a leg amputated. She was sitting up in bed smacking her lips at a plate of broth and saying 'My, that soup's guid. They're awfu' kind to you in here. You'll be the new minister, pleased to meet ye, I hope you'll like it in Aldermouth.'

She had never been in hospital before in her eighty-two years and she did not have a word of complaint about herself or the loss of her leg. In due course she was sent home with a temporary leg, a wooden peg leg, and then got her permanent one. Visiting her one day some time later in her home, I found her wearing the old wooden one again.

'Mrs Laurie,' I demanded, 'what are you doing with that old thing on again?'

'Ach, Mr Cameron,' she replied, 'gang into the bedroom; ma 'ither leg's there.'

Wondering somewhat, I did as she asked, and there on the bed lay the proper leg. 'Bring it through,' she called to me. So I picked up the leg and carried it through, wondering ever more.

'Pit it doon there,' she commanded, and I set it upright in the middle of the floor, where it stood up, a weird looking object, but not to Mrs Laurie.

'It's a bonny leg,' she enthused, 'far nicer than ony leg I ever had,' (I wondered if she had been a centipede!) 'but it's too ticht.' She was perfectly serious but I was doubled up in mirth at the picture of two people contemplating seriously one detached leg.

One evening some time later, Dr John, one of our much loved team of GPs phoned me to inform me, 'I've just sent Mrs Laurie into hospital; her other leg's gone gangrenous. I don't think they'll operate and I'm afraid she won't last more than two days.'

So I visited her that evening. By now Mrs Laurie and I were firm friends; I could say anything to her, and, by golly, she said anything to me. I sat with her for a little and as we talked I marvelled at her spirit, courage, yes, and faith, and thought, 'You know, John, I think you could be surprised. She'll cheat the doctors yet.' We had a simple word of prayer and I left. They did operate; they did remove her other leg; she did pull through and eventually came home again to her little two room house, destined forever to sit in a wheel chair. She had a home-help and her granddaughter looked in daily, but Mrs Laurie was independent, wheeled herself around her little home, cooked, dusted, and lived a more or less normal life. I visited her often and never once did I hear her bemoan her fate, nor, blunt woman though she was, did I ever hear her speak ill of anyone. She had the same code as my father, 'if you can't speak well of anyone, stay silent.'

Mrs McDonald was another of independent spirit. She was ninety-five when I first knew her, lived in the old Fishertown part of the town, for her husband had been one of Aldermouth's many fishermen at the beginning of the century when the town was a thriving fishing port. It was a hard, hard life for the men, and for the women who followed the fleet to gut the herring. She had been a widow sixty long years. Often she would talk of the old days, bringing up a family on her own 'an' no help frae the Government either!' The great fear of her generation was to get into debt. One week she had not a scrap of food in the house and not a penny in her purse. She wandered up the street, bowed down with anxiety, wondering what to do, and on the way met an old fisherman. He knew by her face something was far from right.

'What ails ye, quine?' he enquired, so she poured out her story.

'Do you know what he did?' she asked me.

'No, you tell me.'

'He went into his purse an' took oot ten shillings – ten shillings, mind you! That seemed a fortune an' I didna ken whit to say.'

'Noo, quine,' he said, 'dinna worry. Just you pay me back when you can afford it. There's nae hurry.'

Mrs McDonald looked away back over the years.

'Ye ken, it was the only time I owed onybody money, an' I never rested till I paid him back. He was a gran' man, and kind.' I thought of our modern age of buy now, pay later, hire purchase, young folks who must have everything in their homes from the beginning, and the era of Mrs McDonald when nothing was bought till it could be paid. Mostly we just went over 'the clash o' the toon', but one day she told me of her husband.

He had lain ill for a long time in the box-bed in the living room. He was a fisherman of the old school to whom the most important things in life were his home and family, his work, and his Church, for none of the boats put out on a Sunday and all the fisher families were to be found at worship, the men in their thick blue jerseys. This particular day he gave thanks for a good wife and bairns, then suddenly sat up in his bed, his face shining.

'Look!' he called, 'above Maggie Ralph's shop!'

His wife looked, but saw nothing, but her man was seeing with an inner eye, something hid from his wife. What? A band of angels comin' after me, or like Stephen the martyr, a glimpse of Heaven and his Lord?

'Oh, you've missed it,' he said.

Then he lay back on his bed, sang a stave of an old Sankey hymn beloved by fishermen, 'O happy day, when Jesus washed my sins away,' then murmuring the name of his trusted friend, 'Jesus . . . Christ,' he was gone.

To many the story of his passing would seem like something from a Victorian melodrama, embarrassing to modern ears, but for the couple it was terribly real and unforgettable, an experience that can be paralleled many times over by those of our calling who attend the sick and dying. Then Mrs McDonald went on, 'He was awfu sair done to,' and I thought she was still talking of her husband, but she continued, 'A' thae sodgers, an' that muckle croon o' thorns, an' that wound in His side.' She gave a great sigh, paused, and then her old blue eyes shining she said 'An' it was a' for us!' That mark you, from a woman who was an adherent of the Church, who did not consider herself good enough to join or come to the Lord's table.

I was asked to be present at a meal one day, a quiet little celebration for Mr and Mrs McIntosh who were celebrating their seventieth wedding anniversary, a remarkable couple. Mr McIntosh at ninety-six was still in Church every Sunday and down the street daily for the shopping, but his wife at eighty-nine was more frail. Only the family were present, and their minister. What a privilege to share in such an occasion, a Royal Wedding indeed. I was asked to say a few words. Not having been at a seventieth anniversary before, I had no suitable stories, and I knew from experience of them they liked a joke. After congratulating them, the best I could do as a lighter touch was to tell of the couple on their Golden Wedding day. They had lived all their lives in the one place, were highly respected, and both hale and hearty, and the young reporter sent to interview them for the local paper and get a photograph asked the old man what was the secret of their long, happy and healthy life together. The old man replied,

'Weel, son, it's like this. When Jean and I were wed we agreed we would never fa' oot, that if ever a row was comin' on, one o' us would just go a walk, and the reason we've lived so long and been so happy is plenty of exercise and fresh air.'

Old Mr McIntosh smacked the table in glee at the story so I told another Golden Wedding one which I had heard my friend John Baker, minister of Rosebank Church tell. A certain couple on their great day went back to Arran where they had spent their honeymoon fifty years before. It was a glorious day, and passed all too quickly, but at last it was time to go and get the boat. They found it had gone, so they were forced to stay the night on the island, and managed to get fixed up in the hotel where they had honeymooned. As the wife was preparing for bed and combing out her hair, now silvered, she said to her man,

'Aye, John, the winter's in my hair but the summer is still in my heart,' to which her gallant swain replied:

'Mary, the winter's in your hair richt enough, and the summer micht be in your heart, but if the spring had been in your step, we wouldna' hae missed the boat.'

It was a delight to see Mr and Mrs McIntosh, twenty years on from those in my stories, laugh heartily as if I had said something clever. It was a wonderful experience to hear them recount some of the happenings of their long lives together, walking side by side down the years, and now in the golden glow of evening, still, indeed even more one, dependent on the other.

Then there was Mrs Gilchrist, her old face wrinkled like a ripe pippin, in her eighties looking after her grandson Alan, a terribly mentally and physically handicapped lad. He was in his twenties but had the mental age of an infant, always happy and smiling, and dearly loved by his parents and Granny who had brought him up from a child so that his parents would be free to live and work normally. Alan could not speak, had to be spoon-fed, and have absolutely everything done for him. I early discovered he loved music, especially a good-going tune, and every time I called I had to play 'She'll be comin' round the mountain' and 'Daisy, Daisy,' while Alan kept time with his hand. About half way through my ministry in Aldermouth Alan died, and while most would have said it was a merciful release, Mrs Gilchrist grieved for her 'boy'. On the face of it, one would think of such a life as a tragedy, but there were no happier home to enter in the whole town.

The oldest person in the town, and the oldest in any of the Church's Eventide Homes at the time was Miss Catherine Grant, aged 105. I visited her many times, and over the years had many yarns, for she could go back to the 1870s. She told me of her girlhood as a shepherdess in the hills above Loch Ness. She talked of the Battle of Culloden as if it was yesterday, and told tales of 'the Bonnie Prince' she had heard from her great-grandfather. She recalled filling the 'kist' with its supply of oatmeal for the winter, and of how a sheep would be killed for a celebration. It was incredible to think of the changes she had seen. No anaesthetics when she was a girl, no electricity, no cars.

'What about hospital?' I asked her. She was aghast.

'Och now, to go to hospital was a terrible thing, chust a place to die.' She remembered well stories of how after a burial the relatives or Church elders had to guard the grave and the people built a sentry box at the gates, 'for the doctors used to come to take the bodies away to study the internals.' Sometimes the watchers would let the grave-robbers into the Churchyard, then shut the gate on them so that they could not get out again, and her eyes twinkled at the recollection. She had survived three leg breaks since her seventies, the last when she was a mere youngster of 102. I never thought it would heal, but it did and she walked again.

Always in her room, beside her bed, was the Bible, several individual books in very large print given her by the Bible Society for whom she had been a collector for many years. The books were well thumbed, she could recite many passages by heart, and treated 'The Book' with the reverence of a bygone age. One day she surprised me by an apparent criticism of a Bible character, 'You know, Mr Cameron, I sometimes think that St Paul was chust a little hard on the ladies,' then, as if she had gone too far she added, 'but likely they would be needing it.'

I asked her what was her favourite chapter. She had no doubt, John 14! 'In my Father's house are many mansions. I go to prepare a place for you.'

So on her 105th birthday we celebrated, just a few of us, the matron and Superintendent of the Home, the Provost, the senior doctor, my wife and I and one or two others. In the middle sat the grand old lady, surrounded by cards, flowers, telegrams ('and one from the Queen no less'). She was resplendent in a frilly blouse and black hat, 1900 style, her face powdered, but a little bemused by the popping of flash bulbs, yet regal in her bearing, a queen in her own right, in full control of her life, body, mind and spirit.

Then there were the Campbells, a grand old couple who had, like so many of their generation, raised a large family on very little. They too had been spared to one another well beyond the three score years and ten, and to enter their snug little cottage was to be treated like a prince. Immediately I would be shown to the best chair, mother would give a nod, and the two unmarried girls would immediately rise to put the kettle on and prepare a cup of tea which was really a sumptious feast of home baked scones, pancakes, gingerbread, currant cake and a host of other delicacies. They too were adherents, but in Church twice a Sunday, a humble, gracious, God-fearing family whose like are the salt of the earth. Every Christmas, knowing their minister's sweet tooth and special delights, the two daughters, Grace and Mary, would arrive at the Manse door laden with good things, all their own marvellous baking.

So one could go on. Our senior elder was Mr Hammond, also in his nineties, who had had a family of daughters, and then lastly one boy, Sandy who was the former Session Clerk and my dentist – a wonderful, talented, generous, welcoming family. The first time I called, old Mr Hammond was in bed, but his violin was handed down to him, and he entertained his new minister to a selection. Great folks! There were our near neighbours, Jim and Jean McLennan, who had a special interest in the Manse boys growing up, and who put up with a ball often landing over the wall in their garden.

One of our old folk we had known before coming to Aldermouth was Mrs Burns, Granny to everybody, especially a succession of young doctors who rented the house next to her. She was the mother of Nan Archibald, whose contact had first turned my thoughts from Moorton to Aldermouth and who had visited us with far flung members of the family, home for a visit to their native Ayrshire from Canada. They included a call at Moorton Kirk, where Granny Burns' father had been minister for many years. She was a wonderfully bright, indomitable soul, interesting and interested in all that was going on. A similar 'character' was Mrs Mackenzie, again over the ninety mark, who lived with her daughter Helen, and whose other daughter was married to our marvellous organist, Jim McMichael. She was always as bright as a new pin, alert, informed, and regularly with a twinkle in her eye informing me of course she was English and proud of it, proud too that her late husband had at one time been Provost.

There were well over 200 really elderly folks on our Church roll, and one could speak of them all, but space does not permit. To know them was a privilege and a delight.

Mind you, age does not of itself bring goodness or sanctity. I have known some awkward, difficult and bitter old folks, demanding too, like the old boy who asked me to visit him in hospital. The visit consisted of a list of instructions from him of things he wanted me to see to, including an enquiry about his investments. He was not seriously ill, had no Church connection, but like many another, alas, did not hesitate to use the Church for his own ends when needed. 'Not bad,' I thought as I left his bed 'for one who usually has not a good word to say about Kirks or Kirky folk.'

But for the most part, I have greatly enjoyed my contact with our older folks and still do, and look back over the years to some wonderful people I have known, who, though twice my age, accepted me without hesitation as their minister and friend, and from very many of whom, goodness simply shone out. The golden years indeed!

Years ago there were three famous Methodist ministers – Weatherhead, Sangster and Soper, all spiritual giants, close friends with the redoubtable Lord Soper still, at eighty five in 1988, alive and active. It was said of them, 'Weatherhead loves the people, Sangster loves the Lord and Soper loves an argument!' Sangster was a really saintly man, other wordly, deeply spiritual, a man who was used to point many on the pilgrim pathway, a man just plain good right through. Pulling his leg one day, Weatherhead said to him, 'Suppose you had to interview either an old wrinkled woman or a dashing young blonde in a low cut dress, which would you choose?' Sangster thought seriously for a time, then replied, 'I think the older lady, for she would have seen so much more of life and could teach me so much.'

I can well understand Sangster's choice, and like him I too, though far, far short of his saintliness, have been taught so much about life, in sunshine and in shadow, from those walking in the soft, fading light of evening.

Of course I knew many old folks in my years as a vet too but my relationship with them was different, for it was their animals that concerned me then, but one could not treat the pets or farm animals without getting to know the owners.

My partner of the early years at Bristacombe, Major Kenneth Davidson, was on holiday and I was holding the fort on my own. The summer months saw a reduction in farm work, but this was balanced, as visitors flooded into the town, by a rise in the small animal side of things and in cases at the zoo, so one was never idle.

My first visit of the morning was a very easy one, I thought, to call at the home of a Miss Huxtable and clip the nails of her dog. I duly found the house and an elderly lady came to the door.

'Yes?' she enquired.

'I'm the veterinary surgeon. I've come to clip your dog's nails.'

'Oh – oh my – well, I suppose you better come in.'

I wondered at the hesitation, but followed the old lady into a very comfortably furnished sitting room, where another elderly lady was sitting nursing a Pomeranian, which, at the sight of me leapt from her lap, made for my ankles and caught hold of the bottom of my trousers.

'Oh dear, isn't he the little monkey?' said lady number one. 'This is my sister,' she went on, 'but we were expecting Major Davidson.'

'I'm sorry, he's off on holiday at present. I'm his partner.'

'Oh, but I'm afraid,' spoke up the seated sister, 'we always have the Major. You see, he really understands Peter and Peter is used to him. He is such a sensitive little fellow.'

'I understand, but I think I could manage to clip Peter's claws.'

'Oh no!' said the dominant sister, 'Peter gets so excited with strangers. I'm afraid it will have to be the Major. We will just wait till he gets back. Good day to you, Mr er . . . er,'

'Cameron.'

'Mr Cameron,' and before I knew it I was being shown out, pursued by a yelping Pomeranian.

Some years rolled on, Kenneth Davidson moved to Kenya, and Bernard Paterson became my partner. Here was a problem for the sisters, but it seemed it was not so much the Major they demanded, as always the senior partner, for when next summoned to the Huxtable abode, I was welcomed like a long lost cousin.

'Ah – Mr Cameron! How nice to see you! It is Peter's usual problem of his nails and we have heard *such* good reports of you. Now the Major has gone we had no hesitation in sending for you. But you'll always come yourself, won't you?' Peter was a spoiled little lap dog, and yap dog, but while one sister held him and the other murmured endearments, I managed successfully to do the job.

'Now come and wash your hands,' I was commanded, and ushered into a very luxurious bathroom with a brand new bar of Lux toilet soap and a white, fluffy, expensive towel laid out for my use. That operation completed, I was handed, on my way out, a parcel, 'for Mrs Cameron and your dear little boys.' It proved to be a large box of chocolates, something I received on every visit thereafter, for Peter had regular problems of a minor nature in addition to the nails which needed frequent clipping, for he never walked on hard roads, only being allowed a little romp in their enclosed garden. A new bar of soap and my special towel always awaited me. Poor Bernard never got a look in until I left for the ministry, but there was always rejoicing with our laddies, Neil and Ian, whenever I visited there. They even got to asking,

'Is Peter not sick yet, Daddy?'

'When do you go to cut Peter's nails again?'

Many old folks keep pets of different kinds, and particularly for someone living alone, they can be a great boon. Sometimes it is astonishing to what lengths people will go for the sake of their companions, be it budgerigar or Boxer, cat or canary. I visited a lonely old soul at Martincombe one day. She lived in a little one-apartment house, a bed-sitter, and was possessed of a bad-tempered large Collie cross dog of which she was clearly distinctly nervous. She was no help at all in restraining it as I prepared to give it a distemper innoculation, so I had to muzzle it and continue to hold it tightly by the scruff of the neck while I slipped the needle in. I looked around the little room and asked where the dog slept.

'Oh, it sleeps with me,' she explained rather shamefacedly.

'There can't be much room,' I suggested, looking at the small single bed.

'No, there isn't,' she acknowledged, 'sometimes when he turns over bed I'm frightened to touch him and push him back, so I end up sleeping on the floor.' That, I felt, was carrying one's devotion and self-sacrifice for a pet a bit far, but clearly this little woman was more frightened of intruders than her fierce dog, for no one would have dared beard that hound in its den.

But this kind of thing is the exception. Most pets, particularly dogs and cats, give back all they receive in love with interest, and some unexpected people, I found, lavished a great deal of tender loving care on their animals. Miss Inglewood, for example, was an elderly, man-ish, no nonsense spinster who had an old cat. It had a heart condition, was deaf, subject to eczema, was troubled by its kidneys and had not a tooth left in its head. But she loved her sixteeen-year old cat with a passionate love. She was never away from the surgery with it for the least thing, or for a restock of its many pills, and there was no more precious feline in Bristacombe. A famous, well known, world renowned author was another who unexpectedly showered extravagant devotion on his dog, a Dachsund. He and his wife lived in a lovely house above the dunes at the far end of Mortecombe's famous beach, three miles of clean, golden sand. He was very much a man's man, an old soldier who had a great hole in his leg from shrapnel in the First World War. Twice every day he waded in the sea to keep that old wound clean from which came periodically a sliver of diseased bone. He doted on that dog, and like Miss Inglewood, at the least sign of trouble was on the phone. Aunty Violet, as she was, and is to our boys, for she often thirty years ago baby sat for us, was another who lived for her cats and any strays in the area, and after her husband's death, and particularly after suffering a stroke herself, it was her cats alone, who by their affection gave her the will to live. That is the great thing about domestic pets; they normally ask for so little and give so much in return, and in my years in practice I saw many folks in the evening of life who were given an interest (sometimes it seemed the sole interest in living), by their little companions.

Of course the trouble is that animals do not live so long as people, and there can be great heartbreak when a loved companion dies. I have seen it so often and normally encourage the owner to get another pet as soon as possible. Nearly always they would initially say, 'No! No other dog could take the place of Rex, or Tiger or Trixie or whatever,' but I tried to point out that while that was true, in time the new animal would make its own place.

I remember the phone going about 9.30 pm one evening and a voice telling me she was phoning for Mr Chugg, 21, Fore Street, and could I come as soon as possible as his dog had collapsed. Fore Street was a steep street leading down to the harbour and made up of cheaper class Guest Houses and old dwellings of the terrace type. An elderly man opened the door of number 21 and ushered me into a very humble abode. There, on a mat before a meagre coal fire was an old dog, lying on its side, its breathing very fast and laboured.

'I hope you can do summat for Rover, sir,' said the old man. 'He seems far through. He be nought but a little mongrel but you see, sir, since missus died last year, he's been ma only friend.'

'We'll see what we can do, Mr Chugg. How old would he be?'

'Ah! Rover be a good age, bout 15 an' a've had 'im since a pup.'

I bent down and took the old dog's temperature. Rover scarcely moved, only his eyes following me around, and at the sound of his master's voice, his tail giving a half-hearted little thump on the worn old carpet.

'Can't make it out,' the old chap went on, 'he had 'is tea as usual, like, bout 7, then us 'ad 'is little walk down to t' harbour. He comed in an' just kind of fell down where ee be lyin' now.' The old dog's temperature was subnormal, his pulse fast, thready and irregular. I had a listen at the chest with my stethoscope. There was fluid on the lungs, the heart-beat was weak, and of course, irregular. Just then the little dog gave a whimper and the old man was down on his knees cradling its head in his hands, and stroking it gently.

I straightened up. This was always the hard bit.

'I'm very sorry, but your dog's had a heart attack, Mr Chugg, and he's very ill.'

'Do ee mean he's dyin'?'

'I'm afraid so, Mr Chugg.'

'Can nuthin' be done, like?'

'Not really, I'm very sorry. If he had been a younger dog, and just had a kind of heart spasm, bit like angina in people, we could have treated him. But he's had a proper heart attack and his heart's very weak. There's fluid in his lungs too which means his heart is failing fast. It's just like a pump – but a very wonderful pump – but it's come to the end of its working life.'

'What do ee advise then, sir?' the old man asked.

'Well, I don't think he's suffering too much pain, but he's very distressed. I think I should give him a little jag which will take away all discomfort and he'll just go to sleep.'

'You mean he won't waken up?' the little man quavered. I hesitated to choose my words.

'He might, but I think it likely he'll just sleep quietly away. It's a painkiller, you see, I'm giving him, what we call a sedative, which will quieten his breathing and ease his distress. We can't allow him to go on fighting for breath like that, can we?'

The old man looked at his companion of the years, tears coursing down his cheeks, then he got down on the rug beside his friend and buried his face in its coat while the dog's tail gave a few weak little thumps on the floor.

'Aar, you'm there, old fellow. You've been a wonderful pal. You and me's had some great times, us 'ave.'

Slowly he straightened up and said with a catch in his voice.

'Alright, sir – give 'im 'is jag now.'

I gave the dog a shot of omnopon and scopolamine which would make him drowsy and comfortable, and in sleep would most probably just pass on. It was not really euthanasia, just making an animal as much at ease as I could, but I was certain he would not waken up. The old man was fumbling with a purse.

'What do I owe you, sir?' he asked.

'Oh – that's alright, Mr Chugg. Let's just see how Rover gets on, shall we?'

So I left the little old man, a quiet dignity about him, as he got down on the carpet again, stroking his friend of the years. I called the next morning, and Rover had, indeed, quietly slept away in the night. I asked Mr Chugg if he would not consider having another dog and offered to get him one, but his lip trembled and he said, 'Ah, but it wouldn't be Rover.'

It so happened that several times in the next fortnight I saw old Mr Chugg out doing his bits of shopping, for Fore Street was just round the corner from our surgery. He looked forlorn, lost, desolate. Then I remembered a Border terrier bitch I had whelped about three months before and thought there might just be a chance. I called at the Border's home, whose owner I knew well.

'How are the pups going?' I enquired after a bit.

'They've been slow this time, Mr Cameron, and we're left with one still which we just can't get rid of. We may have to get you to put it down.'

'Dog or bitch?'

'Oh, dog.' I thought this was all providential.

'Would you consider giving it away to a good home?' I quizzed, and told them about the lonely old man. They listened carefully and to my great delight agreed. Now for the difficult part. I called on Mr Chugg that evening just at the darkening, perhaps the loneliest part of the day for an old person living alone.

'Ah, Mr Cameron!' he greeted me, 'it's nice to see you. Come in so that I can square up what I owe you.'

I went in, sat down and chatted for a bit. Eventually he rose and took his purse out of a drawer. The purse looked pretty empty.

'No, Mr Chugg, I haven't come for that. As a matter of fact I've come to ask you if you could help me. You see, I have two friends whose bitch had pups and there's one they can't get rid of. If they don't find a good home for it, they're talking of having it put to sleep, and I thought maybe you could do me a favour and give the wee fellow a try. It's a pedigree Border terrier, just about the same size as Rover.'

'Oh, Mr Cameron, I couldn't, no, it wouldn't be Rover.'

'Seems a shame to have it put to sleep, though, don't you think?'

'Aye, it be a right shame.'

'Tell you what,' I rushed on, 'have a look at it. It's out in the car. You can always say "No".'

It was a kind of blackmail, I realised, but I thought the end justified the means. So I went out to the car, carried in the little pup, which promptly did a puddle on the floor.

'That's torn it,' I thought, but Mr Chugg laughed.

'Rover did that the moment I brought him home too,' he said. The bright little bundle of mischief went over to where the old man was sitting in an ancient broken springed chair, looked up at him, then leapt on his knee and licked his face, and I felt certain I had won.

And so it proved. A lonely old man got a new companion, and being a puppy, the training kept him busy, and in due course I saw him proudly going along the High Street with the little dog on a brand new lead. I called one day to see how things were going for he had promised initially he would just give it a try. The dog was curled up at his chair, its chin resting on his foot, a picture of contentment.

'Well, Mr Chugg, how about it? Will he do?'

'Aar, Mr Cameron, he be a right topper, an' pedigreed an' all. Never had a pedgireed dog before. I've called him Mac, because he and you are Scotch. I hope you don't mind.'

'Mr Chugg,' I said in all sincerity, 'I'm highly honoured.'

I thought, as I drove home, of the contrast of the old man that first night I had seen him and of the change wrought by a four legged bundle of mischief. Of course the dog could not replace the close companionship of his recently deceased wife, but in their own innocent way, many an animal has brought gladness, joy and all the love of its heart to someone in the golden years, providing its own kind of companionship. Indeed more than once someone has said to me something like 'I'd rather have a dog than a husband/wife, for you can depend on a dog. It's loyal, always the same, and doesn't talk back to you.'

That may be true of some relationships, but much as I love animals, I cannot agree that a dog or cat can take the place of a deceased partner. I can think of nothing more beautiful than an old couple, who have weathered many a storm together on the way, still walking hand in hand in the golden glow of evening, one through the years, one for ever.

When I was signing copies of my first book *Vet in the Vestry* a couple came up to me clutching their book and said, 'You won't remember us, but you played the organ at our wedding in Crosshill Church forty-four years ago, and as we went out at the end you played *I'll walk beside you*. It has been our favourite song since.'

I would only have been a laddie of seventeen when I played at their marriage, but I could well understand why the song had remained a favourite, and it sums up all I've tried to say in this chapter.

> 'I'll walk beside you through the passing years;
> Through days of cloud and sunshine, joy and tears;
> And when the great call comes, the sunset gleams,
> I'll walk beside you to the land of dreams.'

And like a great echo, I hear the voice of *the* constant companion and friend say from that land of dreams, 'Lo, I am with you alway, even to the end of the world.'

The least of these, my brothers

EIGHT

Years ago I read in *Reader's Digest* an article about a family in Canada who were seemingly untameable, living in their own style, and for the most part a law unto themselves. They were called McKie. On the very night of my induction to the Old Parish Church of Aldermouth, I was warned by a ministerial colleague about a local family who would plague the life out of me if I did not choke them off right at the start. They too were called McKie, their notoriety had spread far and wide, and sure enough they were at the Manse door within days.

The father was dead, but there were five sons and five daughters and the mother who was the head of the clan in no uncertain terms. She always dressed in black and looked somewhat sinister, but she had a gentle face and manner. However, I soon learned that looks deceived for she had led the family to ruin after the father's death, prior to which they had been law-abiding citizens. Their affection for mother and atttachment to her was astonishing and in its way, admirable, but under her leadership they had gone to complete wreck and ruin. Her every wish was obeyed. The Police Sergeant told me that Mrs McKie had been overheard issuing her instructions about which house to burgle, and they would go out and do it. Never have I known a family, alas, more attached to their mother, whose every desire was paramount. The eldest son, Dan, had been in prison more than a hundred times, could be violent, and indeed most of the family had a 'record'. One of the exceptions was a girl who had married early and got out of the tight-knit family circle. She was living a perfectly respectable, humble life in a local council house. The rest of the family, male and female, were almost constantly under the combined influence of drink and various forms of tranquillisers which a compassionate local doctor, who clearly did not know what to do with them, dished out freely.

They had been evicted from several houses because of the disturbance to the neighbours, and when I first knew them, were living in a large caravan down by the harbour. From the beginning there was scarcely a week we did not have them at the door pleading for help. Early on I realised that to give them money was fatal, for with a scarcely concealed grin of triumph they simply headed for the nearest pub.

One evening, in my first months, the steady member of the family came to see me.

'I'm worried about our Bobby,' she said.

'Bobby? I haven't met him yet.'

'No, he's just coming out of a young offenders' institution and he's sure to go the way of the rest unless somebody helps him.'

'He's really got to help himself, Agnes.'

'Oh, I know – but I thought if somehow he could get a job away from here, he might, since he's young, go straight.'

I thought for a bit. Agnes was a caring girl, and clearly very fond of the baby of the family, and finally I agreed to try to help. I wrote to a Roman Catholic group in the south of Scotland that specialised in helping lads like Bobby, they generously agreed to have him, and the day he came out of the Institution I met him, told him all about it and the lad, a fine, big, good looking fellow in his mid teens agreed to give it a try. I paid his fare south and off he went.

Meantime the rest of the family were going from bad to worse. They ripped out most saleable items from their rented caravan to sell in exchange for drink, and were to be seen daily lurching along the streets, and very frequently at our door. We sometimes gave them a meal, but refused, apart from the occasional bus fare, to give them money. They had relations in Elgin and Inverness, and would periodically disappear for a time, to the infinite relief of the citizens of Aldermouth. There was peace for the harried folks of the town only when the McKies were away, usually in prison. I visited Dan in jail for although my common sense told me it was a losing battle, my conscience kept jagging me to try to help such pathetic human beings. I was told Dan, indeed all the McKies were model prisoners, and really they seemed happiest when 'inside' – well clad and fed, clean, sober and human again. But their sentences were normally short and always they drifted back to mother, seeming docilely to obey her every wish and command. Bye and bye there was no caravan left, somehow they set fire to it, and they were out on the street.

They arrived *en masse* at the Manse one summer evening. I was picking raspberries in the garden and hidden from their view, and I could hear them making their plan of attack as they came along the path.

'Ask for £5!'

'Too much.'

'Try for it anyway.'

They were somewhat startled when I leapt out at them from between the high rows of raspberries and asked them what they wanted.

'Oh, Mr Cameron! . . . er . . . it's a grand nicht.'

It's that alright, and as you can see, I'm busy in the garden. What's the problem tonight?'

'Well, you see, Mr Cameron, you've been awful good to us and we don't like to ask you again, but there's this big tent we can get to stay in – eh – for £5.'

I laughed. 'Where do you think I'd get £5? I've a wife and family to keep, and ministers have not a great pay.'

'Oh, we ken, Mr Cameron – it's a crying shame, so it is – aye, a richt shame, but if you could just give us £5, we won't bother you again.'

'For a tent, you say?'

'Aye, that's richt.'

'Well, tell you what. If you tell the man who has the tent to contact me, I'll see what I can do, or better still, tell me who he is and I'll go and see him and get it for you.'

'Oh no! That wouldna' dae at a', Mr Cameron. The man's no there the noo but he's promised tae keep it for us. If you could just give us the money, you see!'

'No money!'

'£4?'

'No!'

'£3?'

'Not a penny.'

So it worked down till they were asking for ten shillings, but despite the lovely night, the grand crop of rasps *and* my conscience, there was no money forthcoming, and at last, with mutterings and long looks, the deputation departed. Of course it was all a fabricated story, but some time later they did, in fact, somehow acquire a large bell tent, pitched it beside the burned out caravan, and there they lived. It was shocking that any family, however difficult, should live like that and I constantly badgered the Social Work Department to try to house them, preferably away out in the country which I felt was the only hope, with no neighbours to disturb with their wild drinking bouts and fights, but nothing seemed to be done.

In the midst of one of their many crises, young Bobby arrived home. He came to the Manse looking fit, well, sober, an upstanding young man, and announced that he was changed, had got religion, and was going to live a different life. We rejoiced with him and for him. Alas, within a week he was back in jail.

We tried again with Sandy, who was the smallest of the family – a quiet, subdued, shauchly, pathetic little creature, the one we saw most often. I managed to get him fixed up with the Salvation Army in Glasgow, and as the months passed and Sandy did not return, I began to hope. However, one day after nearly a year, a year of happiness for Sandy among the good folks of the 'Sally Army' where he had helped in the canteen, he arrived back and went to stay with Aunt Mary, who, though a humble woman, was honest, kindly and straight.

Aunt Mary, like the McKies originally in their father's time, earned her living as a kind of hawker, but she was a decent soul, and deeply concerned about her nephews and nieces. She surprised Janet one day and showed that the giving was not all one way when she arrived at the door with a large, green, three cornered fruit dish 'to show my thanks for all you've done for the boys'. The dish has graced our dining table annually at harvest thanksgivings filled with fruit, and a token forever that even in the wildest and worst, as my father maintained all his life, there is some good. There was an even bigger surprise one day when Mrs McKie herself, who had often been at our door pleading for bus fares to Inverness and been given the latest one on condition that she paid it back (something she always promised), actually paid it back. Janet nearly dropped the money in amazement, but took it and said, 'I'll lay this aside for you and when you need it, it'll be here waiting for you.' Mrs McKie thanked her and departed. She was always most gracious in her thanks. Two days later she was back for her money!

Sandy struggled to keep his head above water for a time, but eventually, to the great sorrow of Aunt Mary, he was sucked back into the vortex of the family and their way of life, and before long, bruised and battered, for they were forever in fights, he was back at our door looking for money. Neither of us was in at the time, but he was given short shrift by Ian, for by now all our boys knew the family well and had been involved in their own way in our attempts to reform and rehabilitate.

Then came tragedy of a high order. On Games Day in Aldermouth when crowds flocked into the town from near and far, old natives of the area came home for the annual big event and there was general festivity and rejoicing, two of the McKie boys were found lying helpless in the street. I suppose, in retrospect, they should have been taken to hospital but being the McKies, the police, who found them, took them to the lock-up where one, the one least known to us, Billy, died in the police cell of that lethal mixture of alcohol and drugs, choking on his own vomit. There was an immediate outcry from the rest of the family about police brutality, one of the popular 'dailies' got hold of the story, published an interview with the sorrowing mother and there was general indignation in the rest of Scotland which knew nothing of the family and cries of 'why doesn't the Church do something for this poor neglected family', for whom nobody seemed to care. A post mortem confirmed the diagnosis, the brother was buried by me amid tremendous wailing, many of the mourners, who seemed to have flocked from all over the north, being drunk. Dan was escorted to the graveside by two prison warders, for he was undergoing one of his frequent stays in Inverness prison. I felt deeply sorry at the waste of Billy's life, and also felt keenly the tragedy of a life lived without God. How different, I felt, not for the first time, is the funeral of one where there has been faith. I thought back as one always does, should I have done more for the family? Eventually the episode passed. Though somewhat sobered for a time, the death of one son made no real difference to the lifestyle of mother or family.

So the weeks and months passed. One night in the dead of winter, mother and three of the family arrived at the Manse door 'drookit' to the skin and with nowhere to sleep. I had greatly hardened my heart by this time, for we had helped as best we could so often, but I simply could not turn anyone away in such a state on such a night. So we bedded them down in the BB hut, gave them dry clothes, blankets and food, with instructions to be out early in the morning or the Kirk Session would have my head. They kept their bargain, apparently sleeping soundly all night long, which was more than I had done, for I was up umpteen times parading over to the hut to make sure it was not on fire, for in addition to their other 'gifts', the McKies had quite a record as fire raisers. They still had the remains of the tent for their home, for it too had been damaged by fire, but very frequently practically the whole family, including finally the old mother too, were guests of Her Majesty in prison.

Then came a telegram to every clergyman in the town from the Director of the Social Work Department, which read 'For the sake of Jesus Christ, do something about housing and helping the McKies.'

With one accord, the brethren felt highly indignant at that, when we thought of what *had* been done, and how indeed we over the years had been doing things which we felt were the responsibility of that same Director. In time the furore died down, nothing was done by the authorities, another brother Sammy died in the same tragic way as Billy – drink and drugs – and I had a terrible feeling of utter helplessness. Of course the answer was a change of lifestyle, but that could only come from a change of heart, and yet could one continually preach the Gospel which could change, to those with empty stomachs and no roof over their heads? So things just drifted on. I kept vowing this was the last help they would get for almost everything went on drink. I regularly told them to go and work, go out and earn a living. But I knew in my heart that work was really out of the question for two reasons.

One, they were so weakened and drained mentally and physically, they simply could not work and two, no one in the area would employ them.

Usually it was the sons we saw. The girls, for the most part had other fish to fry and went their own ways, always however reporting back to mother. Oddly enough, women did not enter into the boys' scheme of things at all, except mother. If ever I saw a mother's influence for wrongdoing in her family, it was in Mrs McKie. Yet their concern for her was deep and basic, and without her, they felt lost.

After wee Sandy, Dan was our most frequent visitor, a Dan whose face was now battered almost beyond recognition. Every now and then he would break into a house, but his method of operation was always the same. He would take out the light bulb, leaving his fingerprints on it, then burn newspapers for torches, escaping with £5 or a brooch. The police simply went and picked him up without difficulty or resistance, and for a while again, he was at least warm and well fed 'inside'.

Many times I told them there would be no more assistance, but one day Bobby arrived at the Manse, a different Bobby, well dressed, polite, sober, clean and with an independent air about him, a Bobby who could look the world in the eye. He had been out of circulation for a while and I had wondered where he was. Apparently he had been staying in a monastery, and undoubtedly something had happened to him.

'I've been converted,' he explained, 'and I'm going to go straight. Will you help me?'

I was mightily impressed by the obvious change in the wild, and latterly very violent Bobby, and rejoiced that where I had failed, some brothers in the Roman Catholic Church had succeeded. Despite my vow to do no more for the family, I felt I must have one last try with Bobby.

'Bobby! I'm delighted to see the change in you and I'll try to help, on one condition, that you keep away from the family or you're sunk!'

'I know, Mr Cameron, I feel the same myself. They've made a mess of their lives' (so had he!), 'but I'm different now from them.' (A wee bit uppish, I thought, but said nothing.)

'Well, you can have a bed here for a night or two till you get fixed up somewhere else and try for a job. But every day will be a struggle for you now that you're back home.'

We managed to get him fixed up in a caravan that was advertised to let, paid a week's rent, gave him basic food to take away with him, bought him a new pair of boots and some more clothes. With amazing rapidity, mother and the rest of the family converged on the Manse. Somehow they had heard Bobby was home, but we refused to tell them where he was staying. He did, in fact, to my complete amazement get a job, and he would come to the Manse each evening, often dodging in the back way to escape his searching family, and have his dinner with us. Janet and our lads, though like me thoroughly fed up with the whole McKie clan, were wonderful in their forbearance. In addition to his dinner, it seemed Bobby nightly needed a top up of his faith. But alas, the great reform lasted about 10 days, the family found him and off he went with them. Bobby's new found faith and resolution speedily crumbled before the onslaught of mother and the rest, and in no time he was in the hands of the law again.

Eventually, after many years, the authorities housed them in a cottage away out in the country where there were no neighbours to disturb, and Aldermouth, including the Manse, breathed again. The last I heard of them before leaving Aldermouth for my present Charge was that they had somehow succeeded in setting fire to their country cottage. Well, not quite the last, for after my first book *Vet in the Vestry* was published, I had a very warm-hearted letter from one of the girls, telling me that another of the boys and two of the girls had been killed in accidents, thanking me for what I had done, informing me that their mother was settled in her old age in Elgin, and wishing I was back in Aldermouth again! I was grateful for that letter, because, looking back, it has always seemed to me a story of unmitigated tragedy, a waste of lives, and massive failure on my part. I could only console myself with the thought that we, my whole family and a series of Assistant Ministers, Ben, Peter, Richard, Campbell and Donald, had tried very hard for twelve long years, and even the great 'Physician Himself' sometimes could do no mighty works because of people's unbelief, and unwillingness to follow His way in life, and was comforted a little by His promise, He who loves all mankind,

'Inasmuch as you did it unto one of the least of these my brothers, you did it unto me.'

'It's chronic'

NINE

I would be about twenty-four when I discovered there was something abnormal about me. Whether it was a hereditary condition and some oddity was locked up in my genes, an undiscovered virus or possibly, as one consultant suggested, I was a carrier of Bacterium automobilis, could not be determined. Again a homespun philosopher was quite adamant that the whole thing was a series of coincidences, though this, of course, was impossible to establish. Whatever the reason, it is indisputable that over the years my presence in the vicinity of any form of internal combustion engine has sooner or later produced alarming symptoms in the creatures. Autocylces refused to budge when I was around; lawn mowers, be they two-stroke or four-stroke, the latter formerly considered an immune species, splutter and give up the ghost, and cars of any age, size, colour or make invariably show signs of distress. I myself am inclined to think it is an allergy, not that I am allergic to cars, but they most certainly are to me, for in time, any who have had contact with me just give up and refuse to budge. It is not that I ill treat them, nor have I actually caused grievous bodily harm to any of the species. They are regularly supplied with food and water, but inevitably they contract this automobilitis from me and turn ill, usually on some deserted stretch of road with no auto-hospital for miles. Another frequent manifestation is specifically in the morning when they are quite unable even to leave the stable. I have never understood what exactly it is about me, and the experts are baffled, but the disease or disability is now so long established as clearly to be chronic.

The symptoms vary considerably. At times there is necrosis and subsequent amputation of exhaust pipes, a catarrhal, wheezy condition of the air passages, due sometimes to over much oxygen (O_2) or Carbon Monoxide (CO), then sundry groans from all parts of the external anatomy suggestive of rheumatoid arthritis, severed tendons in the CV joints affecting the limbs, an arteriol sclerosis of the main arteries causing clotting or other interference to the flow of life-giving fluid. Perhaps, commonest of all, is a stroke or other cerebral incident leading to complete paralysis.

The first indication that all was not well was on a cold, wet, November night, when, with my girl friend beside me, I was returning from my weekly evening off from the Mochrum Practice where I started my career, in the ancient but trusty Standard. We had, as always, spent the evening at an Ice-Hockey match, when half way home, the car just gave a quiet little moan and stopped. I suspected some form of disc or perhaps nerve trouble, for though I pressed the accelerator vigorously, and my foot would go right to the floor, no response came from the Standard. A telephone call to my brother Fergus brought him hurrying to the scene. Though not qualified medically, he had a working knowledge of first aid, and speedily, and extremely cleverly, I thought, discovered that a severed ligament was the trouble, the said ligament linking the accelerator or foot to the throttle or leg. A piece of wire provided a temporary artificial ligament, till some minor surgery next day put things right.

On the second onset of my condition, the symptoms were dramatic. The boss at Mochrum having taken delivery of a brand new Land Rover, I fell heir to his Ford Prefect. As was customary, I assumed that I could use it for pleasure, as well as business purposes, and was somewhat surprised when Mr Buchan hesitated, said a guarded 'yes', then added, 'but I wouldn't go too far'. It may be that he intended to retain the Ford in reasonable health and appearance for his own use periodically, since a Land Rover is hardly suitable for social occasions. On the other hand, I think, looking back, that he already realised all was not well with me. At any rate on my next monthly weekend off, Janet and I departed on the Saturday for Glentrool, some fifty miles away, there to enjoy a pleasant day in that renowned beauty spot. All went well, till we decided it was time to head for home, when to my utter astonishment and dismay, the gear box loudly protested, uttering the most frightful groans whenever I tried to coax it into action. I at first suspected cartilage trouble, but later decided it was some kind of brain disorder, for the poor Ford could not go forward, but readily would go backward. So we reversed over many a mile of rough, twisting road to the nearest phone box. I hesitated. Should I phone a garage or the boss? Recalling the latter's injunction, I tried all the garages around, but being Saturday evening, all were closed. So the boss it was, who, Mrs Buchan informed me, was out on a case, and not expected back for some time. She would tell him of the Ford's serious condition when he returned, and she was sure he would speed to the rescue. We should just sit tight, and bring what consolation we could to the sufferer. I spoke to it in soothing tones, hoping it would enter into the spirit of the thing, and gallop off, but no, so I kicked it, told it this was ridiculous, and to get up off its hind legs, but this proved equally ineffective. Backwards it would go, and no other. The daylight faded, the evening shadows gathered about the stricken creature, and as a night mist descended Janet and I were forced to huddle together for warmth, which I found helped my morale considerably! Eventually the Land Rover ambulance arrived, carrying the boss, and bring welcome sustenance to us in the form of a flask of tea and food. The sick car was taken in tow, and supported by the strong shouldered Land Rover proceeded up hill and down dale the long way back to Mochrum, with me at the wheel, thinking dark thoughts and feeling pretty desolate, for my best girl had deserted me for the warmth of the Land Rover, and I was pretty sure that Mr Buchan, though he had been perfectly civil in the presence of a lady, might be rather less so on Monday morning when I reported for duty. I was quite correct in my assumption, and the boss made it absolutely clear that anyone with my record should never be allowed to take any vehicle, any distance, since he considered the risk of contamination was considerable. After some time in dock, the invalid eventually recovered, though I never fully understood the final diagnosis, something about bearings or big ends, whatever they may be!

Since both these incidents had occurred when Janet was present, I thought it just possible she was the source of the trouble, and this would have eased things somewhat for me, for to deliver a girl to her home at some unearthly hour and say 'the car broke down' was so familiar a tale to parents as to be unbelievable. But since the next happening occurred when I, and I alone was involved, it was clear where the fault lay. This time it was our Devon Morris, COD 330, which suffered at my hands virtually from the first. It was a very ancient creature, my first car at

Bristacombe, so I suppose it was understandable that regularly in the mornings it was too stiff to move, until assisted by Kenneth's Triumph. Perpetually the little van groaned and wheezed on its daily toil. Then something went wrong with the autonomic nervous system controlling the petrol gauge. The bug-allergy-virus-coincidence or whatever had struck again! It was dashed awkward, for I never knew whether I had a full or empty tank, so had to resort to rocking the car, and ascertain by its bowel sounds whether anything was present or not. Normally I carried a spare can for emergencies. But one day early in my stay in Bristacombe, I was returning for a late lunch after a full morning of work dehorning some thirty to forty Friesian cows for Alf Spicer. Dehorning, particularly in dairy cattle, had become very popular. It was safe, and apart from a headache for a few days in each hornless beast, was not normally too painful, and it had been shown that the herd milk yield increased since the timorous members of the herd had no longer anything to fear from the bullies, and so, thus liberated, were able to realise their full potential. There is nothing complicated about the operation, being rather like pulling thirty to forty sets of human teeth in one morning! Nerve blocks with some form of cocaine knocked out all feeling in the horns, usually, then a saw, horn shears or embryotomy wire applied vigorously did the rest. The choice of weapons largely depended on the thickness of horn and the state of the operater's muscles. As the hours pass, the rate of progress tends to slow up as the biceps seize up. The common feature of all dehornings is that there is a fair bit of blood flying about, and the surgeon tends to cop it in the eye, ear, or even if he stops to speak, the mouth, till the little horn arteries are sealed off. It is I imagine not unlike the scene after the Battle of Waterloo! Alf was clearly tired and ready for his lunch, the cattle were pretty fed up at being denied their morning ration of grass, and since I had surgery waiting for me in early afternoon, the closing events tended to be a bit hurried. Through wringing with sweat under my protective clothing, I was satisfied that a quick wash in a bucket would do me till I got home. Home was seventeen miles away, and half way there, the disease struck. COD 330 gave a few gurgles and expired. The tick, tick, tick was diagnostic of an empty stomach. My own was making much the same noise. I reached into the back for the spare gallon, to find no can! There was nothing for it but to walk to the nearest garage, beg for a can, pay up, and promise to return the container. The garage proprietor looked at me long and earnestly before supplying my need, then came a weary trudge along the busy highway, and through holiday crowds, who seemed to me to be acting most peculiarly. As I appeared, they would cringe away from me, and stand in little groups, pointing and chattering. I could make nothing of all this, but in the end put it down to the fact that as I was a Scot in Devon, I still had a 'foreign' look which marked me out, just as the citizens of London can pick out Wembley bound Scots instantly. The old van, having been supplied with its life-giving fluid, wearily took up the struggle once more. Dropping off his can, I was again scrutinised by the garage man, who seemed to be jotting something down on a slip of paper as I departed. It was all very mysterious, till I looked in the mirror at home! My hair, face and neck were liberally spotted and streaked with blood, and clearly those beholding me were undecided whether I had tried to cut my throat, or someone else's, hence the garage man's bit of paper. COD 330 was the getaway car for number one suspect should any murder be reported in the West Country in the immediate future!

But the criticial point of my allergic properties, or the zenith of my powers, depending on the way you looked at it, occurred on our honeymoon. For this Kenneth had graciously offered his brand new super Triumph, while he, for a fortnight, crammed his large frame into 'Coddy' (COD 330) and devleoped a crick in his neck which took some time to straighten itself. On the very first day of our honeymoon, the disease, allergy or whatever, struck once more. Not even expensive new cars were safe. Proceeding in leisurely fashion, the morning after our wedding day, we had a whole lifetime ahead of us so why hurry, we were enjoying the beauties of the road to Morar, when some way past where Bonnie Prince Charlie had rallied the Highlanders to his cause, we picked up a hiker. He was not a hitch hiker, since that was still a rare breed, but a genuine hiker stepping it out with pack on back. I have always felt this was one of the most worthy acts in my life, and considering we were less than twenty-four hours married, it has seemed to me our deed almost warranted a mention in the New Year's Honours list, and was certainly not deserving of the events which followed! It may be, since we were near Cameron country, the influence was particularly powerful, or the allergy at its most potent, for shortly afterwards, great clouds of steam billowed from the Triumph's bonnet. It was a hot day, but hardly hot enough to account for this extensive sweat. Lifting his bonnet, it needed no thermometer to tell me that Triumph had a raging fever. We decided a rest might help him cool off, and this having taken place, I discovered that where there should have been water, there was none. The sufferer was completely dehydrated! We had an empty bottle, the hiker a Dixie can, so while the lady, now a Mrs of almost twenty-four hours, took life easy, the two males trudged up hill to a Highland burn and stocked up with water, which the patient absorbed like a sponge. It took several trips to satisfy his phenomenal thirst. Clearly the fever was very acute, something like Anthrax, Malaria or Bracken poisoning, I suspected. Eventually his recovery was sufficient to let us proceed maybe ten more miles, when the whole range of symptoms was repeated, and the two men again took to the hills. So we proceeded, with many a stop, till eventually we limped into Morar, our destination, where we bade goodbye to the hiker who was glad to see the back of us! It is a moot point as to whether he would have made better time hiking along the highway, than driving, and certainly the number of hills he climbed that afternoon probably more than satisfied his hiking instincts for several days ahead.

Having deposited lady and luggage at our hotel, I hurried with anxious heart to the nearest expert on the internal organs of a car, and explained the symptoms in detail. I feared the worst, and was already reckoning that all our holiday money would have to go on a new radiator, which I understood was the car equivalent of a kidney transplant. The country car doctor had a quick examination, grunted, looked at me as if in all his years he had never met anything so ignorant, and said, 'Fan belt – you haff no fan belt, man!' I gave a nervous little laugh, said 'Oh-ah- and made a mental note that cars needed a fan belt to keep their cool, or serious disease could occur in the whole abdomen. I was learning! The fortnight passed all too quickly, and from fields of Eden we had to head once more for the fields of Devon. On the way, we crammed every wedding present we could, including a luxury armchair, into the car's rear, left a little tunnel for a view in the mirror, and took the road south, at that time innocent of all motorways, and infinitely more pleasing to the eye, even allowing for the rose-coloured spectacles we were both wearing! Some way on our trip, we encountered Kidderminster, where we decided it was tea-time, and parked the car outside a restaurant, having carefully observed that there was not a 'No Parking' sign anywhere around. With the calories stocked up once more, we meandered forth, to find a young PC, hands on lapels and clearly meaning business, standing guard beside the car. We were tempted to dart back inside the tea room, in the hope that this new trouble would just go away, but his eagle eye had spotted us, our anxious looks having betrayed us. In that cool, competent voice which is the first thing they teach budding 'bobbies' at training school, he enquired,

'Your car, sir?' Strictly speaking, it was Ken's, but I replied,

'Er . . . yes!'

'You have been parked for almost an hour in a "No Parking" area!' Immediately I was all innocence, mingled with an aura of outrage, and having glanced hurriedly around again and failed to see any indication to the contrary, informed this senseless Sassenach of the fact that there was no sign to support his accusation. He looked at me doubtfully, and asked, 'Are you a stranger here sir?'

'Yes, never been here before, just passing through.' He paused a long time. I wondered what this latest car trouble would lead to. It was bound to be jail, for we had not the price of a fine left between us. I wondered fleetingly if we would be allowed to share a cell, or if we would be allowed a phone call, shouting 'Help' to Kenneth or the folks at home. All crime films seemed to indicate that a prisoner was allowed to make one call. The constable seemed to be pondering his next step. He took a long time at his pondering, but at last, with a voice full of regret and disappointment, and a look on his face like that of a fox hound which has just seen its fox disappear over the horizon, sighed,

'Oh, well, I suppose you wouldn't know, but "No Parking" was painted on the road here before they re-surfaced it.' Well! He was not finished yet, seemingly determined to add another 'pinch' to his case book.

'Your car is very heavily loaded. Are you able to use your rear view mirror?' The car was, in fact, packed to the roof, and the cargo having slipped a bit, the view in the mirror was now about the size of a postage stamp, but I assured him we had come all the way from Scotland like that, could see behind us, and in a moment of bravado invited him to sit in the driver's seat, and see for himself. For one dreadful moment, I thought he would, but at last he nodded curtly, and said 'Well, the next time you are in Kidderminster, remember you cannot park in this place.'

'Oh, I don't think Kidderminster is included in our travelling plans for some time, is it dear?' I appealed to Janet. She backed me nobly.

'No, we hadn't thought of coming this way again in the near future,' she replied, with the air of an experienced globe trotter. So we were allowed to proceed. I should like to have helped the poor PC, for he was clearly disappointed, and one never likes to cause hurt to a fellow human being, but then, disappointment is one of the character-forming facts of life!!

Many years have passed since these early attacks of the disease. it persisted at Moorton, and indeed very strongly at Aldermouth, and every car we have had has produced further examples of this odd syndrome. Apart from a Rolls Royce, which I would not care to risk, almost every other make of vehicle has proved my point about this being an allergy to something in me. Because of this condition, we have had to resort to binder twine, string, sellotape, chewing gum, ropes, children's school belts, coils of wire, pins, elastoplast and a host of other items essential to our first aid kit. I would strongly advise any fellow sufferer never to set out on a journey without the items I have mentioned, even if it means having to store the luggage on the roof. Thousands have been spent seeking a cure. We have sought the advice of many noted consultants, but the plague persists, so that at Aldermouth, whenever our local car GP, Chicky, heard my voice on the phone, he would merely groan and say, 'Won't start again? Alright, I'll be along shortly,' and he would arrive with his rescue wagon carrying about twice the normal number of spare parts. It appears that he, like me, realised that the condition was incurable. In fact, having been so long with me, I have to admit bitterly, it is chronic and as every GP in practice, human or animal, knows, such a condition is indeed the most difficult to cure!

Once bitten-twice bitten

TEN

It was question time after a talk I had given to a Church Women's group on the work of a vet. I had been asked how to keep a dog from moulting, how to trim a poodle, how to stop dogs begging for scraps, how to stop a dog chasing cars, and other questions which were not really a vet's business and which I had waffled through. At last came one I could freely answer.

'Mr Cameron! Yours is quite a dangerous job, are you often bitten by a dog?'

I smiled a superior smile, looked around my audience, straightened my tie and smugly answered,

'Never! If a vet is reasonably careful, there is no reason why he should be bitten by a dog, or for that matter a cat.' Thus answers youth and inexperience, but pride, as the old adage has it, goeth before a fall, and soon I was to have to eat my words.

He looked harmless enough, indeed I was delighted to see a Scots terrier walk into my surgery in far away Devon. Not at all a common breed in that part of the world, and my heart warmed to him.

'He's a handsome fellow! What's his name?' I asked the owner who was a stranger to me.

'McTavish,' came the reply, 'and he's a perfect darling.'

'What's his trouble?' I enquired.

'Well, we're on holiday in Bristacombe and he's dragging his rear end along the ground.' The voice, unlike the breed of dog, was very clearly English, a big, florid woman, heavily made up, one of these who worships her dog, I mentally tabulated her.

'I expect it's his anal glands,' I replied. 'Let's have him on the table.'

'My own vet usually lifts him up for me,' so I proceeded to do the same, and as soon as I put my hands under him, he was round me like a flash, his teeth coming together with a sinister click as he just missed my hand. He stood on the table glancing round him solemnly, taking me in from under beetling brows, not a ghost of a smile anywhere, the caricature of a typical Scot who has just had to part with some money very much against his will.

'Has he had his glands expressed before?' I asked.

'Once, yes, by our vet in Pinner. A wonderful man! He really understands dogs.'

Maybe I was over sensitive, but I felt the implication was obvious. I did not measure up to my colleague in Pinner, even though I had not done anything yet.

'It's a simple, but a little bit uncomfortable procedure, as I'm sure you know. Perhaps I better just slip a tape muzzle on him.'

'Good gracious, no!' came the shocked reply. He's as quiet as a lamb and as harmless too. Mr – never muzzles him.'

'Just you steady his head, then, please, while I squeeze his glands.'

The glands are situated just inside the rectum, produce an oily substance which assists lubrication, but in some dogs, often, though not always those fed on an unbalanced diet, the oil dries up, forms a brown cheezy substance, and produces discomfort in the rear. The remedy is simply to take a wad of cotton wool, and gently squeeze the anal ring, which clears the obstruction.

The lady took hold of her dog, if you could so describe it, her hand gently resting on his head while she purred to him

'Mummy's darling! – a good little man – a nice boy – who's a baa lamb then,' and other terms of endearment, while McTavish just stood there, glowering at all around him, especially me, and muttering imprecations in his throat. I lifted his tail, grasped the anus in the wad of cotton wool and squeezed. The dog gave a growl, the lady a yelp, and I a louder yelp as the stolid looking McTavish sprang into action and his teeth, a fine set he had, sank deeply into the back of my hand.

'Oh! You cruel man! You must have hurt him!' was the response.

'Well – he certainly hurt me,' I protested as the blood welled up in the wound. McTavish stood as if nothing had happened, making little noises in his throat which sounded very like satisfaction at a job well done. It even looked to me as if he was smiling. The owner was not one whit concerned except for 'Mummy's darling boy, bad man hurt you, did he?' I held my hand under the tap for a bit, dried it and clapping a bit of sticking plaster on it, turned back to my patient who was still muttering to himself between cuddles and kisses from his owner.

'While we are here, could you look at his ears? I think they need cleaning out.'

'Right, but I'm sorry, he's got to be muzzled for that. If he could catch me good and proper at his rear end, he'll not miss at his head.'

'Is that necessary?'

'Yes, I'm afraid so.'

'Mr – never muzzles him, but then he really understands McTavish. He's Scottish.'

'So am I, and I like Scotties, but this one doesn't seem to like me.' I raised my voice 'Ann!'

Our attractive and very efficient secretary/assistant came through from her den.

'Just give me a hand with this dog, Ann, will you, and watch yourself.' Ann took him by the scruff of the neck, I dangled a tape muzzle over his mouth and between snaps managed to slip it over his jaws and tie it behind his head. McTavish frothed at the mouth in frustrated rage. Mrs McTavish did not like it one bit either and was more or less frothing too, but we ignored both. I peered in his ears with my auriscope, and duly cleaned them out, inserting a few drops of oil, while my fellow countryman struggled and cursed continually. My love for Scotties slipped down a peg. The job done, we removed his muzzle, and the owner immediately rushed forward to console her 'poppet', to be bitten smartly on the thumb! Her endearments were cut off in mid flow.

'Oh, you bad, bad, bad boy, doing that to your mummy!' I managed to restrain a smile, and while Ann held on to the 'poppet', I dressed the lady's thumb for her. Somehow I felt the visit had not been a success.

After surgery that afternoon my first call was to an Alastian puppy who was described as poorly. I duly found the house, down in the old Fishertown part of the town. It was a poor little place, a two-room dwelling, with a large double bed in the living room. The room was none too clean, dirty dishes on the table, paper peeling off the wall, and a smell of dirt and dampness. The mother of the family and several grown up sons and daughters were standing around, but I could see no dog. I was sorry for the people and realised yet again how hard was life on the dole, for Bristacombe, even then in the 1950s, had a high unemployment rate, with virtually everyone depending on 'the season' for a living. It was then the season, but this family seemed to be still out of work and I wondered that they had taken on the added commitment of a large dog.

After mutual greetings, I asked:

'Where's the patient?'

'He be under that bed like,' responded one of the sons.

'Just get him out, will you then,' I asked.

'Us can't us 'as been tryin' all day, like, an' he just won't move. Oi think he likes the dark.'

'Let's move the bed then.'

So we did, but the dog kept moving with the bed, and we were no further forward.

'Look! I'm sorry, but I can't treat your dog unless you can get him out of there. Whoever knows him best get down on your knees and call under the bed.' So they tried, one by one, and all together.

'Whisky! Here boy! Good lad!', but all that issued from the hiding place were growls and snarls. I did not like the sound of it at all. I grew more and more impatient for I had a long list of cases waiting to be got round. Finally, in my agitation, I broke one of the cardinal rules of vets, never tackle a sick dog when it is cornered. I should have used a dog catcher, a long pole with a noose on the end, but I had none with me, and was in a fever of haste to get on. I crawled under the bed, calling 'Whisky, here boy, good lad', and reached for his collar. Even in this dim light I could see he was a nearly full grown pup, but very sick indeed, his eyes filled with pus, his rib cage heaving. Distemper for sure.

I got him out alright, his jaws clenched tightly over my wrist. The blood spurted, the pain was considerable, and I felt faint. He clung to my wrist, even when dangling in mid air. While the family looked on, none offering to help, I managed to prise open his jaws with my other hand and release my wrist. I thought I was going to be sick, and one glance at my wound showed me it was a hospital job, stop bleeding, stitches and tetanus injection, and probably an antibiotic since his mouth was also filthy with pus. Somehow I managed to pick up my case, told the silent onlookers ('after all – it be vetnary's job') someone would call next day provided they had the dog under control, and with one hand drove myself to the local hospital. I staggered in, feeling I would collapse any minute and in considerable pain from my lacerated wrist. Fortunately a doctor happened to be at our little Cottage Hospital, and after a glance at my pale face and bloody wrist, he made me sit down before I fell down. Then followed the usual procedure of cleaning, disinfecting, suturing, dressing and bandaging, a shot of anti-tetanus serum, and instruction to go home and rest. I was surprised at how shocked I was, but mighty glad to get home and collapse into a chair, and be coddled by my equally shocked wife. Poor Bernard had to complete the cases for that day, mine as well as his own, and as I lay back in my chair, I suddenly remember my words to the Women's group.

'If a vet is reasonably careful, there is no reason why he should ever be bitten.'

Well, I had been bitten twice in one day, on the second occasion through my own folly. I was never so foolish again, but did over the years accumulate a few more minor bites, always from small dogs, and usually ones the owners were adamant 'wouldn't hurt a fly'.

I have been bitten a few times in the ministry too. As at Moorton, in Aldermouth too, we had a regular flow of gentlemen of the road at the Manse doors at all times of the day till late at night. One drunk phoned me at one o'clock in the morning and informed me he was a member of Kirkconnel Church, a great buddy of the minister and it was my duty as a minister to provide him with a bed for the night. I knew all about that passage in Matthew concerning visiting the sick, being hospitable to strangers and lifting up the fallen, and indeed had preached on it, but with a young family I was chary about who I had sleeping in the Manse. Over the years I listened to the most wonderful collection of hard up stories the mind of man could devise, many cups of tea were dispensed, clothes were given away, money for bus fares, and while I gradually grew harder and knew that often, quite simply, I was being conned, frequently we helped in some way or other.

I came home one afternoon to be met by a somewhat excited Janet.

'Darling, I've had here the most interesting man for much of the afternoon!'

'Oh?' suspiciously.

'Yes, he's one of the Murray-Fitzgeralds and has been giving me his story, and he's the most marvellous pianist you ever heard.'

'Sounds as if you've had a good time. Is he still here?'

'Yes, he's been playing Beethoven, Chopin, Elgar, and oh I don't know who else.'

'How does he come to be wandering the countryside?'

'Oh, he's fallen on hard times and the rest of the Murray-Fitzgeralds have kind of shut him off. Come and meet him.' So I was led through to our sitting room where sat a little, shabbily dressed man.

'Ah, Padre!' he exclaimed at the sight of me, 'how nice to meet you! Your lady had been listening to me play. Would you like to hear some Mozart?'

'Oh, ah well, alright.'

So he sat down and played, apparently brilliantly, something that might have been Mozart or Murray-Fitzgerald. Not being up in classical music, I could not tell, but he certainly could handle the piano. After reams of music, for he just went on and on, I managed to get a word in.

'Are you on your way somewhere?'

'Yes – to Inverness. You see, I'm a scion of the Murray-Fitzgeralds but I've been cheated of my share of the estate and have fallen on somewhat difficult times. I should be much obliged if you could give me the price of a bus fare and I'll be off after the tea your lady has kindly promised me.'

We talked for a bit while Janet went to get tea, and as we talked my suspicions grew. Murray-Fitzgerald he might have been, but there was something curiously off-key about his conversation. I excused myself and went in search of Janet at the other end of our immense home, in the kitchen preparing the meal.

'You know, lass, I'm sure all that's a load of rubbish.'

'But his playing, Alec?'

'Oh sure, he can play alright and he seems harmless, but I'm sure his stories are the fruit of his imagination.'

He had his tea and talked incessantly, always with that odd, peculiar quality to it, which unlike his handling of the piano, was off-key. At long last he departed for Inverness. We found out later he was an inmate of Craigdunain, the big mental hospital, and had escaped for an afternoon, and for whom they had been searching. If only he had said he was Winston Churchill, or Napoleon or Gunga Din, we would have cottoned on more quickly. Thankfully, he did not think he was Al Capone or Mussolini?'

Our sons were long suffering, never knowing who would be in the house when they came in from school, nor with whom they would be sharing a meal. Actually in the middle of lunch one summer day the front doorbell rang and Neil, our eldest, went to answer it. He came back and reported it was two people, a man and a lady, quite young and wanting to see the minister. (Neil was always polite, everyone of the female species has always been designated a lady, a delightful trait in him, while his younger brothers usually referred to them as 'wifies'). I duly went to the door to be met with a tale of woe. The couple were from Bristol, I was informed, and their car had got a puncture just outside our house. They had no jack, and wondered if I could help. I went out and had a look, and they certainly had a bobby dazzler of a flat tyre. The car was no great shakes, either, looking as if it had recently escaped from a junk yard. It was heavily loaded with luggage and it appeared as if front and rear portions were not on speaking terms and liable at any time to sue for divorce. Across the back window was scrawled the announcment 'Just married', though whether this applied to the car or the couple was not at first clear. it appeared it was the latter who were young and seemed respectable enough. Remembering the car trouble we had had on our own honeymoon up north years ago, I immediately felt for them and invited them in while we got the car fit for travel again. I phoned my garage to come up and see to the tyre and ordered a new tyre, for the sufferer and the spare were completely bald.

By now anxious to help the cause of true love, I chatted to them and questioned them, for the garage had indicated it might be an hour before they could come to the sufferer's aid. It seemed the couple came from Bristol alright, had been honeymooning in the Highlands, touring, but had found troubles descend thicker and faster than usual in the state of matrimony. Somewhere in the far north the wife had gone into a ladies' room to wash, and had walked out, leaving her bag behind. Later on the journey they had realised their loss, raced back, but the bag was gone. This was disastrous for all the holiday money was in it. I thought the little husband was very trusting indeed, handing everything over to the wife thus early, but it appeared he just never carried a wallet, and produced from various pockets reams of documents which confirmed his wallet-less state. He showed me his driving licence, receipt for the car and sundry other bits of paper, all in the name of Henry James.

'I wouldn't mind just so much,' said the young gallant, 'but my wife's ring was in the bag too.' (I had noticed her ringless state and been suspicious.) 'The ring was too tight, you see, and hurt her finger, so we were meaning to get it enlarged when we got back to Bristol. The police at Dornoch were marvellous,' he went on, 'and gave us some money for petrol. A minister helped us out too with some money, a kind man. Here's his card,' and he produced it.

By now thoroughly sympathetic, I called Janet through and told her the story, and she too shared in the sympathy. She prepared a meal for them and while doing so the wife had a bath and the husband a shave with my razor, for it seemed they had slept in the car the previous night.

Eventually the car was ready for the road again, we gave them £7.00, enough then for petrol to Bristol (I had already told the garage to charge the tyre to my account), pored over maps about the best route south in those days of few motorways, and clutching two jars of Janet's bramble jelly, at last they departed, with multitudinious thanks ringing in our ears. We felt good, we had helped a genuine couple in genuine trouble, even though it had cost a pound or two.

They were picked up by the police the next evening near Aberdeen, having come a similar story to another minister who was more suspicious or less gullible than me. Aberdeen was nowhere near the road to Bristol, of course, and it turned out they were a notorious pair of con experts, working this racket as a team and already with a prison record. Well!

So over the years we saw many 'patients', and no doubt were bitten many times, I found it by no means easy to pick out the genuine from the crooked, and I suppose one's consolation, if consolation it be, was that though we did get harder, more sceptical, more worldly wise, the Manse door was always open for those in need and I felt that was the way it should be. Big softie!

Night life

ELEVEN

Brm, Brm . . . Brm, Brm, . . . Brm, Brm . . . Brm, Brm. . . .

I awoke to a ringing in my ears, and realised with a groan, it was not the angelic music of a dream, but the very opposite, the phone. The bedside clock showed 1.30 am. It was the month of March, the height of the lambing season, and this was an almost nightly occurrence.

'Hello! Bristacombe 250,' I sleepily announced, hoping for that 100-1 chance it was a wrong number, faint hope at 1.30 am unless it was someone trying for a doctor or the police. At first there was just heavy breathing coming over the line.

'Great Scot!' I thought, 'not one of these.'

Then a voice sprang to life, a familiar voice with its splutter like the car engine sometimes on a damp morning.

'Mr C.c.c.c.c.c.c. Cameron?'

'Yes, speaking.'

'This is B..b..b..b..b..b..b..Bert Williamson. Sh..sh..sh..sh..Sheila's had an accident. Can you c..c..c..c..c..come please?'

I had it clearly now. Bert Williamson was a thoroughly decent man but with a very bad stammer. He was, moreover, a good client with his lovely English setter dog, Sheila.

'Right, Bert, I shan't be long,' I told him, put the phone down, rolled over and swung my legs out of bed all in one go, a familiar technique I had perfected over many a night call. I always tried to be as quiet as possible and dress in the dark so as not to disturb Janet, but invariably she wakened.

'Lambing, dear?' came a sleepy enquiry from beneath the blankets.

'No, lass, an accident case, Bert Williamson's dog.'

She grunted and turned over on her other side. The only time I envied my wife her life and work was when a night call came in. As I drove the mile to Bert's house, I recalled the last time I had seen him, just a few days before. He had the only English setter in town, a bitch, a beauty, and she had come in season. Very much wanting to breed from her, he had taken a taxi to kennels in Exeter, sixty miles away, and introduced Sheila to her husband to be. She was apparently not impressed, and would have nothing to do with the dog. Bert had waited all day, the taxi meter going all the time, then reluctantly returned to 'Combe. He stood beside the taxi driver counting out the considerable fare, and when he turned round, Sheila was being mated by the most scruffy old mongrel imaginable!

Bert appeared in my surgery a short time later, practically frothing at the mouth and spluttering like a machine gun. I have seldom seen a man so livid, and in his incensed state, with his stutter, it took him some time to explain what had happened. I had never heard a man with a stammer curse before, and in broad Devonshire, it was an impressive performance! I really could not refrain from laughing at the thought of him going all that way to Exeter and back, Sheila turning down a highly pedigreed show winner, and accepting a ruffian. We had given her stilboestrol, the recognised treatment for misalliance in those days of the early 1950s, and assured him all would be well, there would be no Heinz 57 puppies, but her heat period would be prolonged somewhat. Now it seemed Sheila was in more serious trouble, and I knew just how upset the likeable Bert would be for he adored his bitch.

A sobbing Mrs Williamson answered the door to me, and mourned 'Sheila seems bad, Mr Cameron, and Bert's in a terrible state,' Bert was, he was crying too as he knelt beside his bitch who was stretched out on the carpet before the fire. Mrs Williamson, to my relief, acted as the speaker. She took less time and was infinitely easier to understand.

'Sheila somehow slipped out when us was sayin' "good-night" to some friends us'd had in, and she runned right in front of a car. Oh, the horrible screech of its brakes.'

'Did the car go over her, Mrs Williamson?'

'No-o, I don't think so, but hur seems right bad.'

I turned to my patient. Her breathing was fast, her pulse fast, but the colour of her membranes was good. Gently I felt her over.

'Broken leg, Bert, but we can put that right. Let's see what else.'

'Hur's b..b..b..b..-bl..bl..bl..-bleedin' at the mouth,' Bert exploded into speech.

'That might not mean much, Bert. She could just have bitten her tongue, but let's have a listen at her chest.'

Out came the stethoscope, no lung damage I could detect, and so far as I could ascertain, no major abdominal problems either. She had a nasty gash on the shoulder which would require stitching, but that was no difficulty.

'I think she's been lucky, Bert. We'll soon fix her up.'

So the common routine was carried out. First an injection for shock, then a sedative to ease pain and make her sleepy, and I set to work with the old Gypsona plaster of paris bandages, soaking them in water and warpping them up and down the leg like splints – nothing difficult about it, only messy, and the sole hazard being to make sure the bandage was tight enough, but not too tight. Then a scrub of the hands to get rid of excess plaster, dressing her shoulder wound, and while the gentle bitch lay there unmoving and the plaster on the leg hardened, stitching up the cut shoulder.

Meantime Mrs Williamson had been clattering about with cups and plates, and as soon as I was finished, the tea was on the table.

'Us be right grateful to ee, Mr Cameron,' said the little woman, 'comin' out of youm bed an' all, but if owt serious like happened to our Sheila, I don't know what us ad do.'

Bert nodded in agreement. They were a childless couple and the dog was their family, their pride and joy.

'Don't worry, Mrs Williamson, Bert,' I assured them. 'That kind of clean break heals well. She shouldn't have a limp at all, and the hair will soon hide the scar on her shoulder. She won't breed this time round, but she's young enough to wait a bit. I'll look in tomorrow, or rather later today and see how she is,' I yawned prodigiously and apologised.

'Sorry, folks! I had a long day today, or yesterday and it's time for me to be off.'

So I left these kindly, humble folks and headed back for bed. It took me a few minutes to drop off, and I had scarcely fallen alseep, it seemed, when the phone went again, 3.30 am this time.

'Hello, Mr Cameron,' said a bright, perky voice. 'Arthur Hazlett here. Got a ewe bad to lamb. Will you come out?'

'Yes, Arthur, of course,' I grunted, as I groaned quietly to myself and yawned at the same time.

'She's in the top field. Leave your car on the main road and walk across two fields. That will be your quickest way. You'll see my lantern waving. I'll be up there by the time you get out.'

So with the old corduroys, a thick jersey this time, and out into the darkness once more. A drive of just five miles through the night mist, a walk across the two fields, sheep scurrying before me like wraiths in the mist, my objective, the waving lantern just visible in the distance. The patient was in the shelter of a typical high Devon hedge-cum-wall, and Arthur there waiting with a tattie bag for me to kneel on, a bucket of water which had been hot when he left the house, but was now barely lukewarm, soap and a towel. I poured some disinfectant into the water, rolled up my sleeve, soaped an arm, knelt down and felt inside the ewe. What kind of trouble would it be this time? Why type of presentation? Almost at once I realised with relief that this was one of the easier ones, indeed my favourite lambing problem.

'Twins, Arthur, locked and intertwined, but the ewe has plenty of room. This shouldn't take long.'

Nor did it, for basically all you do, in case, dear reader, you ever have to deliver twins is say to one,

'Just you wait there a minute, my dear' and to the other 'up you come.'

Putting it in more technical terms, you sort out the tangle of legs, then repel one lamb and advance the other, and in ten minutes the job is done. As I dried my arm I grinned at Arthur. This was the good bit, the job done, a healthy ewe already on her feet licking her offspring and giving that lovely, throaty chuckle which you get only from a sheep after lambing. It was a cold, damp night, but we waited to see the lambs stagger to their feet, heading for the milk bar for that first, all important drink of mother's milk, finding their way with unerring, inborn instinct. This was the little miracle that made the toughest lambing worthwhile and that never palled on me or grew commonplace.

'Would you mind very much, Mr Cameron, coming down to the farm when you're here anyway and seeing a lamb with joint ill?'

Somewhat wearily I said,

'Alright, Arthur, lead on with the lamp.'

We reached the farm to be welcomed by Arthur's wife, Kathleen who was equally as bright as her husband, and I marvelled at the stamina of these farmers and their wives which would keep them going day and night for six weeks in the lambing season.

'You'll have tea, Mr Cameron, won't you. The kettle just has to boil.' The table was already laid, as it nearly always was in our Devon farms, where the hospitality was quite tremendous. I had a look at Arthur's lamb, a big one, which had joint ill right enough, all its joints being swollen and stiff, and a discharge coming from the navel.

'That's where the infection gets in, Arthur.'

'I know. I must not have dressed this one right.'

I gave the lamb a hefty injection of penicillin and left Arthur the bottle to give a shot for several days, for joint ill can often be tough to shift. Then we drew our chairs into the table, which was laden with food, as if it was a normal tea-time instead of half past four in the morning.

'We had an interesting man at our Bible Study tonight, well, last night,' said Arthur, 'a missionary from the Congo. What stories he had to tell! I admire these men who go off to wild places like that. They must have great courage.'

'And faith, Arthur, that's the main thing,' said his wife. Not to be outdone, I chipped in and said, 'and love. Did Paul not say somewhere that was the greatest thing?'

'1 Corinthians 13,' immediately retorted Kathleen. She knew her Bible from cover to cover. They were members of the Plymouth Brethren, but unlike some of the Brethren, not at all narrow or hidebound and as they talked, I sat back and marvelled. The Hazletts were a delightful couple, their farm was too small to enable them to pay a man, but no matter how busy they were, they seldom missed the Sunday worship or the week night Bible Study. It was an education to listen to their talk. Their faith just shone out of them. It was as if they had found the secret of life and were totally content. I had seen this in a number of farmers and friends in Devon, and though I did not know it then and had not the slightest thought of becoming a minister, it was, I realised later, when I did feel drawn to the ministry, people like the Hazletts who had turned my thoughts to life's basic and lasting values, and made me in the end want to share with others this faith in their Lord.

But the night was going on. I looked at my watch, 5.30 am. We had talked for an hour and as always, with people who are the salt of the earth, kindly, sincere, genuine, just plain good, the time had flown. I trudged back to my car, somehow lightened and cheered, even though soon in that raw night air I was chilled right through my thick jersey.

Then home, and that delicious moment when I would snuggle into my wife's warm back. She never complained even though I often came in like an icy blast straight from the North Pole. In my contented frame of mind, a good dog repaired, lambs delivered, a sick lamb helped, and a kind of inner peace through just having spent an hour with Arthur and Kathleen. This time I was alseep in an instant.

As with all vets, the phone call at night was a regular disturber of the peace, but on one occasion the peace was well and truly shattered, and the phone had not given the merest little peep. The occasion, which came more into the category of things that go bump in the night, was one night when our friends Mike and Audrey Hutchison were staying with us in our little, jerry-built house grandly called Chade Lodge, which we rented along with the buildings behind from the local council. The whole thing had once been the town's abattoir and the buildings were ideal for kennels and for keeping poultry in deep litter. Mike had been at Vet College with me, and he and Audrey, now in Ulster, have been lifelong friends. Our adventures at the kennels have been recounted elsewhere, but this night call was in the house alone. Chade Lodge still had gas lighting, which was the crux of the problem that night.

What happened was that I was awakened by a stealthy creak on the stairs as someone surreptitiously ascended. It was about two o'clock in the morning, pitch dark, and as I heard this sinister creak, my flesh crept and my hair stood on end. Clearly we had an intruder of some kind. I put my hand over my sleeping partner's mouth to prevent her screaming, and whispered in her ear.

'There's somebody coming up the stairs.'

She too was instantly awake, listening to this slow creak, creak which gradually seemed to be getting nearer. We lay where we were, the terror of night and the unknown gripping us. We were a petrified pair! Slowly and quietly I slipped out of bed and fumbled my way over to the gas light which had a pilot jet on it which burned all the time, so that when one pulled a little chain the light popped on, but the pilot jet had gone out, a bad habit it had in our room. Often a box of matches was kept on the mantel shelf for just such an emergency, but no matches could be found. Here was a fix. We were about to be attacked in our bedroom, it seemed, by a burglar, and we could not see a thing. By now the 'footsteps' seemed to have stopped just outside our door, so Janet leapt out of bed and stood by the window, ready to jump out of our upstairs room if somebody entered. I was no braver and thought I would call for help. So quietly opening the window, I stuck my head out and in a voice that was no more than a croak called across the few yards. 'Mike, Mike,' to their window, 'put your light on.' I knew their pilot jet never went out. As is by now obvious, I am not particularly brave, and in the dark, having been rudely wakened from sleep, I was frankly terrified of the unknown. I called and called but Mike and Audrey were apparently sleeping the sleep of the just, or had already been murdered in their beds, and they never stirred. We could only wait, it seemed, till our door handle turned and our visitor was in our room.

Then I remembered the box of matches that was always kept on the ledge on the landing, outside the three bedroom doors which were all adjacent in our pokey wee house. So, having to show my manly courage before my young wife, I suddenly opened the door, dashed out a pace to the ledge, grabbed a box of matches, and slamming the door behind me, rushed for our gas light, and with trembling fingers, lit the wretched thing. Now we were more brave. At least we would be able to see our assailant, but no one came in. So I quietly again opened the door and peeped out, nobody, nothing. While Janet remained at her window, I searched the house, but all seemed in order. There appeared to be no unauthorised inhabitants. Finally we went back to bed, and put the light out. However, the creaking sounds began again on the stairs. We lay and trembled. We had not heard that Chade Lodge had a resident ghost, but maybe there was one, perhaps the shade of some long-gone cattle slaughterman who had met a sticky end on the horns of a bull, or shot himself by mistake with his humane killer.

So the out of bed, light the gas, search the house procedure was repeated. All was still. Every time the light went on, the creaks stopped. Once more back to bed, creak, creak, and as we shivered under the clothes, it seemed to me the sounds were not on the stairs, but actually in our room. This, if anything made matters worse. It could only be a supernatural visitant. By now we were angry at this person or thing playing tricks on us, and anger overcomes fear. I opened cupboard doors, pulled out drawers, and as I opened our wardrobe door, I saw him. It was a mouse nibbling at the wood! I leapt back, the mouse leapt out into the room, and Janet leapt on the bed. A mouse scurrying about our bedroom in the middle of the night was less frightening than a burglar or a headless shade, but we clearly would get no sleep till we had dealt with our little four footed frightener. So in traditional fashion, I grabbed a poker and chased that mouse round the room, poking under the bed, round and round we went until the little animal was in a corner. It would be more terrified than we had been, but it had to go, and a poker was a quick death. I got a shovel, removed the body, and then giggling with pent up nervous tension, and somewhat ashamed, we finally got back to bed. Our little family and Mike and Audrey had never heard a sound and slept through it all, and there was hilarious laughter at breakfast time at our reaction to this thing that went, if not bump, but creak in the night.

Of course, working hours for a minister are rather different from that of a vet, and night calls in our first Charge of Moorton were practically unknown. At Aldermouth the phone would often go late at night when we were preparing for bed or just into it for people knew, in that extremely busy Church, that practically the only time they could guarantee to get the minister himself was late, when he had finished his round of evening visits, or come in from some meeting. Frequently colleagues in the ministry would phone up about something, for they worked similar hours. But calls through the night were almost unknown. It had to be someone very ill, a death, or a person stranded for the night and wanting a bed, to disturb our sleep. I have sometimes explained to people, to their obvious disbelief, that I often worked a longer week as a minister than a vet, but one could usually guarantee a peaceful night and undisturbed sleep, which was a great boon.

One night, however, about two o'clock in the morning, Janet and I were roused with a loud peal on the front door bell, followed by hammering and thumps at the door. Somebody seemed also to be calling out or moaning. I jumped out of bed, threw on a dressing gown and had a peep out of the turret window of our bedroom from which we could see the front door, but in the dark all I could make out was a shadowy figure with its finger fixed firmly on the door bell. I went to the door, and before opening it, suspecting a drunk, called out 'Who's there?' There were various mutterings from the other side of the door and constant cries of 'Help me!' I cautiously opened the door and peered out and immediately a man rushed in, fell at my feet, grasped me round the knees and cried, 'Oh Father, Father, you've got to help me. My father's come back. He's a ghost now!' I managed to free my imprisoned legs, got the man to his feet, and he more or less fell into our large hallway. He was in sheer terror, but I could make nothing of his explanations, so took him into the study, switched on the electric fire, sat him down in a chair and tried to unravel the mystery. He said his name was Dawson, so I knew him to be a cousin of the notorious McKies, but I had never seen him before. He was a tall, round shouldered, lean individual with a pale face, though whether naturally pale or from his fright, I didn't know.

'Tell me what the trouble is, slowly,' I commanded.

'Oh, Father,' he kept pleading. 'I need help. Something terrible has happened. I want you to help me and pray for me for I've done terrible wrong.'

'I'll help you if I can, and I'll certainly pray for you, but if you want a Father, you've come to the wrong house. The priest stays just round the corner. I'm a minister.'

'No, it's you I want, Mr Cameron,' he pleaded.

He really was a pathetic figure, cringing, whining, in terrible distress. Clearly something extraordinary had nearly unhinged his brain. At last I got him calmed down a bit and his story came out in spurts, between cries for help and confessions that he had been a bad son.

'My father came through the wall of my bedroom tonight,' he said with a shudder.

'Your father, *through* the wall?'

'Aye, that's right.'

'But your father's dead.'

'I ken, but he came back the nicht. Oh, it wis him a' richt an' he came into the room and just stood lookin' at me and pointing.'

'Now calm down, Mr Dawson. It couldn't have been your father and why would he point at you.'

'Well, you see, I promised him I wouldn't drink and I've been drinking tonight. I've been a bad son, and he just stood looking at me.' He sobbed with his face in his hands, then again fell at my feet, grabbed me and begged me for help. Now, while my business, in a sense could be said to be supernatural, I had had no experience of ghosts or other-worldly apparitions, had never been asked to exorcise a house, and I felt baffled. He clearly had drink in him, and I suppose in retrospect he was having a bad attack of the DTs, but though, of course I had seen the typical DT before, after a drinking bout, this was something new. That man was utterly and completely convinced his father had returned to rebuke him, and sheer terror looked out of his eyes.

'Coffee,' I thought, 'get him some coffee and calm him down. Play it naturally and coolly.'

But he did not want coffee. He screamed at the suggestion of my leaving him to go to the kitchen. Just then, Janet's startled face appeared round the door, clearly wondering what in all the world was going on, with screams and other odd noises not usually heard in the Manse.

'It's alright, lass,' I said. 'Go back to bed. This is Mr Dawson come to talk about a problem.'

Janet shared completely in my life and work. Indeed without her I doubt if I could have given myself to others as a minister has to do, and I had often wondered how bachelor ministers or priests could do their work in full.

So it went on that night. I am not at my brightest or most patient in the middle of the night, but I had to listen to his story which I did several times over. Finally I said,

'Now, I'm sure it will be alright. Your father will have gone by now. We'll have a prayer together . . . ,' he interrupted me

'You'll pray for me?'

'Alright, I'll pray for you.'

So I did, and whether it was the prayer, or something I had said that was the healing medicine he needed at that moment, I know not, but he calmed down and asked me for a book to help him to be a better son. No doubt a psychiatrist could explain the whole business in a minute! I got up.

'Come, Mr Dawson, I'll run you home,' which I did, to be rewarded with voluminous thanks.

Janet was awake when I got back.

'What was all that about, dear?' she asked.

'A kind of lambing, lass. At least I've been at a delivery.'

The weekly trial

TWELVE

Perhaps the most effective sermon I have ever preached was not preached by me at all! Perhaps I had better start at the beginning to satisfy the questing mind!

It began when we returned from our holidays to be met by John Duggie, our Church Officer, with a distinctly worried look on his face, not at all his usual cheerful self was John as he announced to us while we were parking the caravan, 'Granny's disappeared!'

Here was not merely mystery but calamity of a high order. We had gone off, confidently leaving John in charge of the Manse, including Bruce the dog who was greatly attached to him. Granny was not accompanying us on holiday, but we were not worried about her, for she was an independent old lady, and John had promised to look over each day and make sure all was well, but on the very morning of our return, there was no sign of her anywhere about the place.

We all sat down with a cup of tea to revive us, and trying to console ourselves with the thought that she was sure to turn up. But she did not, so we searched everywhere. Night came, but still Granny did not appear. Here was crisis indeed! The next day a full scale search was instituted, but she remained missing. Days passed, then relief, she had been found, and in a most unusual place. In the field beside the Manse were dozens of bags of sticks waiting for me to deliver to our old folks. Covering them was a tarpaulin, and there, sitting beneath it, quite unconcerned and totally unharmed, was the old lady herself. The weight fell from our shoulders, the world took on a brighter hue, life returned to normal! Granny was safe beneath the tarpaulin and safe beneath Granny were ten brown eggs. Our venerable bantam had decided to become a mother again!

In due course the chicks arrived, pecking their way into the big wide world, and you never saw such a mixture. They outheinzed Heinz! Some were black, some white, some speckled, for Granny's ancestry was a bit doubtful and her husband was grey and white. It seemed a heaven-sent opportunity for a lesson to the children in Church the following Sunday, so, ignoring the glances of my predecessors whose portraits hung on the vestry walls, and whom I felt might not have approved, I took Granny and two of her offspring into the pulpit with me, the birds well concealed in a box. They kept very quiet during the opening hymn and prayer, and then I began my talk to the large crowd of children. We thought of how we were all different on the outside, some black, some white, some brown, different kinds of noses, different eyes, hair and so on but we were all the same inside, 'for boys and girls, "man looks on the outside, but God looks into the heart".'

Then I showed them Granny, to gasps and laughter from the very big summer congregation, and like the superb actress she was, she looked around the vast throng and clucked straight into the microphone, playing her part to perfection. I am certain it was the first time a hen had addressed an audience in Aldermouth. Briefly her story was told, then the two chicks were shown. I did not dare risk any more lest they escaped and had 600 people scrambling about to catch them. One chicken was white, one black, but both were equally dear to their little mother, 'just as precious to her, boys and girls, as everybody is to God our great father. Different colours, but the same parent, you see.' Her duty done, the old girl and her two bairns were restored to their box, and removed by one of the Cameron boys back to her field, and the remainder of her loudly cheeping family. I did not dare keep poultry in the pulpit for the rest of the Service lest they got out or kicked up a shindy in the middle of the sermon. For I had once seen a sermon ruined by an animal. It was at Maryshall in the little village Church we attended, situated about a mile from my home. The Service was held in the afternoon, it was a hot summer day and the Church doors had been left open for air, when plumb in the middle of the minister's discourse in trotted my Collie dog, Glen, which I had been given for passing my Highers, purchased for the large sum of £1.00. Glen trotted right up to the choir area and stood there smiling, panting, and wagging his tail, as he looked up at all the Cameron males in the choir. The audience was convulsed, the minister tried gamely to carry on, finally in a far from pleased voice saying, 'Take no notice of it. The Devil has sent this creature to divert us from the Word of God.' I was not in agreement with the clergyman that *my* dog could be an agent of 'auld Nick', but I saw his point and removed my dog from the Church.

This business of Granny, a gimmick, I can hear many say, but I prefer to call it an audio-visual aid, went down well. Come to think of it, the Master Teacher used plenty of these too, you will find them in the four gospels and they were well received by His congregation too! Certainly for weeks folks stopped me in the street to comment on the mother hen and her chicks. My sermon to the adults was soon forgotten but Granny had put over a message that gripped every one of her hearers, poultry in the pulpit had achieved more than the minister!

Unfortunately such an act is hard to follow. Some preachers are very fond of the gimmick, which is valid, if it really has a worthwhile point to make. Even in a bygone age it seems some used a visual aid like the old minister on Temperance Sunday who was preaching on the evils of drink. Into the pulpit he took two jelly jars one with water, and in the other, gin. At the appropriate point of the sermon he produced them and from a tin took two earthworms. He dropped one into the water and it wriggled about quite happily but the one in the gin had a quick demise.

'Now,' thundered the preacher, 'what lesson does this teach us?' From the body of the Kirk a voice called out,

'If you've got worms, drink gin!' There was one lesson that had gone awry!

I suppose only another preacher realises the difficulty of sermon preparation and delivery, particularly in these days when people are attuned, not to listen, but to watch scenes on 'the box'. I remember Andrew Eastham telling me he found preaching got, not easier, but more difficult as he got older. Certainly the weekly trial by public exposure as it has been described is totally different from any other form of address. For a start, one is conscious of one's own failings, and sometimes I feel we have no right to preach to others. There is the awareness that there will be criticism, and many families have roast preacher for Sunday lunch! Difficult too, weekly to have something worthwhile to say, and to hold a congregation's attention without their going to sleep.

The story is told of a certain Church where the senior elder, who sat right in the front seat, always had a snooze during the sermon. One day a student was taking the Service, and in the vestry he found some notes from the regular minister who was away on holiday. Among them was a PS.

'If an elderly gentleman drops off during your sermon, don't worry or take offence. He does it every week.'

But the fiery young student was determined nobody should sleep during his discourse. Sure enough, during the sermon, the old boy dropped off, so the preacher, in the middle of his address, in a quiet voice, said,

'Stand up, all those who want to go to Heaven.'

The whole congregation stood except the old man who had not heard the words. Consternation in the Kirk! The senior elder did not want to go to heaven. The preacher carried on for a bit, then said, 'All those who don't want to go to heaven, stand up', bellowing the last two words. The old elder got to his feet and looked around him, then looked at the man in the pulpit and said 'I dinna ken whit we're votin' aboot, meenister, but you and I are in the minority.'

Then there is the tension, the stress, of standing up before a group of people, be it twenty or a thousand (and it is easier to preach to the latter for the atmosphere lifts one), and most ministers are afflicted with pre-pulpit nerves on a Sunday. I think most of us find it easier to give an after dinner speech, or a wedding toast than to preach, for preaching is totally different from other forms of public address. I recall speaking to my New Testament lecturer, the famous Dr Barclay who was the best communicator of the gospel and teacher I have known, making it viable, reliable, relevant, understandable, real, to the most ordinary mind, and doing this in the pulpit, on the radio and in his many TV series, which had the whole of Scotland watching. I asked him when he lost his pulpit nerves for he always seemed so calm and unruffled, never stuck or lost in his discourse. Like a flash he answered me, 'Alec, I haven't lost these butterflies before I go into the pulpit, and I hope you never will, either, for the day you do, it has just become a job to do and you're no further use to the Lord.' I am sure Willie Barclay was right. I personally, and I think most other ministers too, like to be alone and quiet for a few minutes before entering the pulpit, a quietness my Beadle John saw that I got every Sunday at Aldermouth before he would come, in his understanding way, and ask, 'Alright, Mr Cameron?' I often felt like the late, great Tom Allan who had a Beadle like John. One day as he was going out the vestry door for the Church, Tom hesitated, and his Beadle, anxious, asked, 'Alright, Mr Allan?' Tom Allan smiled and said, 'Yes, Bob, I'm just marvelling that the Lord trusts someone like me with His message.'

Willie Barclay, however, in contrast to most of us, always preferred to have someone to talk to right up to the moment he entered the Church.

But, of course, pulpit nerves can be excessive and embarrassing. I know of one young man who had to give up the ministry for a time because he was actively sick before facing his congregation, not that he had a congregation that made him sick, let me emphasise, just an acute case of nerves.

Then there was another young fellow about to preach his first sermon. The Beadle, and the Scottish Beadle is often a real character, advised him, 'If you stick at any point, just put your arm up and say "Lo, I come". It doesn't mean anything but looks good and gives you time to think.'

Sure enough, when it came to the sermon, the young minister's notes were a blur, the congregation seemed a sea of hostile faces and he wanted to run away. But he tried the Beadle's recipe. Up went the right hand and he intoned 'Lo! I come.' Still nothing happened. He was stuck. So he tried the left arm with the same negative result. Finally he thrust both arms heavenwards and bellowed 'Lo! I come' and as he did so he stepped back and tumbled down the pulpit stairs, landing in front of a lady sitting in her pew and minding her own business. He got up covered in confusion and full of apologies to the lady, who tried to comfort him with the words, 'Think nothin' o' it, son. You tellt me three times you were comin'. I should have been ready for you!'

But *the* great difficulty is the content of the sermon. What am I to preach about this Sunday, morning and evening? Of course there are books of sermons by the dozen, but I have always felt it dishonest to use another man's work, though many a good illustration has been 'borrowed' from another. The great events of the Christian year, Christmas, Easter, Whitsunday are a help in their seasons, but, like Andrew Eastham, I too have found preaching gets no easier as one gets older and I still have the butterflies. Many a time I have sat with a blank sheet of paper in front of me in my study, and after an hour it is still blank. I have, however, had two guiding principles over the years. 'Preach the gospel, the great certainties of our faith, for maybe there will be someone there hearing it for the first time, and someone hearing it for the last.' The other guide has been, 'remember at least one person in your congregation has been going through a hard, or anxious time, so try to strike the note of comfort.'

I recall one of my Assistants at Aldermouth phoning me one Thursday in a panic. He was due to preach one of the Sunday's sermons. 'I'm stuck!' he wailed, 'I've known for a month I had to preach this Sunday, and I've spent days on it, but I'm not getting anywhere.' I went round to see him, had him preach what he had to me, made a few suggestions on his theme, then tried to comfort him with the words an old divine had given me.

'The manna falls when it is needed.'

'I wish it would,' said the lad plaintively, 'when I came here I had only two sermons and I've preached both of them. How in all the world can you do this twice a Sunday year after year?'

I doubt if one in a hundred of the average congregation appreciates the travail and anguish that goes into making a sermon. The old adage about a sermon being ten per cent inspiration and ninety per cent perspiration is not far off the mark. It is a notable week when the sermon just falls into place, but now and again it does happen. I recall in my vet days, when I was doing a bit of lay preaching, getting an idea as I drove down a farm road with about six gates on it to open and shut, an odd place to get inspiration, but somehow as I bumped along an idea just flashed into my mind complete with three points, and I stopped briefly at the last gate and jotted down the headings before the idea, as quickly, flashed out again. But that is the exception. Over the years I estimate that each sermon has taken up to ten hours preparation, and with two of these to prepare, plus perhaps a Bible Class talk and most weeks school talks or addresses to Guilds, Rurals, Women's Institutes, Rotaries, Men's Fellowships and so on, this hidden work of the ministry is something of which few in the pew are aware. But somehow, week by week, the manna does fall. Sometimes a sermon is well prepared, well illustrated, as perfect as an imperfect pastor can make it. On another occasion, in a busy week, something has to be put together in a hurry, and sometimes that is the one that clicks. The late A J Gossip, one of the great names in the Kirk forty or fifty years ago, a master preacher and teacher, used to tell how one week he had been simply over the head with work, so his sermon was hastily put together at the last minute. As he turned the bend in the stairs of St Matthew's in Glasgow, Jesus met him and asked 'Is that the best you could do for me today?' Thinking back to the kind of week he had had, Gossip said, 'Yes, Lord,' and that day, that hastily slapped together address was a word of tremendous power, enthralling his hearers. A strange experience, yes, but those who heard Gossip tell that story could not doubt the reality of his experience.

But there are the special occasions when one simply *has* to be well prepared in advance, like a Broadcast Service. I remember well my first experience of this in my Moorton days. In these years of the early 1960s, Services went out live, not pre-recorded. There had never been a radio Service from Moorton before and the whole community was buzzing, but faced with a problem. They did not know whether they preferred to go to the Kirk and take part or stay at home and listen to *their* Church on the radio! I remember on the morning of the Service walking in the quiet of the garden to calm me before going over to the Church and one of our young elders, Maxwell Watson, came strolling along. When he saw me he stopped suddenly, hummed and hawed a bit, then said,

'Is it no' time you should be in the Kirk?'

'Och, Maxwell,' I replied, 'I thought I would just stay at home and listen to myself on the radio.'

I can still see Maxwell's puzzled face as he worked that one out!

Much work had gone into the preparation of the whole Service, readings being practised by the readers, hymns rehearsed and everything down to the Lord's prayer and Benediction timed to seconds to make sure the whole Service would be included and time given at the beginning for the Church bell and at the end for the organ, played by a young teenager called John Bell who went on to become a minister, Rector of Glasgow University, a noted hymn writer, expert with young people, and one of the leaders of the Iona Community. On our broadcast day, most of the community finally came, sat like mice for the last few minutes before we went on the air, their eyes and mine fixed on the red light to tell us it was zero hour. Many of them also bought a record prepared by a company, which went round all the Churches having a Broadcast Service. Little Moorton was put on the map.

Quite early in my stay at Aldermouth we had two radio Services, one in August for Radio Scotland, and the other in October for the World Service. By now Services were being recorded in advance and one was not quite so terrified at making a mistake. I recall the engineers having great difficulty with a buzz they could not trace. They tested all their equipment and the microphones for some considerable time before discovering the mysterious noise was coming from an elderly gent's hearing aid! Again everything had to be timed almost to the split second, one's prayers and sermon submitted in advance for approval, and again the Record company had a bonanza in sales. I was told afterwards that a quarter of a million people had heard the first Service, and I felt a tremendous sense of privilege and responsibility in having such an audience. Apparently the overseas broadcast went all over the world and I had letters from Canada, New Zealand, South Africa and the West Indies.

But none of the radio Services, tense though I was, compared to the first time I had to do 'Late Call' on Scottish Television. I had submitted my notes in advance along with a number of slides of hills, valleys, rivers, sheep and shepherds to weave into the talks for I was speaking on the Shepherd Psalm – Psalm 23. I was assured all I had to do was read my words off the autocue. The studio was the size of a barn and in one corner sat technicians playing cards or reading the paper, while in another was the camera, autocue and me – trembling like a leaf. Half way through the first talk the autocue broke down and I was left stuttering like a machine gun and finally gaping like a stranded goldfish. The producer came galloping down from his lofty abode above my head from where he surveyed proceedings, and looked at me with pleading, 'Mr Cameron, for goodness sake try to look a bit more pleasant and happy. Remember it's the Good News you are supposed to be putting over.'

I found it far from easy to look pleasant, let along joyful, with the card playing technicians who between 'takes' shuffled reluctantly over to the camera to do whatever technicians do, looking bored. The cameraman and the autocue girl looked equally bored, but after three hours of rehearsals and recordings I staggered out in a daze. It so happened that my week's series went out particularly late that week for there was a bye-election on somewhere, but the good folks of Moorton sat up to see their man on the box, and five minutes after I said 'goodnight', every light in the village was doused. I imagine they had all been sitting in pyjamas and dressing gowns, but bless them, they *did* wait up.

Of course the more one is in the public eye, or ear, the more criticism one can expect, but I was fortunate, for most of those who wrote to me were at least civil, some congratulating, some seeking help, but always I had one from some bigot condemning me for not using my opportunity to berate the Roman Catholic Church as of the Devil and the Pope, the anti-Christ himself.

On the whole, though, I escaped lightly, not like my New Testament lecturer, Dr Barclay, whom I have quoted several times already and who influenced generations of students from home and overseas. In the Spring of 1961 he was doing a Radio series for Lent, and outstanding I thought it was. One day I was standing studying the Notice Board in the students' Common Room at Trinity, looking at the football team to play New College, Edinburgh, our deadly rivals, and also reading the draw for the Table Tennis competition, with both of which sporting activities I was involved. Suddenly I was aware of a voice hailing me.

WB had come quietly into the Common Room, unnoticed by me, and I realised he was addressing me.

'Can you spare a minute, Alec?' he asked.

'Certainly, sir,' I replied, wondering what was coming.

'You know this radio series I'm doing leading up to Easter, Alec?'

'And very good it is too,' I replied sincerely.

Dr Barclay gave a wry smile. 'I'm glad you think so, for apparently quite a number do not. I've had a lot of stick since my last broadcast, been condemned as a heretic by a Wee Free minister, oh, and a lot more besides.' The Doctor was plainly hurt and my heart went out to this, the kindest of men, but I wondered why he was telling me about it.

'This week I'm taking the following line,' and he proceeded to give me the bones of the address.

'Now! What do *you* think of that, Alec?'

'Great stuff! I don't know how you keep doing it.'

'But is it scripturally sound?' he asked.

I gasped and goggled somewhat. 'You, the greatest New Testament scholar in Britain today are asking me, a very ordinary student what I think?'

'Yes, Alec. I don't willingly hurt anyone or wish to cause dissent and I know you are pretty evangelical, so I thought if you approved, that would give me the green light to go ahead.'

I gasped still more! 'Dr Barclay, in my opinion, for what it's worth, your message is superb, is certainly sound, and I wouldn't lose a minute's sleep over any of your narrow-minded critics, Wee Free or otherwise!'

'Thanks, Alec, you've been a great help,' and Willie toddled off, leaving me gazing after him in astonishment. Here surely was the mark of true greatness that a man of his stature, experience and knowledge should seek the opinion of a humble student.

And then I remembered! Jesus had done something the same, seeking the views of his fishermen friends.

'Whom do men say that I am?' The million dollar question for every man and woman, and the answer that opens doors to a land we have only dreamed of before.

'You are the Christ, the Son of the living God.'

And not to yield

THIRTEEN

The match was well through and we were down 1-0 at home. Playing centre forward, I had just missed a 'sitter', putting the ball over the bar and the crowd was not slow to express its feelings:

'You'm 'opeless, Cameron!'

'Go back to Scotland!'

'Oi could have put that in with me eyes shut!'

I cringed and tried to shut my ears to the raucous voices. After all, I thought, I'm doing my best, and I'm doing it for fun. I get no pay as I'm not a professional. But football crowds are only interested in one thing and that is seeing their team win.

My football career with Bristacombe Town in the Western League (one of the so-called non-league clubs of England), had begun some years back. When I first came to Bristacombe, having played Junior football in Scotland and loving the game, I had joined 'the Ammies', the local amateur team. A few good performances and write-ups in the press had brought me to the notice of the professional team, made up in the main of old has-beens from English or Scottish League Clubs, and young hopefuls who played in the chance of the long shot that would bring them to the notice of a bigger league club.

Harry Bartholomew, the player-manager and some of the committee had visited me, persuaded me to put pen to paper, and I had signed for 'the Town'. However, since I could not, as a busy vet guarantee every Saturday off, I had decided to remain an amateur. Every second Saturday I was free, and tried to plan for the away games while on the others, at home, Bernard, with typical generosity covered for me for the duration of the match. I worked like mad on Saturday mornings, and since Saturday afternoons were usually quiet, cover was needed only for the odd urgent case.

I enjoyed my football, and being reasonably fit in those days, fast off the mark, and with a shot in either foot, I had been moderately successful and in fact for several seasons was the team's leading goal-scorer, though much of this was due to the excellent service I received from the inside men, now dubbed the midfield, crafty players like little Billy Spalding who had played for Aberdeen at one time, and the tall, deceptively lazy Horace Pickard. I was sorry I had not been with the team my first year at 'Combe, for they had enjoyed a run in the FA Cup, losing finally away to Llanelli, whose centre half was the famous Jock Stein, to whom I would have been directly opposed.

In the game of our story, with five minutes to go, I managed to put the ball in the net and the jeers turned to cheers, 1-1.

'Good ole Alex!' (As I was always referred to in Devon).

'He be a right good 'un, that Scotchman!'

'Well done, my dear!'

No further goals were scored, and as we trooped off the field, the Club Secretary said, 'You've to phone your wife right away.'

My spirits sank, a case, when what I needed after a hard game was a bath, my tea, and maybe forty winks. Janet's voice came over the line.

'You've to go to East Challacombe right away. Bernard has been at a calving for nearly two hours and is having trouble.'

I tore off my football boots, put on my shoes, threw on my jacket on top of my football strip, and gathering my clothes into a bundle, flung them into the car and headed for the farm in question. My arrival created a bit of a sensation, a vet arrayed in football shorts and blue shirt was, to say the least, unusual.

'Good life! What have we here?' said Charlie Coles, the son-in-law. 'You'm like summat from a circus!'

'?? .. !! .. zz .. vrooh .. ar .. !? .. chooch,' said father-in-law Lerwill, the owner, whose broad Devon accent I could never decipher, even after several years, the more so since he wore no teeth. He was a perky little gnome of a man, no longer young, but tough and wiry. Another mouthful followed the first, and I gathered he was describing the calf's position. I looked in mystification at Bernard who was himself looking pretty weary, and he explained.

'It's a big calf, head way back, and just no room in there at all. I've got the chains on the forelegs, but just can't get one round the head. Maybe your longer arm will reach it.'

I stripped off my football shirt, soaped my arms, and looking even more peculiar, a vet in shorts and wellingtons, lay down in the gutter, for the cow was down and too exhausted to rise. Immediately my shorts were soaked, the contents of the dung channel oozing their way up the legs of my voluminous football pants. Ugh! I groaned even more when I reached away far in and was just able to touch the pool or head of the calf. Heaving about in the gutter, I gained a few more inches and ran my hand down ito the mouth. 'Ouch!' – I yelped, as sharp little teeth bit my fingers. The calf was still alive anyway, and if I could only gain just a fraction more, I could maybe slide a calving chain into the mouth and round the neck. So I scrabbled and heaved and grunted, having to change arms every few minutes, for there was just no room in that womb at all and in no time an arm would cramp. It was a big calf and a very deep cow, and I must have splattered about for an hour. We pumped soapy water into the uterus, for all was by now very dry, and Bernard had another go, while I leaned wearily against a stall partition, feeling my bruises from the game. No joy! We were beaten,. Three hours between us and we had not gained an inch.

'Look, Mr Lerwill,' I said, 'I'm afraid the only hope is a caesarian, though I don't like doing one when the mother is so exhausted.' I said it with some hesitation, for caesarian section in cows was still something of a rarity, and with two tired vets, both extremely muddy, and with an exhausted cow, an operation was not a cheerful prospect.

The old man looked at me with the perkiness of a robin, head on one side, muttered, 'zz..!!...uur...oh...xx... No.' I got the last word clearly enough. One of the old school, farmer Lerwill was not on for these new fangled ideas at all. I tried to persuade him, but in vain. The idea of taking a knife to his cow was absolute anathema to him. He looked at Bernard and I, both draped over a partition, filthy, limp, exhausted, muttered a screed of indecipherable Devonshire, soaped his arms in the bucket, and got down behind his cow. He pushed, heaved, grunted, sweated, while I looked on in amazement and with some shame. He had not a hope of calving her, but here was this little old man refusing to admit defeat when two much younger men, both professionals, and his strapping son-in-law were ready to throw in the sponge.

After a few minutes of watching, I was shamed into action. If that old man could go on, surely his vets whom he trusted and who were being paid to get that calf out could not yield. So Bernard and I got busy again. Taking a great gulp of air, I lay down, buried my face in the cow's back, reached as far in as I could with a rubber tube, while Bernard pumped in a fresh supply of soapy water. That would give us a few minutes, but only a few before everything became dry again. I have often found as I lay behind a cow at a calving that all sorts of thoughts would go through my mind. I found myself thinking of my missed goal at today's game, and near despair, then a few minutes later my goal from a far more difficult position. I simply *had* to get that calf's head round, and in that moist, well lubricated womb, wonder of wonders, I felt my hand reach over the calf's poll with the chain, and down into the mouth. In imagination I could hear the crowd roar as the ball had hit the net. We had not won, but it was now a draw. It seemed the same situation with the calving. It was a case now of repelling the forelegs and shoulder of the calf as far as possible, and while I guided it, Bernard pulled on the head chain and to my immense relief, slowly the head came round. We were nearly there. Now it was time for pulling, and with big Charlie Coles on the head chain, Bernard and little Mr Lerwill on a leg chain each, and my hand inside directing, bit by bit we eased the calf towards the big wide world outside. The poor cow bellowed as the pain gripped her, but as if sensing that things had taken a turn for the better, she gave a great heave which was worth far more than all our pulling. With a plop the calf arrived, while the men on the chains collapsed together on the seats of their pants in the dung channel. Seldom have so many men become so wet and dirty in one instant! But in a moment it was all forgotten as the calf gave a splutter, a sneeze, and started breathing.

Old man Lerwill was instantly busy rubbing it with a wisp of straw, seeming as fresh as when the whole operation had begun, and in the midst of a flood of toothless Devonshire giving us to understand it was a heifer too. Bernard, bless his heart, who need not have been there at all, was streaked in blood and filth, while I, still in my football shorts which were practically hanging off me, was an even more gory mess. I would have to drive home like that, and hoped fervently I would not get a puncture on the way, for I am sure the police would have lifted me instantly for being indecently attired. The car would also probably smell for days, but what matter all these things, we had won. Inspired by an old man who had refused to yield, we had well and truly won!

That was over thirty years ago, but oddly enough the scene came back to me as I left our little Cottage Hospital at Aldermouth one afternoon, where I had been doing my weekly rounds as Chaplain. I had, like the crowd at the football match, my critics there too. There were two patients, who reckoned I had neglected them, even though I saw them at least once a week, in addition to our many folks in the hospitals of Inverness. I had gone up to one new patient in the corner bed, an elderly woman.

'How are you?' I enquired.

'No too bad. Who are you?' came the response.

'I'm the chaplain.'

'Aye, but who are you. Whit's your name?'

'Cameron, and I'm the minister of the Old Parish Church.'

At this she gasped, then snorted, and fixing me with a beady eye pronounced.

'The auld Kirk! The worst thing that hapened to the Kirks was the union in 1929!'

Whereupon she turned her face to the wall, and refused to speak to me further. For all these years she had carried bitterness in her heart, and would not forget or forgive.

Then I had come to the bed of Mrs Wilson where all was smiles, and that was astonishing, for Mrs Wilson was nearing the end of a long battle with an incurable condition, a battle she had fought with immense courage. She had faced surgery several times, had undergone all sorts of treatment, and with never a complaint had endured it all. Only in her forties, with a husband and family who loved her and depended on her, she had refused to yield to this disease, even though she knew the end was not far off.

That day she had astonished me, as I stood, feeling tongue tied and helpless beside her bed, by describing the holiday she had planned for herself and her family in a month's time, a camping holiday of all things. When I saw her she was so weak she could scarcely raise a hand, could not get out of bed, could not stand. She knew well her time was short, but with great determination and a total refusal to yield, and with thoughts only of husband a family, she was planning a camping holiday! I was amazed, and humbled, but I should have known by now. I had seen Mrs Wilson over many months fighting her own private battles with dogged determination and courage, a courage born of her sure faith that knew her life was in God's hands, a faith which in turn had given her a wonderful serenity and calm even when all seemed hopeless. I had watched her stage by stage and been constantly amazed and humbled at what her mighty spirit had achieved when her body was weak, weary, and sometimes in pain. But as I left the hospital, I felt that not even Mrs Wilson could achieve her final goal of her last holiday with those she loved and for whom she had fought her battles. A camping holiday in four weeks, impossible! I should have known better.

Mrs Wilson had her holiday a month later, as she had planned from her sick bed, a holiday where her fun and gaiety had lifted her anxious family. Then, a few days later, she slipped quietly away to that place where all the hard things of this life are understood and made clear. She had not yielded. She had won. She had well and truly won!

Collar off

FOURTEEN

'Come away in, boys, Alec, John, Gordon, Ben, good you could all come,' said David. 'I thought we would have a discussion on Bonhoeffer today.'

We made our way into David's sitting room where several others of the brethren were already assembled, the first-comers getting the deepest armchairs. The occasion was the monthly meeting of our area ministers' fraternal when we met in one another's homes for a couple of hours of chat, fellowship and relaxation. Sometimes we had a topic for discussion, at other times we just shared experiences and incidents, cheerful or sorrowful. David, the host today, an enthusiastic scholar and a fine pastor, despite his disability and poor health, had obviously prepared a paper on Dietrich Bonhoeffer, the German theologian who was executed for his opposition to Hitler. All the denominations were represented except, sadly, the Wee Free minister who would not join us. What we never did at these fraternals was what two women, seeing a clutch of clergymen entering a Manse, thought they were about.

'Where are a' the meenisters goin' the day?' queried one.

'Och, they're away to a thing ca'd a fraternal,' replied the other. 'Whit's a fraternal?'

'Oh, it's when they a' meet an' swap sermons wi' yin anither.' The first woman thought for a bit and then lugubriously announced,

'My! Oor man's been awfu' unlucky lately!'

David's wife brought in the coffee and cakes and we rose to greet her. While we were passing things around, Dan the priest announced.

'I heard a good story the other day. Three men were at an ecumenical conference in Paris, all of them from the same country town. One of them was of the true faith, Dan, the friendly Father, twinkled round at us all, 'one was a Piscy, one a Church of Scotland minister.'

'In Paris, did you say?' asked Gordon. 'Unusual place for an ecumenical conference.'

'Don't say they went to the Follies bergères,' said Donald.

'Look! Don't interrupt,' Dan commanded, 'or I'll forget the story. It seems the conference ran from Wednesday to Wednesday and they had the weekend off.'

'Even the Sabbath?' asked Hamish.

'Look! It's my story, let me tell it. Well, on the Friday night the priest said to the other two "I've a confession to make. I'm fond of a dram and I'm going to sample quite a selection of these French wines."'

'Always knew you boys liked the bottle,' laughed Donald. Dan pushed on with his story.

'The Episcopal rector said, "I've a confession to make too. I like a flutter on the horses and the pools, and I'm going to have a dabble at the Casino."'

'Must have had more money than I get,' muttered Joe, the representative of the Scottish Episcopal Church.

'The Church of Scotland minister said, "I've a confession to make too. . . ."'

'Neffer!' said Hamish in his delightful highland voice, 'No minister would be haffing anything to do with a confession!'

'This one did,' said Dan, now red in the face. 'He said "I've a confession to make . . ."'

That makes two confessions he had,' quipped the other Alec who was a Congregationalist, and his denomination not involved in the story. Dan bellowed, 'I have a confession to make and I can't wait to get home. I'm the biggest gossip in Scotland.'

Dan sat back with a sigh, his story at last completed, and there were chuckles round the room.

'I know one about three ministers too,' said John, 'a Baptist, a Piscy and a C of S,' John was retired, a father figure, and was shown more respect than Dan had been in his story. Besides, everyone was well into coffee and cakes by now, tucking in happily. John went on.

'They were close friends and keen fishers and were out on a loch one day.'

'If it's a fishing story, I'm off,' said Joe, the irrepressible. John ignored him.

'After a time the Baptist said "I need more bait", stepped over the side of the boat, walked across the water to the bank and returned, to the astonishment of the other two. Bye and bye the Piscy said, "I'm hungry. I'll just get my sandwiches from the bank", and he did the same. Now the poor Kirk man thought "I must keep the flag flying", so he said "It's getting cold. I'll just go and get my coat," stepped out of the boat and disappeared. When he was coming up for the third time, the Piscy said to the Baptist, 'do you think we should tell him about the stepping stones?'

'Aye, good John,' said Donald, 'that's an old one but I'd forgotten it.'

So the talked ebbed and flowed, until the coffee was consumed, then old Hamish leaned forward and said.

'You young ministers are a disgrace to the cloth!'

'No doubt, Hamish,' acknowledged Donald, 'but in what particular way?'

'Look at you, you and your check shirts, hardly one of you hass the collar on. A man of Got should always be properly dressed!'

'Oh, but Hamish,' I was moved to protest, 'we're off duty. Surely we don't need to wear the collar this morning?'

'A minister or priest is neffer off duty,' pronounced Hamish.

'Oh, come come!' 'Nonsense!' 'That's a bit much!' came various exclamations. 'Christ didn't have a special uniform, did He?'

'Look you,' went on Hamish, 'a soltier iss not ashamed of hiss uniform and you are soltiers of the Lord.'

There was instant and vociferous protest, except from Joe, who supported Hamish and reported 'I only take my collar off when on holiday.'

Hamish persisted, 'If effer a preacher of the Word is to be seen in public, he should be in uniform.'

'What about in the garden?' queried Gordon.

'Yes, in the garden too. I always wear mine in the garten. I tell you, you are ashamed of your calling.'

'I heard about a minister who was seen bringing in the morning milk in pyjamas and dog collar,' said the other Alec.

'And I know a young minister who went his honeymoon in his,' said Ben, my assistant.

My mind boggled at the thought. 'The idiot,' I exclaimed.

That statement of Hamish's got us going and the talk ranged far and wide on Bishop's gaiters, cassocks, surplices and all the paraphernalia of the preacher.

'Bonhoeffer was a wonderful man,' came in David hesitantly.

'Aye, and I don't think he wore a dog collar,' said Donald.

'Look at that now,' said Hamish, 'maype iff he had, Hitler woult have hat more respect for him.'

We finally agreed to differ, though I'm afraid I shocked dear old Hamish, a real saint, despite his views on the collar, by saying,

'I still feel more at home in a calving coat than a collar.'

'Och, now, but you are the queer one, yes indeed,' said Hamish, and eventually the subject died down.

'Eh, about Bonhoeffer,' David tried again.

'Before we come to Bonhoeffer we've got a few things to arrange,' said John. 'Whose turn is it to take the Service at the War Memorial this year?'

'Not mine,' said Gordon, 'I did it last year.'

'And I the year before,' said Joe.

'Must be yours, then, Alec,' concluded John, and in this easy fashion the duty was arranged.

Dan piped up again.

'Oh, Alec, about that mixed marriage you've asked me to share. The Bishop hasn't given his permission yet, and I can't do anything till he does. Sorry!'

This led to a discussion on the desirability of Bishops which brought Joe bounding out of his seat in defence of his denomination.

'Judging from the arguments you boys seem to have in your Presbytery, we're better off with Bishops.'

'Nonsense, Joe,' said Donald, 'we're at least democratic and where did you hear of a democracy without arguments?'

'But the Bishops are in the Apostolic Succession,' said Dan, to which Joe added a 'Hear, hear.'

'Now, you've both got Bishops in your Churches who claim to be in the Apostolic Succession. How can they both be?' pointed out Donald.

'Bishops! Bishops!' expostulated old Hamish, 'look at the palaces they live in. That can't be right, and how can someone appointed by maybe a Jewish or atheist Prime Minister haf the cheek to say the Holy Spirit appointed them?'

So the talk switched to which form of Church government was most agreeable to the Bible. We were thoroughly enjoying ourselves, and as always, though we often differed, it was good natured and not in any way divisive.

'Why do you fellows insist on couples at a wedding both being baptised?' queried Ben.

This brought a long, complicated explanation from Joe, while poor David looked sadly at his notes on Bonhoeffer. As so often happened, we found plenty of topics for discussion and in one another's company felt our own particular problems lessen or even disappear. The two hours sped past and we did not get round to David's prepared paper. I felt sorry for him for I knew he would have spent considerable time preparing it, and having had to do an essay on the German theologian at college, I was interested to hear what the refreshing David would have to say. We apologised for not having Bonhoeffer, discussed where the next fraternal would be, promised without fail to hear David's paper next time, and thanking David's wife for the refreshments, departed to our several parishes, instructed, relaxed and brought closer in real fellowship.

On the way home I thought of our talk that morning, and particularly old Hamish's remarks about the collar. Of course it has its uses, if, for example, you want a railway compartment to yourself! It is a relatively new garment, but useful on occasion, as an entry to hospitals at any time without explanations, and of course, on formal duties, I feel a must. I recalled an instance where it had a salutory effect, back in my Moorton days.

My friend Bob was minister of Ibrox Church and Chaplain to Rangers FC, and one week invited me up to a game. Rangers were playing Hearts and with me were our two eldest, Neil and Ian, beside themselves with excitement for they had never been to a big match. We were given a seat in the stand and sat with the élite, and for some reason that day we were both wearing our clerical collars. Behind us were two very vocal supporters, true blue fans. Even their adjectives were the same colour as the team's jerseys, and they became bluer, in direct proportion to the amount, (which was astonishing), of whisky they consumed. Finally, by the second half, it was just beyond bearing, my sons' eyes were getting bigger and bigger as they listened to words they had never heard before, and suddenly, at exactly the same moment, quite unrehearsed, Bob and I turned round to protest. The two somewhat inebriated gentlemen were confronted by two wrathful dog collars. There was a moment of speechlessness, followed by abject apologies,

'Sorry, Father, so sorry, if we had only kenned, Father, who you were . . .' I do not know whether they thought we had wandered into the wrong match, or were Celtic spies viewing the opposition, but at any rate their style was severely cramped for the rest of the game and the air was a bit cleaner.

But there were many other occasions when I had the collar off. I cannot think of anything more uncomfortable, despite Hamish's assertion, when digging the garden. When the boys and I were having a game on our little nine-hole putting green on the Manse lawns, off would come the collar. After all I was known by most people in Aldermouth. I often visited in an ordinary shirt, flannels and sports jacket. The truth was, and is, that having come late to the ministry, and as a vet, being a casual dresser, I simply cannot see the importance of the black and white ensemble that others feel a must. My friend, Alec, the Congregational minister never on any occasion wore a clerical collar, even in the pulpit or at funerals.

Once a fortnight it was certainly discarded. This was when we had our ministers' foursome at golf. Early in my days at Aldermouth, Dr John, our much loved GP had laid it on the line that in a Church of our size and with the multifarious demands of the many organisations (over twenty I counted once, organisations or departments), with the sorrow of two funerals weekly, the anxiety of over twenty in hospital weekly, and the stress of trying to help people with their personal problems, not to mention the long hours of sermon preparation, Dr John had said, 'You *must* learn to take time off. You *must* make time or you'll crack up.'

He was a wise and good man, and the years have shown, too late, that I should have listened to him. However, discovering that Gordon, Alec and John had all played golf at one time, I routed them out and once a fortnight, usually a Monday, we disported ourselves on Aldermouth's famous championship links. We sometimes talked 'shop' on the first fairway, but after that it was strictly serious business as John and Gordon challenged the two Alecs. The golf varied between bad and terrible, but we enjoyed ourselves immensely, and there was a deal of leg pulling. Most important, we relaxed, which was more than the greenkeepers did for when they saw us coming, they immediately fled for cover as if we were an approaching cloud of locusts, getting themselves behind a hut or 'coorying doon' below their tractor. We played summer and winter, sometimes on a cold day being the only folks on the course, and the professional was heard to say one day to a visitor enquiring if the course was busy, 'There's nobody out there but four mad ministers!'

Golf in winter could be difficult with three jerseys on, scarves, bonnets, gloves, but we would stop after the ninth hole, Alec would produce a flask of coffee or bovril and some biscuits, and in the lee of whin bushes we heated ourselves up and prepared for the homeward battle. Never on a golf course was assembled at one time such a motley collection of hooks, slices, duffs, fresh air shots pulls and for a time that dreadful discease which no golfer will mention . . . shank, which sorely afflicted me. Weather conditions varied, like the golf. On one occasion it was so misty that we could not see where the ball had gone, but we drove on regardless, and John played the game of his life. The mist lifted and his game went to pieces! He got into a bunker and had eight hacks at the ball his face becoming redder and redder, but not a comment was made. Eventually ball and club came hurtling out of the trap, John picked both up without a word, then collapsed hilariously. I was reminded of the Bishop on a similar occasion who, playing with some of his flock, and having similar bunker trouble, requested, 'Would one of you laymen say the appropriate words!'

We were all keen, if very indifferent golfers, the 'Clerical Clowns' as John's wife, Nan dubbed us, but the fun and fellowship were immense. I particularly admired John, for though well into his seventies, he was as keen as mustard, so much so, that one day when his ball was on the downward slope leading to a ditch, despite our pleas to lift and drop, he refused, tried to play it, fell and broke his arm.

Eventually Alec and Gorden moved away and John felt he could no longer play, so I had to look for other partners. In time a new foursome of Willie Edwards, a retired minister who had gone to the same school at Mochrum as me, and two of my elders and very good friends, Arthur Menzies and Bob Anderson teamed up. Usually Willie and I played together, saints versus sinners, though which was which was never specified. Two other friends, Henry and Peter, were members of the other course, and from time to time would treat me to a round there. Of the whole bunch, Willie was the finest golfer, having played all his life. He seldom veered from the straight and narrow, never visited a bunker and could putt like Gary Player. He had a degree in English, loved poetry, and would always crown a particularly good shot with an apt quotation, sometimes in Latin to me, and I had left my Latin thirty years behind me! Occasionally, as I was lining up a putt, out would come a screed of poetry in a dolorous voice, meant to encourage but having the effect of making me want to brain him with a brassie!

These were happy days, days of real undiluted joy and friendship, when we would return home tired, but also relaxed, and sometimes on a round with a shot to savour for an hour or two.

I was such a dreadful bunker player that I once preached a sermon in Golf Week on 'the bunkers of life', and I recalled an experience of the late Tom Allan, who influenced a whole generation, including me, with his powerful preaching, deep pastoral concern and practical Christianity. He was a keen golfer and one day things were not going well for him. He kept visiting the sand traps and his caddie said to him, 'Ah doot the Lord's no' wi' ye the day, Mr Allan.'

Tom merely smiled and played on, but at the next tee he said to his caddie.

'You know, Bill, you were wrong back there. The Lord doesn't promise to save us from life's bunkers, but He's right beside us when we're in them, and helps us play the right shot.'

Tom Allan was right. He knew life. He knew plenty about life's bunkers, and he knew his Lord.

Ah me, enough of this dreaming. An hour till Barbara's wedding. Collar on!

Seeing now

FIFTEEN

One day an elderly couple came into the surgery with their Labrador dog, which was also elderly.

'It's his eyes,' they said, something that was at once obvious for they looked terrible. I lifted the old dog on to the table and had a look at them. Both eyes were filled with pus, they were half closed, and the dog kept blinking and pawing at them.

'How long has he been like this?' I asked.

'Oh, he's been bothered with them for a long time, and we've had him to a vet several times before. He gave us ointment to put in them, but we've just retired to Bristcombe and they seem to have gone worse.'

'Did your other vet tell you what the trouble was?'

'He just said it was inflammation, conjugal, or conjunction or some name like that,' they explained.

'Well, his eyes are certainly inflamed, but I'm afraid no ointment will put them right. You see, it's more than conjunctivitis, he's got a condition called entropion where the eyelashes grow inwards and irritate the eyes, then germs get in, and cause all this matter. It's a very painful condition, like having something in your eye all the time, only worse.'

'Oh dear! Can anything be done?' asked the wife.

'Certainly! There's a quite simple little operation which can turn the eyelashes outwards and take away the irritation.'

'An operation!' they both gasped in unison.

'Oh, it's quite a little one, and it would make all the difference to him. What's his name, by the way?'

'Terence!' said the wife, and at the sound of his name, the old dog's tail beat a tattoo on the table.

'Couldn't you just give us ointment like the other vet?' asked the husband. 'You see, he's old to have an operation.'

'Yes, I could give you ointment, but it would not cure the condition, only soothe his eyes a little for a time. I strongly advise you to let me do the operation. It would take away all the pain, make his eyes clear again, let him see properly, for he's really a handsome old fellow, and it's a pity to see him like that.'

'Would it be safe?'

'Yes! It means an anaesthetic, of course, and there's always a very slight risk with an anaesthetic, but it's maybe 1 in 1000. I'll just sound his heart,' which I did, and got a fine, strong, regular beat.

'Sound as a bell, Mr and Mrs . . . eh?'

'Murgatroyd,' said the man.

'Er . . . how much would such an operation cost?' he asked.

'Oh . . . about three guineas.'

'Oh . . . is that all,' said the old chap. 'What do you think, Celia?'

'I don't know, Cyril, but if he was going to be operated on, I'd want to be there. I think we should both be there.'

'Oh, I wouldn't advise that,' I hastily exclaimed. 'Most people get upset to see their animals being operated on. There's bound to be a little blood, you know.'

So they talked to and fro, finally decided on surgery, but only on condition that they could stay with their 'dear old fellow'. I did not like the idea one bit, but for the dog's sake, agreed. Our operation day, apart from emergencies, was Wednesday, so Terence Murgatroyd was duly fixed up for 11.00 am, the next week. I decided I had better take some precautions, so Mrs Drury, our original Secretary/Receptionist/Assistant/Book-keeper, who was with us in my early years with Kenneth as partner, was despatched to lay in a bottle of brandy for the surgery, and two chairs were placed in position, a bit from the table, on the morning of the operation. The dog was lifted onto the table, and I cleaned up his eyes, then explained to Cyril and Celia the procedure to be adopted with Terence.

'First I give him an injection of anaesthetic into a vein, and he will just go quietly to sleep. Then I cut out carefully a little elliptical piece of skin above and below each eye. This has the same effect at tightening up a piece of elastic, and pulls the eyelids outwards, so that the lashes no longer rub against the eye. Perhaps you would find it more comfortable to sit down to watch.'

But they did not, Mrs M in particular, a stout woman, wanted a close up, and her small husband, not to be outdone also hovered nearby, so four heads were bent over the now recumbent Terence. The operation is not difficult, but requires care and concentration, and I was wrapped up in what I was doing, as was Mrs Drury, constantly swabbing the area, when after a short time, I heard a faint voice saying, 'It's awful warm today!' and engrossed as I was, it took a moment to sink in. When it did, I turned quickly to say 'sit on the chair', but I was too late. There was a mighty crash and I was just in time to see large Mrs Murgatroyd sit down on the floor, right on top of her little husband who had tried to catch her, both of them missing the chairs. The little man peered out from underneath and murmured, 'My wife appears to have fainted!'

I had seen many people faint at surgery, even big husky farmers watching a Caesarean in their sheep, but never quite a situation like this. There was nothing for it but to suspend operations, and while Mrs Drury and I eased the wife up, for her husband's ribs would be in dire peril, the little man crawled out from underneath, like a tortoise coming out of its shell. Between us we carted the unconscious lady into the Waiting Room, and not without difficulty, deposited her on the couch. Mrs Drury produced the brandy, and since poor little Cyril looked as if he was about to faint too, gave him a little, then left him sitting beside his wife, lying in a heap on the couch, her hat askew.

'Best just to leave her as she is,' I said (I didn't really know!) 'and when she comes round, perhaps a little sip of brandy.' Poor Cyril nodded, and Mrs Drury and I left him patting his wife's hands as we trooped back to our patient.

In due course the operation was finished, just in time, for with the interruption, the effects of my short-acting anaesthetic were wearing off. I dressed the wounds, and squeezed some chloromycetin ointment into the dog's eyes, for the long standing irritation had produced a great deal of inflammation and keratitis, but fortunately no ulceration of the cornea that I could detect. We lifted the old dog down, laid him on a blanket, then hurried through to see the other patient. She was a little bit ahead of Terence, being able to sit up, though pale, and with the hat even more askew, her eyes a bit glazed, and a glass of brandy in her hand, she would hardly have qualified at that moment for a temperance advert! Cyril, I noticed, was also at the brandy again, and I thought the profit from the operation had already been drunk! We were able to cheer Mrs M up a bit by telling her Terence had come through his surgery well, and when they were ready, we would carry him out to the car and they could take him home.

They returned in ten days to have the stitches removed, and this time they both stayed in the Waiting Room. I was agreeably surprised at the improvement already in the old dog's eyes, the chloromycetin twice daily allied to the removal of the irritation having worked wonders. They came back a fortnight later, and it was lovely to behold. Terence was frisking along like a young dog, looking about him everywhere. I imagine it was a long time since he had seen the world properly, but he was seeing now alright, and had a lot of catching up to do. His eyes were clean and bright as a puppy, a complete transformation.

I have seen this transformation in the ministry too on numbers of occasions. Alec Mullen grew up in a large housing scheme in Glasgow in a street where every single house had somebody with a prison record, including Alec's home, although he, the eldest of a large family, was a steady sort of lad. He had a younger brother who was a real tearaway, but Alec was very fond of his wild brother.

One day the younger lad, a fellow in his early twenties by then, took seriously ill. The doctor was called, and visited daily, but as time passed the doctor became more grave, and informed the family that things could go either way. Why the boy was not removed to hospital, I know not, and as he saw his brother lying helpless in bed, Alec too felt very helpless. Surely something could be done, but what? Alec thought of prayer, but he knew no prayer, had never prayed, and never been near a Church in his life. But that night, Alec did the only thing he could think of. He said Psalm 23 . . . 'The Lord's my Shepherd', which he had learned at school. The sick lad, in time recovered. This set Alec thinking. Maybe it was just luck, coincidence, chance. Maybe he would have recovered anyway, but maybe, just maybe, there was something in this prayer business after all.

Some time later, Alec himself was ill, and advised to get a job in the country air away from the then, smoky city. Thus he came into my parish at Moorton, where he worked on a farm as a general handyman. In time he became a shepherd to the kindly Dalgliesh family. Old Mr

Dalgliesh was one of my senior elders, a kind, gentle, good man, and they encouraged Alec to come to Church. He attended every week, and eventually, though much older than most of the others, came to a Young Communicants' class for prospective Church members. After the course, I had a long chat with Alec, and my delight was like that when seeing the old dog's eyes clear again after surgery. The great surgeon had clearly been at work in the young man's life, and now he not only knew the shepherd psalm, he knew the Shepherd. He was seeing, now, things he had been blind to before, and the world was a wonderful place. It was like all successful surgery, no spur of the moment thing. The cure was permanent.

One evening in Aldermouth, years later, my phone rang.

'Is that Mr Cameron? My name is George Gray and I'd like to join the Church. Could I have a chat with you sometime?'

Now every minister is delighted to get that kind of request, and since I had already to visit in that particular street that very night, I called on Mr Gray, who, with his wife and family, was a comparative newcomer to the town. He was a man in his thirties, and welcomed me warmly, if somewhat shyly. We talked of this and that, and then he told me his story.

He had been brought up in the Shetland Islands by his grandmother, a real godly, severe warrior of the old school. The young George had been sent or taken to three Services every Sunday, Church of Scotland in the morning, Methodist in the afternoon, and Plymouth Brethren at night. He grew up with a considerable knowledge of the Bible, but a hearty dislike of the whole business. At the age of sixteen he went off, like so many of the islanders, to sea. As he left, his granny gave him a Bible which he put in his kit bag, and there it remained, unopened, for years.

He prospered at sea, rapidly climbed the promotion ladder, for he was a clever, highly intelligent man, and when he met me that night, was First Officer on one of the huge supertankers, shortly afterwards indeed becoming Captain. In the course of the years he had married, the daughter of a Methodist minister, and in time they had two children. Though his wife and family would go off to Church, not George. He had had enough religion to last him a lifetime, he reckoned.

'And what has made you change your mind?' I queried.

'Difficult to explain clearly, Mr Cameron. It's been a gradual thing, but over a period of time, often when I've been on watch on the bridge away in the Persian Gulf or some such ocean, with the vastness of the sea all around me and the even more vast starry sky above me, I've felt very small, and also somehow as if I was part of some great master plan. So many of the things I learned long ago in the Bible, and thought I had rejected for good, have come back to me, and the interesting thing is that now they make sense. It's been like a giant jigsaw puzzle falling into place, and all I can say is that I'm seeing now, and want to be part of God's Church, for I like what I see.'

So one could go on, instance after instance of people who had found a faith. In Alec's case he started from scratch; in George's case, there was a background of knowledge and a Christian wife. But the end result was the same.

The operation had been successful, and dim eyes were now seeing God's wonderful world, and His plan for His world, in all its splendour.

Of course such 'surgery' has been going on from the beginning of the Christian era. Most famous was the man Saul, an upright man who kept to the letter of God's laws for His people, the Jews, but a man with a deep and bitter hatred for these upstart Christians. On a mission of destruction of these pestilential Jesus people, he was met by the Master surgeon Himself, was actually, literally blinded for a time by the brightness of the Shekinah glory of the risen Christ, and when he recovered his sight, he was no longer Saul the persecuter, but Paul the apostle, and the baiter of Christians had become one himself, a complete about turn, or to use the word beloved by evangelists, a Conversion.

Over the long centuries of Christendom, many have experienced this spur of the moment encounter and change, like laser beam surgery, a change evidenced by a completely different outlook, different set of values, different code of behaviour and most of all a deep compassion and caring for all mankind. In my ministry I have seen this apparently instant about-turn on a number of occasions. I have also to admit to some cases where the surgery was only successful for a time, and eyes were clouded again so far as commitment to Christ was concerned.

Much more frequently, though, has been the gradual change, as if bit by bit scales fell from the eyes, till people saw differently. Jack Miller was like that. I knew Jack first when in my summer holidays as a vet student, I worked in, of all places, an Income Tax office. My first summer holidays I worked on a farm and there was no prouder teenager in Scotland than me as I carted hay ricks into the stack-yard on the old hay bogeys with my very own mare for the summer, Pearl. These were happy, halcyon, carefree days, but unfortunately they did not pay very much, and in the closing years of the war and immediately after, there were few student grants. True, I supplemented what little my parents could afford by playing the organ in Crosshills Church, and got £1.00 a week for playing football for Maybole Juniors. But much more was required, so, finding that His Majesty's Inspector of Taxes employed students and paid about twice that of the farmer, reluctantly, on several occasions I worked at this, to me, hateful job. Jack was on the permanent staff at the Ayr office, a happy-go-lucky, devil-may-care, extremely likeable man, nothing bad about him, a man typical of millions who lived his life without thought of God or Church and saw no need for either.

Every night after work, he would head for the pub before going home, and on Sundays, while his wife and two daughters went off to Church, Jack usually headed for the Golf Course and after his round spent the rest of the day at the nineteenth hole, until one day some words spoken with the innocence of a child changed things. He was pottering in the garden that Sunday morning and as his wife and little girls went out the gate for Church, Jack overhead one ask, 'Mummy? Does Daddy go to a different Church from us?'

Just that! A child's question, but somehow it stung Jack and set him thinking. Hell-raiser though he undoubtedly was, he doted on his family and he thought, 'I'll go along next week to keep the children happy.'

He did, feeling very strange going in a Church door, and hoping none of his nineteenth hole pals saw him. He had the uncomfortable feeling that everybody in the place, big building though it was, had their eyes on him alone. But as he came out he thought, 'That wasn't so bad. Folk seemed really friendly, as if they were glad to see me, and that fellow in the pulpit talked some sense, even raised a laugh, didn't think folk ever laughed in a Church. The kids were pleased too. I'll give it a month's trial.' The month passed, and another, and another, and Jack, to his utter amazement, found he was enjoying himself, actually *enjoying* himself in that bright Church where there were many young couples and a superb minister.

I met Jack many years later when I was myself a minister and had been preaching in his Church. He was the same cheerful chap, the same friend of all, but yet there was a difference too. He seemed to be seeing things differently, he had a verve, a sense of purpose, a joy about him that seemed to go deep down. He told me he was leader of the Youth Club, was Session Clerk and involved with old folks in the area.

'Alec,' he said, 'I know now why you became a minister. I'm seeing now in a way I never did before!'

Another operation by the celestial Surgeon had proved a complete success, and the great Consultant's still at it.

Patch up job

SIXTEEN

'Hello, Alex,' came the voice over the air of Charlie Trevelyan our local zoo keeper. 'It's ham.'

'Beg pardon?'

'It's ham!'

'Eh?' I was completely puzzled.

'I want you to come up and look at ham.'

I really could make nothing of this at all.

'Charlie, have you got a wrong number or something? Should you not be phoning a grocer or a butcher?'

'Eh? What's that, Alex?'

'Well, why do you want me to look at ham?'

'Because it's off colour.' The mystery deepened. I looked at the phone in perplexity. 'Charlie, ham comes from pigs, I know, but it's usually live ones I see.'

'Oh! Ah! Ha, ha, ha. Oh, that's a good one,' Charlie roared with laughter. Eventually he composed himself and said,

'I mean Ham, the lion cub. You know, Shem Ham and Japheth, Butch and Mary's cubs.'

'Ohhhhhh . . . now I understand. I didn't know you had gone back to the Ark for names. I'll certainly have a look at that kind of Ham, though I'd rather it was something safe like your goats. What seems to be wrong with it?'

'I'm not certain, Alex. He's going about with his head all to one side and he's off his food.'

'These cubs must be a fair size by now, Charlie. How are we to get near him?'

'Oh, don't worry, we'll net him.'

'Well, make sure Butch and Mary are well out of the way or they'll make ham of us.'

'Don't worry, Alex, and while you're up, I'd like you to see a young llama I've bought.'

'A llama! That's more in my line. I'll be up shortly.'

So I headed for the zoo, not exactly looking forward to the visit, for in these days of the early 1950s we had no knock out darts. To treat an animal, you had to get in beside it while it was still in full possession of its faculties and restrain it as best you could. True, you could sometimes slip nembutal or some other anaesthetic or sedative into its food and hope it would not notice it, but since wild animals seldom showed symptoms of disease until they were really ill and by then off their food, most often this ploy was not on. I tried to remember on the way up the steep hill to the zoo perched right on the top just how old these lion cubs would be by now and concluded they must be very well grown. My spirits sagged somewhat!

Charlie was waiting for me at the gate and hurried me through his large zoo at his usual break neck pace, past the sea lion enclosure, the many pavilions of tropical birds, the pets' corner, the ostrich pen, many cages of monkeys, the black bears and finally the lion's corner. There were Butch and Mary in their cage, Mary looking a bit thin and careworn, so, since the lion and lioness were together again, clearly the cubs were weaned. My spirits sagged even more!

'Mary's got the European record,' Charlie proudly informed me, 'she's had forty-three cubs.'

'She's beginning to look it too, Charlie. Do you not think she should stop now?'

Charlie hesitated. 'Her cubs sell well. Maybe she'll manage one more litter, Alex.'

In a cage next to father and mother were two well-grown cubs.

'That's Shem and Japheth. We've got Ham separated in the next cage,' Charlie explained.

I stopped abruptly at the next cage, gazed, gulped, swallowed a jagged lump that seemed to have suddenly sprouted in my throat and murmured.

'He's big, Charlie, a lot bigger than the other two. Do you think we can hold him in a net?'

I found I was sweating somewhat, especially as Ham at that moment gave a roar which sounded pretty grown up to me. In fact, I am sure he was past adolescence and his voice had broken!

Charlie gave me a slap on the back.

'Don't worry, Alex! Never had a vet eaten yet! We'll hold him.'

'Let's just watch him a minute, Charlie, and see if we can get some idea of his trouble.' You can learn much by just observing an animal's behaviour and it was also postponing the dreaded moment when I had to go into that cage. Our vet course at College had said not a word about lions. I could control a horse weighing a ton, had little fear of a bull weighing fifteen hundred weight, but a much smaller lion had not been mentioned. I kept telling myself 'it's just a big cat' but somehow myself was not convinced. I watched the cub for a time. He was prowling around continuously, growling to himself all the time, his head tilted noticeably to one side. Clearly he was in considerable pain. 'Ear or tooth', I thought. Just then he lay down, groaned loudly and pawed at his right ear.

'It's obviously that ear, Charlie. Where's your net? We'll need to have a closer look.'

'Irene, Michael and Tom are bringing it.'

'Irene? will she go in there?'

'Oh, Irene would tackle Butch single handed. She's got no fear, that girl.' That made me feel a bit ashamed of myself and a bit braver. If that slip of a lassie could go in there, surely a six foot vet could too. Just then the trio arrived with a large net, Charlie opened the cage door, and in we went, brave me last, but then I had my cases to carry! Ham retreated before us into a corner, Charlie shouted, '1-2-3-now,' and the net was flung over the young lion and quickly pulled up tight. It was slickly done, except that somehow Tom got caught up in the net, and I doubt if either he or Ham appreciated the skill. Tom was out in ten seconds flat, looking a bit pale about the gills. Ham roared ferociously, which started off Butch, Mary and the other cubs, and outside the black bears joined in the row. The whole line of cages vibrated with animals pounding about and leaping at the bars, the whole din not calculated to calm one's nerves.

'Sure these connecting doors are well fastened, Charlie?' I yelled.

'Certain sure.'

There was no way that Ham was going to lie absolutely still, but enmeshed in the net as he was, his movements were limited and I was able to get a fair look at his ear and inside it. I would have appreciated a drug like Immobilon to knock him out, but it was not around then either.

'It's an abscess, Charlie,' and as if to confirm my diagnosis, at that very moment there was a gush of pus from the lion's ear. The struggle with the net had probably caused a 'ripe' abscess to burst, to my and Ham's great relief. I did not like lancing in ears, even in anaesthetised, still animals, let alone a struggling, fighting fury. I got out some cotton wool and through the mesh of the net, with a pair of forceps, cleaned out the ear as best I could, then, when the pus was down to a trickle, squeezed in a whole tube of chloromysetin ointment. Then back to the black case, a syringe and a dose of long acting penicillin which I jabbed into a rear leg.

'That'll keep him covered for three days and hopefully will be enough, but at best it's a bit of a patch up job in a lion this size.'

'He must have suffered some with that ear,' said Charlie.

That was typical of this man whose first thought was not what money he could make from the various attractions at his zoo, but the well-being of his animals.

'He certainly did, Charlie,' and I marvelled again at the stoic courage of creatures of the wild. 'Never show weakness' was the law, for 'the weakest goes to the wall'. I remembered as I closed my case the agony my father had suffered with a similar condition in his ear, almost climbing the walls with the intensity of the pain.

'Right, Alex, out you go, and the rest of you. I'll get the net,' and typically Charlie was last out of the cage. The young lion was still crouched in his corner, but already his head was less tilted. The pressure in the ear had gone, and much of the pain. In a domestic animal there would have been daily dressings, but that was not very practicable with a young lion, but I had hopes that my patch up job might suffice, and so indeed it proved. Ham was reunited with his brothers, next day was back on his food, and shortly afterwards was sold and grew to full manhood, or lionhood, in another zoo.

I went into the house to have a good scrub up before I touched another animal for my hands were well splashed with germ laden puss. I had a cup of tea, listened to our zoo keeper's enthusiastic talk of his various charges, proposed extensions and future plans and thought as he rattled on that if ever there was a man happy in his work, it was Charlie Trevelyan.

'How about this llama, Charlie? You haven't had one of them before.'

'No, Alex, it were goin' cheap, like. It ben't full grown yet . . . came from a Pets' Corner kind of place.'

'Right! Let's have a look at him.'

'It's a she,' he corrected me.

We made our way round to an open air enclosure and as I saw the llama, I stopped so suddenly, Charlie coming behind, bumped into me. I stared, amazed, a bowly legged llama!

'You know, the last time I saw anything like that was in the streets of Glasgow during and after the war when you would see wee men and women with legs like that, caused by lack of a proper diet.'

'Be that the cause then?'

'Yes! It's rickets, of course and it's a deficiency of vitamin D, and also calcium or phosphorus. I don't know what your Pets' Corner place fed this poor beast on. No wonder you got it cheap!'

'Oh, I'm sure you'll be able to put it right, Alex.' Charlie was always good for my ego. He thought I could do anything and after I left for the ministry, he had even more confidence in Bernard, my partner, who although very quiet, unassuming, and perhaps giving the impression in the early days of lacking in confidence became an outstanding vet and absolutely superb surgeon, as he still is.

'Charlie, rickets is irreversible. The damage has been done. The bones have grown and are setting in that curved way. I don't know whether a first class orthopaedic surgeon would break these legs and try to straighten them, but I doubt it.' I had said the wrong thing! 'Right, Alex. Have a go at that!'

'No, no, no, Charlie! You don't understand me. First, I don't know whether its ever been done, second, I'm sure it has never been done in animals, and third, I'm not going to risk laming this poor beast for life by trying. You can always put a football jersey on her and bill her as the only football playing llama in captivity. Lots of the best football players are bowly legged!'

'Surely something can be done? Come on, Alex, I've never known you stuck before.'

That was not true, but our ebullient zoo keeper was the most generous and enthusiastic of men. I gazed at this creature from South America, now resident with animals from all over the world in North

Devon. I, obviously, just to keep Charlie quiet, would have to try something.

'Well, she's not fully grown and her legs could get even worse as she grows. First, we'll get her on to a course of minerals, calcium, phosphorus, vitamin D. Keep her outside. The sunlight helps. Feed her well, be good to her, and to stop the legs bending further, I'll put them in a light plaster for a few weeks. It won't straighten them, but might, hopefully, keep them from getting worse as she grows, but at best it's a patch up job.'

'Right, Alex! I knowed you wouldn't be beat.'

Charlie was quite content; something was being tried, and if any of the public complained, and he was very sensitive to, and hurt by complaints, I knew he would say he had a top class vet treat them! Yes, Charlie was good for the ego!

I had to nip back down to the surgery for a large supply of gypsona, the plaster of paris bandages. We got the team of keepers assembled again, caught and cast the gentle creature, and after soaking each bandage, swathed her legs in gleaming white plaster. The llama looked distinctly odd with four dazzling white legs, and when it walked it seemed as if it was on stilts, and went clump, clump, clump round its pen. For two months it was one of the principal attractions of the zoo and daily there was a crowd highly amused by this high stepping, gentle-eyed, friendly beast which soon realised it was a star. She would come up to the fence hopefully and be given all sorts of tit-bits. If it had been starved and neglected at its previous home, it made up for it at Bristacombe. I do not, to this day, know whether I did the right thing or helped at all, and there were no llama experts in Britain to consult. All I know is that the legs became no worse as the animal grew to its full size, and I am sure it was sorry to lose its plaster legs, for it then also lost its daily crowd of spectators. It was, like many treatments in animals, especially creatures of the wild, or immigrants from other countries, a bit of a patch up job.

Some days later a Mr and Mrs Fordyce came into the surgery with their fine Golden Retriever dog, called simply Goldie, though having come from a long line of champions, he had a much more impressive kennel name. The couple, who were strangers to me, seemed pleasant folk, and clearly very attached to their handsome dog.

'We're new to the district, Mr Cameron,' they informed me, 'and have just come to live at Birleton. We've always had animals and you and your partner were recommended to us for our vets by our farming neighbour, Mr Huxley. In fact he said you were the best vets in Devon.'

'Good for Len!' I laughed, but I think he's exaggerating more than a little. Now, how can I help you today?'

'Goldie is limping and we think it's his paw. He's a bit sorry for himself too.' They lifted the dog on to the table. He really was a lovely creature, soulful brown eyes, proud carriage of the head, straight back and that glorious sweep of golden, wavy hair which is a feature of the Retriever. He was obviously as good-natured as he was handsome and a long tongue came out and washed my face while his tail swept across the table continuously from side to side. His trouble was not hard to find, nor very serious.

'He's got an interdigital cyst, see here, between these two toes. It's all swollen and inflamed, a very common condition. We don't really know what causes it but we have an injection which should put it right.'
I reached for the bottle, measured out a dose, and like all well mannered dogs, Goldie never moved as I slipped the needle in.

'That should clear it up in a few days, but if you like you could soak his foot in warm water and epsom salts morning and night which will hurry things up and soothe the foot.'
They paid cash, observing that their vet in a London suburb would have charged three times as much, and threw open an invitation to call and have a coffee with them any time I was at Birleton. Clearly they wanted to make friends and I thanked them and promised I would call one day.

I happened to be at Len Huxley's farm of High Yeoford only a week later to treat a cow with Red Water and Len spoke highly of his new neighbours.

'They be proper gentlemen, both of 'em,' he told me earnestly. 'They're from away, o' course, but I dare say they can't help that.' I smiled at the friendly Len's verdict on his new neighbours and thought there was quite a contrast between the well groomed Fordyces and Len in his braces and ancient bonnet, but clearly they were already well acquainted. Len was a rough diamond, swarthy of complexion, but with a heart of gold.

'Thanks for the testimonial, by the way, Len.'

'How do ee mean, Mr C?' he always called me Mr C.

'Telling them we were the best vets in Devon.'

'Taint naught but the truth.'

It was a fact that I had never had a failure on Len's farm, and true to form, the Red Water soon cleared up in his cow. Len Huxley was a first class farmer despite appearances and I was glad he was on our side for his word carried considerable weight over a wide area. Like all vets, I had found there were farms where everything always seemed to go right, and others where, despite similar conditions and similar treatments, things went wrong. Success meant a lot to us as we continued to build our young Practice, and expand it steadily year by year.

I had time on my hands so decided to call on the Fordyces in their lovely old manor house, walking up a path through lawns dotted with flowering shrubs of various kinds, and admiring a glorious pink and white Clematis montana growing up the wall of their home right to the upper windows. I was warmly welcomed by the couple, Goldie and two Siamese cats, regaled with coffee and given a brief synopsis of their background. Mr F was a company director in London, but now, in his fifties, had decided to fulfil his yearning to escape to the country, and although he had periodic trips to the capital, much of his business was conducted from his home. They had a family of six, all away from home, except the youngest, at present studying law at Cambridge. After coffee they said, 'Now come and meet the other members of the family.'

They conducted me around, Goldie bouncing along in front of us, and asked me to inspect two lovely Toggenburg goats and three hunter horses in a field behind their home. Ducks, hens, geese, guinea fowl and turkeys wandered around at will, a real pastoral scene. Referring to the horses, they said,

'We don't hunt, but ride a bit,' then asked,

'Well, what do you think of our little estate?'

'Lovely!' I enthused. 'What a delightful place to live and work.'

'It's heavenly,' breathed Mrs Fordyce, 'we've dreamt of doing this for years, but we're pretty ignorant, real townies and we'll be calling on you for advice frequently.'

'Any time,' I assured them, 'don't hesitate.'

'*Do* call whenever you are passing, Mr Cameron,' and they obviously meant it.

That was the beginning of a growing acquaintanceship with the couple. I did call several times in the next few months for our farms at little Birleton had a spell when they seemed to be in regular need of a vet, and over the summer I met most of the Fordyce family on visits to their parents. They were really grand folk whom it was a joy to know. To see people so blissfully happy with their lot was a delight to behold.

Summer passed, and autumn was just beginning to give way to the first cold touch of winter's hand. The prevailing south westerlies had all but stripped the trees of leaves, and I was glad on night calls that the modern cars, unlike my first, had small heaters in them. One night late the phone rang. It was Mrs Fordyce, clearly very upset.

'Oh, Mr Cameron! I'm so sorry to call you so late but I'd appreciate it if you could come out. Leonard's away and Goldie is very ill.'

'Sorry to hear that, Mrs Fordyce. I'll be out right away, but what exactly seems to be Goldie's trouble?'

'Oh, several things . . .' She started to sob. 'It's horrible. Please hurry.'

I drove to Birleton Manor wondering what calamity could have overtaken the dog sufficient to cause such distress in a sensible person like Mrs Fordyce. One of her daughters, evidently home for a few days, opened the door to me and conducted me to the kitchen where the never-out Raeburn gave a cosy glow on that cold night. As at the zoo, once again I stopped, as if smitten, and stared in concern at my patient. He was certainly not the Goldie I had come to know. The big dog lay on a carpet in front of the stove, his neck stretched out, his rib cage heaving rapidly, his coat dirty and dishevelled, but what really transfixed my eyes was his near hind leg. It was grossly swollen and on the end of it was a foot that was no longer a foot but a huge, club like appendage, just barely attached to the leg. It was black in colour, about four times the normal size, the toes swollen and distended like huge sausages. A great deep groove above the foot went right down to the bone, over which skin and muscle had disappeared, revealing the naked bone. I did not need the voice of Len Huxley to say at that moment,

'Gin-trap, Mr C. Ought to be a law against it!'

I had not noticed Len till now, and glanced round the comfortable, well appointed kitchen. Mrs Fordyce was sitting in a chair, twisting her handkerchief in her hands, sobbing quietly to herself, and the daughter's eyes were also swollen from weeping. Mrs Fordyce looked up and said,

'Thank you for c-coming so quickly. Leonard's been in America in business for ten days. What a homecoming for him! Goldie went missing the day he left and only came back tonight. We've been searching everywhere for him every day, reported his disappearance to the police, and I was just g-going up to bed tonight when I heard him crying at the back door. He was lying there with that dreadful thing on his leg.

Oh, . . . it was horrible.' She broke down and cried again at the recollection. 'There was just Fiona and me and we couldn't open that awful trap. We phoned Len and he came over and got it off, bless him. He'd been in bed too.'

Len looked a bit embarrassed, took off his bonnet, twisted it between his hands and muttered, 'Taint nuthin! What be neighbours for?'

I examined the dog's foot carefully and gently. It was clear at a glance that nothing could save that paw and the bottom part of the leg. Blood vessels, tendons, nerves had all been severed and the bone was roughened and gouged out with the iron jaws of the trap as Goldie had tugged and twisted to free himself from this terrible object that was cutting deep into his leg and causing indescribable agony. It was an all too common picture in these post-war years when gin traps were still widely used. I wondered what, if anything, the person who had set that trap would feel as he looked at this end product of his handiwork. Possibly nothing for 'taint agin the law be it?' The dog had presumably been caught ten days ago as he wandered off to search for his master. He had had nothing to eat or drink as was obvious by his lean frame, and when he had finally uprooted the trap he had clearly dragged himself a long way. Obviously, the trap setter had not checked this trap for at least ten days, which was criminal, and this . . . this obscenity was the result. It would mean an amputation, but Goldie was also far through, with a temperature of 106°F, the lungs under my stethoscope giving the ominous sounds of a raging pneumonia, the stress of the terrible, constant pain, total exhaustion, hypothermia, starvation and toxaemia from that wholly gangrenous paw. The whole thing added up to a very sick animal indeed.

'Will it mean him losing the leg?' asked Fiona.

'I'm afraid so, though dogs can manage fine on three legs, but first we've got to save him. He's very ill tonight.'

'Do you really think you can cure him, Mr Cameron?' asked the lady of the house. 'I'd rather you told us straight.'

'Mrs Fordyce, I can only try. The leg looks horrible, but more serious tonight is this bad pneumonia, the poison that's swirling through his body, and the shock of it all to the system. I know that you'll give him the best possible nursing and if we can get over the next few days, there's a fair chance. We'll ignore the leg tonight, for I doubt he could stand an anaesthetic right now, but first thing in the morning when Ann my assistant comes in, we'll consider surgery. We'll leave him with you in front of the fire for he's warmer than he would be in our kennels, treat the shock and general condition, give him something for the pain which will also make him sleep, and perhaps in the morning you can bring him down to the surgery. I'm sure Len will help.'

'O' course, anything at all. Now don't 'ee worry, Mistress. Us's had three cats lose legs in gins an' they all got over it, caught mice again too.'

So I gave the big Retriever a shot of morphine which would take him away from pain for the night, a hefty dose of mixed antibiotic, and an injection for shock. I stayed till I saw him drop into a deep sleep, we covered him with a blanket, and left him.

'Try to get some sleep, ladies,' I said, but I knew that mother and daughter would probably sit up all night.

'Thank goodness Leonard will be back tomorrow,' Mrs F murmured, then recollecting her duties as a hostess, exclaimed, 'Oh, I'm sorry, I haven't offered you or Len any tea. I can soon get it.'

'Nay, missus, don't ee bother,' said Len. 'Oi be off 'ome to bed an' don't ee worry. It'll be alright, you'll see. Mr C saved our cats,' and the kind hearted but far from genteel farmer awkwardly patted the lady's hand. 'Same with you, miss,' he said to the daughter, 'these traps be works o' the devil, but animals can stand a lot. Your dog will be running around in no time.'

Len's prediction proved partly true. It was a risk with such a sick dog, but next morning, with Ann assisting expertly and watching the anaesthetic with great care, we amputated Goldie's leg high enough up to give us non-gangrenous tissue which would heal properly, and enough healthy muscle and skin to stitch and give a good pad for the stump. It took a bit longer than Len's 'no time' for Goldie to be running around, but eventually he was. Bernard and I were responsible for the fact that quite a number of dogs, and even more cats in the area were going through life on three legs, and coping wonderfully, but it was the kind of surgery that gave me no satisfaction, always, I felt, a patch up job.

The Fordyces were very grateful and said so, Goldie gradually adapted to life without one leg, and as I stroked his head at Birleton Manor a few weeks later I thought, 'Better a patch up than no job at all.'

There were many occasions in my ministry at Aldermouth when I was called to try to 'patch up' some problem too. When first I arrived, I discovered there were no Social Workers or Marriage Guidance Counsellors in the town. Our Kirk Session wrote to the authorities, pointed out this lack, two post-graduate students used our premises as headquarters for a whole winter's survey, and to our astonishment the town was flooded with, initially, six experts. Previously all the problems labelled under Social Work had been devolved to the ministers and doctors. Ministers were, of course, not really trained for this particular kind of thing, but after the initial rush to the Social Workers, I found a curious thing happened. Many with problems seemed to prefer the minister to the professional Social Worker. I am not sure why. Perhaps it was because I was by then well known; perhaps the minister was preferred to the professional because they did not become cases on files, no notes were kept, and no details repeated to anyone and maybe, just maybe, in some cases, excellent though the work of the Social Workers was some felt, wrongly I'm sure there was a more sympathetic, listening ear with the minister. Whatever the reason, the crowd kept coming. I remember in one week, after the oil boom hit Aldermouth, three young wives came separately to me to ask if I could help in their marriage problems, three girls who had not the slightest connection with any Church, but were at their wits' end. This sort of thing went on all the time.

Typical were Billy and Sylvia, whom I had married in my early days. Billy was a wild loon, had come from a broken home in a nearby town, and not without some misgiving, I had married him to Sylvia, who was from a good, steady home, but, like Billy, had not the slightest interest in Church except as a 'nice' place to be married. Billy was one of the boys, a hard drinker, rough and ready, by no means unintelligent, but evidently felt that life, whether as a bachelor or a husband, was for living, for him alone, and proceeded to do so in his own swaggering manner. From early on there was trouble and several times Sylvia or her mother came to see me to talk over problems that had arisen. Mind you, the faults were not all on one side. They seldom are. Eventually, I would speak with Billy and things would be patched up for a time.

Then a baby arrived. Billy was delighted with his wee bairn, and all was serene for a time. But only for a time, alas. Periodically I would visit them and try to talk some sense into the situation, and in particular make Billy realise his responsibilities. I was constantly patching up. Then Sylvia's father died, a good man, quiet, unassuming, a mediating influence. Now Billy became the man of the family, now he would decide everything. Regularly he would break out into an orgy of wild living . . . and yet there was a likeable bit about him despite his rough ways and mode of life. To my great delight, he got involved with one of the youth organisations of the Church, became a junior leader, and the responsibility seemed to steady him. It was marvellous to see him in Church weekly and I hoped we had turned the corner. So indeed it seemed for a time. The baby grew, the couple got a new house, and in due course a second child was well on the way. But gradually Billy drifted away again, and Sylvia came to me one evening in an appalling state. She had clearly been misused, told me, what was obvious, that Billy was beating her and the night before, though over eight months' pregnant, had knocked her down. I had patched and patched at that marriage and now I saw red.

I went straight out to their home and confronted Billy. He was brash, cocky, wild, 'what's it to you' in his attitude. By now I knew them so well I felt I could talk like a Dutch uncle, and gave him a piece of my mind in far from gentle, distinctly non-ministerial language. I pointed out it took a really brave man to knock down his pregnant wife, as he had done. He rose from his chair blood in his eyes, mouthing curses as he came towards me, and I really thought he was going to strike me, and rather hoped he would! I was much more a wild vet confronted by a bull at that moment than a gentle minister. I am afraid in that situation I would have found it difficult to turn the other cheek, but then the Bible also tells us to defend the weak, and speaks of righteous indignation.

'Go on, then, Billy, have a go at someone your own size. Have a go at me.'

I really do not know what I would have done if he had, but I am afraid I would have flattened him. He glared for a time, mouthed more insults, and then threw himself in a chair. Once more I tried, calm again, to mediate and patch up what had become an almost hopeless situation. On the way home I thought with some shame, of my reaction, then remembered Dr Barclay's words.

'Anger for oneself is nearly always wrong for a Christian. Anger for others might very well be right.'

There was no more wife battering, but a fortnight later when Sylvia was in hospital having their baby, Billy nipped off to live and sleep with someone else. That, alas, was the end of things. Separation and divorce followed. The trouble with patches, I felt sadly, is that they do not always hold and if the garment they are patched to is rotten, they tear away, which, after all, is what the Master Teacher said about it.

Many were the patch-up jobs I tried. Some, praise the Lord, succeeded, like the middle aged wife who came to me in great distress to say that her man was out drinking till one o'clock every morning, and then going out next day and working an enormous crane at the yard, high up on the platform, and putting lives at risk. That patch seemed to stick, but sadly, as I look back, though I did a lot of stitching, hour after hour, days and days of reasoning, counselling, advising, pleading, praying, many, like Goldie, finally resulted in an amputation. But I felt I had to try, spending much time and nervous energy, often with people with no Church connection, like the woman who came to me with a black eye and announced,

'My man gied me this last nicht. I didna ken whether to come to you or go to the polis but I thought I'd try you first!'

It was wearing, wearying, often disappointing work, but I felt that where there was any hope at all, I must try, and after all, there is no disgrace in a patch, as my mother used to say, provided it holds.

I sometimes felt guilty in my later years at Aldermouth that I was in danger of spending more time with non-Church members than with my own flock as my life would be taken up with social or personal problems, but then I would remember the words of the great healer.

'They that be whole need not a physician, but they that are sick', and from time to time, as I saw a couple sitting together in Church or walking as a family in the High Street, a patch up job, like Ham, the llama and Goldie, this kind of surgery, seemed quite a worthwhile thing after all.

The constant question

SEVENTEEN

Like, I suppose, most people, my favourite months of the year are May and June. The winter is past, the days have grown longer and warmer, trees are bursting into new life, fields have greened with their covering of that marvellous crop, grass, roadsides and banks are aglow with a multitude of wild flowers, providing homes and nurture for a myriad of tiny creatures. In Devon the lanes would be spangled with bright yellow primroses, making them a delight to drive along, and on the road to the little village of Lee, just outside Bristacombe, by June, fuchsia was growing wild along the hedgerows. The annual miracle of nature had occurred once more and the earth was touched with a fresh beauty, like a young girl prepared and adorned for her first party.

In our veterinary world, the noises of the lambing pens had died away, spring calving cows had produced their offspring, end of winter conditions like acetonaemia in cattle and twin-lamb disease in ewes were over for another year, and in the Practice, we would have time to draw breath once more. It was a period of rejoicing and relaxation for Bernard and I, and for Ann and Janet, on the end of the phone. In fact it was marred for me by only one thing. When May and June came along, farmers thought it was time to have their yearling, or sometimes two year old colts castrated. I dreaded this annual event as on castration days I was tensed up in the morning as I contemplated the day ahead. The reason for this tension was that I was not really a horseman. Oh yes, I could treat horses and in my ten years in practice and my years as a student treated many hundreds, for all sorts of conditions, and for the most part with success. I knew as well as the next man the symptoms of the various equine diseases and disorders, and how to cope with them. But I early came to the conclusion that a real horseman was born, not made, one who seemed instinctively to understand and empathise with a horse, and was absolutely at home and at ease around a stable. For myself, although I could admire the beauty of a handsome young colt or filly, I was more at home with other animals so far as understanding them and treating them were concerned. In our vet course, oddly enough, the horse was still king, classed as number one, and everything else a poor second.

In many areas of the land there would be someone who had the reputation of being a horse expert and he would travel the countryside for weeks cutting the colts, rigs and even sometimes full grown stallions that had not made the grade at stud. This was particularly so in the true horse breeding districts of Britain, and in places like Newmarket where there were dozens of thoroughbred stables. But North Devon was off the beaten track for these experts, and for the most part our horses consisted of ponies or hunters, which were on every farm, the occasional thoroughbred and the surviving working horses, the great majestic heavy breeds like Shire, Clydesdale or Suffolk Punch. So the farmers were quite content to use their own vets. They did the job perfectly well and cost a lot less than the horse consultants in their Bentleys and Jaguars.

For years the traditional method of castrating a horse was to cast it with ropes, chloroform it, truss up its legs to expose the site, and then operate, but surgery in the standing position had become popular with many owners. It was less trouble provided the horse was quiet and behaved itself; it required fewer men to assist, and being carried out under local anaesthetic, it avoided the slight risk attached to chloroform. However, I hated it, it was a dangerous business for the operator and I was convinced it was also a less efficient surgical procedure. Normally Kenneth or I, or after Kenneth left, Bernard and I would go out together to do the job, and I can still hear the rattling of our instruments in their dishes in the back of the car on our way to castrations. It sounded to me like the knell of doom. Occasionally, if the horse was being done in the standing position, I would go by myself to do the job.

That was the case one May morning at Park farm where Dr Fulton had a fine herd of Ayrshires, a flock of North Country Cheviot sheep, which he had brought south from Sutherland, and a few horses. Dr Fulton was a nationwide figure, having been Principal of an Agricultural College in Scotland for years, then agricultural adviser to a large Arab country, until he finally settled in a very fertile area on the edge of our practice. I held him somewhat in awe at first, for he was a clever, knowledgeable man, well versed in all the ways of animals, and while he always treated me with courtesy, I was conscious, senior partner though I was, of my relative youth and inexperience compared to him. He was probably our biggest and most lucrative client, and in the early days when he came to us, I was always apprehensive lest something go wrong. But I had done quite a bit with his sheep, treated many of his pedigree Ayrshires for all kinds of ailments, and also his horses, with complete success, until the week before I set out to castrate his colt which he specified be done in the standing position.

I had been treating a cow with a bad Staphylococcal mastitis, a very serious condition, even with the advent of the wonder antibiotics. Mastitis is, of course, inflammation of the udder and most cases responded to treatment since most were caused by the Streptococcal organism, which penicillin soon cleared up. But a Staphylococcal mastitis was a different kettle of fish. The udder would become as hard as a board, the discharge be foul smelling and teeming with organisms, and very frequently and very quickly, the infection would spread throughout the whole body until the cow was suffering from septicaemia, or blood poisoning. One of Dr Fulton's best cows had developed this as soon as it calved, and despite daily visits, massive doses of serum, antibiotics and other drugs, had grown rapidly worse, and when I had seen it the day before, it was just clinging to life and no more.

I arrived at Park farm to be given the news the cow had died that morning, which did not put me in the best of spirits for my surgery. However, work has to go on. The colt, a beautiful bay, was brought out of the stable by Dr Fulton's son, and positioned with one side against a wall. I laid my instruments in their steriliser and enamel dishes on a bale of straw, and scrubbed up to begin. A twitch (a stick with a loop of rope on the end) was applied to the pony's upper lip by the son, and twisted till it was really tight. This was an age old method of restraint and the idea was that the horse would be so taken up with the wretched thing on his nose, he would not pay too much attention to what was happening elsewhere. I cleaned the scrotum and inguinal area thoroughly with antiseptic, gingerly injected local anaesthetic into testicles and spermatic cord, all safe so far, scrubbed my hands again, then reaching for a scalpel made my incision. Just then, though feeling no pain, the horse realised what was being done to it, and proceeded to rear, kick and plunge about.

'Screw up that twitch,' I shouted to the son, who had the twitch in one hand, a halter in the other. Still the animal pranced about, at the worst possible time, with the incision made, bleeding, and liable with its kicking to get dirt into the wound. Dr Fulton whistled up a couple of men and they leaned against the little horse's side, pressing it hard to the wall. Then I used the emasculator to crush the cord, artery forceps to stop the bleeding, and the testicles were removed. I again cleaned the whole area with antiseptic solution, puffed sulphanilamide powder into the wound, gave a shot of penicillin and an anti-tetanus jab, checked that the haemorrhage had more or less stopped, and proceeded to gather up my instruments with a sigh of relief.

'A bit tricky, Mr Cameron, but a nice clean job,' said the Doc. 'I'm very fond of that little fellow, you know, and glad things have worked out so well.'

'Oh, he should do alright. I'd turn him into a nice clean paddock where you can keep an eye on him today, or if you prefer it, keep him in a loose box, but they usually do better outside. Let me know if he bleeds or if you have any trouble.'

I was taken into the house where Mrs Fulton had a welcome cup of coffee ready, and being both Ayrshire men in a 'foreign' country, we talked of home and discovered mutual acquaintances. Then for the road home and a couple more straightforward cases on the way, the instruments this time, I felt, playing a merry tune in their dishes.

Three days later I had a phone call to say the pony was very swollen and stiff, and scarcely grazing at all. I called, not worrying over much for post-operative swelling and stiffness were not unusual, but a temperature of 105°F had me worried. I examined the wound, with difficulty, for he was very tender there. I did not like the look of it; there had been a little bleeding which was collected in a sac of the scrotum, so, using the twitch again, I enlarged the wound and drained it. I did not like either the colour or the odour of the discharge and so really hit him with a massive dose of antibiotic, bathed the wound, and left instructions to bathe it twice more that day, and I would call again. Next morning he was worse, the swelling was spreading down his rear legs, the whole inguinal area a dirty colour, and the poor little fellow a thoroughly miserable animal. I syringed out the whole of the scrotum with a powerful antiseptic solution, then dusted the wound again with sulphanilamide, and again giving a large injection of antibiotic, departed, a worried man. So it went on.

I could not sleep for thinking about my patient, nor could I understand it. I had never had this trouble with any castration before, went over the whole procedure in my mind again, and concluded that somehow, in his prancing about during the op, or perhaps from the soil of the paddock, he had got that same Staph bug which had killed the cow.

On the seventh day when I called, I was met by a somewhat frigid Dr Fulton.

'He's just died, I'm afraid,' then he went on, 'You haven't had much success here lately, have you, but some people are like that. Maybe you've just been unlucky.' I fully understood the implied criticism in his remark, but in my gloomy state I felt just a little hurt by it when I considered all the previous successes I had had at his farm, and that I had tried to save his colt. All I could say was, 'I'm sorry; very sorry. It's no consolation, I know, but I've never lost a colt before.' Nor did I again.

No coffee appeared that day, and I felt sure I had lost our biggest client, but I imagine as he thought things through, for he was a fair man, he must have decided I could not entirely be held responsible. Despite disappointments, life has to go on, and I had plenty to occupy me for the rest of the day to keep me busy.

Getting back in the early evening from my afternoon round, I found a large dog tied to our operating table with a piece of string. There was a note on the desk to say he was to be put down, having more or less gone berserk at Martincombe where he lived, bitten several people, and terrified the whole terrace. Now I knew that dog. I had visited him once at his house for some minor complaint, and even with a tape muzzle securely fastened and the owner, a big, husky fellow, holding him as firmly as he could, he had struggled, fought and snarled in a pretty terrifying fashion. Apart from a St Bernard and Newfoundland I had treated, he was the biggest dog I had ever seen, an alsatian crossed with, I suspected, a tiger, and here I was, alone with him in the surgery, and somehow I had to get near him and give him an injection. Why not shoot him, I can hear you ask? Well, I did not possess a gun, and even if I had, shooting in a surgery with a dwelling house above is somewhat frowned upon. Even my humane killer was no better, for that still required holding the dog and putting the instrument to his head.

He was uttering the most fearsome snarls which confirmed my suspicion of his tiger ancestry, showing his teeth, ears laid back, lashing about on his restraining bit of thick string. I filled my syringe with Euthatal, and paused to consider how I could get near him, when lo, I did not need not wonder any more, for suddenly he was near me, his cord having parted like thread. He leapt for my throat and I leapt back in considerable alarm, and before I knew it, he was chasing me round the surgery, and somehow I did not think he wanted to lick my face!

I kept on the move, being careful to have the operating table between us, and praying fervently I would not slip or trip, for without question he would have torn me to shreds. I realised I had only one hope, being all alone in our premises, and that was to somehow get a dog catcher and restrain him with that. We possessed several of these, long hollow metal tubes with a rope running through them, ending in a loop which you tried to drop over a dog's head and pull tight. Unfortunately, though, the dog catchers were all kept hanging on a hook in the passage outside the surgery and I wondered how I could reach the door in one piece, and at all costs I must not let this mad creature out of the door and possibly on to the street. So I went on the offensive, roared and snarled at the dog, pushed the table on its wheels in his direction and leapt for the door. Collecting the strongest catcher I could find, I cautiously re-opened the door. He was waiting for me just inside, and sprang at me. I fought him off with the metal rod, then the positions were reversed, as I started stalking him around the room, trying to drop the noose over his head.

I don't know how long it all went on, but it seemed forever. eventually the dog stopped, clearly puzzled about what to do next, and I had him. The noose went round his neck and I pulled it up as tight as I could until he was half throttled. It was far from scientific, in fact it was downright brutal, a horrible way to treat an animal, but this animal was prepared to kill, and it was him or me. He struggled with immense strength and ferocity, and I kept on pulling the cord, cutting off his air supply. Eventually, in his struggles to free himself, he fell on his side, and immediately I threw myself on top of him, reached up for my loaded syringe, and injected the Euthatal into his peritoneum. This was a slower way to destroy a dog, but it was quite painless, and I had no hope in our wrestling match of hitting a vein to produce instant death.

Gradually he relaxed as the drug took effect, and I was able to slacken the rope. He passed into a sleep, and when unconscious, I gave him another dose into a vein and in seconds he was gone. At least his end had been painless, which was more than mine would have been, I was sure, if he had succeeded in catching me.

It took me some time to stop trembling, but eventually I drove home, had a late tea, recounted the day's work to Janet, who was horrified at my encounter with that wild dog, and shared with me in my disappointment at losing the colt. As always, when talking to her, and reliving the fight to save the horse, things looked better, and seemed less like the end of the world. That has always been one of the wonderful things about my wife. She would share to the full with me in the happenings of my work, but always have the ability to point out certain basic things, make me see events in a different light and lift me up. Life with her has always been a total partnership.

Although my whole life as a vet was concerned with disease, sickness and death, I cannot recall ever philosophising much about the whole question of suffering. Only occasionally was I moved to wonder, or indeed to anger. Perhaps when trying to save a sea bird burned through and through with oil because of man's heedlessness or carelessness in its vast world of the ocean, and suffering with the silence of its kind, occasionally the whole moral dilemma came home to me. Again, when having to put down a perfectly healthy dog which was just unwanted or as when watching Dr Fulton's colt suffer, and go down fighting, just on such occasions I would ponder and question. But although the constant question of *why* suffering was there in the animal kingdom, it was only as a minister it came home to me, and became, indeed *the* constant question. Why all this suffering?

Of course there were the many glad occasions in the ministry like weddings, baptisms, work with children, seeing young people grow up straight and true, and the constant joy of preaching the glad news of the gospel. Yet was the gospel not also about one who had suffered and died? In addition, hardly a week went past without some family knowing illness, pain, anxiety and death. In Aldermouth we had a hundred funerals a year in our Church, two a week on average, and this became *the* constant question of my ministry, the thing I have been asked times without number. 'Why? Why suffering? Why sorrow?'

Sometimes one could give a ready answer. I recall at Moorton one day heading for the hospital for my weekly visits, and being overtaken at speed on a corner by a Mini. It was a wet day, the road was slippery with a sort of skin on top of it, and care was required. Just around another bend, about a mile on, I came on the Mini right across the road, lying on its side, its wheels still spinning. I stopped my car as did several others, and we helped the occupants of the stricken car to safety. Fortunately no one was really hurt, but all were shaken, and out of that little car came five adults, three children and a dog. The car's tyres were bald as a coot, obvious in its upside down position. I was wearing my clerical collar, and at the sight of this, a middle aged woman from the tilted car rounded on me in anger and demanded, 'Why did your God do this to us?' An overloaded car, going too fast on a wet road and a bend, with bald tyres, and it was God's fault that they had crashed! I thought, as we pushed their car upright again, they should have been on their knees thanking God they were still alive despite their folly.

There are instances in life when we can see the cause of suffering very clearly. If a man gets behind the wheel of a car with drink in him and kills a child, the source of blame is clear. If I smoke, despite the government warnings, I must be prepared for the consequences. If a person is promiscuous, can he or she really wonder if they get *Aids*, and so on. Many instances where we bring suffering or eventual death on ourselves. But there are the many others. As I have noted, sorrow came to some Aldermouth family virtually every week, and many times I have stood at the graveside with a question in my heart, and visiting the bereaved family later, seeking to bring the consolations of the gospel, feeling very helpless in the face of their questions when the heart is broken. Studdart Kennedy, 'Woodbine Willie', the famous Chaplain of the Great War, once said, 'the person who is not moved by suffering and grief is either hard in the heart or soft in the head', for every death brought heartache to somebody.

I suppose, after doctors, ministers see more of death than anyone else, and many people feel we get used to it, even get hardened, and after all it is our job. I have never 'got used' to the fact of death, and on innumerable occasions have stood beside the bed of one of my folks who over the years had become a friend, and would willingly have given my right arm to relieve them. Especially I found the death of a young person hard, and we had a spell in Aldermouth when it seemed as if every day was bringing bad news.

Three bright young men, at about the same time, contracted

leukaemia and one looked on in wonder at their courage as they fought this thing whose very name produced a pall of fear. They battled, and were at times amazingly cheerful, but all were taken, and terrible indeed to behold was the parents' grief. I had only to look at my own young sons of the same age range to know how the parents felt. Then there was John, a brilliant young man in his early thirties who developed a particularly virulent form of cancer, and had the whole range of treatment. After some months he came to my Vestry Hour one week with a young lady, and announced they had decided, despite the circumstances, to go ahead and be married. I concurred in their decision to have some happiness together, however long or short, for both knew the situation to the full. It was a particularly poignant wedding, and was, understandably, totally desolate; folks spoke of the foolishness of their marriage, but I was glad that they, like so many couples in the war, had even these few months together.

In rapid succession three of my younger elders died, one the local schoolmaster who was one of my closest friends, a man who had so much to give to school, Church and community. I remember the tremendous shock to staff and pupils when I had to announce his death to the whole school one morning. Fit, strong, in the prime of life, he had been golfing the evening before. Why Lord?

Eric trained the local Highland League football team, have given our own son Ian his first chance in senior football at the age of fifteen, as he had done with many other young people. Yet this man, who was infinitely gentle and kind, but would not countenance either dirty language or dirty play, no matter how great the star player, and had an immense power for good in many lives, the most respected man in northern football, was taken. Why Lord?

Donnie, a quiet, unassuming man had brought up his four daughters well, and they, with their parents, were in Church every Sunday and involved in the life of the organisations, and in addition, as the town gardener, had annually created so much beauty for locals and visitors alike to enjoy, yet was also snatched away young. Why Lord?

One evening I had a phone call informing me there had been an air crash at Sullom Voe and included in the casualties was an Aldermouth lad of nineteen. I did not really know the boy, they were a non-Church family, but I recall well that message given by the boy's aunt.

'I believe in God, Mr Cameron, and I know death is not the end, but I don't know what my sister and her husband believe, but could you please come down and try to help, and would you be willing to take the funeral?'

I went immediately to the house, wondering, as so often, what I could possibly say. Often, I am sure, I failed, but often too it is amazing how one is given a word that will help. I met with that family in their deep grief, and among other things told them of Willie Barclay, my old New Testament lecturer and his experience. He too had lost a nineteen year old daughter in a drowning accident, his only girl. At the time he wrote a letter to a friend which included the triumphant words.

'We who believe know that while this is the end of the chapter it is not the end of the book. Barbara has many chapters still to write.' There speaks the confidence of faith, and without that same belief, I would never have dared take a funeral.

It has been said that sorrow either drives us to God, or from God, and I have seen both often. In the case of the lad in the air crash, his parents were drawn to seek consolation from a Father who had Himself lost a Son, and such a seeker never seeks in vain. I took the funeral when our large Church was filled to its 1000 capacity, hundreds of those attending being young people meeting death for the first time. I have never forgotten the tremendous hush and stillness, which was later repeated at the graveside. Even the hardest of hearts could not fail to be moved and to feel that even in this stark tragedy, the Lord was truly there, for 'in all their afflictions He was afflicted.'

Two brothers, sons of a widow, were killed together in a car crash and as I again conducted this funeral and visited the mother regularly afterwards, she said to me one day, 'I didna' think I could get through, Mr Cameron, and I couldna' see hoo I could manage to go on and wasna' sure I wanted to go on, but He gied me the strength one day at a time,' . . . a sentiment many have expressed to me over the years . . . one day, even one hour at a time . . . but why, Lord? Why the sorrow? Why so often the best people who seem to be taken? Many times I felt like weeping with the family at the funeral, but somehow one has to keep going for the sake of all the mourners present, and one does.

The death of little children; cot deaths, the death of a baby, were all particularly hard and the grief of the mother often so terrible and so private, that I felt I could not intrude, only be available.

In the face of all this weight of sorrow, what does one say, for even in the passing of someone who had lived a full life there would be a wife or husband left, or a family. It is hard and I have often felt I did no good at all, as hard though one tries, as with Dr Fulton's pony, it is a losing battle. Many times too, recalling my fight with that big, vicious dog, I felt there was something evil, something demonic, at the heart of things.

One morning our Dr John phoned me. He had just come from the home of Mrs Baxter, for her husband had gone into the bathroom that morning to shave, taken a massive coronary, and died instantly. They had to break down the door to get in. The Baxters were a retired and retiring couple, closely knit and childless. Mrs Baxter in particular, though she was a fine woman, being a shy person by nature, not outgoing, and with perhaps few close friends in this new area.

'Can you go out?' asked Dr John, 'and tell Mrs Baxter what you said on Sunday in your sermon. I think it might help. I couldn't recall it exactly for her.'

'Oh, John,' I protested, 'I can't remember my sermons. They aren't worth remembering. What was it you had in mind?'

'That definition you gave of death. It's the best I've heard,' said our good and godly doctor.

I remembered now. I had come across it in a book written by a young minister's widow, and she had included this description. I don't believe it was hers originally, for Joyce Grenfell quotes the same words, but I had latched on to it as both practical and beautiful.

I sat with Mrs Baxter for a time, then she said, 'The Doctor said you had some words that might help me.' The Baxters were normally in Church every week and would have heard the quote, but had missed the previous Sunday. So I gave her the definition which had helped me, and I believe it helped her:

'Life is eternal' (it does not end here)

'Love is immortal' (it does not end here either. 'We'll meet again')

'Death is but a horizon, and a horizon is only the limit of our sight.'

That sums it up, and is true to the teaching of the only One who ever Himself conquered death and who said, 'In my Father's house are many dwelling places. Why, if it were not so, would I have told you.' I like that confident assertion, 'if it were not so'. So, in the confidence that her man was but out of sight over the horizon and that death could not destroy, only separate in the body for a time, Mrs Baxter and many another, have laid their loved ones to rest.

'Now you're preaching, Cameron,' I can hear many readers say. 'Of course you ministers would say something like that.' Maybe, but over the years if I had not believed in Life Eternal before, I would have been forced to by the experience of countless souls I have known in the vale of tears. But still there remains that 'why suffering?', that constant question. You know, I think for us mere mortals, it will have to remain for the present.

Dr Sangster, the great Methodist preacher, and a saintly man who himself died quite young, put it well in a little story. A boy had gone off to an organised camp with some of his friends. He was given enough pocket money to last him the week, but in two days it had all gone. So he wrote a hurried postcard home, which basically said, 'Out of cash, send by return, RSVP instantly. Love Tom'. But no reply came. His pals, who were also bankrupt and hoping to share in the loot said,

'He can't have got your card.' Tom did not think that very likely.

'Well, your Dad's forgotten all about you.' Tom knew that was not so.

'Well, it can only mean he doesn't care about you.' Tom was certain that was not true. Finally they asked,

'Well, what do you think yourself? Why has he not done what you asked?' Tom thought for a bit, then said,

I don't understand it, but I'll ask him when I get home.'

I too am content to wait till Home to learn the answer to that constant question, why?

The hand that feeds

EIGHTEEN

'Hello!' bellowed the phone at me.

'Hello!' I subconsciously bellowed back.

'Hello!' double forte, came the roar. I held the instrument further from my ear.

'Yes, hello!' I managed to keep it quiet this time. 'Bristacombe 250.'

'Hello! This danged machine be'nt workin.' There was a thunder in my ear. The speaker had obviously banged the receiver on something. 'That's better! Ah can hear it speak now. Be that the vetnary?'

'Yes, Cameron speaking.'

'What's that? Dang me, it be'nt talkin' yet! This is Bill Narracott,' came a roar like a bull, which nearly burst my ear-drum.

'Hello, Mr Narracott,' I shouted, 'Mr Cameron speaking. What's your trouble?'

'Trouble? It be this blasted talkin' thing. It don't seem to speak straight!'

Despite my tingling ear-drum, I smiled to myself. Bill Narracott and brother Bert, in an old-fashioned part of the world, the West Country, where life was slower than in many other places, were even more old-fashioned than most. They were middle-aged bachelors who lived in a tumble-down farmhouse with ancient buldings. They still had horses for work and a minimum of machinery. Their farm and stock was their sole interest in life. They dressed in the thick trousers popular years ago, had for their top an ex-army tunic or some old flapping jacket, their caps were green with age, they appeared to wash but seldom and shaved maybe once a week. I did not think they had the phone installed in their farm of Barton Mill over Mortecombe way, and consequently they generally approached the instrument with mystification. Mr Narracott's next words proved me right.

'Oi be speakin from Ossaboro, Vetnary,' (the neighbouring farm) 'Us 'as a dead bullock – struck with lightin'. You'll 'ave to come out.'

'Right, Mr Narracott, I'll be out as soon as I can. Lightning eh? That's a surprise. I don't think we had lightning in Bristacombe last night.'

'What's that, young man?' came the bellow, angry now.

'I just said I'm surprised at the lightning. We had none over here.'

'No? Well . . .' came the voice. (There was no actual lightning but plenty of thunder over the air, I thought) 'Us 'ad it here. Must 'ave, else how could our good bullock be dead, eh?' It was undeniable logic to Bill!

'Righto. I'll be with you shortly.'

I was glad to put the receiver down. My head was singing with the assault on my ear-drums, especially first thing in the morning. We were at breakfast and our boys were clearly puzzled.

'Shout! Daddy shouting in a big voice,' said young Neil.

I smiled at our eldest son, aged at the time about three, sitting at his breakfast that June morning. Little Ian, some seventeen months his junior, was propped up in his high chair and he proceeded to show he could shout too.

'Quiet, Ian!' I said, my voice inadvertently still raised.

'No need to shout, dear,' said Janet.

'Och – I didn't mean to. My brain hasn't settled down yet.'

'Are you worried about the case, Alec?' queried my wife.

'A bit. I hate these lightning stroke cases for they are so vague and are always liable to get you into trouble with the client.'

'What a client, Daddy?' piped up Neil. He was always surprising us with his vocabulary, and as typical proud parents, we felt he was very clever for his age, almost in the genius class.

'A client's a man with a sick animal, son, usually a farmer,' I explained.

'Milk comes from farmer,' Neil informed us.

'That's right, drink yours up.'

He obeyed, and Ian, trying to do the same, promptly spilled his. Altogether it was a bad start to the day, and with brothers Bill and Bert Narracott to come, I felt it would very likely get worse.

I set off on my visit, having gulped the rest of my breakfast, and as I drove my little Austin 8 van, I mused that lightning stroke was hardly the best way to get in the good books of farmers and the Narracotts had but recently come to us as the Practice steadily grew in size. Actually they seldom had a vet, using the old remedies peddled by the reps of the old drug firms, and only when a beast was on its last legs did they call the vet. Practically all I had done for them was their annual tuberculin test, when I had got into trouble, for they had one cow that was doubtful, and had to be isolated and re-tested. They were clearly not pleased and it was equally clear they thought I was responsible for this 'blasted red tape'. Fortunately the beast had passed second time round, when they announced that they had known none of their bullocks could possibly be reactors and the whole thing had been just a waste of time, 'a load o' govment nonsense'. Lightning stroke was sometimes impossible to diagnose for there were often just no symptoms nor post-mortem signs. The book said, 'There is generally some amount of scorching, especially about the bases of the horns and at the coronets. There may be an irregular "lightning mark" connecting these places. On removal of the skin, there is generally a streak of bruised subcutaneous tissue seen under the scorched areas, but in other cases there may be no visible signs of the electric shock.' No visible signs, I thought. Helpful! Farmers knew about the 'irregular lightning mark' and some had been known to try to scorch the skin with a candle or even a blow lamp to produce this and convince the vet. If the animal was found under a tree that was sometimes a pointer, but all in all it was an unsatisfactory and unscientific business to diagnose the condition. The great concern of farmers to have lightning stroke diagnosed in every sudden death was that their insurance covered such an emergency, and the vet had to fill in a form for the insurance company testifying lightning as the cause of death and putting a value on the animal. The companies were generally very good at paying up, but often the vet's valuation did not come up to the farmer's expectations and this could lead to trouble.

Bill and Bert were waiting for me outside their antiquated farmhouse, their pipes drawing well, traditional hob nailed, turned up toed boots on their feet, their ancient trousers hitched up at the knees with string, the flapping khaki jackets and even more ancient bonnets, the lining of Bert's sticking out so much it seemed to be outside in. I was dressed in my usual garb of corduroy trousers, unlike some vets of the older school who still wore breeches, and when I pulled on my wellingtons and donned my black waterproof coat, I was ready for the fray.

'Right, gentlemen, where's the beast?'

'Hur be in the paddock,' and they led the way. I followed with my black case. To be exact, the animal was in a fairly deep stream that meandered through the paddock, the water flowing over all but the head, which was resting on the steep-sided bank. Sadly, there was no tree anywhere near, only an electric pylon just over the stream. The animal was a well grown Ruby Red, as the native North Devon cattled were called, about two years old and in good condition.

'Has she been ill at all, off colour, poorly?' I queried.

'Nay – sound as the Bank.'

'Had any trouble with Staggers this year?'

'Nay, but look 'ee here, that thar bullock was killed with lightnin', a'm zertain zure,' said Bert, pointing with his pipe.

'It could well be, Mr Narracott, but you see, in any sudden death we have to make sure it isn't Anthrax first of all, then look for something like Staggers or a Heart Attack, and if we can find nothing else, then it's probably lightning. I'll just take a little blood from her and test it for Anthrax.'

There was nothing for it but to go down into the brook and soon the water was over the top of my wellingtons. I nicked the ear and drew a smear of blood on to a glass slide, stuffed a bit of cotton wool into the ear and scrambled back up the bank.

'I'm afraid we'll have to go back up to the car so that I can look at this blood under the microscope.'

'Blasted nonsense!' exploded Bill, 'a tell ee, it be lightning.'

'You could be right, but you see there are no burn marks on her, and although she's not yet stiff, which points to lightning, where *rigor mortis*, that's stiffening is slow, I would be in deep trouble if I let an Anthrax case go to the knacker's yard.'

'Aar,' grunted Bert, 'that thar govenment has just a lot o' new fangled nonsense.'

I fixed and stained my smear of blood, put the microscope on the bonnet of the car, and in the already bright sunlight of a glorious June morning, had sufficient light to see by. I knew it was no use going into the house to have an electric light shine on the slide, for electricity was one of the many things the brothers did not deem necessary. My procedure was far from satisfactory, but the best I could do, and as I peered down the microscope, I was relieved to find none of the square shapes of Bacillus anthracis, one cause of death eliminated.

'No anthrax, gentlemen,' I spoke up cheerfully, endeavouring to spread a little light around, for Bill and Bert were far from a sunny pair. Thunder was in the air, I felt.

'Back to the bullock now.'

'Now look 'ee here, Mr Vetnary,' said Bert once more, emphasising his words by poking me on the chest, 'oi be zertain our good bullock was killed by lightnin', so why can 'ee not say so now without all this 'ere fuss. That bullock be worth a tidy bit to us, an' us means to have our due.' It was quite a speech for Bert. I nodded and replied, 'Don't worry, Mr Narracott, but you see *I* have to be sure too. Did you hear any thunder or see any lightning through the night?'

'Well . . . no,' reluctantly admitted Bert, 'but the only thing I hear o' nights is Bill snoring.'

So we trudged back to the paddock, I slithered down into the stream, and once more looked at their beast.

'Can you see any marks on her, gentlemen?' I asked.

'Hur hair be kind of standin' up just behind shoulder.' I peered at their bullock and decided Bill was seeing with the eye of imagination, or hope. I looked in the beast's mouth. Sometimes animals were struck down while actually chewing grass, but sudden deaths in June were also common from Staggers, magnesium deficiency. I had no wish to deprive the brothers of their rights, but I had to be as sure as I could be. By now, they were becoming apoplectic as they awaited my decision, puffing their pipes furiously. I scrambled up the far bank, the one where the electric pylon rested, and immediately got a considerable electric shock, even through my rubber boots, which mercifully I was wearing. I gave a yell and hastily splashed back through the water and up the other bank. Why I had not had at least a mild shock in the water I know not, but I was at one and the same time more than a little startled by my narrow escape from electrocution, and relieved that I had a positive diagnosis, very positive.

'Your beast's been electrocuted!' I shouted at the brothers, seemingly quite calmly studying my antics. 'It's a mercy none of you went over that stream, for with the nails in your boots, you could have been killed too. There's been a leak from that pole and the sooner we get the electricty people out here the better. You'll still get your compensation, for your Policy covers electrocution.'

It was hard to tell whether Bert and Bill were more relieved at their escape from possible demise, or delighted at their prospective cheque, for they merely took their pipes from their mouths and gave forth a few 'Aars and Uurs'. We hastily got back to the farmhouse, and while I despatched Bill back to Ossaboro to phone the Electricity Board to send men out at once, Bert and I went into the great stone flagged kitchen with its enormous open fireplace and rough hewn furniture, and after considerable rummaging about in drawers, he eventually extracted an insurance form, which I promised I would fill in that very day.

I went home for a dry pair of socks and my spare wellingtons and while Janet dispensed coffee, I decided to fill in the form and get it off. 'You have to treat the client', we had frequently been reminded at College, and I thought some prompt action might make the Narracotts a little better disposed towards me. The last question on the form, however, had me worried, the estimated value of the animal. I have always felt this was an unfair question for vets. The easy way, of course, was to ask the owner, but while most would give an honest valuation, others would bump it up on the principle that insurance companies were able to afford anything. I have never kept up with the weekly market prices of livestock, so I phoned two Devon cattle owners I knew I could trust, and asked them the current price of a two year old Ruby Red. One, whose cattle were a bit of a mixture, said £50, the other with top class animals said £90, so, rightly or wrongly, I decided to take the average and put down £70.

A few days later I had Bill in my surgery, a Bill so incensed he was almost foaming at the mouth. There was certainly lightning now, I thought, and it looked as if I was in for a shock!

'Us 'as just heard from that thar insurance an' they said you said our bullock was worth £70. Now look 'ee here, Mr Vetnary, we expect our rights, for our bullocks allus top the market and us an 'ave gotten £90 or £100 for our beast. You'm bitin' the hand that feeds you, Mr Vetnary.'

I looked at the incandescent Bill, and decided that rough and ready though he was, he was honest. I explained I was not an expert on prices and told him how I had worked out my valuation, without, of course, saying which farmers I had contacted. I then apologised and said I would contact the insurance people and have it put right. I made discreet enquiries after Bill had stumped out, somewhat mollified, but still repeating like a litany his phrase about 'bitin' the hand that feeds you'. He obviously thought that was a good one! My enquiries revealed that despite outward appearances, the brothers Narracott truly had just about the best North Devons in the area, so I immediately informed the Company of my error, and the farmers duly got £100. We also, as a Practice, saved a client I was in danger of losing, and I mused wistfully that one's honesty, ability as a vet, not to mention risk to one's life were all poor second bests to money.

I had a similar accusation levelled at me one never to be forgotten week, many years later, at Aldermouth, though the circumstances were different, and the subject not money.

Frequently we had visiting groups to our large and very beautiful Church, Scouts, Guides, Boys' Brigade camping in the district, Drama Groups, Bowlers' Federations, companies of golfers, visits from the Glasgow-Aldermouth or Toronto-Aldermouth Associations and many others, and almost invariably one or more of the visitors would read a lesson in a Service. Lessons were also read by Sunday School, Bible Class, Youth Fellowship members, representatives of the women's organisations and frequently by elders like Henry, Arthur, Bob, Bill, Andrew, Peter, Sandy, Dave or Alastair my quiet, gentle, wise, humble Session Clerk and others, all fine men and fine friends. The congregation, furthermore, seemed to enjoy others taking part in this way. In addition elders like Arthur, Ashley, Malcolm, Bill, David and the other Alastair also conducted whole Services, to the delight of the congregation and the relief and gratification of the minister. Never was there a word of protest till 'that week', and here we must have a little political history.

When we went to Aldermouth, the MP was a Conservative, and also the Secretary of State for Scotland, a good man and a good friend who would help anybody, especially the handicapped, for whom, being disabled himself, he had a fellow feeling. He was actually a member of the little country Church of Croy, but often he and his wife, sometimes with a pew of visiting friends, would worship with us, partly because, I am sure, of our magnificent choir and the marvellous singing of a congregation of many hundreds. He told me too, that he looked on Aldermouth Old as the mother Church of the area, and on one occasion he took part in a Service. A leading member of the Conservative Cabinet had grown up in our Church, once in my time being involved in a special Service, and his mother was, in fact, still one of our members. She was a dynamic woman who did an immense amount of good in the town and country, but a formidable person who at first terrified me, for she barked at you. I eventually discovered that she only respected you if you barked back!

I recall visiting her in her delightful home in the country one day. Quite by chance, it happened to be the day the Tory party was voting for a new leader, and her son was one of the candidates. She was rumbling like a volcano that day, and suddenly erupted,

'*That* woman Thatcher. It seems nobody can see past her, she's done this and done that. What about my son and what he's done and they're making him seem a nincumpoop!' As all the world knows, *that* woman won the vote, and for twelve years afterwards had no more loyal supporter or wiser adviser than our son of Aldermouth.

Now I am a strictly non-political animal, certainly in public. I have never agreed with colleagues who use their pulpit for a party political platform and claim that the Tory or Labour manifesto is the latest edition of the Sermon on the Mount. I did not even discuss politics on visits if I could possibly avoid it for I recognised that people can be committed Christians and hold opposite political views. Sometimes, in a sermon, I would speak out on a topical moral or ethical issue which did not involve any particular party, but despite my forbearance and attempts to remain non-political, I have in my time been labelled everything but a Communist!

In the election of the early 1970s which saw the SNP win many seats, our highly respected Tory MP was one of the casualties, and a well known, redoubtable lady of the SNP became our MP. One Saturday long after the election, and with no other election pending, I was informed by two elders that our MP was to be in Church the next morning, and what about getting her to read a lesson? I could see nothing wrong with this. After all, others had done it, and she *was* our MP. It was the Sunday after Games Day, the Church was crowded, the lesson selected by me was read, in fear and trembling, the MP told me, 'for this was the Word of God and not some rubbishy parliamentary speech.' I had no inkling that I had trodden on toes nor of the storm immediately brewing. But the next morning, the storm, of gale force, hit the Manse. My phone started ringing early.

'Is it true,' demanded the voice at the other end, 'that *that* woman read a lesson in Church yesterday?' The tone was, to say the least, biting.

'Yes, that's right,' I answered.

'No! That's wrong!'

'Beg pardon, why is it wrong?'

'Well, she's an . . . eh . . . eh . . . she's an SNP.'

'She's also our MP and the Church has room for all political opinions.'

'Not *our* Church.'

'I have to disagree with you, but *our* Church is very much for all.'

That was just the beginning! It went on and on, the phone was red hot, some callers enquiring, some openly abusive of me, one demanding to know what lesson had been read, and finally the remark from one pompous gentlemen that 'I had bitten the hand that fed me'. I pointed out that my stipend was paid, actually from Church headquarters, and privately thought that if I had been depending on that particular man, I would long since have pined away to nothing. Then the letters started appearing in the local press, and even in *The Scotsman*.

'On Sunday last the Church of Scotland showed its true colours. I have been a member all my life, but now that the Church has become SNP, I will never darken its door again.'

Another was of the opinion that the minister of Aldermouth Old 'should be hailed before the General Assembly, publicly rebuked, if not indeed unfrocked.'

I was flabbergasted! All this about one single Scripture reading in a Service totally devoid of any political content, but obviously something had to be done for the town was buzzing, the elders distraught, people taking sides, and I was being treated to some strange looks when I walked down the street. I hastily convened a meeting of our Kirk Session, read them a letter for their comments, a letter I had very carefuly drafted to answer the critics, I thought a very reasonable and moderate letter. The Session agreed with it, I sent it off to various newspapers, and gradually the furore died away, thought I was aware that many comments were still being made behind my back. It had been thunder and lightning with a vengeance. Undoubtedly a case of electric shock like the Narracott's bullock, though without the compensation at the end!

Two things I had noticed, and one suspicion I had held had been confirmed. First all the criticism perhaps understandably seemed to come from members of the defeated party, for all anybody knew, perhaps my party, folks who were clearly sore that their much-loved former MP had lost his seat, though no criticism of me came from the man himself, thorough gentleman that he was. Second, the great mass of caustic comments were uttered, or written, by folks who were seldom, if ever in the Church, but who knew from their superior knowledge what the Church should be doing, or in this case, not doing. My confirmed suspicion? As with the Narracott brothers long before, the only thing that seemed to matter to most of my critics was 'me', 'my point of view', 'my Party', 'my interests come first', and for the non-committed or half-committed Christian, when there is a clash between faith and politics, politics wins every time.

But life goes on, and after all, I consoled myself, Christ had plenty of critics too, and when the powers that be hounded Him to death, was not it, at least in part, a question of politics?

I have never knowingly bitten any hand, whether it feeds me or not, but when self-interest is involved, who believes a 'vetnary or a parson'?

If only they would talk

NINETEEN

Times without number as a vet I have had it said to me,

'Yours must be a hard job for your patients can't talk,' to which I have usually replied,

'Touch the sore spot and they soon let you know.'

But, of course, it *was* true that one of the difficulties of being a vet as compared to a doctor was that the animal could not tell you what was wrong. Oddly enough, I found this one of the fascinations too, making every case like a jigsaw puzzle or a crossword, taking the bits of the puzzle, the clues, and fitting them together. Diagnosis was all important before one could treat, and while the owner could tell you a certain amount, you had to depend on the signs and symptoms to reach a correct diagnosis, and usually, eventually did, but there were cases when one longed for the patient to tell you exactly what was what.

Take Fran, a lovely little Dachsund belonging to Kay Wilcox. Kay often acted as a baby sitter for us at Chade Lodge when our family consisted of two wee laddies, Neil and Ian, and I knew her dog well. Both Bernard and I had been treating Fran for fully a week for what we thought was tonsilitis, throat inflamed, husky cough, off her food, temperature and a total unwillingness to have her mouth opened. She had had pencillin and then streptomycin, but grew worse rather than better. We were puzzled and at last decided we would X-ray the throat. Bernard was the X-ray expert (I'd had not a word on how to work the machine at college) and he came up with a very clear picture of a darning needle lodged across Fran's throat, just beyond where one could see, looking in her mouth. There was nothing for it but to operate which, after administering a general anaesthetic, of course, I did, to find, no needle! I looked again at the X-ray plate. It was as plain as could be. You could even see the eye of the needle, so I searched about a bit more and found, no needle! I was mystified. Where was the wretched thing? Then I had a thought, 'X-ray her stomach, Bernard', which he did, and there was our needle. Clearly the relaxation of the muscles of the oesophagus under anaesthetic had allowed her to swallow the needle. We left it at that for once a needle is in the stomach, it normally finds its way out alright, and indeed this happened.

About the same time in Bristacombe, whenever I think of Fran, I recall a little eight year old boy called Graham Harris, who was playing with his meccano set one day, making a car. Now, as everyone knows, when making a meccano car, two hands are not enough and Graham had a bit held in his mouth, when suddenly he gulped, and lo and behold, swallowed it. Panic stations! Rushed to the doctor, then to hospital for X-ray, and there was the meccano, snug in his stomach. The doctor decided to try to oil it through with liquid paraffin for a few days, but that first night when saying his prayers Graham said, 'Lord Jesus, please send my back axle up or down.' Which way the ambulant axle took I never learned, but a further X-ray a few days later showed it had disappeared. Of course, it would probably have gone anyway, but little Graham had learned the lesson which as adults, in our wisdom, we soon forget, that there's nothing too small or unimportant to 'take to the Lord in prayer.'

On another occasion I recall a Labrador dog, a big, strapping, normally full of life animal, which was brought to the surgery. As always, one depends initially on what the owner says, but all he could tell was that it was completely off its food, constipated and vomiting. Palpation of the abdomen revealed a fair sized lump; what was it, cyst, abscess, tumour or what? It was in our pre-X-ray days and when two days' treatment failed to bring about an improvement, there was only one course open, exploratory laparotomy, go in and see. The dog was duly anaesthetised, the abdomen opened up, and there was the lump in the small bowel, a medium sized hard rubber ball.

'We wondered where his ball had gone,' the owner said when I showed him the evidence. The dog recovered uneventfully, but did not get his ball back, for while I am all in favour of dogs having toys, as with children, they have to be sensible, safe, danger-free articles.

Only two cases, the needle and the ball, where, if only they could talk, would have solved the problem.

But of course there is communication in other ways, body language, an animal's behavioural pattern, the pained look on the face, a complete change in character, a dog licking a sore paw, whimpers and many other means of 'talking'. Indeed sometimes communication is as clear or clearer than mere speech.

I think of one of the most obvious ways of communicating, a limp. Prince was a very big Clydesdale gelding and had a decided limp. The first task always is to ascertain which leg is affected, which is not always as easy as it sounds. Where in a human a footballer can say to the physiotherapist 'it's my left knee', or a husband 'my wife asked me to get a spider off the ceiling and I fell off the chair and hurt my back', one has to decide the affected leg by the way the horse nods as he walks. In Prince I decided it was his right foreleg, but where was the injured part, shoulder, knee, fetlock or hoof? By examination and a process of elimination I arrived at the hoof which to the touch felt warmer than the other front hoof. A gentle tap with a hammer had the big horse raising his foot from the ground where he held it trembling for a bit before putting it gingerly down again. So out with the hoof knife, pick up the foot, hold it on or between one's legs, and proceed to pare the hard horn. There was, as there usually is in such cases, a dark line running across the horn. It was along this that I pared. It was mighty hard work as Prince obviously thought this kind man had just come for him to lean his weight on, and soon the sweat was blinding my eyes as I pared away slivers of horn. But at last eureka, success as a trickle of pus came out of the hole I had made. It is all a bit like a child digging in the sand on the shore till water bubbles up. I enlarged the hole, till the pus from his septic foot, caused undoubtedly by a nail prick, was flowing freely. Then a shot of tetanus antitoxin, an injection of penicillin, and instructions to put a bread and epsom salts poultice in the corner of a sack, put the foot in it, and change it twice a day to draw out all the pus. Two more visits and shots of penicillin sufficed, and the big horse was almost sound again, all because he had communicated his woes with a limp.

A cow standing with elbows out, a pained look on her face, off her food, running a temperature, and producing a grunt when the diaphragm is poked, and she has told you in nine cases out of ten that she has a foreign body, a nail or wire in her reticulum, or the second of her four stomachs.

A dog sitting over its drinking bowl all day long or drinking from puddles, with this excessive thirst the dog is practically saying it has nephritis (inflammation of the kidneys) or diabetes.

I remember a four month old puppy I had been treating at Bristacombe. There was nothing to go on except the owner's information that it was vomiting. I had wormed it, given it our usual stomach mixtures, but the little animal grew steadily worse. It was a pathetic, thin little creature, able to keep down hardly any food. Then one day on the surgery table it vomited while I was examining it, the stomach contents coming out in an arch, like a fountain, and it had 'told' me its trouble, that type of vomiting being symptomatic. It had pyloric stenosis, a narrowing of the exit of the stomach, requiring a simple but delicate operation to put right. This was duly done and in an incredibly short space of time, we had a healthy, thriving and soon quite fat little dog.

But there are other forms of communication which have proved a great boon to thousands of men and women. I remember at Bristacombe one day in Church. It was a weekday evening, the Church was crowded, for there was a very notable visiting preacher. He was certainly worth listening to, and watching, for he was an 'active' preacher, using his arms to the full, pounding the board, pointing and clearly a master of the art of holding a congregation's attention. Suddenly, to my utter amazement, I heard a snore coming from further along my pew. I could not believe anyone could fall asleep with such a preacher, but clearly someone had. A few moments later the snore, a real prince among snores, was repeated, and startled, I looked along the pew and saw the culprit, a lovely wavy haired blonde fast alseep *under the seat.* I had a quiet smile to myself, for I knew that blonde well. She was called Sheila and regularly she walked into my surgery on all four feet, a beautiful, light coloured golden retriever, but a very special one. Sheila was a guide dog and she had transformed the life of her young owner, who, until Sheila appeared on the scene, had been virtually housebound. I used to watch them going along the busy Bristacombe streets, the dog weaving in and out of the crowds, and communicating its instructions via its harness to its mistress. At the kerb she would halt, look right, left, then right again, and if the road was clear 'tell' her mistress to cross, a wonderful empathy, oneness and trust existing between dog and girl, except for mutual agreement on the matter of sermons! it was as if the dog was saying, 'I know your eyes are no good to you, but don't worry, as your Good Book says, mistress, I will guide you with my eye!', a communication every bit as good as mere talking.

So the many thousands of species can 'talk', alright, not only in a wide variety of ways to one another, but also in the animals we have domesticated, to man.

But in the ministry I confess I have often sighed, and said of my fellow Christians, and the members of my congregation, 'if only they would talk'. The Gospel, the good news first spread round the world in days without television, radio or newspapers because those who had found this wonderful new faith 'gossiped' the gospel in their homes, in the market place, in caravanserai as they journeyed until they took it from its cradle in Palestine to the heart of the civilised world, Rome, and spread far and wide across Asia, Europe and even heathen Britain. It is still happening! In China, for instance, a Church is re-opened every day and in non-Muslim parts of Africa, many thousands become Christians daily. Yet in so-called Christian Britain, and the western world generally, numbers are on the decline. Churches are closing, the Church is like an army fighting on the retreat. Now not for one minute do I suggest that talking about Christ or His Church is the only way to influence or impress, as I shall try to show, but it *is* important, and my, we have become unco blate in Scotland about speaking of life's basic values and Christ's truth.

One of the delights I had in Aldermouth was to go off on several occasions to the nearby conference centre of Kilravock with my Elders and over a weekend of fun and fellowship discuss the affairs of the Church and what we should be about. We played together, laughed together, ate together, prayed together an talked together. I remember people like Eric Gilchrist, Dave Peterson, Jack Rodgerson, Eric Rae, Peter McIntosh, Henry Dow, Robin Kerr and many others speaking out, many of them speaking in company for the first time about 'my faith and my job', 'my faith and my home', 'my faith and my recreation' and many other topics. It thrilled my heart to hear these good men, who previously had felt they could not talk openly about their faith do just that, it showed, as the Church grew, newcomers came in, some who had lapsed came back to the fold and several visitations were paid to a large new housing area in our parish. As I have noted elsewhere, some of these men even took the pulpit on occasion and I recall Arthur Menzies' talk on our faith faculty, and I have in my possession still two sermons preached by Ashley Thomas and Alistair Campbell.

The revival of the Church in China today can be traced to great souls like these two intrepid spinsters Mildred Cable and Francesca French who went to the Gobi Desert, Gladys Aylward, that amazing little housemaid turned missionary, men like Eric Liddell and the spiritual giant Hudson Taylor so that a Church was built up of ordinary men and women who withstood thirty years of clamp down, persecution, imprisonment and death inflicted by the State. In Africa the story has similar beginnings, and a harvest is being reaped today of the seed sown by greats like Mary Slessor, David Livingstone and hosts of lesser known souls who had the motto 'each one win one'. Alas in Scotland as Lord McLeod has so vividly put it 'while Jesus Christ called the disciples to be fishers of men, we in the Kirk have tended to be keepers of the aquarium.' If only they would talk, the great Master story-teller must sigh. But, as with animals, there are also other ways of communication, and I saw many of them at Aldermouth.

Every Sunday morning I would sit in my vestry waiting for that dread moment when I had to climb the pulpit steps and face a congregation of hundreds, and as I sat musing and meditating on the Service ahead, I would thrill to the music of our blind organist Jim McMichael as it soared to the heavens and brought calm, healing and inspiration to me, and I am sure to many of the assembled throng. Jim was communicating alright as only he could. But even prior to the organ's melodious message, our Beadle, John, would have climbed up to the tower and for ten minutes rung the great bell there, inviting people to come and worship their God. It is not easy to ring a large bell. I tried it but could never get the dings and dongs in their proper order as John could. In my time alone at Aldermouth, his great bell 'talked' to the whole town some 1200 times.

The Service would commence with a rousing Hymn or Psalm and people, hundreds of them, who would have hesitated to speak their faith, cheerfully sang it, led by our magnificent choir which contained men and women who had sung there all their lives. To hear them in the Anthem each Sunday, with perhaps a soloist like Billy Fowler singing 'Seek ye the Lord' was indeed to listen to people expressing their faith. One could mention so many who had cheerfully given a lifetime to that choir and I would sit back in the pulpit and listen, to the sopranos soaring to the heights, the contraltos balancing them perfectly, the tenors with Bill Crooky and the others coming in and the solid rock of the bass section giving body to it all. One could mention all thirty who were certainly 'speaking' their faith alright and I used to feel that even if my sermon was rubbish, the congregation was fed, instructed, cheered and challenged by Jim and his merry band.

Another way of communicating his faith, as I have already alluded, was that of John, the minister's man's way, a Church polished, shining, heated just right, sitting in its neatly kept grounds. A master baker, John need not have become full time Church Officer at a lesser salary, but this was his way, and his wife Elizabeth's, of witnessing and worshipping.

After the evening Service, the two 'girls', Marian and Jean, both in their sixties, would wait for their minister's suggestions as to who should get the Church flowers that night, and miles they walked delivering their floral message, presented with a suitable card and a big smile of encouragement by this cheerful, faithful twosome, lifting up the spirits a little of many a lonely or weary soul. Then of course there was the beautifying of the Church week by week, done by a succession of Flower Convenors in my twelve years, the fruits of God's good earth in the hands of experts or just willing folk. This was yet another way of communicating one's love for God and His Church. When Norah Ferguson was Flower Convenor, she organised a Festival of Flowers, blooms of every conceivable colour and scent arranged all round the Church by many willing and expert hands, even the umbrella holders at each pew being filled with flower heads by young Nessie Archibald and other youngsters. As we rose that Sunday, a great throng singing 'How lovely is Thy dwelling place' was undoubtably true, surpassing lovely, and again in flowers and Psalms communicating the faith of these women, like the woman in the New Testament anointing her Lord with her most precious gift.

Another means of communiction, of showing one's love, was in gifts the Church received. The Archibald family contributed a beautiful blue Pulpit Fall in memory of Nan's parents. Mr and Mrs Gunning, to give thanks for twenty-five years of happy marriage, gifted two exquisite Communion chairs, matching perfectly the existing ones. The craftsman who delivered the chairs from the Lord Robert's workshop for disabled ex-servicemen gazed at the glistening wood of the pulpit and gallery fronts and commented that then (in the 1970s) it would take at least £40 000 to replace the wood alone and the whole magnificent edifice had been built in 1897 for £9000! A tremendously generous gift was from Bill Heard who, after his wife's death, gave the price of a house he had sold, then offered his own large house at about half its market value as a dwelling place for a much-needed Assistant minister.

A remarkable man, Bill, for although long retired, he took a trip to India to fulfil a long cherished dream, and soon found himself helping a company of Roman Catholic brothers, who, like Mother Theresa, scoured the streets of Calcutta for the sick and dying and carried them in to their night shelter where there was comfort and real caring. Bill stayed for years working among these poor unfortunates, many, indeed most of them, dirty, diseased, destitute, and by his every action was 'talking' of the One who in His day cared for such poor wrecks of society, thus showing love to the unlovely.

So one could go on. There were many other gifts, some of them in memory of a loved one, but there was also a great deal of compassionate work by individual Christians, not specifically for the Church, but most certainly motivated by the Head of the Church. I think of hospital visitors like Henry Dow, people who delivered meals on wheels, Winnie Murray who every morning would light the fires and cook the breakfasts of several old folks, all forms of 'talking', of communicatiron in the name of the One who said 'Feed my sheep'. Long ago Struthers, a famous minister in Greenock said 'what is needed most is for Christians to do a bonny thing'. I saw some bonny things done in His name in Aldermouth, and the same can be said of almost every parish in the land. Yes, many ways of 'talking', of communicating one's faith and love.

I remember hearing of a funeral, particularly pathetic as there were only five mourners for the old man who had died alone. One of the five was a high ranking army officer. As the coffin was lowered into the ground, he stood to attention and saluted. Afterwards the minister asked if he was related to the deceased. The Brigadier smiled and said,

'In a way. Long ago John was my Sunday School teacher. I first saw God in him.'

Yes, many ways of 'talking', but still, if only more of the flock would naturally and unashamedly actually talk of their great Shepherd!

Parson's pot-pourri

TWENTY

I was standing at the Marine Hotel overlooking the Links, a natural amphitheatre where annually the Highland Games were held, and where Aldermouth Cricket Club played their matches. It was a glorious July day of sunshine, the sea a deep blue, and across the water the Black Isle seeming but a step away. The vivid green of the Links contrasted with the soft blue of the sky, across whose benign face here and there some puffs of white cloud were meandering, as if they too felt it was a day for taking it easy.

I was really on my way to a wedding reception, having just come from the ceremony in Church, but since there is always a time lag for photos and so on, I felt I could spare a few minutes watching the cricket. I was particularly interested for Neil, our eldest at seventeen, was opening the batting against Leicestershire 2nd eleven, who were making a northern tour, and I had just seen Neil felled by a bumper which a giant of a fast bowler had hurled down, hitting Neil on the chest. It was all I could do to prevent myself running on to the pitch to make sure my son and heir was alright, or thump the bowler! The scoreboard made sombre reading for Aldermouth, four batsmen being out and a mere ten runs showing on the scoreboard. The giant bowler had evidently wrought havoc. Some smelling salts revived Neil, and to sympathetic claps from the crowd, he picked up his bat again and faced Goliath. Down whizzed another short pitched ball and to my great delight, he stood up to it and hooked it for four runs. I was getting quite excited, my chest swelling with pride, and would fain have watched longer. Just then I was joined by a man, totally unknown to me, but who apparently knew me alright, and who immediately expressed his opinion with a sneer, 'Aye, you've a fine time of it, you ministers. Working one day a week and a slap up feed every Saturday.'

Mind you, many times I have had this one day's work business flung at me, but on such a day, with all nature smiling, I did not feel like any explanations, managed a grin and said, 'You're right, friend. The easiest job in the world! Just the one day for working, after all a wedding's not work!' He looked a bit bemused for he had evidently expected an argument, but as Neil hit another bumper for four, I was the little friend of all the world! The wedding reception proceeded like all such functions with the minister, as was nearly always the case, proposing the toast of the couple, and by eight o'clock, I was home. With one or two receptions nearly every Saturday in summer, I seldom stayed for the dance, for Saturday night in a busy Church is required to check the sermons, but as I changed into some more casual and comfortable clothes, the one day's work-a-week business came back to me. So, just for interest, I flipped over the pages of my diary for the past few months to see what I had been doing, and found an infinite variety of 'cases', every bit as varied as in my vet days.

There was the day of the doctors. It had really begun the night before when about ten o'clock I answered a ring at the front door. There stood a man and a little boy.

'Can we come in, Mr Cameron? We've nowhere to go,' said the man. A Manse door is always open, so of course they were invited in. I knew the father slightly, a Mr Spence. He was considerably downcast and explained that his wife had put him and their youngest, aged five, out of the house.

'But you've other children too, Mr Spence, have you not?'

'Yes, two other boys but the wife has always been against young Simon here. Mind you, she's not always in control of herself. She's had several nervous breakdowns.'

We talked for a bit. I promised I would visit his wife next day, and managed to get him and his pathetic little five year old fixed up for the night.

The next day started with a visit to the Clinic for a minor ailment I had. We were very blessed with our doctors in Aldermouth, all of them, but normally I saw Dr John, or, as that day, Dr Bryce. The latter always had a wisecrack or two, but his flippant exterior could not hide a caring heart. From there I made my way to the Spence household, rang the bell, and was very reluctantly admitted by the young wife, who was clearly in a hysterical state. I was only in the house briefly, wondering what on earth I could do to help, particularly with the memory of a sad little five year old face from the night before, when the young wife and mother started shouting and screaming at me, and ordered me out of the house. Her talk was wild and she was in a very dangerous mood, threatening to end it all by putting her head in the gas oven. It is the only time I have been put out of a house, and although I've heard psychiatrists say that those who openly threatened suicide seldom did it, I felt I could not take the risk. I drove straight to Dr Hannah, her doctor, who had a single-man practice in the town. He was at the Spence house in minutes, and in further minutes the ambulance was at the door, the doctor clearly feeling as I did, that this was a potential suicide. I visited the young woman in Craigdunain Mental Hospital a few days later and found to my horror that she had been put in the geriatric ward, surrounded by seventy elderly women, many of them incontinent and mindless. It was a ward that always made my blood boil for the beds were so close one could hardly get between them. I wondered how in all the world Mrs Spence could recover her sanity and calm in such surroundings. I continued to visit weekly. She was in time moved to another ward, then eventually returned home, took her husband and son back, and a sort of uneasy truce between the various members of the family was arrived at.

In the afternoon of 'the doctors' day', I visited Dr Ferguson who with his wife Norah lived in a lovely flat overlooking the heaving waters of the Moray Firth, its waves lapping the shore just at the end of their lawn. Always the welcome there was warm and sincere. The doctor had retired to Aldermouth, quite often stood in for Dr Hannah, but was now himself unwell. I have often thought that it must be difficult for a doctor to be ill for he knows all the symptoms, and likely outcome of the condition. Dr Ferguson was very poorly, but seemed glad of a visit and, in Norah, had a first class nurse.

Then I went to old Dr Matheson, another retired medic. He had practised in England but never lost his lovely, lilting, Highland tongue. It was really Mrs Matheson I had come to see for she was far from well, but the old doctor, well into his eighties, was in his usual sparkling form (In fact he lived to his nineties, still golfing three times a week). He always tried to trip me up with some obscure Biblical quotation, conducting his own version of Mastermind. But that day he told me a story of his youth in Applecross. One Communion season, which lasted from Thursday to Monday, a notable Doctor of Divinity had been preaching at the Sunday morning Service. In the afternoon of a glorious Spring day he was taking a walk when he was accosted by Angus standing in his Sunday blacks outside his croft.

'Are you on an errant of mercy?' demanded Angus.

'No, just having a walk,' replied the distinguished Divine.

'You shoult not be walking on the Sabbath tay,' he was informed.

'But I'm enjoying the beauties of God's handiwork all around us.'

'We are not meant to enchoy ourselves on the Sabbath.'

Angus thought deeply and came up with his judgement,

'Well, if He dit, He shoultn't have.' End of conversation! Dr Matheson chuckled at the memory, then paid me a compliment I very much appreciated from such a cynic as he had become over the years.

'You know, I'm not at all pleaset with you, no, not at all.'

'What have I done?' I asked, wondering what was coming.

'I hat more or less stoppet going to Church for I've seen so much hypocrisy, but, tash it, man, you make me want to come.'

We had a simple word of prayer, and I went on my way, gratified that I had at least one satisfied customer.

I flipped a page of my diary. Ah yes! That was the week I got up at 7.00 am each morning to go to Mrs Evans' house in the Fishertown. She was a loner, a widow with one son the length of the country away. She had had a mild stroke, had shut herself off from her neighbours, so I lit her fire each morning, stocked up with coal gave her a cup of tea and toast, asked 'Meals on Wheels' to call, and the doctor arranged for a nurse to go in daily. In the early evening I looked in each day to check up on her. After a week the son came home. But that is not minister's work, you say. Away with you! Didn't Jesus wash feet? Thinking of mornings in the Fishertown brought to mind one Saturday morning. Our boys all, in turn, had the same paper round in the harbour area. One day one of them, Alan, I think, had to be away early for he was playing football some distance away, and the bus was leaving very early. I said I'd stand in for him, hoping I would not meet anyone. But I did. It was an early morning worker, and one of our members. He stopped, looked astonished, said 'Mr Cameron' and went on his way, presumably thinking times must be pretty hard in the Manse when the minister had taken a paper round.

I flipped over the diary pages to a Thursday. That was the evening I held my Vestry Hour, usually nearer two hours. I had written 'Baptism – Jacqueline Clark – that makes nine for Sunday.' I remembered Mrs Clark's visit well.

'Oh, Mr Cameron, I know you always have baptisms on the first Sunday in the month, and I'm at the last minute seeing you, but I've just had word that my mother's coming up from London this weekend and I wondered if you could do Jacqueline when my mother's here?'

I looked at her with a perfectly straight face.

'Certainly, Mrs Clark, if you don't mind being number nine. In fact on Sunday I'm going to use a hose.' She looked at me uncertainly then gasped, 'A hose!', before, seeing the twinkle, she laughed somewhat doubtfully. So I went over the Baptismal Service with her, though normally I always saw husband and wife together, but since it was not their first child and time was short, I thought mother would do this time.

I always loved baptisms, as did the congregation, though all my ministry I have had a private fear that I would get names mixed up and maybe call a John, Jane. It has not happened yet, but perhaps there is still time! I did not use the method of a certain minister in Glasgow who always, on taking the baby, asked the father its name. On one occasion the odd reply came,

'Spindoner.'

'Eh? Oh well, Spindoner, I baptise you – '

'Naw, naw,' interrupted the agitated father,

'It's pinned on her.'

Another page of the diary was turned. Ah yes, one of my monthly trips to 121 George Street, Edinburgh, Church Headquarters, for a meeting of the Union and Readjustment, (U and R) Committee, which always met in the evening. I had written a piece after that particular meeting, 'Now I know what Hell is like! It's a series of committee meetings going on *ad infinitum*.'

The sample that day was two and a half hours long, during which the committee voted to close Churches, link or unite others, and give others a minister not under fifty-five. I have heard various ministers describe the work of the U and R as an evangelical exercise. You know, that puzzles me somewhat! I cannot for the life of me see how closing a Church or giving a minister four instead of two churches to supervise helps the mission of the Church in John Knox's Scotland, where he and the Reformers had the dream of a Church and school in every parish of the land, and achieved their goal. Of course, there is a twofold reason for the shrinkage, money and ministers, shortage of both, but there have been many times, in my humble opinion, when the U and R have been a bit heavy-handed. They also appear to have the same notion as the education authorities (and what Scottish education owes to the Kirk) that town is better than country, so frequently, they tag one or more country churches on to a town one, almost always to the detriment of the country church.

That meeting was a shambles. There was a Chairman, but flanked by the two full time Secretaries, he seemed like a Mini with a bus on either side, and a Mini that had even lost its toot. He scarcely opened his mouth, even when the Revd Charles in a corner behind me, got so loud in his own private conversation with his cronies that one could not hear the proper speaker. I wonder if Charles checks his children for butting in when others are speaking? Beside me was an expert on Church law and he kept me informed, 'matter for the Synod' he muttered, or again 'clause 14', whatever that might be! Revd Charles, having suspended operations with his pals, broke in to speak for ten minutes on something which mystified us all until he and we discovered it was not on the agenda, and really the wrong committee. Then another brother protested at length about closing a church to find it was the wrong church. I learned it was very dangerous to establish a precedent and step out of line, and other matters were valid by dint of 'use and wont'. The most animated discussion of the whole evening came when there was an interminable argument about whether a clause should be worded 'is' or 'shall be'. That got everyone awake! The Church militant! Almost all the talking was done by the full time Secretaries (mind you, they have a rotten job), but after six years on the committee it seemed to me I was meant to be just a rubber stamp!

The Lord's business done for another month, I drove the 160 miles up the old, winding A9 which, since there was snow about, was practically deserted by that time of night, and more than once my headlights picked up herds of deer beside the road in the Drumochter Pass. Somehow their life seemed simple and uncomplicated compared to our tortuous committees, but who knows, maybe they had committees too! At last, the Dava moor and home on the stroke of midnight.

All my ministry I have served, like most ministers, on a variety of General Assembly Committees. Some have cheered and enlightened, many have informed, some have inflamed, but all are an attempt at democracy in the Kirk, but well, if not Hell, certainly Purgatory could not be much worse than some of them!

A flick over another diary page and I found it was a Sunday, but quite a Sunday, even if it *was* the only day I worked! Perhaps my critic at the cricket would have grudgingly admitted I had earned my corn that day.

It was one of our Communion Sundays, beginning with a meeting of the duty elders at ten. Then the Service at 11.00 am, another Table of Communion in the afternoon, following which I nipped up to the Church Eventide Home for a short Service and Communion with the elderly residents. Half past six and our evening Service of Thanksgiving was followed by a short message over their earphones to our local hospital patients.

Finally I joined Allan Ross at the sixty-strong Youth Fellowship of senior teenagers. When first I went to Aldermouth, I found I had run this lively group all on my own, and it was the hardest work of he day, for almost all the young folk were at the rebellious stage and either hostile to the Kirk or totally apathetic, but it was the only gathering of the week in the whole town for their age group. Just to keep order was an achievement. Early on I had the help of the Police Sergeant, Sergeant Riddock for a year, then Allan, one of our younger elders and a hotelier became my assistant and eventually leader. He had a marvellous gift of getting on a wavelength of 16-19 year olds and many happy nights we had in the Hall, and later Kirkside, premises we bought for our expanding youth work. We had several weekends away with the youngsters, Janet going along as housemother, and bright, happy, fruitful occasions they were. The Youth Fellowship was a handful, but great times they were. How fruitful only eternity will show, but if you think it easy to interest and influence that number of teenagers week after week, I invite you to try. after Allan had to resign through pressure of other work, I had another excellent leader in Bill McInnes, who had tragically lost his wife at an early age, and brought up their lovely children on his own.

Ten o'clock and the working day was over, leaving me limp, played out, exhausted, but happy. To unwind I frequently took a walk down Manse Road and there with Henry and Nana Dow relaxed, drank tea and chatted over the day's happenings. Wonderful encouragers were Henry and Nana and finally at eleven, it was home and a welcome bed.

Every minister needs a bolt-hole, someone he can go to and share his problems, or be encouraged in his work, and I had several such blessed retreats close by. There were Alastair and Margaret, my Session Clerk and his wife, who was Sunday School Secretary. Though disabled from the war and often in pain, there was no more gentle and understanding man in the parish than my fine, efficient and ever willing Clerk, who was also my Bank Manager. He was a straight, upright man, goodness shining from him as kindness and sympathy shone from his wife. There were also the Archibalds, Andrew and Nan, our friends from the Moorton days, always with an open door and an encouraging word. Billy and Cath Miller lived just round the corner from the Manse. Billy, our Church Treasurer, and Cath, leader of the Playgroup. Billy succeeded the long serving George Farm, the Town Clerk, as our Treasurer. Of course I had my Beadle John, and his wife Elizabeth. I saw John virtually every day and his quiet voice and understanding words were like soothing balm when I was 'up tight' about something. One house I visited often was that of Arthur and Cath Menzies. Arthur edited our Church magazine, a gifted man, a tremendously patient man, a man of God, who over many years nursed and encouraged Cath, who most of her life had very poor health. Every Wednesday evening I called at Jim McMichael's home to be greated by Jean's words 'Come away in' and after talking of the praise lists for Sunday, Jim and I would weekly put the world right, for, though blind, he was right on the ball of all the happenings near and far. One could go on, writing more, much more, about each of them, and many many others, not forgetting the Minister's committee, composed of senior elders whose wise advice and constant encouragement saved me from many errors. I was a lucky, lucky, man in the number of encouragers and willing helpers I had for my one day a week job!

A short note in my diary caught my eye, 'Visit Bruce and Rosemary in their new home.' Bruce Bunker and his father were both elders, father Willie being a builder and stonemason and son Bruce, a remarkably successful business man. He had asked me to look in and see them and ask a blessing on their new home, a lovely request I was glad to fulfil.

Bruce, at the time, had a large bookshop in Inverness, having started with a smaller one in Aldermouth, and the various ventures he turned his mind to over the years all seemed to thrive. He had the golden touch, but Church meant much to him and his charming wife, Rosemary, and it was always a delight to call on them. Bruce thought deeply about things. He was not the kind of man whose Christianity was confined to a Church building, and I remember him expressing his dilemma as a Christian business man as to whether he should be selling books on, for example, Karl Marx. A lovely visit!

On the way home I popped into Tom and Moira Hastings' home for a few minutes for they were practically next door. Tom had one of the loveliest gardens in the town, was ever present in Church, but Moira, poor lass, was one of the many sufferers from that cruel disease, Rheumatoid Arthritis, which causes such continuous pain, deformity and difficulty for the sufferer. She had shown incredible bravery through teens of operations, but despite many set-backs, Moira kept trying to be well enough to golf again. Folks like that get little publicity, and sometimes little sympathy, for it is not normally a killing disease, but my, they know what suffering is!

Another page, a Monday, and I had written in 'three months since I have had a day off so golfed with Peter McIntosh, who took me on to the Dunbar Course this afternoon and slaughtered me!' Peter was, and is, one of the finest men I have known. He had worked in Glasgow all his life where he and his wife threw their home open to every youngster from Aldermouth who was working or studying in Glasgow, or to any Scout from anywhere, for Peter had been Scouting for many years. Eventually they retired to their beloved Aldermouth.

I knew Peter had been in the war and a prisoner of the Japanese but he seldom spoke of it, just like Alastair my Session Clerk who had been in a German POW camp. How often the brave keep quiet! However, that day as we walked up the sixteenth fairway, having just trounced me, he told me of a remarkable escape he had had. Imprisoned on one island, Sumatra, I think, he, with thousands of other prisoners was on a boat transferring them elsewhere. At the last minute, he was taken off the boat, for the MO of the camp, which was remaining had insisted he needed Peter as his assistant. That ship was torpedoed with total loss of life. Peter was too humble a man to say God had protected particularly him, but when one thought of the fruitful life he and his gentle, caring wife had lived for the good of others afterwards, there was no doubt in my mind that 'the shade of His hand outstretched caressingly' had indeed held and saved him.

I found myself looking in my diary at one of the success stories and happiest events in our church calendar. I smiled as I thought back to that week and indeed to previous weeks. There was an air of mystery about it too, I found, and the town wondered what we were up to in the Old Presbyterian Church. Certainly the shop attendant looked at me in mystification when I asked for a hair net. She supplied me and remarked that an awful lot of men had been buying hair nets, and was clearly puzzled for all the men were of the short back and sides variety, some even bald. There was also a run on thick, black wool, it was known that John, the Church Officer had borrowed a policeman's uniform and various people were searching for white gloves, man size. Tile hats were also in demand. What was going on? Certainly the annual Church Concert was coming up. Could there be a connection? Surely not, for the previous two years it had all been by the various Sunday School children who had performed in the Church Hall. They were similar concerts to those I had organised at Moorton.

'It's in the Centre this year,' the cry went round, 'bit ambitious if you ask me and they've taken it for three nights! They'll never fill a Hall that size!'

So the opening night of the concert came round with the various mysteries still unresolved. Despite gloomy predictions, the big hall was packed full, parents, grandparents and hosts of non-aligned spectators, all anticipating a good night with the bairns, if the previous two years were anything to go by.

They were not disappointed. The tiny tots began with their simple choruses, though the task of teaching three and four year olds had been far from simple, remembering they could not read. They won the hearts of the audience, it merely adding to the fun that some forgot to face the front, one lad kept coming in too soon in the songs, another young gentleman had bother hitching up his velvet trousers, while yet another had to be led off to the toilet! Chaos? Not if you were a parent or grandparent with eyes for only one child to see how he/she would behave. The artlessness and simplicity of these little ones won over the audience right away, the 5-7 year olds kept up the good work, then came the main Sunday School, exquisitely dressed by enthusiastic parents as they did a selection of Songs from the Shows (they all wanted to sing the

Edelweiss solo!), followed later in the programme by Songs from Ireland, the girls in green skirts and capes, and the boys with a green sash. It was all very colourful and the singing of a high standard. In between acts while scenes were being shifted behind the curtain, our youngest Alan, aged about twelve and two of his pals told a series of Irish jokes in a very fair attempt at the Irish brogue, jokes as old as the hills extracted by father from a book of jokes of various countries, like the far from new,

'I wish I knew where I was going to die, Paddy!'

'Why's that, Mick?'

'Sure and I'd never go near the place!' or again

'Did you know that the last coach was the most dangerous on a train, Mick?'

'Is that so, now. Why don't they just take it off?'

Ancient stuff, but a now thoroughly warmed up audience laughed as if hearing it for the first time, and as the night went on, the three comedians grew in confidence. The Bible Class, superbly directed by Lena Hammond, Aldermouth's equivalent of Joyce Grenfell, and a life long teacher of teenagers in that department of the Church life. On this occasion they performed beautifully a Hans Andersen classic. Then, the audience could not believe it, elders of the Kirk singing 'Oh you canny shove your granny aff a bus' and other 'high class' stuff, including a biographical sketch of most of the office bearers, not sparing the ministers, written by schoolmaster and friend Bill Barnet. The Woman's Guild Choir sang well-loved Sankey hymns, the BB lads leapt and somersaulted all over the stage, and while the stage was prepared for the next item, Alec Campbell, another cheerful elder, had the feet tapping with his accordion, or the three comedians popped up again with more ancient chestnuts in what was a non-stop performance. There were several solo songs by youngsters, thrilled that they were singing into a microphone like Elvis, though without Elvis's wiggle! Among them was David, dressed in rags, bringing tears to mothers' eyes, and a lump even to his father's throat as he sang in a plaintive but very true boy soprano's voice 'Nobody's Child', repeating the part older brother Ian had done at Moorton years before.

It was all great entertainment, but no real surprises till the curtains parted to show the elders again, sitting round in earnest discussion as 'The Vacant Committee', choosing a new minister (something every congregation should study!). It was a skit, which in places, was not too far off the mark. I had written it in a hurry, my first effort as a playwright. It had taken much rehearsal, but went off pretty well, all fifteen parts being played by men, though Willie Birrell and Billy Miller had changed sex for the occasion, dressed in their wives' cast-offs. John was there in his policeman's uniform, there was a farmer in welly boots and with a pet lamb and dog, the Colonel in a tile hat demanding they choose a DD minister. Bruce, the bookseller and Ben, the assistant minister, both quiet men, revealing that they had the loudest laughs in the county, and Bill, Superintendent of the Eventide Home with his 'bunnet' in his hand, his lines surreptitiously hidden in the cap, while Dave Peterson, his hair liberally sprinkled with powder to make him old and wise, attempted to keep order as Chairman. Eric Gilchrist managed to get his bogey line right 'I've had naethin' to dae wi' doos', for in practice it had always been 'do with daes' (doos are pigeons). It was a rip roaring farce, but the *piece de resistance* was still to come, the penultimate item on the programme.

To gasps of incredulity, hearty laughter and much pointing, when the curtains opened the audience saw the Black and White minstrels before them, all looking exactly alike, and providing a puzzle as folks tried to identify the elders. For the elders it was, all wearing white gloves and black, curly, woolly wigs. The hair net, black wool mystery was solved! As all sang and danced about the stage, the two ministers included, singing old favourites like 'Lily of Laguna', 'I'll be your sweetheart', 'Home on the Range' and many others, I think the only positive identification was that of dear wee Bobby Sim, who took the solo parts, but something that took a sore knock was the picture so many have of ministers and elders as dour, humourless creatures.

Then came the closing scene with all on the stage (except the tiny tots who had long since departed for bed), with all the cast joining in negro spirituals, modern hymns with a swing, and 'The King of Love' in whose name and for whose sake we had made our offering of fun, pathos and beauty, after all David danced before the Lord!

Such an event demanded much busy planning, rehearsing, coaxing and cajoling for many weeks, and involved many willing helpers like Stan Walker and Allan Ross as stage managers, Mrs Paterson on make-up, Mrs Temple and Jim at the piano and hosts of others, not least parents and wives. To see so many happy faces on and off stage made it all worthwhile and bound us all in a warm glow of real fellowship. Who said Christ or His Kirk took the spice and joy out of life? But I suppose my critic at the cricket would not have classed all the planning as work! I mean to say, it could not be as I was not wearing my working collar!

My mind had wandered far and wide that Saturday night, as I flicked over my diary pages when I should have been at my sermons but I was caught and held by the bonds of memory. One more page, I thought. I remembered the day well. A funeral from the Church at noon, a quick bite of dinner, then a funeral from the Fishertown at 2.00 pm where I had to stand at the door to try to let those inside and the vast crowd outside hear. Then, as in the old days, all the mourners walked behind the hearse to the cemetery, and in a deep hush, we laid a good man to rest. I went back to the house where the relatives were gathered and over tea, talked with most of them.

I thought I would just go and see Mrs Gilmour on my way home, a poor soul whom I felt might well be my next funeral. She lived in the Queen's Park area of the town, and was far through with cancer. To my surprise I found her sitting up in bed, her face aglow, a strange light in her eyes. We talked for a bit, then she said, very hesitantly,

'Mr Cameron, *please* don't laugh at me, but Jesus came into my room last night and stood just where you are standing. Really it *was* Him. I wasn't dreaming, and I'd had no pain killers.'

'I'm not laughing, Mrs Gilmour. I believe you,' and I did.

Whatever any of us reading this may think in our wisdom, that woman believed she had seen the Lord, and I believed her, for in my ministry on numbers of occasions, people have described similar experiences. But if you are still sceptical, my friend who reads this, let me say that from that moment, Mrs Gilmour, a dying woman, whom I would not have described as a particularly religious person, nor was she a neurotic, from that moment she started to get well. Doctors call it a remission. Call it what we will, the cancer abated, and Mrs Gilmour lived for years afterwards.

So my critic from the cricket, whoever you are, ministers have been known to work on other days besides Sunday, involved in the rich tapestry of all life, every bit as varied and busy as when I was a vet.

We try, in His Name, to hold a torch aloft to reveal the young Prince of Glory, and in all our doings, the joyful and sad, the ordinary and the extraordinary, try to show that great heart of love that beats at the centre of the Universe.

Twists and turns

TWENTY-ONE

'Hello! Mr Cameron? Derek Hocking, High Deane, here. Us's got trouble wi' some fattenin' pigs. I wish you'd 'ave a look at 'em.' It was early afternoon, and while Ann, our secretary/receptionist went home for lunch, the calls were switched through to us at Chade Lodge.

'What seems to be the matter with them, Derek?' I queried.

'Them be dowie like, right poorly, some off their grub, an' most of 'em is scourin'.'

'Right, Derek, I'll be out later this afternoon. I have a call to make after surgery, so I should be with you about four.'

'That's fine, Mr Cameron. I be right worried 'bout them pigs.' Young Derek was one of my favourites, a good client, a prodigious worker, with a large dairy herd and maybe two hundred pigs. Though his father still did a bit, he was one of the old school who thought you should only call the vet when all the patent medicines had failed, but Derek was more forward-looking, and I was often at High Deane.

I got there about four as planned just as they were starting the afternoon milking. I had a walk up the byre, or shippen as it was called in Devon, and found Derek, as always, flying on, looking after about six milking units at the one time.

'See you haven't taken my advice and switched to a good cow, Derek! Still sticking to these Friesians! Man, they just give white water!' I did not really think that about Friesians, knowing full well that since first introduced, the butter fat content of their milk had greatly improved, but it was a standing joke between us, his choice of breed. He laughed.

'Aar – you and you'm Ayrshires. They be just toy bullocks!'

'The pigs be at Upper Down, Mr Cameron. I'll come up with 'ee.' He called for his father and brother to take over the milking, and we set off for the adjoining little village where Derek had a small piggery in addition to his much larger one at High Deane. We got out of the car. Derek threw open the pig house door, and with my first glance at his pigs, I stopped, and felt a clutch of fear in my stomach.

'How long have they been like this, Derek?' I queried.

'Oh – some days. They be pigs I got in the market 'bout ten days ago. They was goin' cheap, like an' I thought I'd got a bargain but don't look like it now.'

'It does not, Derek. I don't like the look of them at all.'

'Serious, then, you think?'

'Could be. Have you given them anything?'

'Aye – I wormed 'em. They was scourin' a bit an' I thought could be worms, but they's gone worse since then.'

There were twenty in two pens, most of them lying half-buried in the straw, but those that were walking about were really sick looking, shivering now and then, and with a foul smelling diarrhoea oozing from them. A description came back to me from my pig diseases textbook, for some parts are stamped into the memory. 'Young pigs affected with this disease have a high temperature, refuse to feed, lie hidden or half-hidden in the litter, and when forced to move do so reluctantly, giving little annoyed squeals. Their backs are arched, their tails uncurled, the brownish diarrhoea is of a foul odour and the whole appearance suggests acute misery and sickness. The breathing is frequently distressed, the sufferer being attacked with a fit of harsh, dry coughing.'

I had hoped I would never see it, but here before my eyes was a classic example of the book's description. I turned to Derek who was watching me intently, for clearly my anxiety had shown in my face.

'What's the cause o' the scour if it be'nt worms?'

'Oh, there's different causes of scour, Derek, wrong feeding and a whole host of germs called Bcoli, Salmonella and a few others.'

'I've heard o' that thar semolina, but be that not wot comes in food poisoning, get it from chickens?'

'Let's catch one or two, Derek, and take their temperatures.' So we did, they were easily caught, temperatures were raised several degrees. I examined the skins carefully, was there a reddening like the book described or was it my imagination? Suddenly Derek shouted.

'Dang me! There be a dead 'un here in the straw!'

'And the way they look, there'll be a few more soon, I'm very much afraid.'

Derek was by now very solemn.

'What do 'ee think it be then?'

'Well, Derek, unless I'm very much mistaken, they've got Swine Fever. I'll do a post mortem on that dead pig and maybe will be more sure then.'

So I did a PM. There were suggestive signs, enlarged lymph glands, pinpoint haemorrhages in liver and kidneys, but there could be caused by other things besides Swine Fever, and thoroughly though I searched, I could find none of the button ulcers in the bowel which are the main diagnostic feature. I straightened up, looked at the pathetic pigs, then looked at the young farmer.

'The position, Derek is this. I'm not the one to diagnose SF, only the Department of Agriculture can do that, but I'm ninety per cent certain that's what you've got.'

'Be there no cure for it, 'en?'

'No, but there's a preventive, called Crystal Violet Vaccine which we could use on your pigs at the farm. This thing spreads like wildfire. You could carry it on your boots or clothes, mice, even lice, can carry it. It's believed to be caused by a virus, and I'm very sorry, but it's the worst possible disease you could get in your pigs. Here's what we must do. First we have to disinfect our boots, and as best we can, our clothes. When you get home, take off what you're wearing before you go near another pig. Don't let anybody else up to these pens here. When you come next, leave your wellingtons and overalls behind you, for it if gets into your main lot of pigs, you're in big trouble, and when I get home, I'll phone the Ministry vet for advice and have him out here tomorrow.'

Derek was by now very pale, twenty pigs condemned, I was sure, and maybe 200 more, though just in case I was wrong, and for the sake of doing something for the miserable sufferers, I gave him a bowel active sulphonamide. I knew it was hopeless, for in my heart I was sure we had this disease all pig breeders dread, but I felt I had to try something for the pathetic creatures. I went to the car, got out a bottle of disinfectant, and we scrubbed our boots, the wheels of the car and my outer black waterproof, and departed to deposit the anxious young farmer at his home. I went home, scrubbed myself all over again, changed clothes which were laid aside for the washing machine, and phoned the Ministry vet.

'Why didn't you post the bowel of the dead pig to the Lab?' he demanded.

'Because by the time they got it at the Department, there would be several more dead. Besides, there were no button ulcers to be seen.'

'That's not for you to decide, Cameron.'

'I know, I know, but just the same I think you should see these pigs tomorrow.'

'I take my orders from higher up, young man, you should know!' I kept my temper with difficulty, and went on.

'I know that fine. It's also true I've never seen Swine Fever before, but I'd still be grateful if you could get permission to come out tomorrow.' He hummed and hawed, muttered 'highly improper', but finally agreed to come. My wife had been listening to all this conversation with dismay, and then said sympathetically, 'I'm afraid you've got more trouble, another case, dear. Ann phoned about half an hour, a cow down in the yard at Higher Chade, they don't know what's wrong with it, and Bernard's away at another case.'

I groaned, for I had started the day with a calving at John Atkin's farm at 5.00 am, and had been at it non-stop, and my first brush with suspected Swine Fever had taken a bit out of me. Bernard had also had a full day. I gulped a cup of tea while I dressed in fresh clothes, then skimmed off in my little Standard 8, the best car I had been able to afford so far. It was still a small and cheap car, but to me as precious as a Rolls Royce.

Higher Chade was only a mile away, and when I entered the yard, there was my patient lying flat out on the concrete with Ivor Huxtable, the owner, standing looking at it moodily. He was a good natured character, young like Derek Hocking, and likewise a keeper of Friesians, famed for his quaint sense of humour and peculiarities. You never knew what he would say or do next but equally one could say anything to him. What he said to me was predictable.

'Did 'ee 'ave a good tea then? I phoned so long ago it must have been nigh yesterday!'

I grinned at him, slapped him on the shoulder, and enlightened him, 'I was at an urgent case, Ivor.'

'Aar! What was that, 'en?'

'A budgerigar.'

'Oh well, that be different 'en, them budgerigars be mighty valuable like.'

He poked his recumbent cow with his toe, his hands thrust deep into his pockets.

'Can't make this thar bullock out. He be due to calve an' some waters come away, but nothin's showin', an' when I finished my milkers an' come out to turn the dry 'uns back to the field along with 'em, there he be – flat out.'

I had by this time got used to the Devon habit of describing every bovine as a bullock, but it still startled me to hear some farmers call a she, a he. The preliminary diagnosis was easy, but coming from Ayrshire where every farmer recognised the condition, and some, even in the 1950s, were injecting their own cattle, I was constantly surprised that so many in Devon had never seen Milk Fever. I got out my calcium bottles and flutter valve and injected directly into the mammary vein, Ivor holding the bottle up for me for the gravity feed, one hand still in his pocket.

'Now, Ivor, if you can bear to take your hands out of your pockets, would you bring me a bucket of warm water, soap and a towel, and we'll see what's happening in here.'

Ivor slouched off and eventually came back with my requirements. I had no alternative but to lie down on the hard, filthy, concrete yard to examine her, for the cow was still down on her side. My hand went just into the entrance of the womb, and then it was all I could do to poke two fingers inside. I groaned, one of these, a twist, a torsion of the womb, a tricky business.

'We've got a problem, Ivor my lad, and it's more than you and I can handle.'

'Ur! What be that 'en?'

'This cow has a twist in her womb. The waters have broken, so she's at her time, but there's no way we can get the calf out till we straighten out that twist.'

'How do 'ee do that 'en?'

'We have to roll this cow over and over while I keep my arm inside her, and hope that we can unwind the twist, for it's a bit like a corkscrew in there just now.'

'Do 'ee tell me that? Will it work?'

'Well, say a prayer it will, or we're in real trouble. Can you get a couple of men to help us?'

'Reckon so,' murmured the unperturbed Ivor, departed, and returned quite quickly with two men from the neighbouring farm, practically next door. By now the calcium was taking effect, and the cow was sitting up on its brisket, but not yet trying to stand. I needed a fit cow for the calving, but I did not want her on her feet just yet.

'Now boys,' I explained, 'you have to tuck in her legs and roll her on to her side, then right over on her back and so on to the other side. But remember my arm will be inside her all the time and I've got kind of attached to that arm, so if I say "stop", stop at once.'

'Right, boss,' murmurered Ivor, 'us'll 'ave a go.'

So I soaped my arm, put it in as far as I could and said 'Now . . . roll!, which they did, and immediately a tremendous pressure came on the arm and I had an awful feeling I would never get it out again.

'Stop!' I yelled in agony, 'we're going the wrong way. Get her back as she was, quick!'

They worked well, and rolled her back to where we had been at the start, as I scrabbled about on the hard, wet, mucky concrete.

'Now try the other way!' which they did. 'Keep going, right over with her, and over she went, and oh the relief, for it was like coming out of a dark passage into the light, ascending a spiral staircase and reaching the top. The womb was opened up now and already a live calf was moving towards the exit. As if realising that things had taken a turn, or several turns, for the better, the cow struggled to her feet. Now it was time for the calving chains, and the pull of four husky men, for the calf was big, and the cow not yet able to help 100 per cent. Even with four of us, it was a tough pull, but eventually out dropped the calf, hitting me on the chest as I tried to catch this slippery bundle of new life, so that I sat down in the yard, the calf on top of me. I got up, and stood grinning at the calf as the young farmer rubbed it down with a wisp of straw. He glanced up at me, covered from head to toe in filth, and streaked with blood, and in his droll way said, 'You best get back to you'm budgerigar. I reckon it would take one look at 'ee and shout for the police, but I be mighty grateful to 'ee just the same. I never see'd owt like that afore', then as an afterthought he grinned and said, 'Come in an' have a wash. Maybe you can straighten missus out too. She be mighty twisted times, specially when I snore of nights.'

So it was home for yet another change of clothing, after a soak in a strongly disinfected and scented bath. The phone stayed quiet, but I could not put Derek and his pig problem out of my mind. I mused on the unlucky twist of fortune he had had to turn a bargain into a nightmare, so I took a run out to High Deane to see him and chat over his next steps. I explained the whole position to him if our worst fears were confirmed, and advised him, since all the affected pigs were in one place and had not been in contact with the others, to have all the rest, boar, sows, weaners, bacon pigs, the lot, vaccinated. We worked out costs of vaccine, cutting this as low as I could, for Derek's losses would already be considerable. I was desperately anxious to prevent this scourge, which had been known to wipe out ten per cent of the pigs in Britain, from spreading.

The Ministry vet came out next morning, when three more pigs had died. He was more pleasant than he had been the night before on the phone, and as he looked at the sufferers, just shook his head in silence. He did a PM on the dead pigs, but again none of the famous button ulcers could be found. He wrapped up the intestines of one to send to the lab boys, who alone were authorised to make a positive diagnosis. I wondered what they did at the lab, remembering the old gag that they threw the guts at the wall, and if they stuck, it was SF, if they fell off, it was not. The Ministry imposed a stand still order preventing movement of pigs over a wide area. The farm was isolated, the police informed and the original source of the pigs checked out. There was a feeling of near panic in the area. We trembled, and waited.

So it went on for several more days. More of Derek's twenty died, more samples were taken, and eventually after a week, a positive diagnosis was given. The survivors of the original twenty were slaughtered and the carcases disposed of in the fashion laid down, buried in quick-lime.

Meantime I had injected all Derek's other pigs with Crystal Violet Vaccine, and about half of all the other pigs in the district. Injection was behind the ear, one of the few areas of thin skin on a pig, and a messy business it was, for sometimes at the crucial moment a pig would struggle free and some of the brightly coloured vaccine be deposited on pig handler or Bernard and I doing the job. For weeks afterwards we were a highly coloured pair of vets. I kept worrying in case I had inadvertently spread the killer disease on my clothes or by car, but no further outbreaks occurred. In time the restrictions were lifted, and the pall of fear in the pig community melted away.

Over the years in the ministry, I have had many tortuous, twisted 'cases' to deal with too, and at times in Aldermouth, especially after the oil boom came to the area, as I have already indicated, I felt I was more of a social worker or marriage guidance counsellor than a preacher of the gospel.

There was, for example, Frank, with whom I had dealings all my twelve years in the town. Frank was an alcoholic, had been 'dried out' innumerable times in Craigdunain, the big mental hospital in Inverness, but invariably he broke out again, sometimes hitting the bottle by way of celebration the very day he was discharged, a celebration that would last for weeks. He was essentially a decent fellow, never violent and when sober a good worker, but what a life he gave his wife! He visited us at the Manse often. More than once, watching a late TV programme, about the only time I saw television, the back door would quietly open, and while everybody's hair stood on end (especially if we were watching a horror film), and our eyes moved to the inside door as it slowly opened, Frank would come staggering in. The children of ministers are frequently thought to have led sheltered lives, but that was certainly not true of our four. They never knew who would be admitted to the Manse, or would admit themselves unbidden. We had trouble the last two years at the Christmas Eve Service at midnight, with a very small number of teenage drunks coming in, being sick in the Church or otherwise disrupting this most beautiful of all occasions of worship. To counteract this, we had to start the Service before the pubs closed, shut the great front door of the Church, and have elders stationed at all points of entry, but still somehow Frank came staggering in late, having found a side door unattended.

He never came for money, not once. It was not a touch or a con, it was a cry for help in his twisted, tortuous soul. Often he would be in tears at night, bemoaning the mess he had made of his life, but I soon learned that these words of penitence were no more than crocodile tears and vanished with the dawn. He had two sons who lived furth of Scotland and who were the apple of his eye, and if ever one of them was coming home, he made a Herculean effort to stay sober.

Sometimes he would come in such a state that he would plead to be taken to hospital, and I would run him in and see him settled in his familar ward. At other times I would drive him home and even put him to bed. He was made redundant from his job (he was about sixty) and for many months he was at the Manse every day, just sitting there and talking, a place to go other than the pub. Janet was marvellously tolerant of him, as were the boys, who regarded him, even when in their impatient teens, with great pity and patience. He was, indeed, for a time almost one of the family, and day after day we would talk, for he never could get away from himself and his problem. We would pray together, he would have a spell attending Church, drink innumerable cups of coffee or have a meal with the family, and I would hope. Then one day he would not appear and I would see him lurching along the street on another of his long lasting benders.

We had others too whose personality had been twisted by alcohol, whose jobs had been lost, whose marriages had eventually broken up, and though often disappointed in failure, fed up at our home becoming a 'shelter', or downright angry at the waste of it all, we soldiered on, and now and again saw a twisted life straightened out, and a sub-human, weeping, weary, sodden sot of a man really overcome, sometimes with the help of Alcoholics Anonymous, sometimes by will power and the grace of God, and feel it was all worthwhile.

Mary's problem was different. That her mind had many twists and turns I realised at her first visit to me. She came when in acute depression and almost suicidal. She was an intelligent, well-to-do young woman in her twenties. She returned every week for nine weeks and quite early I realised there was one particular something which I could not understand, and which was remaining hidden in the dark recesses of her mind. She was not mentally deranged, only profoundly unhappy. No doubt a psychiatrist would have talked to her, and touched the hidden springs of her mind, but I was no psychiatrist, and like so many more she seemed to prefer a minister. So I could only as a person seek to care and help as best I could. There were, indeed, many, like Mary, who came, and whose life, at the time was, like Ivor Huxtable's cow, twisted and in need of straightening. Then one day for Mary it all came out. I felt that, at last, I had reached the bottom line. She had committed a wrong and felt she could not be forgiven, not ever. Very gently I pointed her to One who on the Cross had prayed 'Father, forgive them', who had indeed died that we might be forgiven and like the twisted uterus of the cow straightening up to allow the new life to come forth like light after darkness, as I had thought that day at Ivor's, so Mary too went away with light in her face, a new life stretching before her, 'ransomed, healed, restored, forgiven'. No further need of the minister now, to my and her delight.

We did not have the same success with Trevor and Jeanette, husband

and wife, but a story as twisted as a Devon lane, and constant new revelations at each turning of the road. They visited me together and singly, Jeanette haunted the Manse where Janet did her more good than I could, and in time we unravelled some of the facts. The basis of it all was that Jeanette had been brought up in the closed Brethren in Wales, a very narrow group of believers they appeared, had left them and, as she said 'gone into the world'. After a chequered career, she had married Trevor, and they had three children. But her parents had never forgiven her even though she was now back at worship, twice a week in prayer. Her complaint now was that Trevor was too friendly with a neighbour. I think the poor fellow was only seeking a normal household where he would spend an hour or two, usually playing Scrabble or just talking, for in his own home he was clearly an outcast, and Jeanette would openly tell their children he was bad. She herself had a massive guilt complex even though she had come back 'out of the world', and in addition she could not forgive Trevor, despite her own past, for what she, quite wrongly, I am sure, regarded as unfaithfulness, and in truth resented him because she had married him in her wild youth. I would listen hour after hour to their talk, accusations of one another, claims and counter claims, try to advise, inwardly groaning for something 'simple' like Swine Fever or a twisted uterus, and eventually stagger over from my vestry like a limp rag, for treating twists is an exhausting business!

I had a young couple one Thursday at my Vestry Hour, having a rehearsal for their Saturday wedding. As they left the Church the bride calmly announced she was away home to start to make her wedding dress.

'To *start*?' I gasped.

'Yes – I've been so busy making the bridesmaid's dresses.'

The great day dawned bright and fair, the bridegroom and best man arrived, the whole congregation was assembled including the bride's mother, but at the scheduled time, no bride. Ten minutes late, twenty . . . thirty . . . forty still no bride. By now the groom looked like something left high and dry by the tide, was feverishly lighting one cigarette from another, and in general, not too happy! After forty minutes, I phoned the bride's home and got her father.

'This is the minister here. What's the trouble? I hope she hasn't changed her mind.'

'No . . . nothing like that,' he replied, 'just a slight hitch. She'll be along in due course.'

'When? How long?'

'Oh, about another half hour.'

So I went into Church, told the wondering guests there had been a slight hiccup, but all would be well, and they might care to walk in the grounds for half an hour. The organist, Jim, who had been playing non-stop for an hour, was mighty glad of a rest too. Eventually the bold girl arrived, as cool as ice, an hour and twenty minutes late, and took her place beside her groom, who was in a state of near collapse. While they were signing the wedding certificate, I asked what had caused the delay.

'Oh,' said the bride, 'I was working on my dress to the last minute, and when I put it on, it burst!'

I was not feeling very gracious, but managed to say 'So the hitch was a stitch!'

Ah well, I thought as I made my way back to the Manse, there's many a twist and turn in life, but the trouble is if you don't get them straightened out in time, there's liable to be an explosion!

The Impossible takes longer

TWENTY-TWO

I came out from my weekly visit to Raigmore Infirmary, Inverness, feeling very solemn. I had been the rounds of our sick folks in the different wards of the various hospitals in the ancient burgh, and as always, after sharing with the many each week who were ill or waiting for surgery, and trying to bring comfort and cheer, I was feeling drained and tired. I knew well what that verse in the New Testament meant when it said of Jesus 'virtue had gone out of Him'.

But it was the final visit which had really solemnised me, and a talk I had had with the Sister of Ward 15. My last patient was Gordon. He had been in hospital for a year, and every week either my Assistant of the time, Donald (now serving in Zambia) or myself had seen Gordon. He was a young man in his thirties, an exceptionally fine young fellow, a cheerful companion and friend, and in his long illness steady, brave, patient, a man, who lived for his wife and family and if what the Sister had said was correct, he would not have much longer to share with them. For about ten years Gordon had suffered from a heart condition which had slowly, progressively, become worse until now he was confined to a hospital bed, weak, weary, and if at times discouraged, who could blame him.

He had seen consultant after consultant, undergone all sorts of tests and treatment, but his progress had been steadily downward. Now he was so weak, his heart so failed, that he could scarcely walk. He certainly could not have the least bit of activity for immediately heart pain would stop him. Occasionally he would be allowed home for a weekend, and when at home, he would struggle to Church and the family pew up in the gallery, stopping for a rest every few steps up the stairs. There was no doubt that Church meant much to Gordon, and it had been his quiet faith that had sustained him over the long, hard years, that and the love of his wife, Irene and their two children. I had baptised his children for him, his son about eight years before, and as a fervent Rangers fan Gordon had called him Colin Andrew after two of the Rangers heroes of the time. Many years before, when he was still half fit, I had occasionally golfed with him, for he was a keen and talented sportsman. Really I should say Gordon golfed. I just gave the worms a fright! All in all I had got to know Gordon and Irene well over the years, so that they were, as with so many of our congregation, not just members, but friends.

Of course I had seen his gradual deterioration, but had hoped for the miracle, but the talk with the Sister that day had dashed this hope. Quite simply, but with genuine concern, for Gordon was a favourite with the nursing staff too, she had said that it was impossible for him to live much longer, and there was, in addition, nothing possible that medical science could do for him.

Impossible! The word had sunk deep into my mind. It seemed so final and as I drove slowly the sixteen miles home two things came on the wings of memory. One was the slogan of a certain firm, 'the difficult is our business, the impossible takes longer.' Impossible! That too was the word Mrs Murdoch had used nearly thirty years before when I arrived at the farm of Laigh Buccleugh to treat one of their cows. It had a prolapse of the uterus, a calf bed out as the farmers called it. Her husband and their workman (a German ex-prisoner of war who had stayed on with them after the war) were both out in the hay fields and too busy to come in. I was then a young, inexperienced assistant vet, working with Ian Buchan at Mochrum where I had grown up, and as Mrs Murdoch and I stared at this huge organ hanging down behind the cow to its hocks, and then looked at the little hole through which it had all to go back into the cow, I could well understand her saying, 'I would say you are trying the impossible!'

For this is the big job in veterinary practice, the heavy task, the one that vets of my era had nightmares about, especially when there was no help available. Some prolapses are worse than others, but all are difficult. What happens is that the cow, straining to deliver her calf, then the afterbirth, goes on straining till it expels the whole womb, and having got rid of it, does not want it back. Many were the ploys vets had used over the years to assist in putting the uterus where it belonged, building up the cow's stall at the rear, hoisting up the animal with a block and tackle till its hind end was suspended in mid air, wrapping the womb in a sheet and two or three men lifting it to a horizontal position, slowly tightening the sheet to make the organ smaller, at the same time pushing hard, and a variety of other dodges. Normally there would be several men to assist with the job, but that day I was on my own. I shared the woman's view, it seemed impossible, for that womb was swollen and engorged with blood, big, flabby, slippery to handle, an ugly thing as most parts of the anatomy are, when not in the place the great Manufacturer put them.

The cow in question was standing chewing the cud as if nothing had happened, and occasionally glancing round at me as much as to say, 'I've given you a corker, young man. What do you think you're going to be able to do?' Oh well, get started and try, I thought, can only try. I stripped off jacket and shirt and got into my calving coat.

'Could you please bring me a bucket of warm water, soap, towel, an old sheet you won't need again, and oh yes, a pound of sugar.'

'Sugar! Did you say sugar, Mr Cameron?'

'Yes, a bag of sugar.' Mrs Murdoch went off shaking her head, Then followed the preliminaries to each operation of the kind, a bottle of calcium for it was believed then that calcium deficiency was involved in such cases, a shot of Phenergan to counteract the shock of handling such a large and vital organ, a jab of Pituitrin, an extract of a little gland in the brain, which helped to contract and shrink the womb and finally, an epidural or spinal injection of local anaesthetic to take away all pain and feeling, and hopefully to prevent the cow pressing and straining against me. By the time I had done all this, Mrs Murdoch was back with my requests, and as she clutched the sugar was looking at me in mystification.

'What in all the world are you going to do with this sugar?' I grinned and tried to look cheerful, which I was far from feeling, and said, 'A bit of black, or rather white magic!'

I got the bucket of water, poured in some disinfectant, and began to clean the pendulous uterus, for it had blood clots, dirt and bits of straw adhering to it. Then I took the sugar, slit open the bag, and shook the contents over the womb, like dusting a large cake. 'What does that do?' enquired the little woman, utterly puzzled. 'It's an old trick, Mrs Murdoch, It helps to draw off some of the fluid and reduce the size of the thing. Just watch for a few minutes.'

Sure enough, as we watched, the fluid started to pour off the womb, and we saw it visibly reduce in size before our eyes. But nevertheless it was still big.

'Well, that's a queer use for sugar, right enough,' she said, 'but I still can't see how you can get that big bag through that wee hole.'

'I'll wrap it in the sheet, and gently squeeze. Do you think you could take one side of the sheet?'

She gave a howl and shook her head vehemently.

'Oh no, I couldn't touch that – that thing. It makes me feel queer to even look at it. I'm off.' She muttered again, 'Impossible, impossible,' departed and left me on my own.

'The impossible takes longer', admitted the company in their slogan, and undoubtedly it took longer to replace the prolapse, working on my own. It also took me to the limits of my strength for the womb of a newly calved cow is a heavy organ, but slowly, with the sheet wrapped round it to prevent it continually slipping out of my arms and to apply extra pressure, it eased its way back in. Holding it horizontally in my arms and using my chest to give leverage, bit by bit it was 'fed' back to where it belonged. Without the spinal injection, of course, it would have indeed been impossible, but with the whole of its rear end numb, the cow did not really know what was happening and although looking bored with the whole business, it made no comment! The final foot of uterus disappeared from sight with a plop, I dropped the sheet, and then inserting my arm made sure that the two legs of the V shaped organ were fully extended, and with a sigh of relief turned to the final short task, inserting three tape stitches through the lips of the vulva to make sure the whole thing did not come out again. One can have too much of a good thing and I had no desire to repeat the whole process, maybe at one o'clock in the morning! So while many vets maintained that if the job had been properly done, no sutures were necessary, I always played safe. Mrs Murdoch had, by now, come back to the scene of the action to see how 'the impossible' was progressing, and it gave me great satisfaction to see the disbelief on her face as she saw their cow once more outside in.

I left some sulphanilamide to dose daily and keep down infection, and told the still wondering Mrs Murdoch I would be back in a few days to take out the stitches. Finally, after cleaning up in a fresh bucket of water, I was on my way to the next case, feeling a bit smug at the success of my one man 'impossible' victory.

By now I had reached the Manse and after giving Janet a run down on the condition of our various patients, for she always wanted to know about our ill folks, I told her what the Sister had said about Gordon, and we that night again specially committed him to God in prayer. A few days later I learned he had been sent to some hospital in England where it was hoped something could be done.

Perhaps a month later, one May evening, Irene came to see me at my Vestry Hour. She clearly needed to talk to someone and I felt glad and humbled that so many of our folks knew they could come to me and share their problems, and know also their confidences would be respected. It transpired that the hospital Gordon had been sent to was Papworth, near Cambridge, which had become famous for the heart transplants carried out there by the brilliant surgeon, Mr English. Gordon had been subjected to many tests, and the great surgeon discussed everything with both Gordon and Irene several times for he believed that the wife had a vital part to play in the post-operative care and way of life of the patient, and while many people needed a heart transplant physically, not all were psychologically suited to cope with the disciplined kind of life afterwards. They also needed to be able to handle the media, for in 1980 heart transplants were still big news, and indeed only one patient, Keith Castle, had lived for several years. Irene told me all about their experiences, their conversations, their impressions and I was able to reassure, just a little, for I too had been a patient in Papworth for six weeks, and had been greatly impressed by the hospital. Eventually, she told me that Gordon had been accepted for a transplant, when a donor become available, but meantime he would stay in Raigmore, Inverness, to have complete rest and quietness.

But she was clearly and understandably worried as to whether they had reached the right decision. She wanted a fit husband, of course, but at present she had a husband and who knew what would happen in the state of heart transplants then and the high mortality rate, and she was afraid, quite simply, after surgery, she would have no husband. A dreadful dilemma for the poor lass to be in! She also asked me earnestly not to mention to anyone the proposed transplant, for they did not want the pressure of publicity. So we talked, then it was the most natural thing in the world to commit Gordon into the hands of One, who, when He walked the earth, constantly made the impossible happen.

The weeks went past, and dragged into months, while Gordon waited with what patience he could muster. Then one evening in August, I had a phone call from Gordon's mother telling me that Gordon and Irene were at that moment in the air, being flown to Cambridge, for a heart had become available, in a few hours he would be on the operating table, and would I pray for him. I jumped into the car and drove down to the hotel Gordon's folks owned, and to my great surprise had to dodge reporters who thus early had heard the news and were plaguing the family for a story of Gordon's childhood, work, interests, sufferings and so on as well as looking for photographs. Newsmen have a difficult job to do but at that moment the family were not in a fit state to cope with this kind of extra pressure. I wondered how in all the world the reporters had heard the news and concluded that someone from Raigmore hospital, nurse, porter or perhaps someone from the airport had phoned the press to get a tenner.

I sat with the family for a while and we talked of all sorts of things as the time dragged slowly by and we waited for news. Again I found that my own experience of Papworth, though nothing like as serious a condition as Gordon's, proved to be a blessing and I was able to describe the layout, the lovely grounds, the calm of the whole place, and assure them of the skill and dedication of the staff. After a while we all gathered round, and committed Gordon and the whole family into God's hands for what was going to be a long night for them all.

The next day the papers hit the streets and there was Gordon on the front page, Supermac as they dubbed him, the first Scot to have a transplant at Papworth, I believe. In the Stop Press was the brief announcement that the operation had gone smoothly. Gordon made rapid progress and I had a long letter from him telling me of his experiences, and saying that to be conscious of a strong heart beating inside him was both exciting and a bit frightening, but rejoicing in how well he felt already after all these long years of illenss. I was greatly touched by that letter. We rejoiced as a whole community for our lad and his family and I recalled that talk I had had with the Ward Sister telling me that it was impossible that Gordon should live. Looking back over the years, it was true, as the slogan had it, that it had taken longer, but the impossible had indeed happened.

I was no longer in Aldermouth when Gordon returned home fit and well, and there was great thankfulness in his family, friends and the whole community. But every Christmas I hear from him, and I have, in a return visit to Aldermouth Old seen him, Irene and all the family in their familiar pew upstairs, and had time for a few words with him. As I write this, nearly eight years later, Gordon is going strong, cycling, swimming, golfing, able to earn a living again, the longest surviving heart transplant Scot. He has been interviewed many times on radio and by the press and in this own quiet way has never omitted to testify to the strength and courage his trust in God gave him, allied of course to the love that surrounded him from family and friends.

That slogan about the impossible taking longer? Come to think of it, does the Bible not say with God nothing is impossible?

Family matters

TWENTY-THREE

I was down in the depths, tired, sorry for myself, allied to a feeling of guilt, my health, to say the least, indifferent and generally a poor specimen of a minister that day in 1980. There was nothing wrong with the day, the very opposite, a glorious mid-summer day of blue sky and lazily drifting clouds, as if Nature was calling to one and all, 'Come on out! There's a big, wide world out here waiting to be enjoyed.'

I suppose my mood had started with the funeral, that of a young man with all his life before him, but who had been taken at eighteen. That was the age of our youngest, Alan, and while I had tried to bring comfort to the sorrowing parents in the funeral service and afterwards in their home, I had felt my words were empty things, imagining how I would feel if it had been our laddie, now down in Edinburgh studying for a BSc.

The house was empty when I arrived home, Janet out shopping and David, now twenty one and on holiday away from Aberdeen University at his summer job of Life Guard on the beach, and enthusiastic about his work. David, a Life Guard and loving it! That seemed an unlikely thing, recalling how afraid he had been of the water years before, and how he had cried for days before he had to go to the swimming baths with the school for the first time. Neil, the eldest at twenty-five, was in Edinburgh, an honours degree in zoology behind him, but with precious little demand for zoologists and the outdoor life he craved, and which his friend Peter Archibald had found, was now a Computer

Programmer in the Civil Service. Ian, number two son, had at least found his desired niche as an English teacher, and had also a highly successful career as a professional footballer, first, while a student, with Aberdeen and now with Kilmarnock, then in the Premier Division, a Scottish League Cap and his cherished blue jersey tucked away in a drawer. But whenever I thought of the boys, now men, and now all away from home, my guilt complex came back, that when they had needed him and wanted him, Dad had more often than not been too busy in the Lord's work. Janet told me it was nonsense, I was not aware of any criticism from our brood of four, but I had carried this sense of neglect with me for years, *the* one big regret of my life, that I had been a minister first, and father second, and missed so much in their earlier years, and now it was too late. Yet was that not the way it had to be? Had Jesus not said 'he that loves father or mother, or son or daughter more than me is not worthy of me?' But it was hard, as all pathways of dedication can be hard.

Janet's footsteps sounded on the gravel and in she came, carrier bags in her hands, and, as always, her very presence seemed to cheer. She glanced at me, asked 'How was the funeral?', then, with the intuition that twenty-eight years of marriage had given, she guessed that all was not well with her man.

'Poor Mr and Mrs – ' she said, then softly,

'But you cannot carry everybody's sorrows all the time, my dear. Why don't you go fishing tonight? It would do you good to get out.'

'I've a sermon to write,' I retorted, none too gently.

'You'll write it better after a break.'

In the end, we compromised. After tea, I went into the study and tried to sermonise, but at 8.00 pm gave it up, gathered my tackle, and said, still far from gracious, 'I'll away up to Lochindorb and see what's doing.'

Lochindorb was a large loch twenty miles up in the hills, absolutely full of small, sweet brown trout, so that only a complete dud failed to catch anything. I managed to be a complete dud many times without even trying! But it was, more important, a place of peace, surrounded by its sentinel hills. In the middle of the loch were the ruins of a castle where Edward I reputedly had met the highland chieftains, the whole the scenario for one of Maurice Walsh's books.

I parked the car and made my way down to my favourite bay and patch of shingle. There was not a soul to be seen and all was silent save for the whirr of a startled grouse, the call of a sheep and the soft boom-boom-boom of Lochindorb House's electric generator, a lovely spot, a panacea for tired minds and handmade to help disgruntled ministers. But I did not become less gruntled easily that night even when I realised it was a hopeless night for fishing. The gentle breeze had died away, and its going was the signal for the midges to venture forth, millions of them and in the gathering dusk there was a plop-plop-plop all over the loch as the fish came up to feed. I tried all my favourite flies, Zulu, Blue Zulu, Silver Butcher, Black Spider, Heather Moth, Greenwell Glory, but gloomily thought that only a fish with a very low IQ would fancy my bait when all these midges were there for the taking, that is the ones that were not feeding on me, and who seemed to be wearing tackety boots or had specially sharpened their teeth for my coming! As I tried bait after bait, finally needing a torch to tie the line, I thought of John McEwan's story of a predecessor in lovely Stratherrick above Loch Ness. John was minister there and one of my closest friends and he had told me of this former minister, a widower, with two lovely daughters. One evening he was out walking, in mufti, a daughter on each arm, when he met a fisherman coming up from one of the many lochs in the parish.

'Have you had any luck?' the minister enquired.

'Not bad,' said the fisher, showing his catch.

'Very good, I'd say,' said the disguised minister.

'Are you a fisher yourself?' asked the angler.

'Well, . . . I suppose you could say I was, . . . a fisher of men.' Looking at the two bonny girls, the other replied, 'Ah well, you've certainly got the right bait!'

None of my bait was right, so at last I laid the rod aside, threw myself down on a bed of heather, tried to ignore the midges, and watched the last rays of the sun disappear in the west. I shone my torch on my watch, 11.40 pm sunset. Maybe it was midsummer madness, but I decided to wait in that soft, still night and see the sun rise again, and as I lay there, my whirling thoughts took over once more.

I sighed wistfully as I realised this would be my last summer at Lochindorb. My health had failed, an odd sort of condition that took a lot of diagnosing and caused much pain, the product, said the experts, of years of overwork and stress. If I wanted to go on working, or even living, I must find a quiet Church where the pressures would be much less than in Aldermouth Old. I did not want to go, indeed I hated the thought of it, for I loved Aldermouth, its people and my Church, but go I must and I had been accepted by two linked country Kirks in the lovely Border country, and was due to start in September. It would be very different in scattered rural parishes, but people's needs would be the same and the folks we had met had been warm and welcoming. Besides, after twelve years I felt I had given my all to Aldermouth, had seen the Church grow, and knew it to be in a satisfactory condition, and maybe it was time, for the Church's sake as well as my own, to make way for someone else. So, at any rate, I tried to convince myself.

One tangible thing I was leaving behind gave me great satisfaction. I had been Presbytery Convenor of the Home Board when the new town of Culloden started to take shape, and I managed to persuade Presbytery that the Church should be there from the start. So we had bought an old tithe barn for £600. It was used as the first Church, elders were appointed, and while a Home Board Missionary, Jim Pettie, was put in charge for the day to day running of the Church, I was, at the beginning, minister in overall control and I felt highly honoured in taking the first Communion, first Baptism and first wedding in the old barn, round which eventually grew up a lovely Church served by a very fine minister in Peter Walker. Oddly enough, just before leaving Moorton twelve years before as Home Board Convenor there too, I had a little share in the erection of another new Church in the New Farm Loch area of Kilmarnock. I felt privileged that I had had a share in the erection of two lovely new Churches in large new housing areas.

So I mused as I lay in the heather in the dark of that summer night, but my mind kept swinging back to home, and my sense of guilt, the boys, . . . ah, the boys again! Once more their old Dad was failing them, for they too loved Aldermouth. There they had finished their schooling – there they had become men – that's where their friends were – there was home, and the stupid, weak, old man had not had the sense to pace himself or delegate work to others, and so cracked up. My mind went back over the years.

I remembered Neil, as a wee boy at Moorton asking one night, 'Can you play with my fort tonight, Daddy?'

'Not tonight, son. I've got a meeting.'

'Tomorrow night?'

'Sorry, another meeting.'

Wistfully, 'Next week?' and I realised my whole week's evenings were taken up. What am I doing to my family, I thought? I remembered the great George Duncan in Troon Portland saying one Sunday that early in his ministry he had *made* time from 5.30 to 7.15 pm each evening to be with his family, so for a time I did the same. But soon I slipped into my old ways and would be away out on a round of visits or attending an urgent call before playtime was over. Janet had often had to be both father and mother.

Another memory of Neil drifted like thistledown into my mind. It was Christmas and the boys at school were all pooh, poohing Santa Clause. So on the great night, when all were asleep, I dressed myself in my long gowns (not having a Santa suit), draped a towel round my head and hanging down like a beard, and put all his parcels on his bed. By the light of my little torch, he looked so serene and peaceful as he lay asleep, I stroked his forehead. He stirred and I fled for my bed, jumped in, gowns and all to hear an excited young voice call, 'Mummy, Daddy, Santa's been! I saw a great tall figure beside my bed and felt an old horny hand on my head. There *is* a Santa!'

Then there was the time Neil had come off a bike at speed and landed on one knee which was gashed and lacerated right through to the bone. We shivered when we saw the extent of it, but all the poor wee lad could say through his tears was, 'Sorry I've torn my new jeans, Mummy.' That injury had kept him from running or footballing for two years and permanently slowed him up.

Another memory of Moorton came back to me. Ian had come running in saying there was a crowd of big boys hitting David at the swing park. Dad was out the door like a shot and soon at the scene of the mêlée. There was indeed a crowd of boys up to the age of fourteen hitting little David, mocking him and saying again and again, 'Sweir boy, sweir. Come on, minister's son, we'll make you sweir!' In the midst was three year old David resolutely refusing to swear. I threatened some very un-ministerial things to that crowd if they ever laid a hand on my son again, and as they slunk away, put an arm round our wee lad, and feeling very proud of him, led him home.

I had tried to make it up to the boys with a lot of attention and playing on our annual holidays by the sea shore in our caravan and ancient tent. These were halcyon days when we built sand castles, searched in rock pools, fished off the rocks or pier, played Test matches at cricket and World Cup at football.

Football! That had been *the* great love of all our four, although they were all-rounders. Ian, for example, having a badminton medal and Neil a table tennis one. Even allowing for an old doting father's pride, they all excelled at soccer. I remembered David, young for the team at nine, chosen for the area schools' select, Alan at eleven captaining the school to victory in the cup final against the much bigger Elgin boys (who stoned the bus afterwards), and scoring the winning goal while John Duggie, Bill Barnett the Headmaster and myself bawled instructions and bit our nails between looking at our watches. I remembered Ian at fifteen making his senior debut for Aldermouth in the Highland League (having played also for the school in the morning) and in a mazy dribble, his speciality, as it was Neil's, beating six Hibs players in a friendly match. I recalled David as a ball boy, then later captain of the Youth team, on his eighteenth birthday playing a stormer of a game for the senior team at right back to win the Inverness Cup, in the same game Neil (who came late to senior football, having concentrated on his studies for his degree) scoring a scorcher of a goal from forty yards. I recalled my pride as young Alan captained the Northern Schoolboys in the annual national tournament. I had been at all these games yelling my head off. I remembered the Aldermouth manager and coach saying, 'Alan will be the best of the four.' But alas, a disability in his teens put paid to Alan's football for these vital years. Then all the excitement of football trials for Ian and Neil with, among others, Manchester United, Dundee United and Airdrie. Ian making it with Aberdeen, and Neil, who I am convinced could have also made it if he had started earlier, remaining in the Highland League. They were twins in style, position and inherent ability, while David and Alan were likewise twins, initially, as doughty defenders.

They had played cricket, and all had captained the school team in turn (handing on their 'whites' from one to the other), Ian and Alan being powerful sloggers, while Neil and David were all-rounders, handy with bat and ball. Happy days and a proud Dad!

Then golf. Our sideboard was covered with trophies they had won, Ian chipping the ball into the hole for an eagle three on the eighteenth to win the King Cup at the age of fifteen. Neil winning the big prestigious Open tournament in the handicap section at seventeen, his excited Dad caddying for him. David and Alan had their share of junior wins too, and both could hit the ball out of sight. It seemed no time since I had given them their first, old hickory shafted clubs and they had played with Dad, getting two strokes a hole. Now they all looked pityingly at the old man and asked, 'How many strokes do you want?' I recalled David caddying for me in the only competition I ever entered, being quite excited as I went two ahead, then my caddy looking worried as I lost my lead and finally exploding with a loud groan 'Oh Dad', as I chipped into the burn and lost the match two and one.

They had all worked in their summer holidays, Neil at the Golf View Hotel keeping the grounds and 'hoovering' the outside swimming pool each day. Two days he was away and Ian took over. On the first day he lost a bit of the 'hoover' and had repeatedly to dive for it, while on the second day, walking round the pool and watching some guests, no doubt pretty girls, he had fallen in, fully clothed. David and Alan had worked on the Golf Course, then with 'the squad', the grass cutters and garbage collectors of the little burgh, before David became a Life Guard, a swimming medal to his credit.

Another memory, less pleasant, of Alan, drifted into my mind as I continued to lie in the soft, fragrant night beside the loch. Alan had witnessed a boy vandalising a drainpipe at school. The culprit was a fellow member of the Academy school football team, and Alan, brought up by us never to 'clipe' or tell tales on a friend, had refused to give the other boy's name, though he himself was totally innocent. I had a letter from the Deputy Head Master stating that if Alan did not spill the beans 'he would be invited to remove his presence from the school'. That made me see red. Whether Alan was right or wrong is a moot point, and readers will form their own judgement, but the boy was merely carrying out the code we had taught him. I had a stormy meeting with the Deputy Head, reminded him that none of our four had ever given the least bit of trouble, all had brought honour to the school scholastically and in sport with never a 'thank you' or word of praise from the authorities, and to threaten our son with expulsion for a deed he had not done was like taking a sledgehammer to crack a nut. I did not succeed in convincing the Deputy Head, but at least the air was cleared and we heard no more about it.

So my thoughts drifted on, borne on the wings of memory as I lay beside the loch, enveloped, embraced by a silence that could be felt, till suddenly other wings startled me as a gull swooped over me. I was startled, yes, but also stimulated to recall our episode of the gull at the Manse.

Ian had found a herring gull on the beach unable to fly because of a damaged leg, and carried the bird home to see if Dad could do anything for it. The leg was, in fact, too damaged for any real hope, but I splinted it as best I could, and the bird, dubbed Sinbad remained in the garden, a source of interest, but also eventually becoming a nuisance to numbers of people. For a start it had to be fed, so every evening I went to the river, returning with a catch of minnows or small trout, which Sinbad consumed speedily. Although it stayed around the garden for the most part, in time it would fly short distances, and one day, one of our elders, Bob Anderson came to the door and informed Janet the bird was sitting right in the middle of the road and thus a traffic hazard. So a posse of the boys went after it, and brought it back from the midst of tooting cars. Ian tried to teach it to fly better by throwing it out of his upstairs bedroom window, encouraged or derided by the others watching, or catching below. Sinbad's territory increased, and spotting a lovely patch of green turf from the air about 100 yards from the Manse, the gull landed there one day and produced chaos as it limped about! Janet was again confronted by an elder, little Bobby Sim who spoke rather quickly, and in his excitement was almost incoherent but Janet got the message,

'Mrs Cameron! Ian's bird is sitting in the middle of the bowling green and upsetting all the games.' Again the posse went out and brought Sinbad back. So it went on. Sinbad was the subject of a children's address in Church, and 'Ian's bird' was known to the whole congregation. But things could not go on indefinitely as they were and eventually, though it was still a partial cripple, Ian returned the gull to its native element, thus ending the Sinbad phase in the Cameron history.

There would be no more such episodes, for now the boys were all gone from home. It was Darby and Joan at the Manse, but at least we had them to come home, not like the couple whose lad I had buried that day, poor souls. There seemed to be a strange light behind me and I looked round. It was the sun, rising again at 12.30 am, hardly any night in these northern climes, and my sermonic mind told me, 'That's like life. Sunrise on the other side of the hill follows sunset in life here and hereafter.' For that lad I had buried that day there was already the sunrise of the great beyond of eternity, life all of a piece, now and beyond the hills of time, and for us, with our unknown future, a Hymn came to me like an answer to all my yearnings.

> 'In Heavenly love abiding, *no change* my heart shall fear;
> And safe is such confiding, for nothing changes here.
> Wherever He may guide me, no want shall turn me back;
> My Shepherd is beside me, and nothing shall I lack.'

and the marvellously assuring last verse.

> 'My hope I cannot measure, my path to life is free;
> My Saviour has my treasure, and *he will walk with me*'

I rose from the heather and thought I would try one more cast, even though the midges were still providing a self-service restaurant, and lo! and behold, there was a splash, a tug, and I had my trout, even though it must have been a mentally defective one! Maybe there would still be fishing of all kinds for the minister in the Borders!